T4-ADC-324

Reprints of Economic Classics

THE IDEA OF VALUE

THE IDEA OF VALUE

by
JOHN LAIRD, M.A.
*Regius Professor of Moral Philosophy
in the University of
Aberdeen*

REPRINTS OF ECONOMIC CLASSICS

Augustus M. Kelley · Publishers
NEW YORK 1969

First Edition 1929
(Cambridge: At The University Press, 1929)

Reprinted 1969 by
AUGUSTUS M. KELLEY · PUBLISHERS
New York   New York   10010

By Arrangement With
CAMBRIDGE UNIVERSITY PRESS

Library of Congress Catalogue Card Number
68-30532

PRINTED IN THE UNITED STATES OF AMERICA
by SENTRY PRESS, NEW YORK, N. Y. 10019

PREFACE

In the hope that this book may tell its own story, I do not propose to embarrass this preface with any additional explanations. I have, however, to make certain necessary and grateful acknowledgments.

My colleague, Mr A. S. Ferguson, has read the first proofs in their entirety, to the great advantage of the narrative. Two other colleagues, Mr A. Gray and Mr H. M. Macdonald, have read the parts of the proofs which concerned their special departments of economics and of mathematics. They have done their best to enable me to make my statements tolerably shipshape, if not precisely Bristol-fashion.

While writing the book, I also wrote a tiny volume, *Modern Problems in Philosophy* (Cassell and Co. 1928), and included in it a few pages upon "Values". There is naturally a certain resemblance in the ideas expressed. In chapter VIII of this book, certain matters are treated (not wholly without reminiscence) which I have also treated in a lecture given to the British Institute of Philosophical Studies and shortly to be published in the *Journal* of the Institute.

J. L.

King's College
Old Aberdeen
December 1928

CONTENTS

Preface . . . . *page* v

INTRODUCTION

§ 1.	The technical and the dictionary meanings of value	xiii
§ 2.	Comparison with other languages . . .	xv
§ 3.	Value and disvalue	xvi
§ 4.	"Value" and "good"	xvi
§ 5.	A point in history	xvii
§ 6.	Plan of this book	xx

CHAPTER I. *BONUM UTILE*

Section I. The conception of value in economics . 1

§ 1.	General	1
§ 2.	Value and utility	2
§ 3.	Utility	4
§ 4.	Catallactics	9
§ 5.	Division of economic values	12
§ 6.	Preliminary conclusions	13
§ 7.	"Labour" and "cost of production" theories .	13
§ 8.	"Natural value"	16
§ 9.	"Natural value" and the theory of margins .	23

Section II. Of means and ends 32

§ 1.	Economics and the study of means . . .	32
§ 2.	Mistakes concerning ends and means . .	34
§ 3.	Points to be considered	35
§ 4.	The category of "end"	37
§ 5.	"Instrumental" or "conditioning" versus "intrinsic" values	42
§ 6.	Self-justifying and self-sufficient values . .	44
§ 7.	Summary of the foregoing	47
§ 8.	Complementary, supplementary, alternative and competing ends	49

CONTENTS

§ 9. Heterogony of means and Polytelism . page 52
§ 10. Transvaluations of these values . . . 53
§ 11. Certain tentative conclusions . . . 59
Section III. Of Signor Croce's opinions . . . 63

CHAPTER II. SPINOZA'S ACCOUNT OF VALUE

§ 1. Introductory 69
§ 2. Spinoza's account: the first phase . . . 70
§ 3. Comments on the first phase 72
§ 4. Spinoza's account: the second phase . . 75
§ 5. Remarks on the second phase 77
§ 6. Spinoza's account: the third phase . . . 79
§ 7. The rational good: synopsis 81
§ 8. Remarks on the above. A. The nature of action 82
§ 9. B. The nature of passion 84
§ 10. Action and passion in relation to reason . 86
§ 11. Anticipatory 87
§ 12. Spinoza's account: the meaning of good and evil in the third phase 89
§ 13. Man's beatitude 91

CHAPTER III. THE PRINCIPLE OF NATURAL ELECTION

§ 1. Describing the principle 92
§ 2. The place of the principle in nature . . 95
§ 3. Natural election and utility 98
§ 4. Natural election and consciousness . . . 99
§ 5. Natural election and interest 102
§ 6. Natural election and the principle of perfection 108

CHAPTER IV. THE VALUES OF DESIRE

Section I. General 114
§ 1. The meaning of "desire" 114
§ 2. Remarks upon the above 117
§ 3. Desire and satisfaction 118

CONTENTS

§ 4. Desired and desirable	page 122
§ 5. On an argument of Mr Ross's	125
§ 6. The quality of desires	126
§ 7. Further on the same	130
§ 8. Desire and perfection	132
Section II. Of certain historical opinions	135
§ 1. Hobbes	135
§ 2. Schopenhauer	136
§ 3. C. von Ehrenfels	136
§ 4. T. H. Green	141

CHAPTER V. *BONUM JUCUNDUM*

Section I. General	146
§ 1. Nature of the subject	146
§ 2. Pleasure and satisfaction	147
§ 3. Further on the same	148
§ 4. Fine art and beauty	149
§ 5. Discussion of objections	151
§ 6. The nature of aesthetic experience	154
§ 7. The quality of pleasures	157
§ 8. Pleasure and perfection	160
§ 9. The distinction in aesthetic theory	161
§ 10. Leibniz and Locke	163
§ 11. The metaphysics of felicity	165
§ 12. Pleasure and excellence	169
Section II. Meinong's theory of value	172
§ 1. Preliminary	172
§ 2. "Personal" value	172
§ 3. The emotional basis of value	173
§ 4. The analysis of value-experience	176
§ 5. The "objective" of prizing and of other valuations	177
§ 6. Value and excellence	178

CHAPTER VI. THE ANALYSIS OF APPROVAL IN THE BRITISH MORALISTS

§ 1. Preliminary . . . . . . *page* 183
§ 2. Shaftesbury 184
§ 3 Francis Hutcheson 188
§ 4. David Hume 193
§ 5. Adam Smith 207
§ 6. Price and Reid 217

CHAPTER VII. THE OBJECTIVITY OF VALUES

§ 1. Preliminary 226
§ 2. Values and physical objects 226
§ 3. The values of sensible appearance . . . 228
§ 4. The objectivity of mental facts . . . 230
§ 5. "Subjective" variations 231
§ 6. Recessive and non-recessive approval . . 234
§ 7. The insufficiency of ultra-recessive theories . 236
§ 8. Further concerning subjectivity . . . 240
§ 9. Further concerning objectivity . . . 241
§ 10. The consequence for value-theory . . . 245
§ 11. The "right" kind of emotion 246
§ 12. "Coherence" and value 247
§ 13. Summing up 252
§ 14. Judgment and principle in these affairs . . 253

CHAPTER VIII. *BONUM HONESTUM*

Section I. General 255
§ 1. A retrospect concerning perfection and excellence 255
§ 2. Further concerning excellence 257
§ 3. Perfection and reason 258
§ 4. Reason, perfection and moral good . . . 259

CONTENTS xi

Section II. Of value according to metaphysical
rationalism . . . . . . *page* 260
§ 1. Descartes 260
§ 2. Geulincx 268
§ 3. Malebranche 272

Section III. Kant's theory of value 276
§ 1. Introductory 276
§ 2. Kant's aesthetic theory 276
§ 3. Beauty and goodness 279
§ 4. The sublime and the ideal of beauty . . 280
§ 5. The nature of value or dignity . . . 281
§ 6. Reason as an end 282
§ 7. The good will 284
§ 8. Value and freedom 285
§ 9. The ego or subject of dignity 288
§ 10. The restriction of dignity to reason . . 289
§ 11. The rights of man 291
§ 12. Perfection and happiness 292
§ 13. The nature of human dignity 294
§ 14. Value and existence 297

CHAPTER IX. TOWARDS A CONCLUSION

§ 1. Explanatory 301
§ 2. The legitimacy of the elective theory . . 302
§ 3. Implications of the elective theory . . . 304
§ 4. The appreciative versus the elective view . 305
§ 5. The foundations of the appreciative view . 306
§ 6. The genetic argument 308
§ 7. The appreciative versus the timological view . 311
§ 8. Prizing and evaluation 312
§ 9. Insufficiency of the appreciative view . . 314
§ 10. Prizing and timology 315
§ 11. Evaluation and reason 318
§ 12. Natural election versus timology . . . 320
§ 13. The ambiguity of "value" 321

CHAPTER X. STANDARDS AND MEASURES OF VALUE

Section I. The idea of moral arithmetic . . *page* 323

- § 1. The earlier forms of the explicit idea . . 323
- § 2. Bentham's opinions 326
- § 3. Buffon to Fechner 331
- § 4. Turgot to Gossen 333
- § 5. Jevons 335
- § 6. The legitimacy of "marginalism" . . . 337
- § 7. Problems in the measurement of pleasures . 340
- § 8. Further on the same 345
- § 9. The meaning of pleasure 347

Section II. The general theory of value-measurement 349

- § 1. Axioms of value and of value-measurement . 349
- § 2. The commensurability of all values . . . 353
- § 3. Further on the same 356
- § 4. Lines of preference 359
- § 5. The commingling of values 362
- § 6. The inverse estimation of commingled values . 366
- § 7. Perceptual evaluation 368
- § 8. Patterns and schemata of valuation . . 372

Index 376

INTRODUCTION

§ 1. *The technical and the dictionary meanings of value*

For the purposes of science or of philosophy it is necessary either to apply common words in a technical sense, or to invent new technical terms. For science and philosophy are technical exercises, and need their proper tools.

Both of these courses are followed by writers on value. In their pages, technical terms like "axiology" or "timology" are not uncommon and have their uses. Perhaps, even, something may be said, although probably not very much, in favour of top-heavy compounds like "affective-volitional meaning". On the other hand, the usual technical practice (which need not be disturbed) is to employ, in the main, words that are used in everyday speech.

The chief of these are the words "value", "worth" and "good", although there are many others at least partially synonymous with the members of this triad. Within the triad "value", on the whole, seems the most important word.

For the most part, when "value" is mentioned in common speech, the reference is to exchange-value, or at least to some *equivalence* in value. This use of the word, although not exclusively economic, is very largely so, and is frequently even monetary. As we shall see, economic values form an important part of the general subject. Speaking broadly, however, it is clear that equivalence in value presupposes the values that are equivalent. A very brief effort in analysis, consequently, carries us beyond any *ratio* of values to the consideration of values themselves.

Relinquishing the special implications of exchange or equivalence, therefore, we have to ask what "value" itself means in ordinary language, and we have to answer that there are two such meanings. The first is the character or property of value, the second is the things which are said to possess this character or property.

INTRODUCTION

Let it be remembered that, for the moment, we are dealing with the *prima facie* implications of language. It is therefore irrelevant to contend, as many philosophers do, that when we *say* that something is valuable, we *mean* only that *we* have a certain attitude towards it, the attitude, namely, of admiration, approbation or esteem. The question at present is what language asserts, not whether the implications of the language can ultimately be vindicated. In this *prima facie* sense, then, it is undeniable that the property, quality or character of value is ascribed to certain things and to certain persons.

The property called "value" is, of course, abstract, but is not therefore unintelligible; and it means what is meant by "worth" in ordinary English, except for the circumstance that "value" is wider than "worth". In *The New English Dictionary* "worth" is defined as "high or outstanding value, excellence", and there is no need to go beyond this definition.

Passing, now, to the second sense of value, we find, according to the same admirable dictionary, that "value" in the sense of "a thing regarded as worth having" is obsolete, and also that it is obsolete to take "value" to mean "good opinion", as in the quaint example, "Thus parted those two great men, preserving in their souls such a value of one another as you may easily imagine".

It is to be feared that "value" in this second sense (frequently employed by philosophers) is suspiciously like a combination of these two obsolete usages. For example, I cannot think of any other way of interpreting so high an authority as Mr A. E. Taylor when he tells us that "the 'good' or αὐτὸ τὸ καλόν is, in fact, the *ens realissimum* of Christian philosophers, in which the very distinction between *esse* and *essentia*, *Sein* and *So-sein* falls away".[1] But let us take heart. In the *Dictionary* it is also stated that "value", in a sense not obsolete, means "the relative status of a thing according to its real or supposed worth, usefulness or importance"; and

---

[1] *Plato: The Man and his Work*, p. 231; cf. p. 289.

there is, perhaps, not a very long step from this definition to a conception like Mr Taylor's. In any case, philosophers do say that truth, beauty, righteousness, sentient happiness, together with love and human affection, are "the great values", meaning thereby the facts which have the property of value in a very high degree. And this interpretation of "value", although it may be jargon, is not at all obsolete.

In addition to these two distinct meanings of "value", we also use "value" as a verb. "To rate high, esteem, set store by", says the *Dictionary*, and reminds us of Celia's speech, "I was too young that time to value her; but now I know her".

§ 2. *Comparison with other languages*

The Latin *valeo* and its derivatives in modern European languages show a wide range of meanings, and something very like the ambiguity of "value" in English.

According to Lewis and Short, *valeo*, in its primary significance, designated strength, and, with strength, health. Hence, by a natural transition, the term came to mean "being effective", and, by another transition, equally natural, came to mean "being adequate". Idiomatically the term was used for money value, and for the kind of equivalence which we call the significance of words.

Similarly in French the meanings of the term range between equivalence (la livre sterling *vaut* 124·21 francs) and *valeur* as an optimum or highest excellence.

In Italian there is the interesting development that *valore* tends to be honorific (and signifies excellence, say, in Dante's *Purgatorio*), while *valuta* is used for price and market value.

The Greek ἀγαθός applied primarily to men of rank or valour, and καλὸς κἀγαθός retained this implication. Secondarily, it applied to special capacity, e.g. in a good physician or boxer. According to Liddell and Scott, Theognis was perhaps the first to use the term in the moral sense. This is an isolated instance, the moral usage being seldom found before the great philosophers, such as Plato.

The German *Wert* has the advantage of an alliance with the verb *werten*, and is readily compounded into *Werthaltung*, *Werterlebnis*, *Bewerten*, and other useful terms. In modern philosophical usage, however (although apparently not in Kant), the word has the general sense of the English "value" and not the more honourable significance of the English "worth". Such writers as Meinong prefer to speak of "dignity" or "nobility" when they treat of excellent and not merely of valuable things.

§ 3. *Value and disvalue*

In the technical usage of philosophy, economics, aesthetics and certain other such studies, "value" is usually taken to mean both value and disvalue. It is therefore contrasted with non-value, or with that which is neither good nor bad. This device is a convenient shorthand, and need do no harm. It is similar to the shorthand use of "moral", as when we speak of "a moral being" meaning a being capable of morality but also, as we know, capable of immorality. "Moral-or-immoral" existence, in this sense, is obviously contrasted with non-moral existence such as that of rocks and stones and trees. It is rare for anyone to be misled by difficulties arising from this source.

§ 4. "*Value*" *and* "*good*"

All the words we use in common speech come to acquire a subtle and quite individual flavour. Accordingly, although "good" and "value" (or "valuable") are very nearly synonyms, they cannot be used altogether interchangeably. For example, we should never, I think, use "good" to mean "good-or-bad", although we do sometimes use "value" to mean "value-or-disvalue".

Again, "good" seldom expresses equivalence, although we might, I suppose, speak of a tin of petrol as being "good" for an afternoon's run. What we should mean in any such statement, however, would be that the petrol is "*good-for*" a certain purpose—that is to say that it is an effective instrument.

"Good", the adjective, has sometimes the special meaning of "kindly" or "well-disposed". Otherwise, when we speak of a good man quite generally (and do not intend to signify his efficiency in some particular department, as "a good gardener" or "a good golfer"), we mean by "good" either an adjective of indefinite commendation[1] or else a specific commendation of the man's moral character.

In the main, however, "good", taken simply and without regard to specialised instrumental efficiency, is either the character or property of value, or else that which has this property. To say that beauty is, or has, "good" is identical with saying that beauty has value; and to say that love is the greatest good is also to say that it is the greatest "value".

§ 5. *A point in history*

It seems frequently to be supposed that the philosophy of value is particularly modish and up to date—indeed that earlier writers did not have the advantage of our outlook in the last few decades. If so, our good fortune is a responsibility as well as a privilege. But we may be forgetting a good deal when we rate it so high.

Value is not a new term in philosophy. For example, when Descartes argued that a wise and prudent man should calculate beforehand the advantages and the disadvantages, the good and the evil, of any proposed course of conduct, one of his favourite phrases was that we should estimate such matters according to *la juste valeur* that we found in them.[2] Kant, again, as is very generally known, used the terms "market", "fancy" and "intrinsic" value to signify the salient distinctions in the central phase of his ethical argument.

To be sure, an old term revived and made fashionable may very well become the watchword (or the catchword) of a fresh

[1] Cf. *The New English Dictionary*.
[2] Cf. Brunschvicg, *Le progrès de la conscience*, vol. I, pp. 155 *sqq*.

outlook. Since "good" and "value", however, are so nearly synonymous, it is evident that this claim to novelty, if accepted at all, must be accepted with a pungent pinch of doubt. For if discussions about value are relatively newfangled, discussions concerning the good or the *summum bonum* are manifestly as ancient as philosophy itself.

What has to be maintained, therefore, in defence of this claim to novelty, is that the more recent philosophy of value alters the horizon of the older philosophy of good—and alters it to the advantage of philosophy in general. The new term, it is said, expresses a new attitude, and emancipates us from the well-scoured and unalterable channels of the *summum bonum* with its inveterate tendency to define "good" as virtue, or, at the best, as virtue mixed with luck.

Nevertheless, we should not congratulate ourselves too soon or too easily. The newer theories of value, I suppose, take their rise partly from the influx of economic notions, partly from two teachers at Göttingen, in the middle nineteenth century, Hermann Lotze the philosopher and Albrecht Ritschl the theologian. From the economic standpoint, however, the conception of "value" goes back to Aristotle and was not an invention of Walras, Gossen or the Austrian economists. And Lotze himself did not seem to sniff a revolution in the offing. In the *Microcosmus* he expresses his unshaken belief that "in its feeling for the value of things and their relations, our reason possesses as genuine a revelation as, in the principles of logical investigation, it has an indispensable instrument of experience".[1] At the close of the *Metaphysics*, he says that he had concluded his earlier and imperfect work "with the dictum that the true beginning of Metaphysic lies in Ethics. I admit that the expression is not exact; but I still feel certain of being on the right track, when I seek in that which *should* be the ground of that which *is*".[2] In other words the second statement, which is purely Kantian, is regarded as a description of the argument in the earlier book.

[1] English translation, vol. I, p. 245.   [2] *Ibid.* vol. II, p. 319.

INTRODUCTION xix

Certainly Lotze may have builded better than he knew; or, in the alternative, although his general aim of vindicating the reality of much in the world which is *not* mechanical science may have been similar to Kant's later philosophy, his actual theory, whether he was aware of the circumstance or not, may have carried him far beyond anything that could have been excogitated at Königsberg. And Ritschl, reviving Pascal's *raisons de cœur* (if indeed they were *raisons*), may similarly, like the wizard in the fable, have unloosed a stream which he could not control. How else can we explain Ritschl's immense influence in nineteenth-century theology?

In the main, therefore, it is possible that the current philosophy of value is essentially new; with the wine of adventure in its veins. Value *may* prove to be the key that will eventually release all the human sciences from their present position of pathetic, if dignified, futility. It would be imprudent, however, to cherish this hope without remembering an essential circumstance. In a part, at least, of the older tradition, an "enquiry into moral matters" did not mean an enquiry into virtue and righteousness only, but an enquiry into *mores*. It was an enquiry into qualities "useful or agreeable to ourselves or to others"[1]—or, in other words, an enquiry into humanism and into the human sciences. The analysis of approval among the British moralists of the eighteenth century was, in principle, very similar indeed to most contemporary analyses of value; and there was also less difference than might appear between the British moralists and those with whom they disputed. It is the recovery rather than the invention of this attitude which should be the pride of the newer theories. What they have recovered, let us hope, they have also improved. But it is important to recall these historical matters, and I shall try to keep them pretty steadily before the reader in the discussion that is to follow.

For better measure, in this connection, the opinions of J. F. Herbart (1776–1841) should also be noted. According to this author, "the beautiful", understood in its widest sense,

[1] Hume's phrase.

was the master-key to all these doors. He was concerned, as he explained, with "the καλόν which includes ethical or social good within it".[1]

§ 6. *Plan of this book*

The general outline of the argument in this book is very simple. The first chapter deals with the subordinate (but important) conception of utility, and, at the same time, with economic good. The main discussion begins with the second chapter, where Spinoza's doctrine of value is considered, and ends with the suggested conclusions of the ninth chapter. The book concludes with a discussion of the standards and measures of value—in principle, not in detail.

The reason for beginning the principal discussion with an account of Spinoza's views is, generally, the catholic prospect of Spinoza's theory, and more particularly the way in which Spinoza plainly suggested the threefold division of the subject which (as I think) all subsequent investigation should follow. The three strands in this thread of Theseus are, firstly, the relative values of natural election; secondly, the relative values of psychological interest (i.e. of pleasure and conscious appetency); and, thirdly, the absolute values of excellence or of rational perfection. The meaning and the scope of each member in this triple division, together with the relations between them, seem to me to define the entire problem with which we are concerned.

[1] *Lehrbuch zur Einleitung in die Philosophie*, § 81.

CHAPTER I

BONUM UTILE

SECTION I. THE CONCEPTION OF VALUE IN ECONOMICS

§ 1. *General*

ACCORDING to certain authors—for example, according to Mr Heyde[1]—the treatment of Value in economics has so little (of importance) in common with its treatment in philosophy that it is better, at the outset, trenchantly to separate the two. This opinion, however, seems mistaken on the score of fact and unwise on the score of policy.

The facts are against it both when they are regarded from a psychological or philosophical angle and when they are considered from the standpoint of economic science. Much of the important work upon the subject for which we have to thank the Austrian philosophers—and notably Messrs Meinong and von Ehrenfels—stands in close affinity to the work of the Austrian economists, Menger, von Wieser and von Böhm-Bawerk. Similarly, turning to the economic side, we find an ironical confirmation of the connection in the circumstance that Jevons, in his criticism of Mill's economic theory, really carried the philosophical theory of Utilitarianism, which Mill had done so much to keep alive, to a stage of logical completeness far beyond the place which Mill had reached. "It is surely obvious", Jevons says in one of his sharp attacks on Mill, "that Political Economy does rest upon the laws of human enjoyment; and that, if those laws are developed by no other science, they must be developed by economists."[2] In fine, without multiplying instances, the connection is plain. Von Wieser's "appraisal of future needs",[3]

---
[1] *Wert*, p. 7.   [2] *The Theory of Political Economy* (1st edn.), p. 47.
[3] *Social Economics*, Book I, § 7.

Mr Wicksteed's[1] assertion that *all* preferences are comparable and that the question, "How much of this must I forgo to obtain so much of that", is *always* relevant, are highly general statements with an unlimited application, and in no sense a mere device of scientific convenience.

Again, even if the facts were far more dubious than these considerations suggest, the policy of neglecting all reference to the work of economists upon this subject would surely be imprudent. To be sure, there may be something premature in hoping, as Mr Perry does,[2] that the conception of value will show itself capable of uniting the human, the social and certain of the philosophical sciences or of putting an end to their distractions and untidy makeshifts. It would also, however, be rash to renounce this aspiration without proper trial; and no such enterprise could afford to ignore economic science. Indeed, like Signor Croce, we might be able to discern an economic moment in all our practice, and particularly in everything that aspires to worth, or dignity, or nobility. The science of economics, it is true, must, like other sciences, study its own convenience first, and a general study of the kind attempted in the present volume need not be expected to explore technical alleys. The broader questions concerning the meaning of economic values, and concerning the measurement or computation of these values, on the other hand, concern us very nearly indeed.

The first of these questions—the *meaning* of economic values—in its wider features, is the subject of the present section. The second question, except in so far as it is logically inseparable from the first, will be considered at a later stage of this enquiry.

§ 2. *Value and utility*

By general consent among economists, the crux of the first question is the relation between "utility" and "value". When Ricardo came to deal with the puzzle that gold may

---

[1] *The Common Sense of Political Economy*, p. 32.
[2] *General Theory of Value*, pp. 4 sq.

cost two thousand times as much (per unit of weight) as iron but is certainly not two thousand times as useful, he concluded that utility is absolutely essential to value but that it is not the measure of exchangeable value. Sir Leslie Stephen, commenting upon Ricardo's perplexities, maintained, with an assurance that should perhaps have been tempered, that "a solution of these puzzles may be sought in any modern textbook".[1] In any case, this is where the question lies. And so we have to ask whether there is a puzzle, what the puzzle is supposed to be, and how precisely the modern text-books have solved it.

It is highly probable that Ricardo's difficulties in this affair were to some extent caused, and to some extent aggravated, by the form in which Adam Smith had drawn and developed the distinction between value-in-use and value-in-exchange.[2] Historically speaking, this result was unfortunate in many ways. For Smith was imprecise. On the other hand, the puzzle stands forth clearly in Smith's pages, and tempts us accordingly to begin with his account of the question.

Smith maintained, then, that value-in-use means utility, and that value-in-exchange means purchasing power. He illustrated the distinction by saying that water, which has great utility, has little purchasing power, if any, and that diamonds, which have great purchasing power, have little, if any, utility.[3] The general implications of this point of view are plainly that every economic "value" must be a "utility" of some kind, but that among utilities those which are exchangeable have an altogether preponderating (if not, indeed, an exclusive) place in economic theory. In short, when Mill, at a later date, said that "the word Value, when used without adjunct, always means, in political economy, value in exchange",[4] he was giving expression in round terms to the practice which had been followed during a long tradition. And when he remarked that "happily there is nothing in the laws of Value

[1] *The English Utilitarians*, vol. II, p. 207.
[2] *Wealth of Nations*, Book I, chap. iv.
[3] *Ibid.*   [4] *Principles*, Book III, chap. i, § 2.

which remains for the present or any future writer to clear up; the theory of the subject is complete",[1] he was rashly asserting a confidence that most of his English contemporaries would have felt as strongly as he did.

§ 3. *Utility*

Accordingly, we have to ask, firstly, whether Value in economics is essentially utility (or some species of utility); and, secondly, whether, if economic value is *only* a species of utility, this species is in fact *exchangeable* utility (i.e. in Whately's[2] language, Catallactics, or the science of exchange).

To the first of these questions, it would seem, we must reply unreservedly in the affirmative. All that is necessary is to define what the affirmative means.

It is usual to explain that economics has to do with goods (or commodities) and with services—or, more in detail, with material things which are necessary, useful or agreeable to mankind and with the actions of men which may have a similar function. From the economic standpoint the only important criticism of this general statement would appear to be that it should be definitely restricted. By etymology, economics means household management, and it always involves the provision or the husbanding of resources. Consequently it is not enough that there should be resources, i.e. that material things should be commodious or human beings serviceable. The function of economics is the organisation, management or husbandry of these potential resources, and it can be nothing less.

Assuming, however (as we must), that economics has to deal, broadly speaking, with utilities, and more precisely with the provision and management of utilities, we have still to consider what precisely is meant by "utilities" or by the function of utility. Here, it is plain, lack of precision has been frequent and downright error not uncommon.

When we say that anything is (or may be) useful, we mean

[1] *Principles*, Book III, chap. i, § 1.
[2] *Introductory Lectures on Political Economy.*

that it is useful *for* some purpose, that it is a means to some end or consummation. Accordingly the phrase "value-in-use" might very well be ambiguous, since it might confuse the critical distinction between consummations (i.e. the using *up* which is commonly understood by "consumption") and the property of being a means *to* a consummation. It has to be explained, therefore, that consummations, as such, are not economic facts,[1] except in so far as they affect the amount of remaining supplies, or are to be regarded, not as completions, but as the means towards further activities. (One's breakfast, for example, may be regarded both as a consummation and as fuel for the day's activities.)

Much more than this, however, has to be explained. When we speak of a commodity or of some human action as being useful, we mean, to be sure, that it is a *bonum utile*, a means to some good. But what, in turn, are the implications of this conception?

The Utilitarians said that a utility was a means to pleasure, a disutility a means to pain, and most subsequent economists seem to have agreed to employ the term "satisfaction" in place of "pleasure", and the term "dissatisfaction" in place of "pain". It may be doubted, however, whether the new terms are either substantially different from, or an improvement upon, the old. In England, and particularly by Marshall,[2] they seem to have been chosen as neutral labels which avoided partisanship in the psychological controversies between Cambridge Utilitarians and Oxford Idealists. Whatever the reason for their adoption, however, the new terms hide at least as much as they reveal.

For satisfactions, whatever other properties they may have, must at least have the property of being felt, and it is not true in fact that everything that is useful or good for a man is felt by the man to be so. Obviously there have been many things, like oxygen or vitamines, which were highly useful to the

[1] Cf. von Wieser, *Social Economics*, Book I, § 9; N. G. Pierson, *Principles of Economics*, vol. I, p. 42.
[2] *Principles*, Book I, chap. ii, § 1 n, 5th edn. p. 17.

human species before anyone knew anything about them or suspected their very existence. Again, even if we keep to satisfactions that are felt, we run upon a host of critical distinctions which are manifestly pertinent to the definition of *bonum utile*. In terms of satisfaction, the utility of a commodity must mean the satisfaction which the commodity yields. Do we mean, then, the satisfaction which it actually yields (which is a fact) or the satisfaction which we think it yields (which is frequently but a conjecture and sometimes, at least, a mistaken imputation)? And when we speak of the provision for satisfaction, do we mean the "satisfaction" we expect (which is often based on hearsay or on a vanished capacity for enjoyment) or the "satisfaction" which actually falls to us (which may easily be dust and ashes)? A theory which neglects distinctions of such manifest importance as these can hardly be supposed to be either strenuous or profound. Yet, looking for more, we seldom find it in treatises on economics.

Let us consider the problem from a different angle. In the broadest sense, *anything* must be accounted "useful" which is a means to *anything* that is good. Hence two consequences follow. In the first place a science which is restricted to utilities (or *means*) is in one sense a dependent science. For (by common consent) ends govern means, and consummations govern the steps which lead up to them. A restriction of this order, however, is in no way derogatory to economics. For the management and the husbanding of all these "means" (including all material resources and all professional and public services) is so large a problem, especially in a complicated society, and is so full of acute, yet urgent, perplexities, that it would be a piece of inordinate greed to ask for a wider scope. It follows in the second place that, apart from some further and narrowing explanation, *every* means to *every* end that is good in any defensible sense[1] is part of the subject-matter of economics. And those who consider (not unreasonably) that the means, say, to artistic, religious or scientific

[1] Or, perhaps, indefensible, like Sairey Gamp's gin.

ends need not be always or prevailingly economic are naturally inclined to jib at this second implication.

If so, the obvious course is to maintain that utility, in the economic sense, should be taken to express, not any means to any good, but a means (or perhaps a certain kind of means) to certain kinds of goods. This, in effect, was what Adam Smith did. In declaring water to be useful and diamonds not to be useful he did not mean, and could not be taken to mean, that the possession of a diamond does not normally yield greater satisfaction than the possession of a cup of water, or that the desire for personal adornment is not effective in human affairs. In short, he was thinking biologically, and forgetting perhaps the biological importance of ornaments in sex-attraction. Indeed, from the economic standpoint, he had forgotten more than he should have forgotten. The place of jewels and of other such treasure in Eastern countries or in the mediaeval Church was surely, *de facto*, of high economic importance; and Smith's distinction is at least as confused as the complaint of so many English tourists that the *tesoro* in Toledo Cathedral is a "waste" because it is not employed in industry. One wonders if the cathedral itself is a "waste" also.

Mill, criticising Smith, made this obvious comment, and in making it said also that "political economy has nothing to do with the comparative estimation of different uses in the judgment of a philosopher or of a moralist. The use of a thing, in political economy, means its capacity to satisfy a desire or serve a purpose".[1] If this statement means that moral or even that philosophical standards never have and never can have had any effect whatsoever upon men's actual desires and purposes, it is probably as hard to believe as the doctrine which Mill condemned. Apart from this, however, the original difficulty recurs. Is it true, in fact, that we have more than the vaguest knowledge of men's actual satisfactions, or even of their definite purposes? Have we not to deal instead with presumed satisfactions, obscure inducements, inexplicable although regular vagaries of fashion, traditions which if they

[1] *Principles*, Book III, chap. i, § 2.

have a purpose are not generally understood, rules of health and of nourishment whose correlation with agreeable feeling is largely a matter of imputation?

The Utilitarians maintained, not only that pleasure was the only good, but also that pleasure (together with the avoidance of pain) was the only possible inducement to human action; and they clung to this opinion in the teeth of the evidence. When satisfaction is substituted for pleasure a wider territory is enclosed, and the fulfilment of most of our needs and purposes is included with less palpable violation of the facts. If "satisfaction" however is taken to mean personally felt satisfaction, and utility to mean an accurate knowledge of the causes of such satisfaction, it may well be denied (as we have seen) that the new terminology is appreciably more accurate than the old.

In short, all such theories are faulty, and, from the standpoint of economics, seem to be assumed solely for the purpose of getting the discussion under way. From the economic point of view the essential thing is to reduce all human adjustments and provisions to some sort of common measure or, in the alternative, all except the few that are expressly repudiated as non-economic. Despite Adam Smith's unfortunate discussion of the diamond, it is hard to suppose that *all* our adjustments are *simply* economic in the same single sense. Indeed Mill himself was quite as inconsistent as Smith was when, in the parallel instance of "productive" and "unproductive" labour, he tried to restrict "productive" labour to the production of permanent sources of enjoyment, and gravely maintained that "it would be subversive of the ends of language to say that the labour of Madame Pasta was as well entitled to be called productive labour as that of a cotton spinner".[1]

Thus it would seem in the end that the fundamental notion of utility is accepted rather casually and debated rather perfunctorily in economic treatises. That the utility of anything is its capacity to serve some end and that economics is concerned with the management and provision of such capacities

[1] *Essays on some unsettled questions in Political Economy*, Essay III.

in things and in persons is maintained very clearly. Yet when we ask, What ends? the explanation limps. To say in effect (as Mill did) that every end must be accepted provided that it is actually operative in human affairs seems to many an overstatement. Spiritual, ascetic or artistic ends seem but partially economic although they certainly operate. On the other hand most of the attempts to distinguish what ordinary people would call "utilitarian" ends from others seem (as in the instance of Adam Smith) to fail miserably; and a general and vaguish reference to business, to industry, to the common affairs of life or to utilities mainly material tends to take their place. If all ends were personal satisfactions, and if every personal satisfaction were an operative force and strictly commensurable with every other, these attempts to qualify or to restrict the range of utility would be absurd by definition; and statements of this kind are very commonly made about satisfactions—with what seriousness it is impossible to say. These statements, however, are misleading and unscientific, partly because they are unduly psychological and partly because their psychology is inadequate. They are unduly psychological because much that is said of needs and of their fulfilment is psychologically but a guess and is known, in reality, from experience of a more objective kind. And the psychology is inadequate because a mistaken emphasis is laid upon personal feeling in all matters of volition, conduct and choice. The reality, in these affairs, is immensely subtler and very much more intricate.

§ 4. *Catallactics*

So much, then, for the meaning of utility. Let us now examine the conception of value-in-exchange.

In a venerable jingle Sir Hudibras asks:—

For what is Worth in any thing
But so much Money as 'twill bring?[1]

[1] II, i, 465–466. Cf. Hobbes, *Leviathan*, Part I, chap. x. "The *Value*, or Worth of a man, is as of all other things, his Price; that is to say, so much as would be given for the use of his Power; and therefore is not absolute; but a thing dependant on the need and judgement of another.'

and it is possible that many unthinking people believe that the jingle expresses the marrow, if not the entire substance, of the authentic meaning of value. In other words, they suppose that value means ratio of exchange and nothing else —unless, indeed, they believe something narrower still, viz. that value means this ratio expressed in terms of a pecuniary standard.

As a general theory, of course, any such doctrine is visibly and completely defective. When an exchange is effected, utilities change hands. A commodity or a service is exchanged for another commodity or for another service. And these utilities, as we have seen, are themselves means towards valuable consummations. In other words, value-in-exchange is the exchange *of values*, that is to say, more strictly, the exchange of what is instrumental to consummation values. The ratio of exchange presupposes values and cannot of itself constitute them.

In complicated systems, however, it frequently happens that the logically subordinate portions of such a system obtain, so to say, a strangle-hold over the system as a whole. This *may* be the plight of economic values; and many economists seem to hold that it is. Mr Cassel, for instance, as I understand his argument, maintains that the desires and efforts of men are purely subjective and incapable of being measured. It is the "price-fixing process" which determines all definite value-relations—or at any rate all the value-relations in scientific economics.[1] And certain other economists, if they are not quite so frank, tend to arrive at the same conclusion. Thus Marshall[2] argues that although satisfactions, and the like, cannot be measured, their effects can. When we examine this statement, however, we find that what is asserted is that the *economic* effects of the satisfactions can be measured; and in the last resort Marshall does define the economic effects of economic motives by referring to the money-standard.

In view of these circumstances and of these arguments,

[1] *The Theory of Social Economy*, e.g. pp. 48 and 50.
[2] *Principles*, Book I, chap. ii and *passim*.

BONUM UTILE

therefore, we must be prepared to consider the possibility that the derivative science of catallactics (even in the form which contains the developed implications of a standard currency) yields in fact the proper meaning of value in economics, with the further, if more remote possibility, that economic value, although subordinate in a logical sense to the values presupposed by it, is the only conception of value which, in the end, is definite and intelligible.

Suppose, then, for argument's sake, that value and value-in-exchange are precisely equivalent in economics. It follows, of course, that every catallactical value is an economic value. It also follows that there are no economic values except catallactical ones, and except in the degree in which these values are catallactical. Could this position be sustained?

The first of the above propositions has been disputed, but, it would seem, on inadequate grounds. Thus Mr Cannan has told us that it would be unusual and inconvenient to regard the sale of indulgences as an instance of economic process, whether the indulgences are in the domain of religion or of morality.[1] The sale of indulgences, however, did affect the revenues of the Church. And if "morality" here means sex, it seems plain that "sex for a home" is a thoroughly economic procedure and that "sex for hire" is a very ancient profession. Even bribes seem to be an economic transaction.

It is otherwise, however, with the second proposition; for it is abundantly evident both that economic values are conceivable without either money or exchange and that the exchange-value of very many goods and services does not, in fact, adequately represent their economic value. Robinson Crusoe's provision for the rainy season was an economic adjustment, although without exchange in any ordinary sense; and manifestly without money. A communistic state, again, distributing on the principle of "To each according to his needs" would have to do with, and control, economic values that could not be called catallactical.

More importantly, perhaps, every good bargain contradicts

[1] *Wealth*, p. 15.

the assertion that exchange-value and economic value are one and the same. In a good bargain both parties are economically[1] the gainers, each receiving something more useful *to him* than what he relinquished. If they exchange at a "price", the "price" will be lower for both than the value received by each. This conclusive argument might be extended in several directions. Even if wives could be sold, as in Mr Hardy's story, the exchange-value of a wife is seldom a serious economic factor, although her economic function is obviously most considerable; and even when there are no restrictions upon exchange, as in one's books, or tools or furniture, it is abundantly evident that the personal value of these things *to us* may be, and frequently is, very much greater than the price they would fetch.

§ 5. *Division of economic values*

In short, exchange-values and economic values are not the same. Even from the economic standpoint we need a division of the following kind:

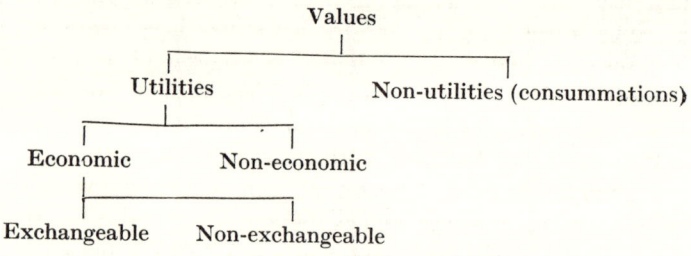

```
                       Values
          ┌──────────────┴──────────────┐
       Utilities              Non-utilities (consummations)
   ┌──────┴──────┐
Economic     Non-economic
┌──────┴──────┐
Exchangeable  Non-exchangeable
```

The only member in this series of subdivisions which has escaped discussion in the foregoing argument is the class of non-economic utilities. This class, however, in any ordinary sense is one of the commonest in our experience, for it includes the greater part of what are sometimes called esteem-values. It is true that a man's reputation for probity, or his distinguished lineage, may be in some measure an economic and even a commercial asset, but the greater part of these

---

[1] Although not usually catallactically.

values is obviously non-economic. It is true, again, that certain esteem-values may show themselves in the sale-room—the manuscript of *Alice in Wonderland*, for example; but, the price in these cases is a sort of economic fantasy. Lastly, it is true that the esteem-value, say, of a treasured lock of hair or of a stem of edelweiss might conceivably have a certain minimal economic function. The hair or the cherished flower is a utility by definition—that is to say, it is a source of personal enjoyment, but it does not usually play an effective part in the management of one's resources.

§ 6. *Preliminary conclusions*

This discussion, it is to be hoped, has done something to clear the ground; for the distinctions drawn have been real distinctions. From a general standpoint the chief of them have been, firstly, the distinction between ends (or consummations) and means (or utilities); secondly, the distinction between exchange-values (more narrowly prices) and other values; and, thirdly, the distinction between what is beneficial or hurtful, on the one hand, and what affords (or is suspected to afford) personal satisfaction or personally felt discomfort on the other. All these distinctions will occupy us in the sequel—the first in many places; the second in connection with the special problems of the standards and measures of value; the third, on the whole, most of all.

§ 7. "*Labour*" *and* "*Cost of Production*" *theories*

It remains to consider some of the more special problems of economic value in the present section; and the next step in this argument seems to be decreed by the course which the preceding steps have followed. Adam Smith's doctrine of value-in-exchange is very closely connected with the "labour" theory of value, and more generally with "cost of production" theories; and it is needless to explain how Marx and Ricardo and a host of others followed (although with deviations) the same road. Let us turn, therefore, to the labour theory.

The origin of the labour theory seems to be ethical rather than economic. The theory is based upon a supposedly "natural" right to the fruits of industry, the doctrine that Locke expounded when he affirmed that a man who had "mixed his labour" with a certain article had, *pro tanto*, a right to the article. This doctrine, for sufficient reasons, must be taken to be obsolete. If we are wise, we do not talk about Natural Rights any longer. On the score of ethics, the most that can be conceded is that anyone who transforms some material thing with the object of adapting it to human uses is probably better entitled to some reward for his action than anyone else. It cannot be maintained, however, that all property rests on this basis under actual conditions, and it would be hazardous as well as over-simple to argue that any other foundation for property is necessarily unjust. Even the *gratis* principle of communism, although it is essentially opposed to Locke's, might conceivably be defended.

Leaving ethics aside, however, we readily observe that the labour theory in economics may be carried a considerable way. While it may not be true, as the Greek proverb runs, that the gods give us *all* good things in exchange for our toil, it is sufficiently obvious that humanity cannot expect very much unless most human beings are prepared to work a good deal. And even if some of us work far too much nowadays, it is impossible to deny that an extensive social economy requires persistent labour on the part of most of its members.

Accordingly the labour theory forms a natural alliance with the catallactical theory. In general, we exchange something which has been partially transformed by human effort for something else which has also been transformed in this way; and if we include transport, advertisement and the like under "labour", it would be difficult to think of anything exchangeable to which labour was definitely irrelevant. Again, if we do not exchange commodity for commodity, we exchange our skill and our leisure for something we presume to be useful. A needlessly gloomy moral has been extracted from this circumstance. Men, it is said, undergo their labour, which is always irksome, because they are impelled by desires which are always painful. In the result, fear and uneasiness are matched against a species of servile drudgery. The truth is that desire need not be painful, and that toil need not be unpleasant. Beneath such exaggerations, however, an essential verity remains. It is a characteristic of work, as opposed to amusement, that we must be prepared to go on with it even when we find it tedious or full of risks.

There is also a natural connection between "labour" theories and "cost of production" theories. In so far as it is labour that transforms crude material into serviceable commodities, the main factors in an entrepreneur's calculations must be the price he has to pay for the hands that are employed.

Clearly, therefore (as we have said), the labour theory is able to carry us a certain way. Equally clearly, it cannot carry us far enough. To be sure, under conditions of ideal commercial freedom, without monopolies, without privileges, without political taxes or embargoes, labour, which makes that which was useless useful, would be mainly responsible for all exchange-values. It is also true, no doubt, that Ricardo and others among the principal exponents of the labour theory were, for the most part, careful to explain that they were arguing under the hypothesis of complete commercial freedom, and that in the case of many great industries the hypothesis corresponded closely to the facts. Even in a market ideally free, however, labour is not *all* that counts, granting that the labour is efficient. There is also the time factor, the necessity for waiting and for abstinence. Mills take time to build. They also take a certain time to grind. Orange-groves do not mature in a day. Even if part of the time factor can be equated with labour indirectly (by reference to the labour required for sustaining those who build the mills before the mills can grind) the whole of it cannot possibly be thus equated.

This important proviso, accordingly, would have to be made, even under conditions of ideal commercial freedom.

Under actual conditions, where there *are* monopolies and privileges, the problem, obviously, is entirely altered. Suppose that the effect of monopoly or of privilege is to restrict the supply of articles which (apart from the monopoly or the privilege) could be produced, and made accessible, with very little labour. Suppose also that there is an effective demand for these articles. It is evident that the exchange-value of these articles will not be affected at all by ethical or sentimental ideals concerning the dignity of labour. In a free market, broadly speaking, the effect of labour is to produce commodities approximately according to the demand. If for any reason labour has not the determining voice in decreeing the supply, the exchange-value may bear no appreciable relation either to labour or to cost of production.

§ 8. "*Natural Value*"

These cogent and sufficient reasons lead, by an easy transition, to the "natural value" of the Austrian economists and to the similar theories of Walras, Jevons and others. Before proceeding to this part of the subject, however, it is advisable to consider a further point in connection with the labour theory. When we speak of labour creating value, *what* labour do we mean? It is clear that not all labour creates value. It may destroy (when destruction is a mistake) and generally it may be misapplied. Efficient labour, therefore, is meant. But when is labour efficient? Not surely in every instance in which it produces something which *might* be wanted or *might* be useful. The possibility of a glut on the market is ruinous to this simple notion. In short, labour is efficient when, and only when, it produces that for which there is a contemporary demand.

Similarly, we have to consider the factor of timing. When goods come to market the labour that has been spent on them is over and done with. Is it *past* labour, then, that creates the value? In most cases, to be sure, the goods would have no value (they would not even be "goods") except for this past labour. Yet the labour is not enough. If, when the goods arrive, there is no demand for them, the past labour may have a sentimental value, but it has no economic value at all. If, again, while the goods were being made, some cheaper and more efficient way of producing them had been discovered and made effective, the past labour would once more be irrelevant. The labour which counts is the labour which affects the prospective supply at the time (or near it).[1]

For all these reasons, we must conclude that labour *may* be a relatively unimportant condition of exchange-value, and that when its importance is predominant, the reason lies not in labour alone but in the ratio of supply to demand. Similar reasoning holds of the "cost of production" theory. But now it is time to pass to "natural value".

In his admirable account of Philosophical Radicalism[2] M. Élie Halévy points out that Adam Smith, by adapting Locke's ethical theory of the "natural right of labour" to his own economic theory of catallactics, made in reality a retrograde step, and obscured certain of the essential points which Pufendorf, and Smith's own teacher Hutcheson, had stated with greater precision. What Pufendorf had said was that utility (or "the aptitude which things or actions have to serve the needs, the comforts and the pleasures of life") was the *cause* of all value, but that the *scarcity* of these utilities had also to be considered in the analysis of market price. Taken conjointly, this pair of considerations may be said to exhibit "natural value" in the germ. Utility, defined as Pufendorf defined it—Demand would be a more accurate term—is regarded as the governing factor. No one will buy or work for what he neither needs nor desires, and although supply, in a minor way, may create demand by arousing wishes which, except for the supply, would have been either mere dreams or undreamt of, Demand, in the last analysis, calls the tune. Yet utility by itself is something less than

---

[1] Cf. H. C. Carey on the Cost of *R*eproduction. *Principles of Social Science*, vol. I, chap. vi, *passim*.

[2] *La formation du radicalisme philosophique*, vol. I, pp. 169 *sqq*. (especially pp. 173 *sq*.). English translation p. 96.

value. For "value" is a function of utility and scarcity taken together.

We may take von Wieser's statements in the first chapter of his *Natural Value* as a sufficient, brief account of the shoot that has sprung, although after a long delay, from this germ. Here the essentials of the first steps in the theory are expounded in four propositions. First: "goods which are to be had in superfluity, and which anyone may appropriate at will, no one will pay anything for, be they ever so useful". Second: "things which have a great deal of use have often a smaller value than those which have little use". Third: "a large quantity has, under certain circumstances, less value than a smaller quantity of the same thing". Fourth: it often happens "that value is in agreement with the exact antithesis of use—namely with costs".[1]

Let us examine these four assertions with a view to determining their truth and what they are evidence of.

The first assertion used to be illustrated by air and water and sun, which were supposed to be nature's bounties and not to enter into commercial transactions. These illustrations, in view of what invalids pay for sun and air on the Côte d'Azur or of what Californians pay for their water,[2] were not perhaps entirely fortunate. Suppose, however, that we neglect all such reservations, and admit the hypothesis of a superabundance ready to everyone's hand. It follows, certainly, that no one will pay for these commodities, but the reason for this consequence does not seem at all abstruse. People will not pay for what they can have for nothing. All that the argument shows is that there is no room for *exchange* in connection with these commodities. The argument says nothing at all, in any proper sense, about their *value*.

For this reason, Lauderdale distinguished between wealth and riches, defining the former as "all that man desires as

---

[1] *Natural Value* (Eng. trans.), pp. 3 sq.
[2] In the matter of sunlight the reader may consider Mr Justice Eve's decisions in Dare v. Strand and Savoy Properties, Ltd. Chancery Division. See *The Times*, May 3, 1928.

useful or delightful to him" and the latter as "all that man desires as useful or delightful to him, which exists in a degree of scarcity." He therefore concluded that wealth diminishes as scarcity increases, although individual riches then increase.[1]

Von Wieser himself seems to have conceded this point, but he went on to argue that the same considerations applied to value-in-use as to exchange-value. For, he said, no one ever dreamed of economising with regard to commodities which are to be had in superfluity.

Here again what he says is true—and nothing whatsoever follows. There is no point in making provision for that which, *ex hypothesi*, needs no provision, or in stinting ourselves of things of which there is always too much.

We may suspect, however, that von Wieser overlooked a very pertinent consideration. When we speak of water as being useful, or as a useful commodity, what exactly do we mean? Strictly speaking, a pitcherful of water which is used for drinking is a different commodity from a pitcherful of precisely the same fluid which is used for washing. It is the particular use[2] of some material thing that makes it a "commodity" at all. The same thing in different employments gives a different accommodation, or, in other words, is actually a different commodity. Hence it follows that such water as is not used at all is *not* a commodity. In other words, being unused, it is not a utility in any sense whatsoever. In short, it is inaccurate to say, without qualification, that "water" is a utility. One might just as well say that "fishes" are utilities and forget what happens when too many fish are caught.

Von Wieser's second assertion, for reasons of a type already sufficiently explained, involves him in a crude and undeniable contradiction. According to him, the utility of anything is neither more nor less than its capacity to satisfy some want,

---

[1] *Inquiry into the Nature and Origin of Public Wealth, passim.*
[2] To be sure, the matter is complicated by the time factor, i.e. by prospective uses which may be alternative.

need, or desire.[1] Therefore (we should remind him), if the majority of human beings desire an ounce of gold more than they desire an ounce of iron, it follows at once that the ounce of gold *is* by definition more useful than the ounce of iron. And there is no occasion to make a mystery of the circumstance. It would not signify in the least whether this general preference for small quantities of gold had a good reason or, for that matter, any reason at all. If the "reason" were only a desire for adornment, the existence of such a desire would compel the "utility". After all (though the point is irrelevant) the desire for adornment is very ancient and very strong.

In other words, what Mill said about the diamond and forgot to say about Madame Pasta is thoroughly applicable here. Utility *may* be defined in such a way as to exclude such services as amusement, aesthetic gratifications, or personal adornment; but von Wieser did not define it so. We *might* say as Jevons did (although he also was inconsistent with himself when he said it) that "it is the lowest rank of feelings we here treat. The calculus of utility aims at supplying the ordinary wants of man at the least cost of labour".[2] If we did say so we might also revise our opinions upon the supposed uselessness of the ounce of gold. For gold is one of the most employable of metals; and its uses even in the form of coin or of bullion are not to be despised.

It is needless, however, to continue these reflections. We have seen enough to recognise that there is no "paradox of value" lurking in our author's second assertion. The ounce of gold satisfies a stronger desire than the ounce of iron; and that for von Wieser should have been all. If he had excluded the desire for adornment (say) from his definition of utility, there would again have been no reasonable suspicion of paradox. For in that case the gold (treated negligently as only a bauble) would not have "utility" at all.

Von Wieser's third assertion may appear stronger, or even decisive, but in reality is not. To select an instance, let us

---

[1] E.g. *Social Economics*, p. 23.   [2] *Theory*, p. 32.

consider what happens when we have too much rubber, too little rubber, or just enough rubber. In the first case, if the rubber really exists in superfluity, we have the same state of affairs as with the superabundant water or fish of our previous examples. Only part of the stock is actually useful or an authentic utility. Comparing the second case with the third, we see that the units of rubber are probably more useful in the third case than similar units are in the second case. For if rubber is scarce the supply of it will normally be put to the more important uses, while rubber, if it is plentiful, may be used for toys and other relatively trivial things. (An exception would occur if there were too little rubber to be effectively employed in manufactures.) We also see that the price per unit in the third case may be so much higher than the price per unit in the second case that the total money-value of a smallish supply of rubber may actually be greater than the total money-value of a much larger supply.

There are no important consequences beyond the last two, and neither of the two seems to be either paradoxical or to define some distinctive and peculiar conception of "natural value". The money-consequence is, no doubt, the more striking—but it is simply a question of money. In other words, its importance is not what von Wieser has declared.

Indeed, the nett result of this argument is to lead us to suspect—what has been growing more and more evident—that "natural value" is really "natural price", and that the doctrine gives an analysis of some of the conditions of exchange-values in general and of prices in particular.

In view of what has been said regarding the labour and the "cost of production" theories, von Wieser's fourth assertion need not detain us long. The alleged antithesis is wholly misstated in his pages. As we have seen, the exchanges that are relevant in this type of instance are *prospective* exchanges. The labourer, prospectively, exchanges ease or freedom for sustenance, that is to say he relinquishes one good in order to obtain what should be a greater good. The entrepreneur exchanges the utility represented by the money required in his outlay for the utility represented by the greater money-value of the returns he expects. To insinuate a "paradox" of exchanging disutilities for utilities is entirely gratuitous.

If these criticisms are sound, their general effect is seriously to curtail the pretensions of "natural value" to be either a distinctive or a fundamental conception in economics or elsewhere. Analysed to the quick, von Wieser's arguments do not seem to tell us much more than that there will be neither production, husbandry, nor exchange in the case of commodities which are not at least potentially scarce in the ordinary course of nature; and that, if supplies of commodities (which are obviously useful) are scarce, greater efforts and sacrifices (in the way of labour or of other goods relinquished) will have to be made to obtain these frugal supplies than would otherwise be likely to occur.

On the other hand von Wieser was right in asserting, as against Marx, that the economy of a Crusoe or of a communistic society "did not become transparently simple"[1] through the mere abolition of exchange-value or, more specifically, of money. As he perceived, the connection between scarcity and utility, in all its complicated interrelations, must remain wherever provision has to be made for human requirements. This connection is the essence of natural value, and Mr Cassel is quite mistaken in calling the conception "vague and elastic".[2]

This same conjunction between scarcity and utility is also correctly stated to be logically more fundamental than any accepted scale of reckoning values, such as the pound sterling, or the oxen in the economic transactions of Homeric heroes. For "natural value" holds under conditions of direct barter; and although it may be historically dubious to assert that barter preceded some sort of standard of reckoning, it seems certain that direct barter may occur at all times along with a money standard, and in partial independence of that standard. It is still more readily apparent that when the

---

[1] *Social Economics*, p. 87.
[2] *The Theory of Social Economy*, p. 50.

currency breaks down there is a return to barter—as in the "butter shifts" of the miners in the Ruhr and other notorious instances in Europe within the last decade.[1] "Natural value" therefore may fairly be said to be *logically* antecedent both to money prices and to many other sorts of prices. Analytically it is more fundamental. On the other hand, it may well be more complicated than it looks. For if it does not quite precisely presuppose a system of private property among the exchanging parties, it presupposes at least some determinate system of distribution such as even a communistic state could not avoid in providing for the needs of its members; and it also presupposes that men have alternative ways of employing their powers with at any rate a relative degree of freedom. The notion of a standard currency, accordingly, is not historically primitive, and it is hedged about with rather notable complications.

§ 9. *"Natural Value" and the Theory of Margins*

We have not, however, made an end of this foray into the domain of "natural value", for we have still to consider its connection with the doctrine of margins.

To be sure there may be less connection than is commonly supposed. The conjoint operation of scarcity plus utility does not of itself require a doctrine of margins; and it is possible, *per contra*, to evolve elaborate accounts of the marginal employment of income, marginal costs, and the like, without any explicit reference to "natural value". In short the alleged connection may be largely historical and due to the fact that Jevons and the Austrian economists based their economic theories upon these two conceptions taken together. Nevertheless, in making the connection, these economists exploited an affinity in the facts, whether or not "margins" and "natural values" might logically be treated separately. It is necessary, therefore, to explore this affinity in the form in which they presented it, although (for the present) only up to a point. As has already been remarked, in so far as the

[1] Cf. Keynes, *Economic Consequences of the Peace*, p. 88 n.

doctrine of margins is a technical device for the measurement of values, it falls to be considered in a later chapter. And even there we have to consider it only in so far as the general purposes of our investigation seem to require.

The affinity between margins and economic values (on which so much stress has been laid) depends in great measure upon the psychological foundations of the type of theory we are now considering. Jevons puts the point very clearly in a letter to his brother in which he gave an account of the main ideas of the book he projected. "One of my most important axioms", he says in this letter, "is, that as the quantity of any commodity, for instance, plain food, which a man has to consume, increases, so the utility or benefit derived from the last portion used decreases in degree. The decrease of enjoyment between the beginning and end of the meal may be taken as an example. And I assume that on an average, the *ratio of utility* is some continuous mathematical function of the quantity of commodity".[1] In other words, once we assume that the utility of anything is an expression for its capacity to satisfy some need, or want or desire, and also take note of the effect of scarcity in quickening desire and in enforcing husbandry, we have to reckon with the further relevant consideration that desires, for the most part, are *satiable*. As the child said about jam-roll in Mr Wicksteed's illustration, "Second helps are never as good as first".[2] There comes a stage when even jam-roll is not a utility for the child.

On this principle it is possible to construct a *Sättigungskala*, as the Austrian economists did, and determine the point at which any given consumer becomes *satt*. The little girl's first mouthful, we may suppose, is enormously more satisfactory than her last. If she were the kind of child whose appetite grows with eating, some of the later among her early mouthfuls might be distinctly more satisfactory than her first. The child's gratification, however, would, sooner or later, begin to decline. Then it would decline pretty steeply; and in the end

[1] *Letters and Journals of W. Stanley Jevons*, p. 151.
[2] *The Common Sense of Political Economy*, p. 40.

would reach vanishing point, even if some of the roll were left.

In this illustration the mouthful just before the child pushes her plate away is to be regarded as the marginal value, and if this marginal utility is reckoned as a unit, it is clear that the earlier mouthfuls have a greater utility than the marginal unit. It may be doubted indeed, in this simple instance, whether the attempt to employ a definite arithmetic is other than specious. Granting that the first mouthful is much more satisfactory than the last there is no reasonable method, our psychologists tell us,[1] to determine the actual intensity of the satisfactions in question. Such figures have illustrative importance, and enable us, for example, to distinguish very clearly between "total" and "final" (or marginal) utility, but they are not ascertainable measurements of actual satisfactions.

It may be otherwise, however, if we consider another of the major applications of this doctrine, viz. its application to alternative uses of the same material substance. Let us suppose, as in von Böhm-Bawerk's classical illustration, that Robinson Crusoe has five sacks of maize—one for his bread, one for his cakes and puddings, one for his poultry, one for a kind of whisky, and one to feed unnecessary companions such as pigeons. If the uses of the various sacks are in this order of importance, the marginal value is determined by the use to which the last sack is put. In this case, the fifth sack is just worth keeping for the pigeons; and if *any* of the sacks was accidentally destroyed, Crusoe would leave his pigeons to starve. If a further accident happened to another sack he would forgo his whisky. And so on.

Even in this instance, however, arithmetical figures seem demonstrably misleading. By hypothesis, the first sack is indispensable and the others not. Its value to Crusoe, in consequence, should *not* be commensurate with theirs. It is also most dubious whether a "marginal" increment can

---

[1] Cf. W. Brown, *Mind and Personality*, p. 99. Brown holds, however that "*contrasts*" are measurable in a sense.

properly be held to occur unless the increment approximates to an "infinitesimal".

Indeed, when we examine this question closely we seem to find, once again, a concealed connection with hypothetical market prices. In the end, the reason for treating the marginal utility as so important is the correspondence of this unit of usefulness with the condition of the retail trade in a stable economic system. What is maintained, in fact, is that there cannot be differential prices for the same quantities of the same commodity. One loaf must command exactly the same price as another loaf precisely similar. Since the "marginal" loaf, therefore, is actually purchased, it must determine the price of every loaf. For, by hypothesis, no one will pay more for any other loaf.

If this, as it seems to be, is the genuine argument, it clearly contains a nest of assumptions. In the first place, there *are* differential prices—for example, doctors' and surgeons' fees, and we have all heard of instances of differential prices among retailers in the same city, although sometimes, to be sure, the possibility is obviated by agreements between retailers and manufacturers regarding the selling price. If people, however, do frequently pay different prices for the same article, the arguments before us have to assume a strangely altered look.[1]

In the second place, the doctrine, at any rate in its simpler forms, would hold only of commodities which can be parcelled out into small portions in such a way that the sale of any one portion may be presumed to be independent of the sale of any other portion. Thus, as Mr Allyn Young points out, it would be unreasonable to assess, or to attempt to exchange, a large tract of homogeneous building-land at the same price as the product of the prices of the constituent building-lots.[2] Mr Young suggests that a different class of demand here comes into operation; and manifestly there is also the time factor.

---

[1] The force of this objection may be partially evaded by the circumstance that differential prices are normally charged to different classes of customers. The marginal method, accordingly, may be employed within each class.

[2] *Economic Problems New and Old*, pp. 210 *sq.*

In any case, however, it is clear that there is a relevant difference between selling goods in bulk to a single buyer and selling them in single parcels to a multitude of independent buyers over a considerable period of time.

In the third place, as von Wieser himself expressly stated,[1] it may happen quite readily that men expend labour and energy with the firm intention of providing a superfluity. A town, for example, may avail itself, at considerable expense, of a supply of water far in excess of any probable computation of its needs, and the town may properly take pride in this achievement. In this case the marginal utility of the water is *nil*; yet no one should maintain that a water supply of this kind has no value. The reason, in brief, is that there are great advantages in not having to economise at all; and consequently that if superabundance is approximately as easy to secure as an adequate supply, it would be mistaken policy, in this instance, to aim at the latter and not at the former. This would not, indeed, be good policy on the part of people who made their living by trading in units of water, but it would be good policy for the town; and the circumstance, surely, involves a most significant limitation of the significance of these marginal theories.

It seems necessary, therefore, to conclude that all such computations in terms of marginal utility properly apply only to some and not to all economic transactions; and that, when they do apply, further complications have to be reckoned with. There are complementary goods, such as pipes and tobacco, each of which is useless without the other. There are substitute goods, such as margarine in place of butter. There is the fact that the price of many articles depends upon the knowledge that only a few of the articles will be offered for exchange; and, as we have seen, the differences between cumulative and alternative employment, or between the demand for large stores and for small parcels, may be very highly significant. It is not to be denied that successive

[1] *Social Economics*, p. 128. The computation according to marginal utility, we are here informed, "leads one astray"!

elaborations of the theory may take account of these relevant distinctions and of others like them, but it may well be doubted whether the initial theory is not over-simplified.

It is also manifest that if, like Jevons, we expect to find some continuous mathematical function for changes in the ratio of exchange measured by "marginal" increments this can only occur, or even appear to occur, in cases in which there is a very large number indeed of purchasable parcels, each to be sold at the same price. As Jevons says, "any one sack of corn or any one bar of iron is practically infinitesimal compared with the quantities exchanged by America and England".[1] In his view, however, there is a failure of his equations when we deal, say, with America's purchase of Alaska from Russia; or with the ordinary sale of houses and factories.[2] For these have to be bought as wholes, and are not "practically infinitesimal" items.

It is time, however, to leave the more special features of the problem and to return explicitly to the general foundations of the theory. How far is it true that the theory, even in a restricted form, is a correct deduction from the laws of human satisfactions? And if it is a correct deduction, how far is this circumstance conclusive?

According to many authors, human desires are insatiable, or at least must be presumed to be so for the purposes of economic science. There is no limit to our acquisitive tendencies, no end to our ambition to provide a more opulent standard of living. Von Wieser, on the other hand, following Gossen, declared that "no sound need is insatiable".[3]

What is the truth in this dispute?

In the latter statement the express qualification that the need must be "sound" seems to savour of ethics in a marked degree;[4] and from the ethical standpoint, as we should all be

---

[1] *Theory*, p. 119.   [2] *Ibid.* p. 120.
[3] *Social Economics*, p. 25.
[4] Cf. *ibid.* p. 30, "Wholly degenerate needs may be insatiable". Von Wieser also asserted that "no economic distinction may be allowed between true and false needs, permitted and forbidden, or moral and immoral" (*ibid.* p. 23).

aware, there has been an age-long conflict between those who maintain that we should seek a life as rich as possible in enjoyments, and those who counsel us to evade the snares of fortune by diminishing our desires so far as we may. Both of these roads may lead to contentment, but the second, perhaps, is the better devised. The cautious Epicurus was probably wiser than the more flamboyant Cyrenaics who preceded him.

Such is the verdict of ethics, but ethics is only doubtfully relevant to these economic issues, and perhaps von Wieser did not intend his statement to be ethical at all. Is it true then, in fact, that most human needs, treated broadly and in principle, should properly be regarded as satiable?

From most points of view the question of fact seems to be at least as perplexed as the question of ethics. It is easy to borrow Godwin's thunder[1] and to declaim against the natural injustice of plutocrats who have more bread than they can eat, more clothes than they can wear, more houses than they can effectually inhabit. If greed and ostentation were out of the way, we are apt to think, these anomalies might readily be made to disappear. Yet greed and ostentation are actual desires and rather stubborn ones too. There are limits, to be sure, to the amount that even the grossest feeder is able to consume at a single meal, but wealthy persons who desire rare foods perfectly served (with the relish of good company added) would not seem to be trammelled by any definite barriers in the way of expense. Certainly, in a stable economic system the majority of mankind may confidently be supposed to be likely to jog their way through life without any active desire to alter their customary standards. A probability of this sort, however, does not seriously affect the question of principle.

In any case, the type of argument on which Jevons, Gossen, von Wieser and Mr Wicksteed were accustomed to rely appears plainly insufficient. During a single meal there may be a diminishing return of satisfactions (especially if the participants overeat themselves), but there is no occasion to

[1] In his *Political Justice*.

remark this phenomenon, in the general case, when we consider recurrent meals which are consumed at intervals during a long period. And, as we have seen, it is only in quantity not in quality that the limits of our satisfaction (in principle) need be supposed to be reached.

In most of the well-worn discussions upon this topic, however, another principle is invoked without any clear indication that the alternative principle is very different indeed from the simple occurrence of diminishing successive satisfactions. According to such alternative ways of reckoning, the margin of utility is computed by reference to the last unit of a given sort which anyone might be supposed to acquire rather than to do without. Thus we get the economic rhapsody contained in the doctrine of an alleged consumer's surplus.[1] Suppose that a woman would give eight shillings for a single pound of tea rather than have no tea at all. Suppose that if she already had a pound, she might be willing to give five shillings for a second pound. Then if she can obtain two pounds at the marginal price of the second one she is alleged to have a consumer's surplus of three shillings.

In this argument the times of the purchase are hopelessly confused, and the effect upon the purchaser's mind of already having a supply of tea is treated as if it did not signify. Our present concern, however, is not with this confusion, but with another oversight still more radical. The actual satisfactions of this tea-drinking lady are one thing, and conjectures about her attitude in the hypothetical case of her supplies being threatened or stopped are quite another thing. To alter the illustration, a man might be willing to give half of all he possessed rather than do without a single skinful of water. He would if he were in the desert; but considerations of this sort do not concern his actual satisfactions in England when he may have access to a whole river.

Let us consider another and most relevant point. It is usual, in these computations, to refer to separable portions of some single commodity. Shipwrecked mariners are sup-

[1] Cf. Marshall, *Principles*, Book III, chap. vi, § 2.

posed to have so many biscuits, or so many casks of water. Since the items are similar, it is easy to begin to do sums; and since mariners are sometimes shipwrecked and have then to exercise the most stringent economy, it is readily apparent that the illustrations, so far, are legitimate. The restriction of the illustrations to a single kind of commodity, however, may be most highly illegitimate. If water were the one thing the mariners needed, they might give their all for very little of it. The same might be true of biscuits if they had plenty of water and hardly any biscuits. Yet neither water nor biscuits would matter if their gravest peril were the immediate prospect of being frozen to death.

In short, many things are necessary to sustain a man's life, and many are necessary to sustain the existence of a community. If any one thing that is absolutely necessary were suddenly annihilated, ruin would follow. If several were annihilated together, the result would be precisely the same. The value to mankind of the requirements of each of these "sound needs" is infinite. The value of all of them taken together is this identical infinitude. What is the point, then, of computing the last unit, in these instances, which a man would strive for rather than do without? If the last unit were inadequate he would do better to let it go. If it were adequate, the question is not what he would give his shirt or his honour for, but what he really needs, quite apart from hypothetical conjectures about his satisfactions in cases of dire necessity or from his alleged satisfaction (which he need not notice at all) when his life pursues its normal course.

The more we investigate such questions, the more the inadequacy of the psychological economics of personally felt satisfactions is brought home to us. To say with Jevons that "the will is our pendulum"[1] is a statement that might perhaps be defended. For economics, understood with any strictness, may always imply effective human choice. To say that the satisfactions *which men actually feel* supply this pendulum, is to say something utterly false. In their practice, economists,

[1] *Theory*, p. 14.

whatever they may profess to believe on this important question, do not employ the pendulum either of private pleasure or of known and ascertainable gratification.

SECTION II. OF MEANS AND ENDS

§ 1. *Economics and the study of means*

As we have seen, the general practice of economists is to draw a trenchant and fundamental distinction between ends and means, and to maintain that economics is concerned wholly with the latter and not at all with the former. "Economic theory and practice", von Wieser declared, "are concerned only with the outward manifestations of the instrument of satisfaction."[1] He further declared that "consumption as such, the satisfaction of needs as such, is not an economic act at all".[2]

In other words (and to repeat), economics is concerned with utilities and with these only. Its fundamental proviso is that the utilities in question require a certain husbandry in their management; and, usually, a certain foresight regarding the quantities which are produced. Exchange-values form a sub-species of these economic utilities and are concerned with the ratio of transference of commodities which in some sense are owned.

Certainly, this conception of the domain of economics has been challenged with some acerbity. "Consumption", Ruskin said in his *Ad Valorem*, "is the end, crown and perfection of production, and wise consumption is a far more difficult art than wise production. Twenty people can gain money for one who can use it, and the vital question for the individual and for the nation is never 'How much do they make?' but 'To what purpose do they spend?'"[3]

This criticism is manifestly *ex parte*. To produce commodities is not the only way of managing resources; and spending,

---

[1] *Social Economics*, p. 22.   [2] *Ibid.* p. 43.
[3] Quoted by H. Kyrk, *A Theory of Consumption*, p. 11.

according to current theory, is as much an economic transaction as saving or making an income. Spending, in fine, is not consumption and it is not satisfaction. What Ruskin showed is only that economics is something different from a complete social philosophy or an adequate social ethics. It is not identical either with the theory or with the art of wise and harmonious living. Indeed, in so far as means are subordinate to ends, the economic study of our resources for welfare must be subordinate to the ethical study of the nature and constituents of welfare. In the alternative, if ethics, as some suppose, is a narrower study than is implied in the statement just made, we have to maintain that (in so far as means are subordinate to ends) the economic study of utilities must (similarly) be subordinate to the ends of these utilities. In the same sense, and to the same degree, economic valuations must be subordinate to the general valuation of all values, or, in other terms, to General Axiology.

As we have also noticed, this admission of the subordinate character of economics in a certain crucial sense does not show in any way that it is advisable to confuse the boundaries between economics and anything else (say, social philosophy). Nothing in fact could be more dangerous or worse conceived than a heady mixture of staff-work concerning ways and means, on the one hand, and visions, enthusiasms and ideals, upon the other. The staff-work is not the whole campaign, but its function is not therefore inconsiderable. If the campaign, in this instance, truly is social welfare, then, if economics is not the whole of the staff-work, these remarks may indeed require a certain modification. But in the main they would stand.

I may be excused, perhaps, for appending an observation of some little consequence. As it seems to me, certain economists (like Mill) attempt to escape from an unnecessary dilemma by a thoroughly illogical device. Being anxious to show that economics has an independent status, they rashly assert that economics has nothing to do with ideals and is wholly concerned with actual desires and satisfactions. This contention (we saw) might be sound if men's aspirations had nothing to do with their wishes or with their practice, and if men's habits and activities were either unalterable, or alterable only by inducements in which sympathies, loyalties and visions had nothing whatever to do. In reality, however, men are idea-driven, both by good ideas and by bad; and they are also ideal-ridden both by ideals of the baser and of the finer sorts.

In any case this suggested principle for distinguishing economics from the pursuit of welfare is utterly illogical. The authentic distinction is not at all between fact and ideal, actuality and dreaming, the plains and the hills, axiology and descriptive science. On the contrary, the genuine difference in this matter is between the hypothetical question, "If the end were so and so, what steps can be taken to bring it into effect?" and the categorical, more decisive, question, "What is the end that should be chosen?"

§ 2. *Mistakes concerning ends and means*

The distinction between ends and means is thoroughly familiar to ordinary thought, and is usually taken to be quite pellucid. Nevertheless, it is not infrequent for writers on political economy and on philosophy to fumble when they deal with it.

Among the former, we may here consider Jevons and Ruskin.

On page 82 of his *Theory*, Jevons spoke of "the nonentity of intrinsic value". Yet he was a convinced utilitarian. Indeed he was so orthodox a believer that he did not so much as mention any of the formidable difficulties which stand in the way of that theory, although he must have heard of some of them. Since the utilitarian thesis is quite precisely that pleasure alone is good in itself, or, in other words, that pleasure is always an intrinsic value and the only such value, it is clear that Jevons's entire theory is based upon this very "nonentity".

A similar and complementary fallacy is to be found in Ruskin's *Munera Pulveris*.[1]

"Intrinsic value," Ruskin there said, "is the absolute power of anything to sustain life. A sheaf of wheat of given quality and weight has in it a measurable power of sustaining the substance of the body; a cubic foot of pure air, a fixed power of sustaining its warmth; and a cluster of flowers of given beauty, a fixed power of enlivening or animating the senses and the heart. Used or not, their own power is in them, and that particular power is in nothing else. But in order that this value of theirs may become effectual, a certain state is necessary in the recipient of it. The digesting, breathing and perceiving functions must be perfect in the human creature before the food, air or flowers can become of their full value to it."

Confusion could hardly go further. Food-values are obviously instrumental, yet Ruskin would have us believe that the strength or "availing" of wheat is *its* intrinsic value, and even that every such "intrinsic" value is relative, at any rate in certain ways, to the condition of the human stomach.

These mistakes concerning "intrinsic" values imply mistakes concerning ends and means.

§ 3. *Points to be considered*

From the standpoint of philosophy the truth is that several allied but distinguishable and subtly varying conceptions intermingle in this matter.

Firstly, there is the distinction between means and end. This distinction itself may not always be so precise or so fundamental as it is frequently taken to be.

Secondly, the relation between a "means" and an "instrumental good", while manifestly very close, may require discussion.

Thirdly, a number of conceptions, more or less intimately connected with "ends", are nevertheless distinct from one another and from the conception of "end".

An "end", we say, is chosen *for its own sake*. Consequently, there is a visible affinity between an "end" and (1) an

[1] I, § 12.

"intrinsic" good, (2) a self-justifying good, (3) a self-sufficient good, (4) an unconditional good.

Yet these four conceptions are not themselves identical. An "intrinsic" good—let us say, a pleasure—may very well have conditions. "Self-sufficient" goods are usually regarded as wide departments of value completely organised, while "self-justifying" goods may be only the dominant and governing portions of such organisations. In both of the two latter conceptions, the goodness in question may be said to be intrinsic either to the whole which is organised or to its governing portion; and both of them apply to goods which, being underivative in point of goodness, may, in one sense, be said to be unconditionally good. Owing to the influence of Kant, however, a "conditional" good is usually said to be something which is good under certain conditions or in certain relations, but is not good under other conditions or in other relations. The contrast, in this case, is plainly between things which are good in *all* circumstances and relations and those which are good in certain circumstances and relations *only*.

If it were legitimate to assume that value is either contained in some pure fountain of excellence or borrowed, with dilutions, from the fountain, these various conceptions might indeed coalesce. In reality, however, there is no warrant at all for any such assumption. Value may grow and not be borrowed ready-made. It may be due to combination, not to extraction. Relations, not the pure substance of a separable essence, may be the breath of it. In a word, many *different* conceptions may enter into its analysis.

More in detail, the conceptions of a *dominant* good (not necessarily underivative, unconditional or universally efficacious), of a *complete* good (however arising), of an *intrinsic* good (which would be good in isolation) and of a *universal* good (which is good in *all* relations and in *all* circumstances) are really quite different, each from every other, and should never be confounded.

Furthermore, an end which is good is always a good which may be sought. For every end is something sought after. Yet there may be goods which *cannot* be sought, and there may be other goods which are always damaged in the seeking.

§ 4. *The category of "end"*

Clearly the first requisite in this enquiry is to analyse the contrast between means and end, and to examine the importance of the entire conception.

The contrast, we have seen, is familiar to common speech and to common thought, yet has led to confusion among writers of repute. Its very familiarity, perhaps, led these writers to their undoing; but some enquiry seems called for.

In the familiar way, we think of a "means" as a process deemed preparatory to some consummation, and it is quite indisputable that a distinction of this general sort is, in a host of instances, as plain as could reasonably be wished. We undergo surgical operations in order to recover our health, and although these weeks in the nursing home, since they put our patience and our fortitude to the test, may have a certain value, it is clear that we would not choose to undergo the operation, and that no surgeon would undertake it, were it not for the promise of recovery or some such ulterior justification. Again, nations go to war for the sake of conquest and the fruits thereof; and although there are a few who have a taste for soldiering when the guns are loosed, and a larger number of arm-chair theorists who extol the value of campaigning, the general view proclaims that war itself is a wretched business, although victory (whatever history has to say on the matter) is a glorious and most enviable consummation.

Assuming then that there is no appreciable doubt about analyses such as these, we have next to ask whether the category of means and end has a wide application of this luminous kind.

The most serious reason for doubting whether the category really has a very broad application lies in the strength of the contention that the category itself, in a wide range of instances, is subordinate to something still more fundamental, viz. our root interests, impulses or instincts interpreted primarily as modes of behaviour.

The doctrine of means and end had taken so firm a hold of Western thought that, until recently, it was customary to define the instincts by saying that they achieved an end of which the agent was totally unaware. The hungry animal feeds, and the amorous bird seeks a mate, without any proper knowledge of the biological purpose of nutrition or of reproduction.

This may be truth, but it is a singular way of stating the truth. To speak in this vein is covertly to assume that the conscious, or even the reflective, choice of ends, and the intelligent selection of means to such ends, is the only intelligible way of explaining behaviour, although we have also to admit the anomaly of apparently "purposive" action *without any purposes* on the part of certain agents or of most agents at certain times.

Surely it is possible, at least, that the terms of all such explanations completely invert the fundamental order of the facts. Plants feed and grow and perpetuate their kind. In their case it seems unnecessary to assume any possible prevision or foresight. The natural and the sufficient interpretation is the rhythm of biological process. Such processes, which are mainly periodic, have indeed a certain integrated continuity, and persist until equilibrium is restored. Their results, again, may be correctly described, in the normal case, as the perpetuation of individual or racial existence. These admissions, however, are of little moment. An end is not a *mere* result but a *chosen and intended* result, and in the case of the plants there may be neither intention nor design. Buttercups and dandelions have no designs, and if we say that nature has planned something for them, we may well be attributing to nature a quality and species of action which is really peculiar to *ourselves*, and in ourselves may be less frequent and less important than we fancy.

We differ from the plants, to be sure, partly in being conscious and partly in being reflective. If *we* lack food or moisture, we *suffer* from hunger or from thirst. We are disquieted as well as restless. We may also design aqueducts and granaries.

There is no need to assume that differences such as these are insignificant. The question is whether they are always or generally decisive, and it would seem that often they need not be. In many instances, at least, these anxieties and disquietudes report and prolong what they do not originate. They are the creatures of appetite, and appetite (which need not be conscious) goes deeper than suffering. What is more, these conscious experiences and these reflective designs may easily be partial and misleading. When we lack we do not always suffer, and when we suffer we do not always lack. More importantly, when our restless feelings report *something*, we may not know in the least what they are saying. We sigh for *something*, perhaps for *anything*, yet may have no inkling of what is fitted to still our unrest. And when we think we know the end that will still our longings, we may easily be mistaken. What else, indeed, could we expect? Before we have experienced the completion of any process, its "end" must be known by hearsay, or be divined, or be a phantom. When we have had our experience, we ourselves may change, or we may find the experience stale and trivial when it is repeated. In a host of ways we are very badly placed for making these estimates with any considerable degree of accuracy.

I do not wish to exaggerate the force of these contentions. I am not suggesting that our conscious experiences are always (or even usually) illusory or otiose. I am not insinuating that all (or most) reflection is a pompous and blundering menial. And I am not one of those who believe that "instinct" supplies a current of pure air warranted to dissipate all psychological fogs. On the contrary, it seems to me clear that what is called an instinct is seldom more than a general name for a rabble of tendencies all of which have, in a way, the same biological function. Man, as Mr Graham Wallas has neatly said,[1] is but semi-gregarious; yet we are supposed to be

[1] *The Art of Thought*, p. 116.

following the modern way if we explain all actions not habitually solitary by appealing to "the" gregarious instinct. A pseudo-science of this order is at the "metaphysical" stage of occult qualities, or, at the best, mistakes the names of classes for authentic causes in nature.

We should rid ourselves, therefore, of these fantasies. Yet, having learned to unlearn them, we find a stubborn residue most pertinent to our present subject. As a piece of simple description, we are bound to admit the existence of a great number of organised "tendencies", patterns or schemata in human beings, some (as we say) constitutional, others acquired without design or foresight in very various ways. These tendencies, in many instances, do seem to describe a natural unity of function artificially disintegrated into the contrast between means and end, and so to be misreported if we insist upon applying this category to them. In other words, what we call an "end" is often in part a reflected image and in part but a stage in a process whose foundations lie very deep. Its significance is therefore heightened in a misleading way, and the significance of the "means" to it is proportionately lowered. The "means" in such instances are parts of the integral process as clearly as the "end" is, and the process as a whole is probably richer than the "means" and the "end" that we commonly see in it.

Accordingly, without necessarily maintaining like Spinoza[1] or M. Guyau[2] that what we call an "end" is really the pale afterglow from a burning vital process, we may have good reason to believe that several so-called ends are aptly described in such terms. Indeed, hints to the same effect crowd in upon us when we look at ordinary conscious experience from this angle. The vicar of Wakefield, believing that the period of courtship is the happiest in a man's life, was anxious to see his son affianced (but unwedded) for as long a period as possible. Most lovers, if their minds were made up, would chafe at any extensive delay. Yet marriage itself is a beginning, and the

---

[1] Cf. chap. II of this book.
[2] *Esquisse d'une morale sans obligation ni sanction.*

effective desire for offspring (occasionally grossly and selfishly misdescribed as the longing for personal perpetuity) is in some hearts the "real" spring of this important affair. In such cases, to be sure, there may be genuine disagreements concerning what is end and what is means, but it is at least equally likely that there is no substantial disagreement and that, in the main, we have a series of snap-judgments according as this or the other aspect of a connected process makes an appeal to the observer. In any case it is uninstructive to make such judgments without carefully defining what is taken to be end and what is taken to be means. And in any case the category of end and means has many alternative, if valid, applications to these tangled processes.

Indeed, we might even say that since end and means are correlative terms, each is incomplete without the other. The completed circumstance can never be anything less than *this* means to *this* end, or in other words, a single connected process. Even in the stock instances of the surgical operation and the rest we have always to ask the question, "Is it worth it?" of the process as a whole, that is to say of end and means together. The reason here is partly that the means, in such instances, imply risk and suffering and temporary disablement, and that these are to be shunned on their own account. Even if the means were neutral in themselves, however, the same considerations would apply in principle. For if the means are carried through we have to occupy ourselves with them, and it cannot be indifferent if we spend our time in an employment of neutral value. We might spend the time differently in ways that were not neutral.

A further and serious perplexity springs from a dangerous ambiguity in the word "end". The difficulty here is a time difficulty and is due to the fact that "end" may mean either termination or climax. There is a connection between the two senses since any natural tendency, if interrupted, is apt to induce profound disturbance. Such tendencies have to work themselves out to their appropriate termination. And of course the termination *may* be the climax as when we climb a hill to see the view. On the other hand termination and climax need not coincide and frequently do not. Yet we often forget this obvious truth.

§ 5. *"Instrumental" or "Conditioning" versus "Intrinsic" values*

A means, in the most usual sense of the term, that is to say, a process designed to be preparatory to some given consummation, is a particular instance of the relation of cause and effect. Consequently, in a more general way, all causes, instruments, tools or media may be regarded as "means".

Any such definition is excogitated at the common-sense level of thought which finds no mysteries in the causal relation, and incidentally distinguishes causes from substances. A cause in this sense is either a substance brought into active connection with another substance (and therefore modifying it) or else an alteration in some given substance which determines an alteration in another substance. Thus, in the first case, the substance alcohol introduced into Jones's system may enliven Jones's spirits, although it would not be enlivening in the bottle; and in the second case, the modification of Smith's environment which we call illuminating his room may enable Smith to read or otherwise occupy himself in ways that would be impossible in the dark.

Assuming, then, that this conception of "instrument" is tolerably clear, we have to distinguish it, at this common-sense level of thought, from the conception of an underlying substantial condition. For example, it would be contrary to the implications of common speech to assert that Robinson's animal life, or the circulation of his blood, or the condition of his thyroid gland was a cause of his estimable moral qualities. The relation here is the relation of part and whole rather than the relation of cause and effect. The incarnate virtuous Robinson is an organisation of mind and body, and his virtues characterise *him*. But although we can point to half a hundred conditions without which Robinson would not be an incarnate virtuous person, we cannot, in general, call these conditions causes of his virtue. Even if we suspect some of these conditions to be genuine causes we do not know enough about the human body-mind in detail to do more than suspect.

This distinction between "instruments" and "substantial conditions" is of considerable moment and will confront us later. Meanwhile we may pass to another aspect of the question.

Anything that is good "as an instrument" and good in no other sense (e.g. a railway ticket) is "good-*for*" some purpose and is not good absolutely, or intrinsically, or *simpliciter*. Thus "virtue is good" is a logically complete or absolute statement, if virtue is an intrinsic good. And "Quinine is good-for" is an incomplete statement. On the other hand, "Quinine is good-for-fevers" is also an absolute or complete statement.

In view of this circumstance, it is sometimes contended that when A is good-for B, the whole value in the case must be ascribed to B, on the ground that A might have no value (or worse) if it were not employed at all or were employed for some other purpose. This conclusion seems uncalled for. The point, surely, is rather that A has value in a certain connection, and not in some other connection.

This alternative explanation, I think, comes nearer to our usual ideas than the other. The mere fact that an instrument is a *chosen* instrument tends to give it value in our minds so long as we continue to choose it—and perhaps a sentimental value thereafter. People usually have an affection for their tools, as a golfer has for his clubs. It is true, no doubt, that very few people ever conjure up affection for a ticket, but tourists have been known, say, to retain their cards of admission to the Salle Privée at Monte Carlo.

If so, our present topic is more complicated than might appear on the surface. If A is good *only* when it is instrumental to B, it is of course *not* good unconditionally, absolutely, intrinsically or *simpliciter*; and B *might* be good in these ways. On the other hand, it is at least possible that B also would not be good without A; and in general that intrinsic or absolute values need not be looked for in all cases in which there is *any* value. If we know, or have very strong reasons for believing, that many values (such as Robinson's virtue perhaps) could not occur without underlying substantial conditions which need not be valuable in some other connection, we should not hesitate to assert that these values may nevertheless be entirely authentic. An absolute or unconditioned value is one which would be valuable apart from any conditions. An intrinsic value is one which would be valuable if it were utterly solitary. These hypothetical statements are not necessarily impugned by the mere fact that no finite values *are* absolute or unconditioned in the sense of such definitions; but if the hypothesis in question is manifestly absurd, like the chastity of some angel who had never thought of a sexual body, it need not receive close attention.

In any case, as we saw in § 3, the contrast between "intrinsic" values, and those extrinsic relations which we call instrumental, is only one of the relevant contrasts in this field of enquiry.

§ 6. *Self-justifying and self-sufficient values*

Let us turn, then, to certain other conceptions.

Anything that is justified, is justified because of its value. If a thing is the best that could exist, it is completely justified; and if we know that the thing is good, although we do not know whether or not it is best, we have, in this measure, a relevant, although an incomplete justification. Contrariwise, unless we can point to some value in the thing or connected with it, we have *no* justification to allege concerning it.

Consequently, as we saw, an "intrinsic" and a "self-justifying" good are closely allied. An intrinsic good must justify *of itself*, because everything *except* itself is excluded by definition.

When we speak of self-justifying goods (or values), however, we commonly think of some organised system of values such as morality, science or art. A moment's pleasure, fleeting, sporadic and forgotten, would be an "intrinsic" value; but many philosophers would refuse to call it a "self-justifying" value on the ground that nothing episodic and impermanent should be dignified by this name.

Keeping, then, to systems of values, we mean, when we call them self-justifying, that they are governed by some authoritative value or set of values, and that this special authority, whatever its origin, is not derived from some other authority. Thus as Bradley said,[1] I should be *immoral* if I tried to give anything but a *moral* answer to the question, "Why should I be moral?" Moral authority lies *within* morality, and questions concerning moral justification can be answered—legitimately—only by analysing and pondering the moral system itself. In the same way, we should usually say, with Spinoza, that truth is its own norm,[2] and that art must be judged by its own canons. A truth that is dangerous or ugly or morally subversive is none the less a truth, and these alarming tendencies, if they exist, are scientifically irrelevant. One's duty may be unaesthetic and still be unquestionably one's duty; and it is art that must judge whether vice or the fabulous is properly an artistic subject. The question, to employ the vernacular, is whether the artist can "get away with it". As we all know, a plausible impossibility is better, artistically, than a genuine possibility which people will not believe in. Horse-sense *may* stand in the artist's way, but a part of his business as an artist is to lull, to overcome, or to make use of it.

The query may be put, however, whether *any* of these systems of value are really self-justifying. Truths, it may be said, are often trivial, and in that case justify nothing however true they may be. It really does not matter where Mons Graupius was, or whether James VI, connived at the closing scenes at the Castle of Fotheringay.

The answer here is that it is for science to settle what truths are or are not trivial. In the matter of Galgacus or of King James it is for historians to explain whether they are playing

---

[1] *Ethical Studies*, chap. ii. I fear Bradley also held "that it is a moral duty not to be moral". *Appearance and Reality*, p. 436.
[2] *Ethica* II, chap. xliii, Schol.

with puzzles, or retailing gossip, or making a substantial contribution to their subject.

There are, however, further difficulties. "It is the duty of a newspaper to tell people the truth provided that the truth was not obtained in an illegitimate manner", Mr Baldwin is reported[1] to have said. The caveat, if admitted, shows that the *expression* of truth need not be self-justifying, and the same would usually be said of other caveats regarding truth and, say, the functions of the press in war time. Thus the public interest, or the morality of the methods employed in ascertaining the truth may override the claims of truth itself. And it is hard, in this affair, to distinguish between truth and its expression.

Similar considerations hold of art. There are memoirs which should never be published, however signal their excellence in their own *genre*. And if certain views should not be expressed in war time, their expression in perfect prose or with the beauty of consummate oratory could not justify them.

It follows that neither art nor science is completely self-justifying in the sense that it has unlimited authority. Each, however, has complete authority within its own sphere. It is for art to say what is artistically good, and for science to determine what has scientific value. The expediency of the orator's eloquence has nothing to do with the question whether or not he *is* eloquent though it may have a great deal to do with the question whether he should be allowed to make a speech at all.

Morality, to be sure, may be differently circumstanced from art and science in this crucial respect; and it must be differently circumstanced if morality governs our whole lives and is always, in idea, the pursuit of the best. This interpretation of "morality", however, carries us far beyond the ordinary lists of virtues and of duties. Indeed, it implies a complete axiology. To be sure it would not *be* axiology for it would be *conduct* directed towards the best, while axiology would be an entirely catholic study of all values and disvalues, and of all possible

[1] See press of 20th March, 1928.

standards of value. Even on this interpretation, however, morality (although of unlimited authority regarding conduct) would be, in another way, the greatest of all borrowers. It would have to go to science to learn what scientific values are and to art to learn what artistic values are. And it would govern these other values, not in the sense that it could intermeddle with them directly, but chiefly in the sense that it might have to declare that any such value, however great it were, should nevertheless have to be forgone.

After "self-justifying", we have to consider "self-sufficient" goods.

The notion of a self-sufficient good plainly differs from the notion of a self-justifying one, and the point does not need much explaining in view of what was said in a former paragraph concerning substantial conditions. As we have seen, morality is self-justifying in the sense that the question "Why should I be moral" must be answered from within the moral point of view. If this be not so, morality cannot be what it claims to be. It does not follow, however, that morality is in every sense self-sufficient. It may well imply underlying substantial conditions which it accepts and cannot alter—much in the way in which Margaret Fuller accepted the universe. To return to our old illustration, the virtuous Robinson is a body-mind in whom virtue resides. His admirable character, we agree, is to be found in the governing part of him, supposing that we could distinguish this part from the rest. A government, however, draws its sustenance principally from its subjects, not from itself. Consequently it is not self-sufficient even when its authority is supreme.

§ 7. *Summary of the foregoing*

Before proceeding with this investigation, we may conveniently sum up the general results of our analysis, and say:

(1) That a value may be self-justifying without being entirely self-sufficient, although a self-sufficient value must be self-justifying.

(2) That an unconditional value is closely akin to a self-justifying or self-sufficient value. In general, however, all our values imply underlying substantial conditions, and what we commonly think of in these cases is a whole which (including its substantial conditions) is absolutely valuable, or, less stringently, is generally or predominatingly valuable.

(3) That self-justifying or self-sufficient values ought to be sought when they can be sought, and are therefore ends. It is possible, however, that certain values, although admittedly authentic and perhaps even profound, are quite incapable of being sought at all. We may acquiesce in them and even long for them but cannot properly seek them. In this case it seems improper to call such values "ends".

(4) That in dealing with the "end" of any process we must always be careful to distinguish between the "climax" and the "termination" of the process. These need not coincide, and when they do coincide, it is the former, not the latter, which is of greatest significance in this matter of values.

(5) That it should never be forgotten that "means" and "end" form a connected process.

(6) That all means are, or are a certain class of, instruments. It should not, however, be concluded that any value not self-sufficient, self-justifying or absolute is therefore "instrumental". Instrumental values, strictly speaking, are the *causes* of certain effects, and the conceptions of self-sufficient, self-justifying or absolute values are not derived from the causal relation or in principle reducible to it. In general, the most precise form of division is the division into values, on the one hand, which always or usually occur whenever a certain dominant value is present, and into values, on the other hand, which occur in certain specific relationships only.

(7) That the conception of an "intrinsic" value is obviously very closely connected with the conception of self-justifying, self-sufficient or absolute values and with ends which should be sought for their own sakes. On the other hand, it is to be noted (*a*) that such intrinsic values might quite well occur without being sought, perhaps even without being amenable

to search, and are therefore not ends; (*b*) that in the usual instances of self-justifying or other such values the important point is not so much whether the values could exist in isolation, or would be valuable if they so existed, but that they *are* values *when* they occur. If so, it may be also true that they occur in some context and have underlying conditions which, although they may not be absent, need not have any obvious or direct relevance to the problems of value.

§ 8. *Complementary, supplementary, alternative and competing ends*

If confirmation were needed for the statement that the potential isolation of "intrinsic" values might be relatively unimportant, it would be found in the analysis of complementary ends. For these, in so far as they are complementary, are *not* to be treated in isolation. It is better, however, to treat this and kindred conceptions without any *arrière pensée* of a polemical kind.

In Section I, § 9, of this chapter a brief reference was made to complementary utilities, substitute utilities and the like. A fuller treatment would have distinguished between joint demand and joint supply, and would have shown that the possibility of alternative uses of the same material thing leads both to competing demand and to competition in production. There is a demand both for milk and for milk-products such as cheese; and petrol, once a waste product, has become a by-product of commercial value, and finally a product in chief. It would also be necessary to distinguish between direct and indirect utilities (e.g. the effects of lighting or ventilation firstly upon output and secondly upon health and general contentment) and also to consider the extent to which disutilities are or are not separable from utilities (e.g. the extent to which industrial life must be huddled as well as urban, and the *pros* and *cons* of urban existence itself).

We have now to ask how far these considerations apply to ends as well as to means.

It is abundantly evident that there are alternative ends, and that these ends may compete. This is so plain that the point would not need any discussion whatsoever, were it not that certain authors falsely suggest or maintain that material or possessive goods are the only ones which give rise to competition. Any such idea, of course, is utterly mistaken. Some material goods, like a man's waistcoat or a piece of bacon, cannot (or should not) be shared. Others, like parks or libraries, may very well be collectively owned and used. Apart from this it is simply not true that there is no competition regarding spiritual or creative ends. To be sure, one man's activities in these cases may seldom actively hinder another's, although it is hard to see how a co-operative enterprise, in science, for instance, could be undertaken without a great deal of voluntary subordination and spade work which is rather self-sacrifice than anyone's self-culture. Suppose, however, that we neglect these complications, and consider the general issue only. Within himself a man has several spiritual capacities and he cannot develop them all to their full extent. If he tried to do so he would succumb to the aimlessness of versatility, and would incur the historic penalty of those who, in a single month, try to be fiddlers, statesmen and chemists.

With regard to complementary, supplementary, and substitute goods, however, there would appear to be a clear distinction between what is end and what is means. Indeed, it might seem reasonable to hold that these characteristics apply *only* to means and not at all to ends. The nature of complementary demand is that several distinct means are necessary, conjointly, for a single end. Tobacco is useless without a pipe, and a pipe is useless without tobacco. Both are needed for the single end of smoking. What happens again in the case of joint, or supplementary, products is that portions of the same material may be used for different ends —as coke, coal tar and aniline dyes. Finally, substitute utilities are most naturally regarded as alternative means to the same end—as saccharine and sugar may both be used for sweetening jam.

This contention, too, may well appear quite general for it is certainly not restricted to industrial or to material means. Institutional religion serves many spiritual ends, and if adventures in the air or on high mountains take the place of what was sometimes called the Great Game of war, we appear to have one source of excitement, valour, or renown substituted for another source.

I cannot think, however, that these considerations are decisive. The courage, sympathy and team-work implied in the mountaineer's code are, after all, analogous to, not identical with, the courage and other admirable implications of soldiering. If war became an anachronism we should have an alternative activity rather than an alternative means, and the activity would be means and end together. It would therefore be as much a substitute end as a substitute means in terms of this very argument. For the comparison now before us is not between the "ends" of conquering enemies, on the one hand, and conquering mountains upon the other, but between the acquired excellences of the soldierly and the mountaineering characters.

And so of complementary ends. It may be freely admitted that facile optimisms and puerile accounts of the *summum bonum* paint an unconvincing fairyland with their easy commingling of all possible perfections. This, however, is no proof that perfections, and even seekable perfections, may not commingle. The propinquity of the beautiful and the true, we think, is a natural propinquity. In other words, these ends are in principle complementary. And if we think, turning critical, of the defects of great excellences, or of the propinquity which high and serious things have with sorrow and pain in the lives we have to lead, our conclusion, in its essence, is strengthened rather than overborne. This sorrow and this pain are elements in such ends, not means to the ends. The question is not one of instruments helping or hindering one another, but of union or disunion in fruition.

In brief, there *are* complementary ends.

§ 9. *Heterogony of means and Polytelism*

If an end were always strictly correlative to its means, there would be a certain theoretical error in speaking, as Wundt[1] did, of heterogony of means, or, as M. Bouglé[2] does, of polytelism. When we use these terms we are adopting the standpoint of common, uninformed opinion according to which different causes may have the same effect, and the same cause, for unknown reasons, may have widely differing effects.

In other words, according to the language of the schools, we are assuming the possibility of plurality of causes and of plurality of effects. Here difficulties may lie of a pretty obvious kind. We say, indeed, that a man may be killed by poison or by shooting (plurality of causes), or that the jest which appeals so strongly to Debenham may grievously offend Freebody (plurality of effects). Yet even in the common view, as in detective fiction, death-from-gunshot is an event characteristically different from death-from-arsenic; and everyone would admit that there must be differences between Debenham and Freebody to account for their opposite attitudes to the same jest.

Nevertheless, it is at least a tenable view that plurality of causes and of effects have a certain meaning, importance and truth. The shot and the arsenic, although in different ways, do cause the man's heart to stop.

By heterogony of means, then, is meant the familiar process, by which the means to some end become adapted to some other end when the first end falls out of favour. This process, understood in general terms, is as familiar as it is salutary and essential. We have a temporary heterogony of ends when peace-time factories are adapted to the purposes of war, and we should have a more permanent heterogony if spears were turned into pruning hooks after war had been outlawed. Folklore and anthropology supply innumerable

---

[1] *Ethics*, Part III, chap. i.
[2] *L'évolution des valeurs*, pp. 90 *sqq*.

examples. Thus the swastika, according to Mr Mackenzie,[1] was developed from the equal-limbed cross which served as a primitive compass to early mariners, became a symbol of the four seasons, and thereafter, being adapted by a solar cult, came to symbolise certain attributes of the new divinity. The Jewish Passover, again, continued to be observed as the Christian Easter, although the early Christians believed in continuous not anniversary celebrations.

M. Bouglé, to whom the name polytelism is due, illustrates his conception by referring to the various functions of a suit of clothes (such as adornment, concealment, warmth and social prestige),[2] or by the various ends, hygienic, aesthetic and economic which an architect has to build for, or by the way in which a weekly day of rest may have the most subtle consequences upon a man's health, spirits, family relations and religious cult and beliefs. We may say, if we choose, that very few actions rest within themselves, and that all tend to spread, frequently in most dissimilar directions. When these branching activities can be induced to conspire together, we have complementary ends. Otherwise, we have a motley or jarring polytelism.

§ 10. *Transvaluations of these values*

Except for the last paragraph, and for a few sporadic hints, our investigations in this section have taken no account of time, or of development, or of change. It is obvious, however, that ends alter and develop, and also that substantive values —that is to say the circumstances, experiences, or pursuits on which we set store—alter in respect of the value which (as a characteristic) we attach to them.

It is necessary now to rectify this omission, but it is also necessary to make an explanation by way of preface. If there is any way in which the process of valuing yields truth, these truths of valuation must, like all other truths, conform to the logical Law of Identity. With them, as everywhere, the

[1] *The Migration of Symbols*, p. xiv.
[2] *Op. cit.* p. 92.

maxim "Once true, always true" holds indisputably—provided, of course, that the maxim itself is properly understood.

In other words, if any given person, say Hodge, values anything, even a fleeting personal experience *truly*, the truth of his valuation cannot be affected by anything that happens subsequently either to him or to anyone else; and although his valuation may have been caused by antecedent events, the valuation cannot thereby be made other than it is (i.e. true). It does not follow, however, that the circumstances, activities or pursuits in which Hodge correctly finds value at one time, necessarily yield him value at another time. The reason is that these phrases are imprecise. A pursuit, for instance, which is fresh and vivid is only generically, not specifically, "the same" when it becomes stale or tedious, and this specific difference between freshness and staleness might be the whole relevant difference between a value and a disvalue.

In short, in so far as transvaluations are genuine—that is to say, in so far as they are not matters of mere opinion or the correction of former mistakes—they deal with entities which change in respect of their value either absolutely or in relation to some particular person or set of persons. In the latter case, what is correctly valued at any time is not a "thing" *simpliciter* or in all relationships, but in some limited or personal relationship and in that only.

In general, when we say that a man's "values" change, we mean that there is a change somewhere in the total state of affairs which we describe by saying that the man finds value there, or else that there is a change in what the man thinks about the matter. These alternatives coincide only in the case in which the man both thinks and thinks truly. Such a coincidence may be comparatively rare, and the problem of its rarity or its frequency is one of the main topics we have later to discuss. For the moment, however, it must suffice to say that, in certain senses at least, men may prize or set store by much that never crosses their minds, and that, when they take themselves to be aware of values, they may frequently be without authentic evidence that their opinions are true.

(Discussions on the theory of value, of course, have to deal with someone's beliefs or opinions on the subject, but discussions about Hodge's values need not be preoccupied with Hodge's views. For Hodge may have no views, or none worth a theorist's attention.)

To resume. A man's values may alter, either because *he* alters or because there is alteration in something with which he has to do, and a man's opinions about values may alter for a great many reasons, most of which need not be considered here. We ought, however, to remember the principal ways in which values may alter through personal or first-hand experience. Such experience, for the most part, makes us, as we think, wise after the event. What seemed bright in prospect may be heavy and sombre in fruition, or may be linked with consequences which destroy the real although partial advantages that were correctly foreseen.[1] The converse too may occur. That of which little was expected may be or become something great, and opportunity may knock at the door of the most listless and careless inmate.

It is enough, however, to recall these feeble platitudes. To dwell upon them should be quite unnecessary. *Per contra*, it is expedient and even inevitable to consider, in some detail, the forms of transvaluation which specially concern ends and means.

The simplest and most notorious form of this species of transvaluation is the process in which a means comes to be regarded as an end. The stock illustration, of course, is the miser who, in defiance of the nature of things, would rather have his money than use it, and so becomes, effectively, the most abject sort of pauper. In discussions of this instance it is commonly assumed that the miser begins by regarding money

---

[1] Cf. Vaughan's lines:
> I played with fire, did counsel spurn,
> Made life my common stake,
> But never thought that fire would burn,
> Or that a soul could ache.

as a means, but becomes so engrossed in the process of acquiring (or of retaining) a competence that in the end he becomes blind to the functions of money altogether. It may happen so; but it is also possible that through hearsay and the perversions of our social system, he makes this mistake from the beginning.

However that may be, it is clearly advisable to distinguish between the cases in which this process results in a perversion, and those in which nothing of the sort need be supposed. If, for example, we choose a man's growing interest and pride in his profession as an illustration less one-sided than the instance of the miser, we see at once how complicated the analysis of the affair may become. Since the aims of a man's life can seldom be fully accomplished in any single profession, it is plain that a man who has nothing to live for except his job must, in a sense, always be a starveling. Yet surely it would be a miserable society, and far more miserable than our actual state, if men's occupations were to be regarded, simply and entirely, as means to the home, or to dining and wining and such leisure as may be spared. The professional activity itself, although in many ways a means, is also a way of living, and may itself be a value. The mere circumstance that work is work and fulfils a function should not prevent a man from loving and taking pride in his work as an activity, not simply as a source of consequences.

To be sure, these statements may be true of the initial stages of the activity as well as of the activity in its developed form. The stripling who chooses his profession may, no doubt, begin by selecting it as a simple means. He has to do something, and it may not greatly matter which out of several possible careers he chooses. He may have a lucrative income in view and little or nothing besides, or he may ardently desire to become the instrument of some good in the world. It would be interesting to know what proportion, say, of medical students falls into each of these three classes and what proportion falls outside them. It would also be interesting to discuss how far the conception of instrumentality in the third class is modified by the fact that its members *choose* to make instruments of themselves. Freely to become a tool is perhaps to become more than a tool. But let us put side issues aside. Pride and joy and interest in the art of medicine must in large measure be acquired, and may be acquired irrespective of the motive which determined the choice of the profession. If the process was begun as a simple means, it does not usually continue such, and the change need not, in any proper sense, be fictitious or perverted.

Means therefore may transform themselves into ends, perhaps abruptly, perhaps insensibly; and similarly ends may transform themselves into means. The publisher's hack and the penny-a-liner may have felt themselves artists in the beginning, and may be the veriest drudges in the end. Some who go to pray remain to keep up appearances.

So much, then, for the transvaluations respecting means and ends. There are clear instances of ends becoming means and of means becoming ends, but for the most part the lesson we should mark and digest in consequence of these enquiries is the need for caution in drawing this very distinction. We can hardly stir the surface of the question without finding "ends" and "means" dissolving and commingling. What from one point of view is an end is a means from another; and it is folly to forget the recoil of our own weapons.

The problem, indeed, should be considered more generally, and I propose to proceed with a more general treatment. In doing so I shall omit the question of repetition, staleness or novelty as being too notorious to require more than mention, and shall deal instead with the expansion, the organisation and the differentiation of interests. I do not suggest that interests and values are the same, but there should be no appreciable difficulty in generalising such results still further.

Our lives become more affluent through the expansion of our interests. In the beginning our experiences are relatively naked and forlorn. Later they are apparelled with imputations, suggestions, and nuances of memory and of meaning. There is at least as much difference here as there is between a line of Virgil quoted in the present House of Commons and the same line quoted there in the eighteenth century, or between the Bible to a Scotsman and to a pagan gentleman. Our interests, in short, may be so transformed by expansion that they are genuinely transfigured. When transfigured they ought to be transvalued.

The differentiation of interests, however, is at least equally important. When interests are simply narrowed or contracted they are therefore impoverished; and this process occurs very often. We become "set" in our ways and we pay the penalty. On the other hand our interests may be the richer because they are deepened and purified, and although no interest is a fixed quantity which must occupy less bulk if impurities are removed, or have its surface diminished if its depth is increased, it is nevertheless undeniable that concentration of attention may also transfigure an interest. Settling *Hoti's* business, I daresay, would be a tedious employment for many of us; yet a good grammarian has a finer interest than most who are avid but undiscriminating; and if the man who renounces his catholic affection for bird and for beast in order to study the herring loses a very great deal, he may still be the gainer. To argue otherwise would be to maintain that all specialisation, being really super-specialisation, is a loss to ourselves and to the world, or that the microscope cannot transfigure as well as the glass.

Fortunately, however, we need not abandon ourselves to the simple alternative of expanding our interests on the one hand and contracting them, through concentration, upon the other. According to the usual metaphor, there is a vertical as well as a lateral movement to be considered; for our interests should come to form a hierarchy. As we shape our purposes we try to fit them into a proportioned edifice. This is the architecture of the spirit, and it is illustrated by the way in which private interests may become part of an integrated public policy or carnal functions are made the foundation of a sacrament.

§ 11. *Certain tentative conclusions*

The intention of this Section has been to explore an intricate subject, not indeed fully, but not quite cursorily. Any such attempt has attendant disadvantages. There would be more than good luck—indeed there would be something suspiciously like a miracle—if a single conclusion emerged from these labyrinthine explorations, and determined all future advance. On the other hand, all these intricate enquiries are undeniably relevant to the central problem of the character of *bonum utile*, and we may conveniently supplement the general summary contained in § 7 by offering a few observations on the situation in which this central problem now finds itself.

Firstly, then, we should consider the extent to which the ramifications of the present section affect or appreciably modify the conclusions of Section I; and here, I think, we should conclude that there should be little, if any, essential modification. To be sure, we spoke, in Section I, of means and ends in the common way, and this language, in view of the later argument, must be regarded as only provisional. Nevertheless, in essentials, it should stand, for the simple reason that the economic doctrine of *bonum utile* has been excogitated with reference to a distinction between means and ends. As we have seen, this distinction is sufficiently clear in a great many instances; and among these instances the economic are, for the most part, the clearest of all. Material commodities *are* means to ends; and human services, from the standpoint of economics, are means also, whether they are regarded from the point of view of exchange or from the point of view of production. It would be otherwise, indeed, if economics purported to be a social philosophy, but so long as an economist keeps to his last and is content to ask those hypothetical questions which are his proper and his most important business, he is entirely justified in framing his hypothesis in terms of this distinction between serviceable means and alternative ends.

On the other hand—and this is the second point—our general ideas concerning the status of *bonum utile*, or, so to say, the general philosophy of it, can scarcely remain unaffected by the enquiries in this section. For in view of what we have seen, we cannot afford to treat all the material conditions of human value as nothing but means, and to concentrate, as philosophers, upon ends alone.

At any rate we should not do so *forthwith*, on the simple basis of some plausible but dangerous dogma concerning means and ends. I am aware that certain authors profess to have intuitive certainty that nothing that is not conscious, or, again, nothing that is not spiritual, can possibly possess intrinsic value, and maintain in consequence that unconscious or non-spiritual "values" are at the best instrumental only. Doctrines of this species must be considered in the sequel, and so it would be improper to examine them now. All that concerns us meanwhile is certain points in the logic of them.

In the end, these doctrines combine a judgment of relevance with a judgment of irrelevance, and rely upon the principle that a justifying value is always intrinsic. Their exponents discern intuitively (*a*) that consciousness or spirituality is relevant to authentic value, and (*b*) that anything else is irrelevant. If this pair of intuitions be accepted it certainly follows that even if spirit or consciousness have underlying conditions which are unconscious or non-spiritual, such underlying conditions cannot belong to the province of authentic values. For the judgment of irrelevance aforesaid expressly forbids this idea.

I do not wish to maintain that spirit or consciousness could not exist without bodily conditions, but it would be a hard thing, I think, if we were bound to prove them capable of discarnate existence before we had the right to maintain that they might have value; and this, as I understand, is seldom contended. Supposing, then, that they do have bodily conditions when they actually have the values we are anxious to ascribe to them in the ordinary way of everyday human experience, it is surely dubious to assert that anything they cannot possibly do without is really irrelevant to their value.

Human nature's daily food is *not* irrelevant to the human spirit, and I have argued that there *is* irrelevance in maintaining that the food has no intrinsic or unconditional value on the ground that it is valueless when unconsumed. The question is whether it is valueless when it is consumed, and unless we can maintain that it is not an authentic value even when it performs this essential service we have no right to assert that, in logic, *all* value must be completely determined by *intrinsic* value. To see this clearly is to gain something.

In the third place, I would repeat that if we insist upon debating these questions in terms of means and of ends we should take the most scrupulous pains to define what is taken to be means, what taken to be end, and in what respects. And I shall attempt to justify the repetition by means of an illustration which itself has great importance. It is commonly held, and often it seems to be very true, that increase of value is largely determined by increase of spirituality. Without in any way seeking to controvert this opinion, I should like to show, on the lines which M. Paulhan[1] has made classical, that much in the opinion depends upon its definition of means and of ends.

Animals feed, and man may dine. That, in sum, is a process both of socialisation and of spiritualisation. Instead of jostling and snarling at one another, those who dine in a civilised way make the meal an occasion for wit and story and other collective amenities. The pleasures of the table, again, are capable of authentic refinement. If the palate is not as noble as the ear or as the eye it should not therefore be called base or swinish, and those who extol the pleasures of the table in a lyrical or even in an epic vein do, in their own way, spiritualise it. Even an exaggerated curiosity in these matters (like that of Huysmans) is more, not less, spiritual, than common swallowing.

[1] In *Les transformations sociales des sentiments*.

Hence many conclude that spiritualisation, in many cases, may be a very great evil, for they assume that nutrition in principle is only a means and therefore conclude that to refine, to spiritualise or to make an end of it is always a species of perversion. Others, to be sure, maintain the contrary; but even they, for the most part, would be inclined to impose pretty stern limitations upon the permissible development of the gourmet's interest.

What has now to be noted, however, is that if the biological functions of nutrition are alone in question, it is very doubtful indeed whether either the gourmet's aestheticism or the incorporated social spirit which, as many think, redeems dining from being a merely animal performance, is biologically advantageous. Even if the best food is plain, the cult of perfection in these matters is not the best way of acquiring a hardy stomach, although, to be sure, the man who is either listless or bolts his food unless he is in congenial company does not properly consult his health. Our vaunted superiority to the animals in this affair does not show that, biologically speaking, we are wiser than they, or that our social or spiritual riches may not prove our undoing. The very hierarchy we establish may be shaky at its foundations.

An even stronger instance is that of sex. There is not merely the danger of being sex-ridden in the most spiritual or introspective way; there is also the danger that the more we mingle sex with enduring companionship or community of interests the more we may imperil its efficacy as a biological means. Perhaps sex is a better means if it is quite frankly a simple means. Here also the animals, except under conditions of domesticity, may be more efficient than we are; and although no one could seriously maintain that we either could or should return to a condition of mere animality in the interests of racial perpetuation, it is advisable for us, in our pride, to consider, with some accuracy, what is means and what is end.

SECTION III. OF SIGNOR CROCE'S OPINIONS

The attentive reader of these pages, if he is also familiar with Signor Croce's writings, will find, despite the differences, a definite measure of concord.

Signor Croce's purpose, as I understand it, is to give an analysis of the economic function, and to show the place of this function in a synoptic philosophy of the spirit. While no such philosophy has been attempted in the foregoing sections, these sections contained an attempted analysis of the economic function. And a philosophy ought to follow.

Signor Croce, it will be recalled, sharply distinguishes between knowledge and action, and applies to each of these categories his doctrine of the double degree. In the case of knowledge, he maintains, we have the two degrees of intuition (whose province is aesthetics) and of conceptual science. In the case of action we have, correspondingly, the two degrees of economic and of moral function. In both cases, the two degrees are distinct but united—distinct because the first degree (e.g. the economic) may occur without the second (e.g. the moral) yet united because the second cannot occur without the first and because the second, when it does occur, is wholly concerned with the government of the first (which is by nature properly subordinate to the second).[1]

The economic function, accordingly, is not technical or applied knowledge—for it is not knowledge at all, but action. It may be "innocent" or non-moral because it may occur by itself and so be self-subsistent, but it cannot be anti-moral, because morality, when it enters at all, enters as the proper governor of this very economic function and of nothing else.

Hence we have firstly a critique of economic science, and secondly a constructive philosophy of the economic function.

The nature of Signor Croce's critique of economic science may perhaps be sufficiently indicated by a brief narration of the four main points he elaborates in his letters to Professor

[1] *Philosophy of the Practical*, Part II, section I, chap. iv.

Pareto.[1] These four points are (a) that economics, in principle, is not mechanical; (b) that it is not hedonistic; (c) that it is not, properly speaking, technical; and (d) that it is not egoistic.

(a) Economic facts, Signor Croce contends, are facts of choice, and they imply appreciation or appraisement since the choices in question may be made well or ill. Economics, in short, ought to deal with certain of the practical activities of a *man* whereas "mechanical" principles apply either to dead things or to something merely animal. The fondness of certain economists for a "mechanical" view results from their delight in measurement and in mathematics. *Homo economicus*, however, is not a term in a mathematical equation. He really is *homo*. In the wooden psychology of the *Sättigungskala*, human motives are treated as fixed numerical entities whereas in reality each is a distinctive reaction to a fresh psychological situation. The thirsty man who has imbibed two glasses of water has not, to speak exactly, just so much less thirst, but has instead a specifically different, although a more languid, relish for the fluid.

(b) When we choose well, and act efficiently, pleasure ensues; but pleasure may arise in other ways than from the fulfilment of desire. It is only one particular species of pleasure, therefore, that is relevant to the economic function; and economics, consequently, ought not to be identified with hedonism.

(c) The economic function is doing, not knowing, just as a bungled action is a practical muddle, not necessarily a piece of ignorance. Technical knowledge, therefore (as we have seen), is not the economic function.

(d) Egoism is wicked. It is the persistent and intentional assertion of the self against all other claims in the world. Hence egoism is quite different from the economic function (which is not wicked but is simply a man's efficiency in his deeds).

---

[1] Accessible to the English reader in a volume entitled *Historical Materialism* (London: H. Latimer), translated by C. H. Meredith, chap. vi.

As a result of these criticisms, Signor Croce arrives at the conclusion that "the data of economics are the practical activities of men in so far as they are considered as such, independent of any moral or immoral determination",[1] and in the second of these letters to Professor Pareto he puts his point in a way peculiarly interesting to the student of value-theory.

"Activity", he says, "is value. For us, nothing is valuable except what is an effort of imagination, of thought, of will, of our activity in any of its forms. As Kant said that there was nothing in the universe that could be called good except the good will; so, if we generalise, it may be said that there is nothing in the universe that is valuable, except the value of human activity. Of values as of activity you cannot demand a so-called genetic definition. The simple and the original is genetically indefinable. Value is observed, immediately in ourselves, in our consciousness."[2]

Signor Croce's critique of economic science is at the same time a critique of certain current opinions concerning the nature of means and of ends. In reality, he maintains, "what is called means is nothing but the actual situation (and the knowledge of it) from which arises the practical act, and to which that act corresponds".[3] In other words, the economic function is really the quality of efficiency in a man's deeds, and so it is misinterpreted in a mischievous way when it is replaced by dissertations concerning causes and effects, and particularly concerning the supposed causal connections between material things and the hypothetical satisfactions or utility of an economic man. In short (as we in our own way have also contended) economic *value* has slipped out of sight when, in place of it, we are presented with certain theorems concerning "instrumental" goods.

It is time, however, to pass from these negative and critical arguments to the positive philosophy of Signor Croce's contentions, or in other words, to the second or moral degree of practical activity and its relation to the first or economic.

The most concise and the most telling summary of this view occurs, I think, in the *Aesthetic* where he says "To will

[1] *Historical Materialism*, p. 173.   [2] *Ibid.* p. 179.
[3] *Philosophy of the Practical* (Eng. trans.), p. 338.

economically is to will an end; to will morally is to will the rational end. But whoever wills and acts morally, cannot but will and act usefully (economically). How could he will the rational end, unless he also willed it as his particular end?"[1]

It is evident that the term "rational" and the term "moral" in this summary require (as of course they also receive) definition; for Signor Croce's statement would not be even remotely plausible if morality or rationality were interpreted in the narrow senses too often ascribed to them. Both terms, in fact, have to be understood in the most catholic and comprehensive way. Reason is totality and oecumenical harmony, or, as Signor Croce also says (although, we may suspect, with an emphasis far too human and planetary, far too little cosmic), it is humanity in its fullest compass as opposed to contingent, individual, self-seeking. Morality, similarly, is *the whole* of reason in action, the very breath and spirit of catholicity, comprising all values, all culture, all profound aspirations, and the very antithesis, in consequence, of a list of prohibitions brought down from some high mountain or a set of rules for living prudently and avoiding social friction. This, and nothing less than this, is the autonomy of the second or ethical degree.

The consequence, one would suppose, ought to be a lucid and entirely unambiguous solution of the problem of the relation between *bonum* and *bonum utile*. For it is plain how the solution would run. *Bonum*, we might say, is goodness or value. It is confined to, and is the essence of, practice or activity. *Bonum utile* is also confined to activity, and it is the quality or moment of efficiency in such activity.

I think this is the solution we ought to expect, but it is not Signor Croce's solution; and I should like to suggest that he should not have offered any other solution. If the first "degree" is simply the moment of efficiency, then it should surely be apparent that "efficiency" cannot conceivably stand by itself. Yet it is an essential part of Signor Croce's philosophy that the first degree can so stand.

[1] *Aesthetic* (Eng. trans.), p. 57.

Any genuine value, he maintains, must be efficient, and must be efficient in the domain of practice where all efficiency occurs. That is the nature of the dominion of the second degree, and, so far, all is clear. As it seems to me, however, Signor Croce's theory has slipped precisely because he has conceded to his opponents what, in terms of his own theory, he ought not to have conceded them. These opponents, in the main, are utilitarians taking shelter behind an egoistic psychology. Utility for them is summed up in private advantage; and they point triumphantly to the fact that people do seek their own personal benefit. Certainly many people do, and Caesar Borgia, to choose Signor Croce's favourite example, differs very clearly in this particular from Giordano Bruno. Surely, however, if we are right in admiring Borgia in any way, it is his efficiency, not his egoism, that we are right in admiring, whereas, in the case of Bruno, we admire, not his efficiency (which was doubtful) but the dignity of his death and the splendour of his aims. In short, utility (or the economic function) is just efficiency and nothing more. It is *entirely* an abstraction and *therefore* incapable of standing alone. It should be treated hypothetically, not categorically. To treat some complete action, like many of Caesar Borgia's, as if it was the *quality* of efficiency is to sensualise and make substantial an abstract relationship which, in principle, repels such treatment.

It is probable, I think, not merely that Signor Croce has conceded more to the utilitarians than he ought to have conceded them, but that, like so many other philosophical architects, he has striven too hard to impose the symmetry of his system upon intractable material. It is no part of our business here to consider the relations between the first and the second "degree" on the side of knowledge or speculation, i.e. to consider the relations between aesthetic and conceptual knowledge, yet we can hardly avoid the reflection that a great part of Signor Croce's immense influence in the domain of aesthetic theory has been due to the fact that he has vindicated (as many think, successfully) the independent status of art and beauty. Nevertheless, his parallel between the aesthetic and the economic degree is obviously, in many ways, a brilliant *tour de force*, and may well be so in this matter of potential self-sufficiency. One may wonder, in short, whether, apart from the parallel, Signor Croce would ever have thought that mere efficiency could conceivably stand alone.

We may also, I think, ask ourselves whether the fundamental distinction between knowledge and action should be drawn quite in the place where Signor Croce draws it or quite in Signor Croce's way. Morality, we agree, is not the statement of certain theoretical principles concerning action. For moral principles themselves are active. And the economic function is not a theoretical application of theoretical principles but efficient choosing and doing. Nevertheless theoretical principles, and speculative and applied knowledge, enter into both and may properly be considered in a theoretical way, provided that we never forget that any such treatment cannot exhaust the question. There *is* such a thing as moral science and there *is* such a thing as economic science. If each of these lacks something, neither of them, in consequence, should be set aside.

CHAPTER II

SPINOZA'S ACCOUNT OF VALUE

§ 1. *Introductory*

WE have already noted, on various occasions, that a distinction must be drawn between what is beneficial, on the one hand, and what, on the other hand, is agreeable or, again, is the object of conscious appetency. This distinction is of critical importance in the theory of value, but it does not exhaust the subject. For other senses of value must be considered as well as, and in connection with, these—especially "value" in the sense of perfection or excellence.

Spinoza's account of good and evil, perfection and imperfection, in his *Ethics*, supplies an admirable introduction to these fundamental topics.

We should note that, although Spinoza wrote some centuries ago, there is no occasion, in consequence, to suppose that what he says is either obsolete or archaic. Anyone, for example, who reads Mr Whitehead's *Religion in the Making* can scarcely avoid being impressed by the Spinozism of the account of value contained in that work. To say, as Mr Whitehead does, that value is "the ultimate enjoyment of being actual"[1] or that "to be an actual entity is to have a self-interest"[2] is pure Spinozism, whether or not Mr Whitehead remembered Spinoza when he said so. To be sure, Mr Whitehead's further statement that "an actual fact is a fact of aesthetic experience"[3] is couched in terms that Spinoza would not have used. When we read, however, in Mr Whitehead's next sentence that "all aesthetic experience is feeling arising out of the realization of contrast under identity"[4] we may perhaps suspect that any difference which subsists between them is an affair rather of words than of substance.

---

[1] *Op. cit.* p. 100.   [2] *Ibid.*   [3] *Ibid.* p. 115.   [4] *Ibid.*

It would be impolitic, however, to linger upon Mr Whitehead's statements because, besides being cryptic, they are condensed to the point of obscurity. Spinoza, on the contrary, defined his terms and elaborated his conceptions.

§ 2. *Spinoza's account: the first phase*[1]

Spinoza's intention, in the first phase of his doctrine, was to erect an impregnable barrier between the vulgar idea of value and the philosophical conception of perfection.

True philosophy, he affirms, is monism, that is to say, nothing is really explained unless it is explained from the standpoint of the One or of the Whole. And the Whole (which is One) is God.

In God, reality, perfection and power are the same. All things, therefore, are produced by God in supreme perfection, because all things flow necessarily from His perfect nature.

The vulgar sometimes maintain that there is nothing good or bad, perfect or imperfect in things, except in so far as God makes them so by His arbitrary will or by His mere good pleasure. This is an error because it implies (which is impossible) that God's pleasure might be mutable or capricious. Again, it is an error because it implies that God might have willed things to be other than they are, i.e. that what flows from His nature might also not flow from it.

A more serious vulgar error, however, is also commoner. According to this prevalent mistake, God is said to act *sub ratione boni*, that is to say for an end or purpose outside Himself. Opposing this mischievous heresy, Spinoza, in the Appendix to Part I of his *Ethics*, expresses himself in terms which, in comparison with his usual severe restraint, are almost garrulous.

Whether in God's case or in man's, Spinoza is astute and sedulous to show, good and evil, understood in the common way, are mere illusions bred from man's ignorant and irresponsible belief in final causes.

[1] In the *Ethics*, Part I.

SPINOZA'S ACCOUNT OF VALUE

Men believe themselves to act for an end, and to have a mysterious faculty of freedom. The truth, however, is quite precisely opposed to these fantastic, if inveterate, prejudices. What actually happens is that man is driven by his appetites and desires, yet is ignorant of the nature and of the causes of these appetitive processes. Because of his ignorance, he takes these processes to be uncaused when, in fact, they have causes. His second mistake is to misread the character of his appetites. Man's appetites are such that they minister to his advantage —that is to say, their normal result is to serve man's interests. Hence men conclude that they act for the sake of their own advantage when in fact they are pushed, *a tergo*, into certain advantageous fruitions. And along with this pair of errors goes a third error. Men magnify the phantom which they have created in their own case, and proceed to presume its influence everywhere in the universe.

Men have eyes that see, and teeth that chew. Concluding, therefore, that eyes come into existence in order to see and teeth in order to chew, they go on to argue that *everything* which is adapted to *any* function comes into existence for the sake of performing that function. Thus "Nature", they say in their folly, "does nothing in vain". Indeed, in their preposterous theories of design and of providence, men try to bring God Himself into the very jaws of their own insatiable greed. God, they think, is helping them. What better could He do? If there are storms or earthquakes or pestilence they think God is angry.

Such, then, are the roots of the vulgar error that Spinoza believed he had exposed, and we need not stay to consider the additional reasons he gives in his various proofs that this "error" really is an error. What does concern us is the way in which he used this exposure of error to clinch his analysis of good and evil according to the vulgar interpretation.

Through the mistakes aforesaid, Spinoza tells us, men call those things the best by which they are most fortunately affected. Thus many vulgar notions come together. Good and evil, beauty and deformity, praise and blame, sin and merit, order and confusion, and the "secondary qualities" such as hot or cold—all these have the same status in this affair.

Men call good anything that conduces to their health or is bound up with the practices of their religion. The opposite they call evil. What suits their faculties they call well-ordered. Anything else they call "confused". What is conformable to the economy of the nervous system they call beautiful. All else is said to be deformed. What suits their bodily senses, as odours suit the nostrils, defines the status in question; and all such matters pertain not to knowledge, demonstration or the intellect, but to a spurious realm that Spinoza calls "imagination".

In short, good and evil have to take their place among the fictions and the phantoms which depend upon, and vary with, man's animal, sensory and emotional nature. *Quot capita, tot sensus.* It is all a sham and an empty play.

§ 3. *Comments on the first phase*

There is, of course, a genuine contrast between the *perfectum* or real, and the *utile* or beneficial. The latter is relative and incomplete, the former absolute and complete. In this first phase of Spinoza's doctrine, however, the contention is that the meaning of this contrast and of the terms which compose it is overlaid and obscured by a pernicious and pervasive error unthinkingly accepted by the mass of mankind.

If Spinoza is right in asserting that nothing in the universe is uncaused, "freedom" or "liberty", in most of the vulgar senses of these words, is a very puerile notion. It does not follow, however, that purpose or teleology is also a puerile notion, because it has to be shown that the conception of purpose conflicts with the conception of cause.

It must be conceded, however, that, to the vulgar mind, there is a definite conflict between the statements that we are impelled *a tergo* by our appetites towards a certain end, and that we *seek* this end because it beckons us *a fronte*. Perhaps then the vulgar are right (as they often are) in taking these alternatives to be not simply different but actually contradictory. If the alternatives are contradictory, teleology must be rejected by all consistent Spinozists *because* causality is true; and even if they are not contradictory, it is open to every Spinozist to maintain that teleology is gratuitous because causality is a sufficient as well as a necessary and true explanation of these matters.

Nevertheless, Spinoza's contentions seem to contain a lacuna. Let us suppose that final causes are an illusion, and freedom a bombinating chimera. It is still impossible to deny (and certainly impossible for Spinoza) that certain things *are* beneficial to the human species, or conducive to the health of particular men and women. Therefore, if good *means* beneficial, the rejection of freedom or of final causes cannot alter the circumstance. It can only alter the way in which we think of the circumstance.

Ultimately, therefore, the gravamen of Spinoza's argument is that our common way of thinking about facts which are true in some sense and over a limited range, is radically vicious in the eyes of philosophy. The reason he gives is that the common way of thinking is perniciously interfused with our senses, and that the senses are misleading faculties pointing to unreal regions.

Here several distinct questions are bundled together—not to the advantage of clear thinking. I do not think it can be denied, indeed, that Spinoza, like so many other rationalists, oscillated between the radically different views that the senses are unreal (i.e. nothing) and that generalisations based upon them are apt to be illegitimate, because such generalisations presume the senses to afford a theoretical message which, in fact, they are quite incapable of yielding. The former view is absurd, because there certainly *are* sensible colours, sensible pleasures and so forth. These facts, therefore, cannot be nothing. The latter view may reveal itself, in the end, to be wrong, but it is not absurd.

Only the latter view, therefore, can conceivably be well-grounded, and even with respect to it, Spinoza's summary inclusion of so many distinct classes of experience into the common genus which he calls "imagination" seems, in this matter of good and evil, to contain formidable difficulties of its own.

He takes the *pulchrum* to be merely the pretty or pleasing; and this, while it is an aesthetic theory not infrequently held, is also hotly disputed.

What he says of order and of confusion is still more perplexing. Even a mathematical demonstration may be well ordered or ill; and the order in things seems as authentic a piece of reality as anyone could wish to find. Accordingly, it is not mathematical proportion or order that Spinoza must be taken to mean, but a vague aesthetic order—something that appeals to our senses without our knowing why. So regarded, his statements are consistent and intelligible, but his way of making them cannot be commended, especially when we remember that, in the bulk of his theory, the falsity and unreality of the senses, passions and imagination are ascribed entirely to their "confusion".

Spinoza's reference to the "secondary" qualities is also puzzling. He meant, we must suppose, that colours, sounds, and the like are relative to our bodies (or "in our heads") while the geometrical properties of physical things are not. If he could have anticipated Berkeley he would have seen that the shapes which we perceive are as much in our heads as the colours.

He did not anticipate Berkeley; so let us pass the point. We know, however, that he strenuously advocated the doctrine of psycho-physical parallelism. From this doctrine it should follow that *all* our thoughts, even when we are geometrising, are matched by a corresponding process in our physical brains. If so, what is the point of saying *Quot capita, tot sensus*, and declining to add *Quot capita, tot intellectus*?

To be sure, reasons can be given for believing that truth and demonstration must be the same for all, whereas many sensible and emotional qualities are highly variable, one man's fancy being another man's abhorrence. Hence it may be argued—there is no experimental evidence to confirm the

SPINOZA'S ACCOUNT OF VALUE

point either way—that the brain correlates of logic are similar in all men, while those of many sensations are dissimilar. Both classes, however, must be matched by brain events and in the same sense.

Again, supposing the essence of the argument to be the fact of variation, Spinoza should surely have noticed that if some sensible qualities are highly variable, others seem to vary very little. When Shylock tried to prove that, although a Jew, he did not differ relevantly from Christians and other men he referred to these very senses and bodily powers. It will suffice, perhaps, if we recall this famous passage.

I am a Jew. Hath not a Jew eyes? hath not a Jew hands, organs, dimensions, senses, affections, passions? fed with the same food, hurt with the same weapons, subject to the same diseases, healed by the same means, warmed and cooled by the same winter and summer, as a Christian is? If you prick us, do we not bleed? If you tickle us, do we not laugh? If you poison us, do we not die? And if you wrong us, shall we not revenge?[1]

§ 4. *Spinoza's account: the second phase*

The second phase of Spinoza's account of value, we may say, is defined in the scholium to Proposition 39 of Part III. Here it is stated that good means every species of joy, particularly the joy that comes from the fruition of any desire, and that evil means sadness, including all the sadness that comes from thwarted desire.

This opinion, although not in itself remarkably striking or original, is the result, in Spinoza's case, of an elaborate psychology of the emotions and of a penetrating analysis of human activity.

The cardinal points in this analysis are joy (*laetitia*), sadness (*tristitia*) and *cupiditas* (or appetition). These, in their turn, are said to be modes or expressions of the fundamental activity, self-assertion or self-maintenance which are the essence of any actual thing. For the reality, perfection or fundamental character of anything is just its endeavour to persist in its own special mode of being.

[1] *The Merchant of Venice*, Act III, Sc. 1.

The term *cupiditas* describes the various forms or patterns which this fundamental endeavour assumes, and is itself psycho-physical. On the bodily side it is called appetite, and on the mental side it is called will. It may therefore be defined as appetite accompanied by the consciousness of appetite.

Although joy and sadness are primarily psychological terms, they are also understood by Spinoza in a wider way. Joy he defines as the emotion wherein the mind passes to greater perfection (III, xi, Schol.), being careful to add that it does not imply any explicit comparison between different degrees of perfection (III, General Def., Explic.). It is increase of power, reality, self-assertion, vital or substantial essence. And sadness is the polar opposite of joy.

Spinoza's views on the mind-body relationship induced him to interpret the connection between our brains and our emotions in the way later made familiar by the by-product or epiphenomenal theory. In other words, he maintained that our emotions are but the recorders and the ineffective companions of bodily processes, and even went so far as to argue (inconsistently with his general parallelism) that the passions were not indispensable companions of these brain processes, since somnambulists act as if they were conscious, although, in reality, they are unconscious (III, ii, Schol.).

This doctrine underlies his entire theory of joy and of sadness. "Whether a man is or is not conscious of his appetites", he says (III, Affect., Def. i, Explic.), "the appetite remains one and the same", and therefore a man's *cupiditas* is simply and entirely his characteristic essence taking some determinate form (*ibid.*). What holds of joy or of sadness, holds also, of course, of value or disvalue, since these (in this phase of the argument) are the same. Spinoza accordingly informs us, with all the emphasis at his command, that "we do not endeavour after, will, seek or desire a thing because we judge it to be good, but on the contrary that we call anything good because we endeavour after, will, seek and desire it" (III, ix, Schol.).

So far, then, the doctrine is one of naked self-assertion,

although expressed in terms of joy and of sadness. We endeavour to bring about anything that conduces to our joy (III, xxviii), but this, in its turn, means that we try to increase our strength, power and actual essence. For the same reason we try to strike an alliance with whatever is favourable in our physical environment (III, xii *sqq.*), thus drawing into ourselves greater strength and solidity. Again, what we do in our human way, brutes also do in their brutish way (III, lvii, Schol.).

It was quite apparent, Spinoza showed, that good and evil in this sense are relative terms, human good being different from canine,[1] and Caesar's from Pompey's. He also maintained that such values are relative in a further sense, because they are merely comparative. Men, he said, judge of good and evil by reference to their own personal condition. We call a man intrepid who does not fear what we fear, and we call him timid if he is afraid of things of which we are not afraid. Thus we form standards of value, forgetting how comparative and how personal they truly are.

§ 5. *Remarks on the second phase*

What I have called the second phase of Spinoza's argument differs from the first phase, not indeed in principle, but in its characteristic elaboration. In a certain sense Spinoza may be said to be explaining what he meant in the first phase when he told us that we were so ignorant of the nature and causes of our appetites. Physically regarded, he maintains, each of us is a unique pattern of movement, a "balance of motion and rest". Psychically regarded, we are the mental counterparts of this pattern of movement. Yet we cannot help being ignorant of much that is highly relevant to the pattern, because our consciousness reflects our physical individuality in a personal and isolated way, although this physical in-

---

[1] Spinoza even says (Letter XIX): "The wars of bees, the jealousy of doves, etc., things which we detest in men, are nevertheless things for which we consider animals more perfect."

dividuality is itself largely determined by causes outside the body of which, for the most part, we are ignorant.

Spinoza's parallelism, in the one-sided form which he defends at this stage of his argument, is obviously full of difficulty. To discuss these difficulties, however, would lead us into a vast region of dubious relevance. We must therefore forgo the enquiry.

It is much more manageable, and it is also necessary, to offer some comments upon the lurking ambiguities in Spinoza's account of joy and sadness in their relation to our essence, actuosity and self-assertion.

As we have already seen so often, it is illegitimate to identify joy or pleasure with augmentation of life or power. It is clear, in the first place, that our vital forces may be augmented without any sensible joy or pleasure at all. Indeed this normally happens during our sleep. Secondly, it is plain that pleasure or joy is not an infallible indication of health, or strength or efficiency. Morbid excitements, the Chinaman's taste for opium or even the small boy's taste for vast quantities of jam or the small girl's taste for a score of chocolates, are sufficient examples. Since Spinoza's time, and especially after the general acceptance of some form of the Darwinian theory, these considerations have become notorious. Biological advantage, we now know very well, may occur without consciousness. What is more, the keenest pleasures and pains attend our finer or "epicritic" sensibility, not the deeper or "protopathic" organisation. There is more pleasure from the finger-tips than from the spleen, more pain from the gums than from the liver. Yet there is less biological importance. Again, although what we like is usually good for us and seldom seriously hurtful, there is no more than a general correspondence under this head.

Another ambiguity in Spinoza's theory is to be found in his sketchy references to the relation between pleasure and desire. Here again subsequent analysis has revealed a gaping set of differences. Desire, so far from being identical with pleasure, is normally restless and uneasy if not acutely painful. Accordingly it is only the "object" or expected fruition of desire that can conceivably be regarded as being necessarily pleasant. And here we have to say (1) that many pleasures may occur without antecedent desire (e.g. the scent of pine-woods or the stimulating quality of streams and graceful uplands). Such experiences may generate the desire to repeat these pleasures but will not account for the original unexpected enjoyment; (2) that, as Bishop Butler showed, the appetite seems frequently to come first and the pleasure to result from its fulfilment. Normally we eat because we are hungry, not because we anticipate the pleasures of the table; (3) that if the anticipated pleasures in any desire are disappointed, there is no pleasure at all either in the desire (which is uneasy) or in its fruition (which is sad and disheartening).

§ 6. *Spinoza's account: the third phase*

Up to the present, the story of value, as Spinoza narrated it, has been manifestly incomplete. The first phase was negative, being the exposure of an illusion. The second phase, although positive, was concerned with man's passionate not with his rational nature; and "reason" is man's distinctive character as well as the principle of his dignity. In the third phase of his argument, however (which is contained in the fourth book of the *Ethics*), we approach the completion of the story and attain its principal instalment.

The result, as the reader may have anticipated, is profoundly to modify the *prima facie* tidings of the first and second phases, and in a sense to introduce discarded notions all over again, although in a transfigured form. Freedom, so absurd in the vulgar way of regarding it, appears now as rational self-determination and in this guise is the chief stone of the corner. Animal self-assertion becomes rational activity; animal joy an acquiescence in the rational self, combining dignity, self-respect and proper pride—in a word, *animositas*. Since the achievements of reason may not conflict, but interweave themselves into a firm and tenacious fabric, this *animositas* is also *generositas*. Otherwise put, animal self-seeking and all the predatory aspects of the *meum* are left far behind. Even finalism or teleology reappears in a way; for rational man is said to be an ultimate end (IV, App. iv). The abstractions contained in so many definitions of good are undone in the overwhelming concreteness of the *summum bonum*, that is to say, in beatitude proper. And similarly over the whole range of this immense subject.

As a preliminary to his extended survey, Spinoza gave certain further explanations concerning good in its relation to perfection, and evil in its relation to imperfection (IV, Preface); and it is best to follow the order of his exposition.

He distinguishes two meanings of the word "perfection". According to the first and strictest interpretation of the term, a work is said to be perfect if it precisely fulfils the intention of the workman. A house, for example, which is built exactly as the architect and the mason meant to build it, is, so far, perfect.

A second signification of the term arises from man's habit of constructing general norms, patterns or standards. Viewing them from this angle, we call the things in nature perfect, or imperfect, according as they do, or do not, attain these standards. This is perfection *in genere*, as distinguished from perfection *simpliciter*. Nevertheless, as Spinoza had already explained in the first phase of his doctrine, these standards are not to be found positively in nature but are the fabrications of men. The "perfect" house of the builder who does what he means to do, and the "perfect" house of the builder who conforms to our standards of what, as we say, a house ought to be, are both, metaphysically considered, the simple consequence of man's appetite and taste for domesticity.

Despite this reiterated assertion, Spinoza, with very dubious consistency, is prepared to modify his earlier definition of good. He now means by it, he says, that which we know *for certain* to be advantageous to our species *as if* it approximated more and more closely to an ideal pattern of human nature (*ibid.*). In other words, although *genera* for him are fictions,

Spinoza permits himself to attach independent meaning and importance to generic perfection.

§ 7. *The Rational Good: Synopsis*

Although our first concern, in this enquiry, is with the conceptions of good and evil, perfection and imperfection, which Spinoza uses in his philosophy, it would be impracticable and pedantic to attempt to separate these analytical questions altogether from the profound and comprehensive survey of nature, man and deity which is Spinoza's magnificent achievement.[1] It is relatively easy, moreover, to avoid any such pedantry, since Spinoza himself gives a *coup d'œil* over the general perspective of his theory in the Appendix to Part IV of the *Ethics*.

The sum of it is as follows: All our appetitive movements follow from our own nature in such a way as to be explicable, either directly by our own nature, or indirectly, if we knew how, by this nature in conjunction with the various external causes which affect it. The first class defines what is, properly speaking, our own actions. It is knowledge, reason, understanding by adequate ideas. The second class is necessarily inadequate and confused and it defines our passions.

In this sense our *actions* are always good; our passions may be either good or bad; and our beatitude consists in the true or metaphysical comprehension which arises from understanding of God or the Whole with consequent acquiescence therein. The perfecting of knowledge or understanding, therefore, is man's greatest utility or advantage. Evil can come only from outside a man.

Men cannot, however, sunder themselves wholly from the influence of external things, and therefore they may and should seek their good or advantage in the sense defined in the second phase of the argument, that is, they must study to conserve their health and physical welfare and security. In this regard, nothing is more advantageous to a rational

---

[1] In Letter XXVII Spinoza says that "a large part of Ethics, as everyone knows, must be based upon Metaphysics and upon Physics".

man than other rational men. And men should seek the advantage of every part of their nature, because they are the better equipped for understanding and thought in proportion as their lives are fuller and richer in experience.

Man's greatest perfection accordingly is the attainment of understanding, and acquiescence in, true and adequate knowledge. He should seek this perfection with the better part of him, that is to say with his mind, in so far as a man may.

§ 8. *Remarks on the above.* A. *The nature of action*

It is advisable, and even necessary, to expand this summary by examining three of its cardinal features. These are: the nature of action, its distinction from passion, and the connection of these with the life of reason.

Since our virtue is our power (IV, Def. viii) our true virtue is our true power or activity; and we are said to act in the true sense when anything follows from our own nature which can be clearly and distinctly understood in terms of that nature alone (III, Def. ii).

Plainly, this is the Stoic ideal of entire self-sufficiency and self-mastery. As Spinoza elsewhere says (II, xiii, Schol.): "The more the actions of an individual body depend on it alone (*pendent ab ipso solo*), and the less the influence of other bodies concur in its doings, the more distinctly does the mind apprehend"—and become active. Such also is the obvious and natural reason why Spinoza maintains that the rational life is our emancipation from a certain bondage. In it we are delivered from the tyranny of outside things, and cease to be the playthings of circumstance.

As with the Stoics, however, this doctrine of Spinoza's may easily reach an impasse when confronted, as it must be confronted, with the problem of the relations between the microcosm and the macrocosm. Spinoza strenuously denied that man is, in fact, an *imperium in imperio*, a self-governing member of nature's empire, yet he speaks as if we could *make* ourselves free, and as if, in becoming free, we became literally one with the Whole. It would be a bold thing to affirm that

SPINOZA'S ACCOUNT OF VALUE

Spinoza, unlike most other monists and most other determinists, had withstood the menace of these perennial difficulties.

Again, there is yet another way in which Spinoza's account of action gives rise to specially harassing difficulties; and this time he is (not indeed alone) but a member of a smaller company. The problem here results from his views concerning the relation between knowing and being—in short from his habit of identifying the two. To say that our strength is identical with our knowledge of our strength, or our sufficiency with the knowledge of our sufficiency, is to say something so little plausible that the marvel must seem how anyone came to believe it. Yet Spinoza believed it and said it. Indeed, without it, his edifice crumbles. Let us ask, then, why he said it.

Spinoza had a dual theory of knowledge. From one point of view, he maintained, knowledge is a species of agreement or correspondence. The mind agrees with its bodily counterpart which *pro hac vice* is the proximate cause of the mental idea. To be caused in this way is just to know, and the accuracy of such knowledge depends upon the proximity of the causes. Remote causes, although not wholly unknown, are known very imperfectly.

Such views have frequently been held from the dawn of serious philosophy up to the present time; yet they cannot be adequate. When Dr Johnson kicked the stone in order to refute Berkeley's philosophy, it seems just as unreasonable to conclude that the stone was aware of the proximate cause of its translation in space (i.e. of Dr Johnson's shoe) as of the remote cause (i.e. Dr Johnson's opinion of the immaterialist philosophy). In other words, not any causality is knowledge, but only (at the best) causality *upon a mind*; and when we come to examine the mind, the causal theory becomes less and less convincing. Mental events seem often to occur whose causes we do not know. When we take ourselves to perceive the causes, it is the remote and not the proximate causes that we take ourselves to perceive; for we suppose that our perception extends to what we can see or touch, and these are remote causes in comparison with the proximate cause (our brain) which we know very imperfectly indeed. Still more importantly, it does not seem to be true that the mind, in fact, knows itself better than anything else, or that it should not know, quite directly, things other than itself.

I think therefore that when Spinoza says that "to act under the guidance of rational knowledge, to live and to preserve one's essence are one and the same" (IV, xxiv), he is saying what is false. A life guided by reason may indeed be the strongest life, when reason organises what we call the vital forces; but our lives cannot be identified with our rational knowledge.

Along with the correspondence (indeed, the causal) theory of knowledge Spinoza holds another and essentially different theory. Knowledge, he says, is self-revealing, just as an illumination reveals both itself and darkness (II, xliii, Schol.). Truth is its own criterion and shines by its own light.

It is this second theory, and not the first, that gives any plausibility at all to Spinoza's theory of action (or to Leibniz's which, in this particular, was borrowed from Spinoza). What is more, the second theory, if it is not true, seems at least very likely to be so, although to be sure, it has still to make up its mind whether this natural light is the self-evidence of particular truths, or the coherence of a world of truths, or both combined. Rational self-evidence comes very close indeed to what Spinoza is asserting. In it our knowledge seems to depend upon itself alone, and to need no other support. Such self-sufficiency, however, is not true at all of our strength and our life; for strength and life do require outside support if only in the way of ordinary nourishment.

§ 9. B. *The nature of passion*

If Spinoza's account of action is hard to accept, his account of passion is also not easy.

Sometimes the main point seems to be that the passions are essentially bodily. To say, as Spinoza repeatedly does, that man must expect always to be subject to passion, is to say that he cannot escape from his body, or his body from its surroundings (e.g. IV, iv, Cor.). Again, the fundamental proposition, so familiar in contemporary British philosophy, that nothing but a stronger and contrary passion can control a passion, is said to be proved by the consideration that nothing but a bodily state can affect a bodily state (IV, vii). Indeed, Spinoza adds that the true knowledge of good or of evil cannot, in respect of its truth, control a passion, but only in respect of its bodily counterpart (IV, xiv).

A second, and for Spinoza a more important circumstance, is that our passions are confused and inadequate. This second characteristic, as we have seen, is connected with the first, because our bodies are not self-supporting or self-explanatory, but inevitably affected by remote causes which must always be imperfectly understood. Whatever the reason, however, our passions, according to Spinoza, are defined, and in a measure condemned, by their confusion.

The difficulty here is that, according to Spinoza, confusion is not a positive characteristic of anything in nature. It is simply something lacking as if one were presented with a ready-made conclusion without hearing the reasons on which the conclusion was based. If, then, it *is* nothing, it can *do* nothing, or, alternatively, the same thing which is a passion when viewed confusedly ceases to be a passion when clearly understood (v, iii *sqq.*). Spinoza even maintains that all passions may become actions in this way (IV, lix, and v, iv).

We need not enquire whether these statements can possibly be reconciled with the others we mentioned just before them. There is a more important question at issue than Spinoza's consistency. For how can a passion (malevolence, let us say) cease to be a passion, simply because it is understood? If malevolence disappears it must be dissipated, that is to say, it becomes *nothing*; and although it may certainly be dissipated by our comprehension of a situation which, when misunderstood, led to malevolent feeling, this is a very different thing from saying that malevolence itself is not a distinctive and perceptible emotion, i.e. that it really is nothing at all. We might as well say that redness disappears when we understand the colourless vibrations which cause the sensation. Passionate experience is as definite a thing as the colour red. To say that it can cease to be a passion and yet be itself is wholly and finally absurd.

A third point in Spinoza's theory is that passions are temporal while truth is eternal. Since it is generally conceded, however, that the unreality of time does not follow from the timelessness of truth (or truths), we need not dwell upon this very characteristic part of Spinozism.

§ 10. *Action and passion in relation to reason*

As we have seen, Spinoza endeavours to prove that our reason and our genuine activity coincide, that our passions are not really ourselves but attestations of our slavery, and so that our strength consists either in ridding ourselves of passion (reason taking its place) or, at the least, in taming and in calming our passions. In general, the purport of this contention is sufficiently evident, but it is worth noting in comparative detail how very various Spinoza's grounds are for his strenuous advocacy of the life according to reason.

Without attempting to be exhaustive, we may distinguish the following distinct arguments:

(1) Reason is our true strength because it is our proper nature. It is a *meditatio vitae* (IV, lxvii).

(2) It is our true strength, because anything that thwarts us must come from some external cause, and our reason does not have an external source (e.g. IV, v).

(3) Whatever arises from reason does not permit of excess, but passion may always be excessive (IV, lxi).

Here reason seems to mean moderation, and we are told to enjoy in moderation not only food and drink, but perfumes, gardens, music and the theatre (IV, xlv, Schol. 2).

(4) In empirical fact the union of rational men is the strongest thing in the world. Man may be a god, not a wolf

to his fellows. In civil society much more is useful than hurtful.

Here it is plainly stated that he has the right to be a wolf to all other animals, and it may not be altogether clear why he might not, on occasion at least, be a wolf to men who are utterly recalcitrant and bent upon evil. As regards the animals, it is stated, without reservation, that although they feel, man should exploit them *ad libitum* (IV, xxxvii, Schol. 1; IV, App. xxvi).

(5) Men, in so far as they are rational, must agree. It is only in their passions that they differ.

In this argument, no sufficient account is taken of sentimental unities, because reason, love and harmony are swept together. There is also no discussion (so far as I know) of what the rational man ought to do, if the supply of food and other necessaries should be insufficient to support all the rational men.

In Spinoza's general theory we find an essentially abstract conception of reason (viz. the view that reason has to do with the common properties of all things) combined with

(6) the "comprehensive" doctrine that the more sources of experience we have, the more adequate our ideas are likely to be. It is very hard to understand why the properties common to *all* things could not be culled from *any*, or from but a few, things. Spinoza, however, combines the abstract and the comprehensive views in one and the same proposition (II, xxxix, Dem. and Cor.).

§ 11. *Anticipatory*

I have said that it would have been pedantic and impracticable to confine our attention to Spinoza's conception of value without attempting to scan the wide horizon to which his conception is adapted. In saying so I employed an intentional meiosis. Evidence is always adapted to its subject-matter. If it is not adapted, it is not evidence, and in these problems concerning value the essential requirement is that we should attempt, at the outset, to employ conceptions sufficiently broad, and sufficiently flexible, for the work they have to do.

In traditional philosophy there are three relevant conceptions of value, viz. *bonum utile, bonum jucundum,* and *bonum honestum,* or, as we may translate these terms, economic, hedonistic and moral good. This rough division may serve, but it should be further subdivided in each instance. Under *bonum utile* we must include, not only obvious means to obvious ends, but (as we have seen) the whole complicated province of underlying substantial conditions. *Bonum jucundum,* again, has at least two species, according as we concern ourselves with pleasure, on the one hand, or with desire on the other. We may call these the agreeable and the hormic aspects respectively. Lastly, *bonum honestum* should not be restricted to virtue and moral goodness only. For it should not contain less than the entire domain which is usually designated "perfection".

Although the outline of Spinoza's philosophy of value which this chapter has attempted to sketch has been bare, I fear, and something pallid, it should at least have indicated the comprehensive sweep and the searching flavour of his ideas; and in the rest of this book I propose to try to steer in the wake of his argument, although in a humbler craft, and, for reasons which have appeared, without being able to avail myself of much that he took to be evident and true. He has charted the course, and if we cannot accept all his sailing orders, we have to navigate the same course in our own way as best we can.

To drop metaphor, the business of a general theory of value is to unite the values of utility, satisfaction, desire and perfection into a single coherent scheme. According to Spinoza, man's strength and efficiency is his virtue. In him, his very strength is hormic and allied with joy, and it may yield his proper and rational perfection, thereby making him one with the spring and the ethos of the entire universe. If, commenting on him, we have to say (as I think we do have to say) that the essential meaning of value does not really grow, but instead is annulled and then fashioned into a new thing during the course of his argument, we cannot, of course, accept his philosophy as it stands. But we should learn the more from noting where we are forced to differ.

§ 12. *Spinoza's account; the meaning of good and evil in the third phase*

As we saw, Spinoza's eventual decision was that our rational actions are always good, and that our non-rational appetites may be either good or bad (IV, App. iii).

The first are good absolutely, for goodness in this sense is our actual reality or perfection (these are the same), considered in itself and without relation to anything outside it.

The second, if they are good, are good only relatively, always bearing confused traces of contingency, external influence, fictitious or comparative standards; and of time which is illusion.

It seems evident, therefore, that the conception of good in Spinoza's philosophy is, in the end, frankly ambiguous. I do not say that there is no way of combining the aspect of goodness which is absolute with the aspect which is relative, but in Spinoza's considered judgment, repeatedly asserted, the relativity of good is taken to demonstrate that it is "nothing positive in things". If that be so, absolute and relative good must be as different as any two things can be. For the first is a thing's positive essence, and the second is nothing positive in anything.

In view of the magnitude of this ambiguity, it seems unnecessary to refer to lesser perplexities, such as the dubious status of the "standard of perfection" in the Preface to the fourth book of the *Ethics*.

Mutatis mutandis, this radical ambiguity in the definition of good is equally serious, and even more apparent, in the case of evil. In Spinoza's view there is no such thing as evil in the absolute sense. It is confusion, error, and mere negation; and these are nothing positive in things. Hence it is natural to conclude that evil and error are nothing at all, and much of Spinoza's argument consists in showing that *in a sense* (and that sense the most important) they *are* nothing. Thus vice is mere weakness; weakness is but absence of strength; and absence is nothing.

The logical error contained in this view did not, perhaps, receive general recognition until Kant wrote his *Essay on Negative Quantities*. Nevertheless it is an error. For opposition is *not* mere absence; and it *is* something positive in things. What is more, there is an ambiguity in the word "positive". Absence may not be a positive description of anything, but the absence, say, of a phial of poison in some particular cupboard is as authentic a fact as the presence of the poison in some other cupboard.

Even if the general point of logic were doubtful, however, the distinction would be readily apparent in the case of relative evil. Spinoza defined evil as that which we know for certain to be thwarting us (IV, Def. 2). Since he held (as most of us would say, falsely) that nothing in ourselves can tend to our own destruction, he denied that evil in this sense could be absolute (i.e. intrinsic to us). Yet even if it were relative, it would surely be different from nothingness. If active opposition is unreal, it would be hard to find even a plausible instance of anything real. Similarly, granting that pain and pleasure are "relative", neither is *therefore* nothing, and each is characteristically (and most positively) distinct from the other.

Indeed we may suspect that the form in which the Spinozistic distinction between absolute and relative is cast—he went so far as to say that anything was absolute which could be considered by itself alone (e.g. in IV, lix)—leads to hopeless confusion; and that relations between things are facts as authentic and as positive as the intrinsic properties of these things. The recognition of this circumstance might have altered Spinoza's entire conception of value.

§ 13. *Man's Beatitude*

Spinoza's argument proceeds to a beautiful and moving close in which man's spirit (it is contended) reaches supreme felicity by attaining that union with the meaning of the cosmos which results from intuitive understanding, and the peace and blessedness which flow from the intellectual love of God.

The intuitive way of knowing, and the way of living and of loving which goes along with it, certainly reveal the bloom and finer essence of his philosophy; and nothing short of them can reveal the truth as he saw it. I do not think, however, that he meant to tell us that the intuitive way of knowing corrected the faults of scientific or philosophical demonstration; for he denied that demonstration, in the strict sense, had any faults at all. In short, I cannot think that the perfection he spoke of in the fortieth proposition of the fifth part is different in principle from the perfection that is discussed in what I have called the third phase of his argument. It is, I think, the same thing transfigured in the eternal radiance of full comprehension and utter acquiescence. And therefore I have forborne from offering any further comments on Spinoza's concluding pages.

CHAPTER III

THE PRINCIPLE OF NATURAL ELECTION

§ 1. *Describing the principle*

IN the fourteenth chapter of the second book of Montaigne's *Essays* (as translated by Florio) we find the following passage:

> It is a pleasant imagination to conceive a spirit justly ballanced betweene two equall desires. For, it is not to be doubted, that he shall never be resolved upon any match: forsomuch as the application and choise brings an inequality of prise: And who should place us betweene a bottle of wine and a gammon of bacon with an equall appetite to eat and drinke, doubtlesse there were noe remedy, but to die of thirst and of hunger. To provide against this inconvenient, when the Stoickes were demanded whence the election of two indifferent things commeth into our soule (and which causeth that from out a great number of Crownes or Angells we rather take one than another, when there is no reason to induce us to preferre any one before others) they answer, that this motion of the soule is extraordinarie and irregular comming into us by a strange, accidentall and casuall impulsion. In my opinion, it might rather be said that nothing is presented unto us, wherein there is not some difference, how light so ever it bee: and that either to the sight or to the feeling, there is ever some choice, which tempteth and drawes us to it, though imperceptible and not to bee distinguished. In like manner, hee that shall presuppose a twine-thrid equally strong all-through, it is impossible by all impossibilitie that it breake, for, where would you have the flaw or breaking to beginne? And at once to breake in all places together, it is not in nature.

Following up Montaigne's hint, I propose to call this principle the Principle of Natural Election, and to consider, in this chapter, the nature of the principle and its relations to the theory of value.

Otherwise described, "Natural Election" is the principle of Non-indifference in nature. I take it to be evident that if two things in nature are utterly indifferent to one another, neither, in relation to the other, has any value at all. If, on the other hand, they are *not* indifferent to one another, it is likely, if not absolutely certain, that a value exists for one or the other or for both of them, at least of a relative kind.

What has to be done in the first instance, therefore, is to describe the essential character of this non-indifference.

By "indifferent", then, I do not mean anything peculiarly psychological, as when Miss Rachael Wardle admitted that Mr Tracy Tupman was not wholly indifferent to her— although, to be sure, the principle frequently reveals itself at a psychological stage. Similarly, I do not mean anything peculiarly biological, although biological examples of the principle abound, as when spiders (I suppose) are indifferent to bees but not at all indifferent to flies. What I have in mind is something far more general—something at least as general as, in the old phrases, "attraction" in physics or "affinity" between chemical bodies. "By no endeavour, Can magnet ever, Attract a silver churn", understood quite simply and literally, is a perfect illustration of the principle. It is an imperfect illustration when we let our fancies roam like the author of *Patience*, and make iron and steel express surprise, needles open their well-drilled eyes, and so forth.

I do not know whether Natural Election is the best name for this principle. There are disadvantages in employing a mere negative like Non-indifference; and Natural Selection, which is perhaps the obvious name for the principle, has a prescriptive claim to quite a different estate. I prefer, then, to speak of Natural Election, using the title for short. In the long the title would be Natural-Election-or-Rejection. That is to say, there are two ways of *not* being indifferent, the positive and the negative, but for convenience and for brevity we refer to the positive when we mean both the positive and its opposite.

For a fuller explication of the principle we may refer to a striking passage in Francis Bacon's *Silva Silvarum*, which Mr Whitehead quotes in his *Science and the Modern World*,[1] the third chapter. The passage runs as follows:

It is certain that all bodies whatsoever, though they have no sense, yet they have perception; for when one body is applied to

[1] P. 52.

another, there is a kind of election to embrace that which is agreeable, and to exclude or expel that which is ingrate; and whether the body be alterant or altered, evermore a perception precedeth operation; for else all bodies would be alike one to another. And sometimes this perception, in some kind of bodies, is far more subtile than sense; so that sense is but a dull thing in comparison of it: we see a weatherglass will find the least difference of the weather in heat or cold, when we find it not. And this perception is sometimes at a distance, as well as upon the touch; as when the loadstone draweth iron; or flame naphtha of Babylon, a great distance off. It is therefore a subject of a very noble enquiry, to enquire of the more subtile perceptions; for it is another key to open nature, as well as the sense; and sometimes better. And besides it is a principal means of natural divination; for that which in these perceptions appeareth early, in the great effects cometh long after.

Commenting upon this passage, Mr Whitehead bids us note the way in which "taking account of" (as a purely physical principle without any vestige of "sense" or consciousness) is distinct from the materialism of classical physics (with its implied philosophy that "matter" is something purely passive). He goes on to say that he believes "Bacon's line of thought to have expressed a more fundamental truth than do the materialistic concepts which were then being shaped as adequate for physics", and that the passage, in its context, is "permeated through and through by the experimental method, that is to say, by attention to 'irreducible and stubborn facts', and by the inductive method of eliciting general laws".[1]

These comments, coming as they do from a distinguished mathematician and physicist, are very encouraging to those of us who believe that the principle of non-indifference, understood quite simply and just as it shows itself, is in reality one of the great descriptive principles in nature, although it appears but obscurely in most of the expositions of classical physics.[2] Without it, we may say with Bacon, all bodies

[1] *Science and the Modern World*, p. 53.
[2] In modern terms, I suppose we might say that classical physics, restricting itself to the inertia of bodies, overlooked the affinities represented by atomic number.

would be alike; or alternatively, with Montaigne, that they would break at once in all places together. In other words, without it we should not have nature at all.

§ 2. *The place of the principle in nature*

One of the major obstacles in the way of accepting this principle of Bacon's and of Montaigne's is the difficulty of comprehending it with the deliberate *naïveté* and vehement innocence which are appropriate to all deep and fundamental things. We have learned, I daresay, to refrain from speaking, and perhaps from thinking, of mystical affinities or magical sympathies in nature, and the lesson, in a certain way, is salutary. Yet very few philosophers are able to bridle themselves enough. Natural Election, in a sense, may be said to exhibit the rudiments of mind, of life and of teleology, because it underlies all of these. In itself, however, it is none of these things, and it is misconceived if it is regarded as, in its essence, the promise and potency of some one of them.

It is also not to be confounded with identity or similarity. Non-indifference, it is true, may be compatible with likeness and, in the extreme case, with identity. In general, we are not indifferent to our peers, our compatriots and our contemporaries; and we are seldom indifferent to ourselves. On the other hand, we need not be indifferent to Chellean man, or to our food or to our utensils—that is to say, to things dissimilar from ourselves. Just as in the case of the objects of our desire, it seems correct to maintain that these have no common property other than the property of being desired,[1] so in the instance of natural election. Or, rather, we should say that desires are a species of natural elections and exhibit the extensive range of utter diversity which is compatible with that principle.

Certainly, we may hold that wherever natural election operates, there is to be found a certain union, or inner connivance and conspiracy, among the things which are not

[1] Cf. McTaggart, *The Nature of Existence*, vol. II, chap. xl, § 447.

indifferent to one another. What is united, however, may be diverse as well as similar. It would be well if the fact were remembered in the interminable disputes concerning the question whether Europeans are too like or too unlike the Chinese to understand them, or whether a man understands his male companions better than his wife.

Yet it is not enough (although it is something) to explain what natural election is *not*; and although, in the end, it is just itself, its expositors have the duty of attempting to show some of the principal ways in which, most characteristically, it *is* itself. I shall consider it, therefore, in two such ways. The first of them is the logical principle of relevance. The second is the physical principle of causation.

Logical relevance, we may say, is natural election in the sphere of evidence. It is the discrimination between what matters in an argument and what is frankly immaterial—between what counts or is to the point and what is "gammon" or "hot air". In detail, of course, such discrimination may be said to be the main part of logic, but in admitting the circumstance we should not allow ourselves to forget the principle which determines it. Discrimination of a subtle and orderly kind between what is relevant and what is immaterial presupposes the truth that there *is* such a thing as relevance; and relevance itself, being a condition of all logic, has ultimately to be accepted in its stark and primitive purity. We cannot "get behind" it and we should not try to do so. Those philosophers who, like some of the pragmatists,[1] try to *explain* relevance (I suppose by relevant arguments) and tell us that it means congruity with our senses, our actions and our passions, have plainly broken themselves upon the wheel of logic. They are attempting to oust a primitive principle by means of *itself*.

Physical causation, as the term is understood in common speech, is plainly selective. And so is all causation. Given a certain effect, usually quite definite and quite definitely limited, we want to know what precisely brought it about.

[1] E.g. F. C. S. Schiller, *Formal Logic*, p. 9 and *passim*.

Given a certain tool, we want to know what precisely can be done with it.

Our conceptions, it is true, are frequently very vague. A "chill", we say, causes a common "cold"; and superficially our enquiries may seem to become rather expansive than selective when we try to become scientific. In studying the aetiology of the cold we may find ourselves rummaging into a man's history, habits and ancestry in order to obtain a plausible explanation of his susceptibility to microbic infection at such and such a time.

Nevertheless it is scientific (as well as good horse sense) to distinguish in all such enquiries between what counts and what does not count. Indeed, if we can be certain of anything in this vexed and vexatious province of discussion, we may be assured that the *whole* context of nature does *not* count in such matters in the telling and intimate way in which certain *specific portions* of the context make a material difference. The problem of induction itself, is, firstly, to learn what counts in every inference from observation, and secondly to discover what counts most significantly in this or the other sphere of determinate investigation.

It is generally conceded at the present time that if events in nature were uniform, featureless things like the balls in an urn so dear to the writers on abstract probability, there could be no valid way of establishing a degree of probability even remotely similar to the degree of probability we ascribe to what we call well-established laws of nature; and that, in addition to the general laws of probability, we require, for the sake of our logical consciences, something like what Kant called the Principle of Specification[1] (*Entium varietates non temere sunt minuendae*), or what Mr J. M. Keynes calls Analogy and opposes to Pure Induction,[2] or what Mr Broad calls the Principle of Limited Variety.[3] Since it is not my business here to discuss the inductive problem on its merits, I need not

[1] *Critique of Pure Reason.* Appendix to Transcendental Dialectic.
[2] *A Treatise on Probability,* Part III.
[3] Presidential Address to Aristotelian Society, 1927.

prolong this discussion of it. I have done enough for my purpose if I point out (as is surely sufficiently obvious) that every principle of the type supposed—whether Kant's, Mr Keynes's, Mr Broad's or some other—is a special form of the Principle of Natural Election.

§ 3. *Natural election and utility*

In the remainder of this chapter I mean to discuss the relations between the principle of natural election and the various kinds of good or value enumerated in § 11 of the last chapter. This plan will have the obvious disadvantage of compelling us to treat of certain matters in a rough and provisional way, leaving their fuller analysis to the sequel. *Bonum jucundum*, for example, will be the proper subject of future investigation, and so will *bonum honestum*. It is only in a clumsy and approximative way that we can now consider their relations to natural election.

On the other hand, we have already examined the conception of *bonum utile* and should be able to perceive its connection with, and its difference from, the conception of non-indifference or natural election.

The general relation, I think, is that natural election is a very broad principle, and utility a rather narrow one. Utility is the offspring of the doctrine of means and ends, or, in other words, a generalisation from a certain level of human experience. This is a knowledgeable and a prudent level and it may well be doubted whether our human experience is anything like so prudent or so knowledgeable as the doctrine of utility suggests. In short, a wider conception is likely to be more adequate and also deeper.

More in detail we may say:

Firstly, that natural election plainly includes all that makes for loveliness, peace and serenity (in beings capable of achieving these) as readily as it includes utility in the vulgar sense, i.e. whatever is necessary or commodious. The doctrine of utility may indeed overcome this embarrassment by expressly admitting "higher" as well as "lower" utilities or in some other such way. There are great advantages, however, in ridding ourselves of such embarrassments from the outset.

Secondly, that natural election includes all substantial conditions in the same easy, unstrained fashion as it includes utilities. The doctrine of utility, on the other hand, finds difficulty here since the substantial conditions of many values do not seem merely to be means, and yet should not be regarded as ends.

Thirdly, that it is forced and incongruous to maintain that a thing is useful to itself (although Spinoza said so). It is pleasantly natural and plain, however, to say that a thing is not-indifferent to itself.

Fourthly, that the distinction between intrinsic and extrinsic is contemplated, according to the principle of natural election, in the way which experience and observation render by far most probable. According to the principle, a thing sustains itself by taking account of other things, assimilating some of them, neutralising some of them, assuming amicable or defensive relations with others—and all non-mentally (as Bacon showed) as well as (sometimes) mentally. The doctrine of utility, on the other hand (*vide* almost all its expositors), is driven to make a violent and unplausible separation between intrinsic and extrinsic, external adaptations and internal consummations, or the like. In short, utility is a dangerous and sometimes a fatal solvent in these matters.

Fifthly, that most theories of *bonum utile* are consciousness-ridden. Natural Election is not. It is convenient, now, to consider this question more generally in a separate paragraph.

§ 4. *Natural election and consciousness*

As we saw, Bacon carefully distinguished between "taking account of" (which he called "perception") and our conscious "sense". The former he held to be infinitely more subtle than the latter; and Bacon regarded it, unlike sense, as something universal in nature. With him, indeed, "perception" is that relevant affinity between particular things which is an initial precondition of any definite action. Montaigne is less precise and less profound, because he speaks of an imperceptible "choice" which "tempts" our senses, although the senses themselves cannot see or divine the minute tempting quality.

To choose a physical analogy, we may say that Montaigne's view of natural election is microscopic, and Bacon's (in principle) ultra-microscopic. By a quantity of microscopic order is meant something which cannot be discriminated by the naked eye, but is discriminable when the eye-system is suitably aided by the lenses of the microscope. The microscope is, so to say, a more delicate eye-system interpreting the waves of light. What is ultra-microscopic, on the other hand, is something too minute for any conceivable extension of the eye-system to discriminate, because it is too minute to be interpreted in terms of light-rays, and is revealed only by waves, such as X-rays, which are enormously shorter (say by ten thousand times) than the waves of light.

It is clear that a distinction of this kind is decidedly important, theoretically, when we come to examine any such theory as the "unconscious" in modern psychology. We have to make up our minds whether this "unconscious" is only a little too subtle for the naked eye or whether it is altogether ultra- or infra-conscious. What I am asserting, then, is that Natural Election may be *altogether* infra-conscious, and discoverable in things that are not conscious at all, although, to be sure, it is also discoverable in conscious beings and in their conscious experience.

It is here, I suggest, that most of our interpretations are apt to go astray. What Bacon called "sense" presupposes what he called "perception" and is, in many ways, analogous to perception. In these significations "perception" is sub-conscious, and therefore we are commonly told that it is a crass form of consciousness or a dim premonition of consciousness. In the same way, because it is sub-organic, we are asked to infer that it indicates the universal presence of a crude form of life; and because it underlies purpose and design (being, so to say, sub-finalistic) we are told, by Mr Driesch[1] and others,

[1] Cf. *The Science and Philosophy of the Organism.*

that we should suppose the general dissemination of "psychoids" or "entelechies" in the universe.

I am suggesting that all such statements, like end and means in the traditional definition of instinct, are committing the logical fallacy which is called a *hysteron proteron*. Instead of trying to explain last things by first things, they are attempting to explain first things by last things. Organisms, consciousness and ends are special and highly distinctive forms of the principle of natural election. In order to understand them we should first attempt to understand natural election. We shall never understand it if we persist in trying to read into it what is peculiarly appropriate to certain of its special forms.

In short, although the principle, in an intelligible sense, may be said to be sub-mental, sub-conscious, sub-organic or sub-finalistic, it is not, unless by mere analogy, necessarily semi-mental, semi-conscious, semi-organic or semi-finalistic.

This, when it is clearly understood, should enable, or at least help, us to give distinctions their due. Always, when we have to deal with a specific, developed, and "higher" form of a general, possibly primitive, and "lower" principle, we are apt to become confused, and to maintain either that the "higher", when all is said, is the same thing as the "lower", or that it is made "higher" by the presence of some new ingredient whose status we can seldom determine clearly.

I do not wish to deny that mind and consciousness may contain or suppose some ingredient which as Aristotle said, came "from out of doors"; for I think there is evidence that they do. What I am urging now is that, supposing they contained no such element, we should have no business to conclude that consciousness is otiose or quite subordinate—that, as Spinoza said, one and the same physical appetite may or may not be conscious.

We ought, in fact, to draw the conclusion precisely opposed to Spinoza's. If anything in these matters is clear, it should be that conscious choice is *not* the same as unconscious natural election.

A very clear statement of the correct inference is given by Sir Henry Head in his recent work on *Aphasia*, when he says:[1]

There is no more difficulty in understanding how an act of consciousness can affect a physiological process, than to comprehend how one reflex can control and modify another of a lower order.

Consider, for example, the conditions which govern micturition. When the fluid in the bladder reaches a certain variable amount, the muscular wall contracts, the sphincter relaxes and the contents are expelled. After transection of the spinal cord, this whole process may occur automatically. Should the cord reach a high state of vigilance, the act can be greatly facilitated by scratching the sole of the foot or other parts of the body below the lesion, and the bladder is emptied at a smaller volume. But as soon as the controlling influence of the mid-brain can be exerted upon the spinal centres, this facilitation ceases; the stimulus to be effective must be applied within the limited field of the bladder itself.

Psychical conditions have a profound effect upon this reflex. It may become urgent and uncontrollable under the influence of fear....On the contrary, it can be checked by an idea.

In other words, one and the same "action" (e.g. the evacuation of the contents of the bladder) may be very different indeed according as it is the culmination of a more or of a less developed pattern of physiological action. The higher system is not the same as the lower although in part identical and in part employing the same muscles and other means. If consciousness were *only* a higher organisation than the highest unconscious physiological pattern, the same conclusion would follow. It would also follow if above mere consciousness we were to place, say, a reflective or an ethical pattern of action.

§ 5. *Natural election and interest*

Contemporary psychologists very frequently regard emotion, on the one hand, and appetition, upon the other, as twin manifestations of a single category which they call interest. The former, they say, is the passive (or pathic) side of affective-volitional disposition, and the latter is the active side of the same thing. Historically speaking, this is a reversion—very

[1] *Aphasia and Kindred Disorders of Speech*, vol. i, pp. 496 *sq.*

likely a well-grounded reversion—to the Aristotelian bipartite division of the mental powers in opposition to the tripartite division (knowing, feeling and willing) of Tetens, Mendelssohn and Kant.

For the provisional purposes of the present chapter it will be convenient to treat the affective-volitional aspects of our nature together in this way.

If etymology were a safe guide it would be reasonable to suspect that "interest" has the closest possible connection with natural election; for our Latin dictionaries tell us that *interest*, as an impersonal verb, means "it makes a difference, interests, concerns, imports"; and Messrs Lewis and Short, among a phalanx of relevant quotations, cite examples from Cicero, in which, although the term "interest" has usually a mental reference, such various "interests" are mentioned as what concerns honour, the reputation and good fame of the republic, or our own dignity and well-being. In brief, *Quid interfuit?* means What did it matter?—and "interest" in the etymological sense is the same thing as non-indifference.

Most psychologists, however, including those who pride themselves upon their "realism" or their "naturalism" and their utter freedom from any mystical or superstitious flavour in their interpretations of the human mind, employ the term "interest" rather in Rachael Wardle's than in the etymological sense, and therefore take it to signify something much more restricted than natural election. Since "interest" in this narrower psychological sense is the very kernel and essence of value according to Mr Perry's *General Theory of Value*, the most important of recent books, in English, upon our general theme, there is a great deal of point in examining what Mr Perry has to say, with special reference to the distinction between interest and natural election.

"In discussing the definition of value", Mr Perry says, "we shall be dealing constantly with the motor-affective life; that is to say, with instinct, desire, feeling, will and all their family of states, acts and attitudes. It is necessary, therefore, to have a term which may be used to refer to what is characteristic of this strain in life and mind, which shall be sufficiently comprehensive to embrace all of its varieties, and whose meaning we may refine as we proceed. The term *interest* is the most acceptable, and will henceforth be so employed."[1]

Thereupon Mr Perry proceeds to argue, firstly, that value without interest is an utter impossibility, and secondly, that value is neither the object of interest qualified in some special way (e.g. an egotistical object, according to the doctrine that we can desire only a state of ourselves) nor the object of some qualified interest (e.g. a "natural", "personal" or "rational" one). The truth is (he contends) that value is *any* object of *any* interest—that is to say, the simple occurrence of the interested relation itself is *eo ipso* the occurrence of value. This opinion, Mr Perry frankly admits, is an experiment in generalisation,[2] not a verity intuitively manifest; but he is entirely confident regarding the outcome of the experiment. "If we take life *interest-wise*", he holds, "as it can in fact be taken...the data and the perplexities denoted by 'good' and 'evil', 'right' and 'wrong', 'better' and 'worse', or grouped within the special fields of morality, art, religion and kindred institutions, then fall into place and form a comprehensive system."[3]

"The view here proposed", he continues, "may properly be termed a bio-centric or psycho-centric theory of value, in the sense that values are held to be functions of certain acts of living mind to which we have given the name of interest."[4] In the end, however, Mr Perry takes a psycho-centric not a bio-centric view. "An act", he says, "is interested in so far as its occurrence is due to the agreement between its accompanying expectation and the unfulfilled phases of a governing propensity."[5] This governing propensity (or so I gather) may be biological. At any rate, we are explicitly told that "the living organism provides the context of interest".[6] But, according to this author, there is something lacking in the

---

[1] *General Theory of Value*, p. 27.
[2] *Op. cit.* p. 126.
[3] *Ibid.*
[4] *Ibid.* p. 139.
[5] *Ibid.* p. 183.
[6] *Ibid.* p. 180.

strictly biological point of view. "Prospicience" or "the capacity to act in the light of expectation" may be widely disseminated in the animal kingdom, but is not, properly speaking, an "interest" until it becomes, as in man, *notably* characteristic of action;[1] and men may rightly conclude that their lives are not *worth* living unless their special interests, not merely their biological existence, are fulfilled.[2]

For Mr Perry, then, interest is *favouring*, and he holds that we cannot *favour* without being aware of what is favoured or favourable, and without liking the same. Regarding the former point, he is inclined to make the requisite of awareness rather stringent. "An element of belief", he says, "is also present in expectation"[3] as well as the fact of being ready for something in particular. Moreover, "to expect an event signifies only a disposition to act *on* it; while to be interested in an event signifies a disposition to act *for* it, or to provide an occasion for acting on it".[4] Indeed, "interest may be said to be a product, derivative or *function* of cognition, in the sense that its satisfaction varies with the truth of the cognition which mediates it".[5] Nevertheless, "although interest cannot exist without cognition, it can and does exist without cognition of itself. An individual may be unaware of his interest at the moment when he is interested. It is true that he must be aware of the *object* of his interest in order that he shall *be* interested, but it is not necessary, either logically or psychologically, that he should be aware that he is interested".[6]

On the latter point, i.e. the necessity for a *liking* actually experienced, it is sufficient to note that Mr Perry expresses his essential agreement with the views of Mr D. W. Prall, who writes:

The being liked, or disliked, of the object is its value. And since the being liked or disliked, is being the object of a motor-affective attitude in a subject, some sort of a subject is always requisite to there being value at all—not necessarily a *judging* subject, but a subject capable at least of motor-affective response. For the cat the cream has value, or better and more simply, the cat values the

[1] *Ibid.* p. 180. [2] *Ibid.* p. 181. [3] *Ibid.* p. 313.
[4] *Ibid.* p. 318. [5] *Ibid.* p. 357. [6] *Ibid.* p. 358.

cream, or the warmth, or having her back scratched, quite regardless of her probable inability to conceive cream or to make judgments concerning warmth.[1]

According to the Prall-Perry theory, therefore, both awareness and liking are essential in all valuing. Mr Perry is a pragmatist and something of a behaviourist in his theory of knowledge, but, as he says, a behaviourist "without psychophobia". While agreeing that psychophobia is a horrid disease (and pretty easy to avoid) I should like to suggest that in this matter of values the Prall-Perry theory is altogether too psychological.

In the first place, a part of Mr Perry's reason for being psychological (and not merely biological) in his account of value, seems to entail claims and standards which imply something more than his psychology. If it is a valid argument against biological theories of value that life, after all, may not be worth *living*, it must also be correct to point out that we may enjoy many things which are not worth *liking*. In *this* sense of worth, a fondness for gin or hashish is at least as much to be deplored as the hollowest of empty existences.

For the moment, however, we are concerned with the lower rungs of the ladder of values, and have to ask whether natural election, which admittedly "provides the context" for psychological "interest", may not itself constitute the *value* in which psychological "interest" may indeed participate (often in a disturbing fashion) but which need not be mental at all.

Here, therefore, we have our second, and, for the time being, our more important question.

There is a presumption, I think, that the Prall-Perry view is mistaken, if for no other reason, because biology is admitted to "provide the context" for psychological interest; and if, as seems undeniable, natural election provides the context for biology, it would seem that we should not stop short at life any more than we should stop short at mind.

[1] *A Study in the Theory of Value*, Univ. of Calif. Publications in Philosophy, vol. III, No. 2, pp. 215 *sqq.*: as quoted by Perry, *op. cit.* p. 117.

Mr Perry thinks that the very meaning of value reveals something notably characteristic of man; and Mr Prall has a predilection for values which are notably characteristic of cats. Yet why should either of them stop where he does? If cats why not beetles, and if beetles why not potatoes, and if potatoes why not magnets and filings? Magnets do concern filings; and if it does not matter whether or not we are aware of our likings, why should it matter whether or not there are any likings at all? If things are concerned with, and take account of, one another, is not that enough? So far as I can see, it is a mere dogma that values *are* peculiarly characteristic either of men or of cats. When human beings think about their values, to be sure, they naturally consult their feelings—naturally, but not, perhaps wisely. If they cherish vipers, it is surely the character of what they favour, rather than their amiable frame of mind, that really does concern them. For "favour", to be brief, is deceitful.

Experimenting with his generalisation, Mr Perry asks us to assent to the statement that "interested or purposive action must be actively selective, tentative, instrumental, prospective and fallible".[1] I suggest that none of these characteristics, except the first, necessarily pertains to value, in the sense of value with which we are at present concerned.

Active selection, together with response to such selection, is the very meaning of non-indifference. It is not, however, peculiarly psychological.

The prospective and instrumental characters belong to purpose; but what reason can be given for the view that all values are purposive? Even if values *were* exclusively psychological, this opinion should not be sustained. For acquiescence is at least as important as seeking, and it may be a condition (say of peace and of deep contentment) that they should not be sought, either directly or indirectly.

The view that all "minding" is referring to the future is the stubborn residue of Mr Perry's pragmatism. He would even have us believe that memory in a way is forward looking,

[1] Perry, *op. cit.* p. 209 *sqq.*

since it is an attempt to recall what, at the time of the attempt, is not before the mind.[1] The process of valuing, however (understood in any ordinary sense), need not be peculiarly prognostic. There is no contradiction whatsoever in supposing, as most of us believe, that we may prize the past or set store by the present.

Again, it may be true that minding (at any rate for the most part) is tentative and fallible, and these characteristics are certainly found in most of our apparent or estimated values. There is a clear distinction, however, between these estimates or appearances of value, and, as we say, "what really matters". The facts of natural election do not depend upon our fancies, or wishes, or opinions. Yet there are such facts, neither tentative nor fallible.

I think we should conclude therefore that value in the fundamental sense of natural election or non-indifference is of far greater moment than the psychological subdivision of it which alone is acceptable to the Prall-Perry theory. The doctrine of non-indifference and the Prall-Perry theory agree in their assertion that value is relative in the sense that it occurs only when some selecting entity (Mr Prall says, "some sort of a subject") meets (or takes itself to meet) with some sort of response; and I do not wish to suggest that this is the only possible significance of "value". I am arguing only that where "interest" (in the psychological sense) has to be distinguished from "interest" (in the etymological sense), the latter, and not the former, must be regarded as the basis and essence of "relative" value.

§ 6. *Natural election and the principle of perfection*

The term "perfection" was something of a scandal in classical philosophy, and Kant as well as some others were probably justified when they found it incurably vague. Vague terms, however, although they cannot solve any problems, very commonly set them, and it seems clear that "perfection",

[1] *Op. cit.* p. 339 *sqq.*

in some at least of its senses, sets very intricate and quite inescapable questions to the theory of value.

In the provisional way which (I think) is legitimate at the present stage of our investigation, we may say that the principal meanings of the term perfection are, firstly, completeness, and, secondly, superlative excellence. In the present paragraph, therefore, I intend to consider the relation between natural election and each of these meanings of perfection.

There is a sense in which everything, being just what it is, is completely so, but, for the most part, when we think of completeness we think either of the maturity that young, undeveloped things may be said to grow towards, or of a typical, generic rotundity of being which the completer members of a species attain and the others, in various ways, fall short of.

Perfection of this order, that is to say completeness *in genere*, need not be excellent at all (unless, indeed, we mean by "excellent" something like "egregious"). For it is entirely possible that a thing, complete in its kind, should be complete in a bad and vicious kind. "This book", some reviewer may tell us, "is an almost perfect example of pompous ineptitude", or in other words a complete exhibition of something radically worthless. If reviewers were to say so, it would be absurd to dispute the verbal propriety of their statements.

The same, however, holds of natural election. The commonplace author shows his quality by his unintended (and by him unsuspected) indifference to all that is not commonplace. He is drawn and tempted to things not excellent by imperceptible but compelling impulsions. And excellent things pass him by.

Indeed, I think we may agree without further argument that the connection between completion and natural election is of the closest kind. In natural election everything either holds what it has or calls for what it lacks, and when we speak of what a thing lacks (what Grote called its *egence*)[1] we mean,

[1] *A Treatise on the Moral Ideals*, p. 27. Grote drew five distinctions in this connection, and with regard to at least three of them, he cannot be accused of splitting the follicles of a hair. The passage runs: "The degrees of *withoutness* are (1) simple *non-habence*; (2) *carence*, i.e. the

not everything it is without, but that which, being absent, frustrates the thing's completeness. A pig without wings or without a classical education certainly does not possess something which sparrows, in the one case, and bookworms in the other, find good and profitable. The pig, however, is naturally indifferent to such things. If his snout or his tail were threatened, his own completeness would be in jeopardy, and his natural election would respond.

Natural election, it is true, seems to be individuating rather than generic. Entities are drawn and tempted by their own affinities, and if their individuating tendency is to be "roguish" and aberrant from type there is nothing more to be said in terms of the principle of non-indifference. Completeness *in genere*, however, although a very usual way of interpreting "perfection", is not always a necessary or always a very convincing way. If the "rogues" were brought to heel and forcibly compelled to conform to the type of their species, they might be less (not more) complete than if they pursued their individual course. As Locke said, "though it may be reasonable to ask, Whether obeying the magnet be essential to iron? yet I think it is very improper and insignificant to ask, whether it be essential to the particular parcel of matter I cut my pen with; without considering it under the name *iron*, or as being of a certain species".[1]

So much, then, for the relation between the principle of completeness in particular things, and the principle of their natural election. It remains to consider the relation of perfection, in the sense of excellence, to either of them.

As we have seen, a thing may go on its own bad way very completely indeed; or, again, going its own way, it may follow

being without a thing when there is at least some conceivable reason why it should be present...; (3) *egence*, where the want is of some particular thing according to the nature of that which wants, and where there exists in nature a possibility of the satisfaction of the want, such satisfaction being probably striven after or provided for in some way; (4) *desiderium*, or craving and yearning, which is the last subjectively felt, and possibly amplified by imagination, etc.; (5) *cupido*, or general imaginative desire, which may be without any egence as fact".

[1] *Essay*, Book III, chap. vi, § 5.

a path that is neither good nor bad. "Good" in these statements means "excellent"; and it is obvious, accordingly, that excellence is a different notion from natural election, since the fullest and most "perfect" of natural elections may be either void of excellence or opposed to excellence. It may not do to say, even, that things complete in their kind are as good as such things can be. For perhaps the things cannot be good at all. And as for perfection *in genere*, it is entirely possible that things which diverge from type may be more excellent, by far, than things which conform.

In any case, if we compare complete or typical members of different species—let us say a typical raven and a typical man—we may significantly enquire whether the typical raven is or is not more excellent than the typical man; and if we say, as most of us would, that a very imperfect man is better than a very perfect raven, better, indeed, than a raven as good as any raven could be, it is plain that there is an ambiguity in the words "good" and "better" which is precisely the difference between completeness and excellence.

In terms of natural election any such question is utterly and entirely meaningless. The raven is drawn and tempted by its affinities, and men are drawn and tempted by their affinities; and there is nothing more to be said. Moreover, although the question whether men are more excellent than ravens seems manifestly one that can be significantly asked, it appears to me that a great many philosophers argue on assumptions which make this question mere empty sound.

They assume, in fact, that value means human value, so that we can only ask with any legitimacy what *human* value ravens have, and never should ask whether they are more excellent than men, or, indeed, whether they are more excellent than any other species of birds or of beasts. I gather even, although here I should like to speak with diffidence, that certain modern theories which call themselves theological are solely concerned with the question whether God and His angels have any *human* value or not.

In reply to this view I can only affirm that even if all the major excellences within the universe happen to belong to human "persons", it cannot be true that excellence *means* something human.

Frequently, however, we are confronted with an alternative view, whose main outline, I suppose, would be to the following effect:

Nothing is excellent in itself, for every excellence is defined by the natural election of this or the other being. Nevertheless we may legitimately compare the excellences proper or possible to one being or species with the excellences proper or possible to another being or species. For of two beings, each of which is equally complete in its own way (as pitchers, in Descartes's example, although of different sizes may all be quite full), one may be much more complete than the other. Thus, because men have fuller capacities and a greater range of activity than ravens, we are told that it is correct to say that they are more excellent than the ravens. Perhaps, even, the philosophers who argue in this vein might go on to say that man is the universe in little in a sense which is more than metaphorical; and that ravens are not. Hence his completeness, or perfection, approaches, if it does not actually touch, the Absolute itself. In short, nothing that can be indifferent to the universe can be indifferent to man: and conversely.

These crowning statements seem to me crowning absurdities, and almost as fantastic, in their way, as Hegel's celebrated dictum that "physiology ought to have made it one of its axioms that life had necessarily in its evolution to attain to the human shape, as the sole sensuous phenomenon that is appropriate to mind".[1] It is true, however, that the range of man's activities makes him a large, not a little, pitcher, when we compare him with his fellow animals. Nevertheless, this circumstance seems irrelevant to natural election and irrelevant also to excellence.

It is irrelevant to natural election because natural election is a differentiating principle, not an expansive one. The prin-

[1] *Philosophy of Fine Art*, Introduction. Bosanquet's translation, p. 150.

ciple states that it is not in nature for everything to be the same all at once. Its basis is the fact of specific variety. One natural election is just as specific as another, and it does not signify how big any of them be. From this point of view, to speak of the "universe" employing natural election is nonsense. The universe cannot take sides or take special account of anything. Natural election, on the contrary, describes the way in which particular things do take sides and do take special account, not of everything, but of certain particular things and *not* of others.

The circumstance, similarly, is irrelevant to perfection in the sense of excellence, because a small or a brief excellence need not be the less excellent on account of its smallness or of its brevity. This is so plain that no argument, I think, is needed, but I may be permitted perhaps to remind the reader of Ben Jonson's noble lines which can hardly be staled by repetition:

> For what is life, if measur'd by the space,
>   Not by the act?...
>   It is not growing like a tree
>   In bulk, doth make men better be:
> Or standing long an oak, three hundred year,
> To fall a log at last, dry, bald and sere:
>   A lily of a day
>   Is fairer far in May,
>   Although it fall and die that night:
>   It was the plant and flower of light.
> In small proportions we just beauties see;
> And in short measures life may perfect be.

CHAPTER IV

THE VALUES OF DESIRE

SECTION I. GENERAL

§ 1. *The meaning of "desire"*

One of the commonest and, in appearance, one of the simplest theories of value is that good and bad are derived from, if not identical with, "desire". If so, it is surely important to ascertain, with some precision, what "desire" means.

Unfortunately, there is great confusion in this matter among several contemporary authors of repute. For example, Mr Bertrand Russell in his *Principles of Social Reconstruction* (1916) draws a provocative, if unsound, distinction between the glad spontaneity of impulse, and the tiring, constrictive fetters of desire.[1] (Here "desire" seems to mean resolution, foresight and accepted principle.) In his *Analysis of Mind* (1921) we find, to our amazement, that "desire" has suddenly become "hormic" and part of a "behaviour cycle" although, in a subordinate way, belief and certain emotions may attach to it.[2] In his *Outline of Philosophy* (1927) "desire" is made the foundation of Mr Russell's entire ethic. He has come to perceive, he tells us, that "good" is derivative from desire, and therefore to abandon the view, which he formerly accepted from Mr G. E. Moore, that "good" is a simple quality.[3]

I am not concerned with the nimble transitions of Mr Russell's successive philosophies. All I wish to show is that "desire" may be interpreted very ambiguously at the present time. And this, I think, is a pity, because very careful analyses of the term were given, say, by Locke, Abraham Tucker and Sidgwick[4] in former times, or by Dr Ward and by Mr Shand more recently.

---

[1] Pp. 12 *sqq.*   [2] Chap. iii.   [3] P. 238.
[4] Especially in *Mind*, 1892, pp. 94 *sqq.*

THE VALUES OF DESIRE

At the present day, therefore, certain authors seem to mean by "desire" any bodily "horme"[1] or "urge" or "appetite" (especially of a persistent kind) together with all beliefs and emotions which chance to be connected with the same. This usage, I concede, may be legitimate. It is consonant with the famous "desire of the moth for the star" and of "the day for the morrow". To discuss it, however, would here be unnecessary, because it has already been examined in connection with the more thorough-going doctrine of natural election.

Assuming, then, that desire, wherever its roots may lie, is to be considered something essentially psychological (as in common speech and in the analyses of careful philosophers) we have yet to admit that certain difficulties in the interpretation of it still remain, and particularly the difference between an interpretation like Dr Ward's, on the one hand, and an analysis like Locke's or Mr Shand's upon the other.

According to Dr Ward, the essence of desire is a certain failure in the efficacy of our ideas. When an idea effectively guides "the pent up stream of action" towards "new channels", desire, properly speaking, is absent.[2] When, on the contrary, the pent up stream growls and calls attention to its own restless, unrelieved turbulence, when nascent movements obscure and occlude the clear enterprise of action, desire makes itself felt. Desire, in short, is the mental incubus of undirected movements. Ideas, in the full sense, are certainly present in desire, according to Dr Ward. Indeed, he is of opinion that an experience below the level of explicit ideas (e.g. the complaint of the proverbial fox about the grapes that were sour) is not, strictly speaking, desire, but only analogous to that condition. Nevertheless, in his considered view, the executive actions appropriate to these ideas do not occur in

---

[1] Cf. T. P. Nunn, *Education: Its Data and First Principles*, p. 21. ὁρμή means impetus, effort or the shock of onset. ὁρμαί was a term used by the Stoics for blind animal impulses. In contemporary psychology the term *horme* is used in a general way for what is less elegantly termed an "urge" or a "drive".

[2] *Psychological Principles*, p. 283.

desire. In their stead we have a bewildering superfluity of inchoate and merely tentative movements.

Locke and Mr Shand, on the contrary, while agreeing that desire has an ideal character, maintain that the essence of the condition is emotional. "I find the will", Locke says, "often confounded with several of the affections, especially *desire*, and one put for the other; and that by men who would not willingly be thought not to have had very distinct notions of things, and not to have writ very clearly about them." Yet "the will is perfectly distinguished from desire; which, in the very same action, may have a quite contrary tendency from that which our will sets us upon".[1] In reality desire is "an uneasiness of the mind for want of some absent good";[2] and its character is most clearly shown in Rachel's passionate plea,[3] "Give me children or I die".

According to Mr Shand, desire implies an impulse relatively highly developed on the intellectual side.[4] Sometimes "the thought of the end arises first, and both provokes the impulse and transforms it into desire".[5] More usually, however, the delay or obstruction of an impulse provokes the intellectual or ideal development which is characteristic of desire. Accordingly desire usually is, as Locke said it was, an "uneasiness", for there is a restless, uneasy feeling when the obstruction occurs. The most noteworthy thing about desire, however, is the way in which, by an immanent necessity, it tends to form systems of desire which may even be more definite than many emotions. Desire has, in fact, a six-fold tendency towards the desiderative systems of Hope, Confidence, Anxiety, Disappointment, Despondency and Despair.[6]

---

[1] *Essay*, Book II, chap. xxi, § 30.
[2] *Ibid.* § 31.   [3] *Ibid.* § 32.
[4] *The Foundations of Character*, Book III, ch. i, § 2.
[5] *Ibid.* (1st edn. p. 461).
[6] *Ibid.* (p. 463) and Book III, chap. ii.

§ 2. *Remarks upon the above*

We might perhaps describe Dr Ward's view of desire sufficiently, although briefly, if we said that desire occurs when a moving idea disturbs us without being able to command effective action. If so, the descriptions of Locke and of Mr Shand appear to contain the same elements as Dr Ward's. By all these authors, desire is said to involve ideas of an intellectual kind which indicate a strong attraction. By all of them, desire is said to bring restlessness and uneasiness in its train (at any rate in the normal case) owing to delay or obstruction in the fulfilment of the attractive idea. The difference between them is that Dr Ward *explains* the uneasiness, not simply by delay, but by the surge of clumsy and bewildered actions which arise during the delay. The other authors are content simply to *describe* the uneasiness of a soul that is baulked or in suspense.

On the whole it seems unnecessary to lay so much emphasis upon the intellectual side of this affair. The disappointment of a kitten which, in its novitiate, has allowed a captured mouse to run just too far away from its paws, does not seem to differ in principle from the disappointment of a racing owner when he sees his fancied colt passed on the post. On the other hand, if we used the term desire still more broadly, and took it to include all that is hormic either consciously or unconsciously, we should have overlooked the essential significance of the term with unjustifiable carelessness. Desire is *not* the horme but the pathic or emotional disturbance and excitement which accompanies some delay or obstruction of the horme.

This necessary distinction between the horme and the desire is highly relevant to the problem of the connections between desire and value. It is plausible, although I do not think it is true, to say that any value is simply the proper object of some hormic or appetitive process; but it is not at all plausible to hold that the excitement of baulked expectancy determines or constitutes the meaning of goodness.

§ 3. *Desire and satisfaction*

In other words, it is the fulfilment or satisfaction of a hormic process—which implies the stilling and the overcoming of restless desire—that is meant in this "meaning" of good or value. This is a part of *bonum jucundum*, the topic of our next chapter; and since the general relations between appetitive process and pleasurable experience have already been noted in Chapter II, § 5, and elsewhere in this book, it seems unnecessary to recur to the general problem. It is convenient, however, to supplement what has already been said by taking note of two pertinent considerations. The first of these is readily shown by examining Abraham Tucker's criticism of Locke. The second is admirably stated by Dr Ward.

It must be confessed that, except in the particulars already related, Locke's views of the relation between desire, on the one hand, and pleasure (or good), on the other hand, are not altogether clear. His main point is that what determines a man to act at any given moment is the emotions (or rather the culminating or "topping" emotions) which he actually feels at that moment.[1] Hence, although good or pleasure is the proper object of desire in general,[2] the mere acknowledgment of the *summum bonum* may be inoperative "until our desire, raised proportionately to it, makes us uneasy in the want of it".[3] In this way "due and repeated contemplation"[4] of the good may make us invariably uneasy when we act ill; and we have the power of suspending our action even during a very pressing uneasiness.[5] "Naturally", however, what happens is that our *present* satisfaction prompts to continuance in a given course of action, whereas nothing prompts to change except a *present* uneasiness.[6]

Regarded as a motive, therefore, pleasure (or satisfaction) leads to continuance, and the uneasiness of desire leads to change. Regarded as an end or result, however, pleasure (or

---

[1] *Essay*, Book II, chap. xxi, § 31 and § 39.
[2] *Ibid.* § 44.   [3] *Ibid.* § 35.   [4] *Ibid.* § 46.
[5] *Ibid.* § 48.   [6] *Ibid.* § 29.

IV] THE VALUES OF DESIRE 119

satisfaction) is identical with good. "That which is properly good or bad is nothing but barely pleasure or pain...but... things also that draw after them pleasure and pain are considered as good and evil."[1] These satisfactions are as individual as our palates are, and those who ask whether riches, virtue or contemplation have the greatest claim to our allegiance "might have as reasonably disputed whether the best relish were to be found in apples, plums or nuts".[2] Regarding the identity of pleasure with good, however, it has to be said that Locke also maintained (as already noted) that "what has an *aptness* to produce pleasure in us is that we call *good*, and what is *apt* to produce pain in us we call *evil*; for no other reason but for its aptness to produce pleasure and pain in us, wherein consists our happiness or misery".[3]

Regarding satisfaction as a result, Tucker's theory does not differ from Locke's in any important particular. The *summum bonum*, Tucker thinks, is a name for the aggregate of satisfactions from whatever source they come.

Why are useful things good? Because they minister to the supply of our wants and desires? Why is this supply good? Because it satisfies the mind. Why is satisfaction good? Here you must stop, for there lies nothing beyond to furnish materials for an answer; but if anybody denies it, you can only refer him to his own common sense, by asking how he finds himself when in a state of satisfaction or disquietude, and whether of them he would prefer to the other. In short, the matter seems so clear that one may be thought to trifle in spending so many words to prove it; and after all, what is the upshot of the whole but to show that satisfaction satisfies? a mere identical proposition.[4]

Regarding the motivation of action, however, Tucker, with great respect, is at odds with his master. In Tucker's opinion "satisfaction always attracts and uneasiness always repels". In affairs of the mind, he argues, there is no such thing as continuance, since every experience is momentary and transient.[5] Where all is change, therefore, *every* motive must be

---
[1] *Ibid.* § 63.   [2] *Ibid.* § 56.   [3] *Ibid.* § 43.
[4] *The Light of Nature*, Human Nature, chap. xxvii.
[5] *Ibid.* chap. vi.

a motive to change. Accordingly, Locke's theory implies that our lives are constantly painful. "The will never ceases working from morning till night; we are always a doing, but should have nothing to do unless to deliver ourselves from uneasinesses following close upon one another's heels."[1] This is not the fact.

Suppose a company of young folks agreeably entertained in dancing; somebody tells them of a fine fire-work just going to be played off in a neighbouring garden: I will not ensure they shall not run instantly to the window. When their curiosity a little abates and before the sight begins to cloy, some one puts them in mind of their dancing, perhaps the rest take the admonition and they run back to their sport as hastily as they quitted it. Surely this is a change of action and a departure from the plan laid down for the employment of the night; yet I appeal to any gentleman or lady, who may have experienced such an incident, whether they feel the least spice of uneasiness either in breaking off their diversion or returning to it again.[2]

In brief, therefore, "while desire runs on smoothly in its course towards attainment, while we want nothing besides the object we pursue, while no bar stands across the way, nor difficulty occurs to check our speed, for my part I can see nothing but continual satisfaction accompanying the progress".[3]

It is plain, I think, that Tucker's examples—I have quoted only one of them, but one is enough—really do prove his point. It is not true, in fact, that every change in human action is preceded by a marked and painful uneasiness. On the other hand, it seems equally plain that Tucker, at the end of his argument, interprets "desire" as meaning all hormic process with the imprudent addition that appetition, understood in purely introspective terms, is the sole determinant of human action.

The dancers who run to the fire-works, it is true, afford a pretty good example of action which may very well be treated in this wholly psychological way. If, then, there is no spice of uneasiness in their conduct, we have to say either that there

---

[1] *The Light of Nature*, Human Nature, chap. vi.
[2] *Ibid.*   [3] *Ibid.*

THE VALUES OF DESIRE

is no spice of desire in what they do, or that there may be desires without uneasiness. As soon as we examine this question, we readily perceive that the essential point in dispute is whether the "uneasiness" must be supposed to be painful or not. If "uneasiness" merely connotes a certain restless and excited instability of spirit, it need not be painful at all; but, on the contrary, may be pleasantly stimulating. And the dancers *have* a spice of *this* uneasiness. They do not, however, have an uneasiness that is painful in the least degree. Nevertheless, this pleasant instability might easily become painfully and resentfully uneasy. Suppose, for example, that the dancers were little children, and that their elders forbade them to break off the dancing in order to run to see the fireworks. Might there not, then, be an oppressive uneasiness?

As I indicated at the beginning of this paragraph, certain opinions of Dr Ward's on the general topic of the paragraph, deserve to be marked very carefully.

"Instances are by no means wanting", he says, "of very imperious desires accompanied by the clear knowledge that their gratification will be positively distasteful. On the other hand, it is possible to recollect or picture circumstances, known or believed to be intensely pleasurable, without any desire for their realisation being awakened at all: we can recall or admire without desiring."[1]

These brief and pregnant sentences seem to me to be wholly true; and for that reason it is to be regretted that their author appends a statement which clearly contains an oversight. Dr Ward's further argument[2] is that because habituation usually stales our gratification (although it may make our desires more imperious), desire, in theory, must be sharply distinguished from expected gratification. The oversight in Dr Ward's argument is that it neglects the negative side of this affair. When a habit is formed, there is pain in breaking it even in matters which, before the formation of the habit, were totally indifferent. The avoidance of this acquired uneasiness must therefore be considered as well as the positive, but diminished, gratification.

[1] *Psychological Principles*, p. 284.　　[2] *Ibid.* p. 285.

§ 4. *Desired and desirable*

Our subject, in the present chapter, is the relation between desire and value, and it has already become clear, I hope, that the problem of the analysis of desire has an important bearing upon our general topic. We have now to consider various aspects of the relation itself.

It is very commonly assumed that "good" and "desirable" are one and the same. To say that some consummation is devoutly to be wished is to say that it would be a most excellent thing if it came about; and if language means anything, it is surely apparent that what is "desirable" is closely connected with what is *desired*.

Without for the moment challenging any of these statements, let us consider why "desirability" may be supposed to express the nature of value more adequately than the simple fact of being desired.

A very clear exposition of this point is given by von Ehrenfels, who argues to the following effect:[1]

The value of anything should not be confused with either the desires or the gratifications actually felt at any moment. A practised swimmer, for example, may be serenely unconscious of the risk of being drowned. A beginner, on the other hand, is acutely conscious of this unpleasant possibility. Both, however, are equally averse to drowning. What is important or valuable to both, therefore, is the same, but it should be defined, not by what happens to be prominent in the swimmer's consciousness, but by what *might* be prominent under special circumstances. It is the desirable, not the desired as such, which accurately expresses value.

In view of the course of our previous exposition, we need not, I think, linger over this argument. Value, in the sense of von Ehrenfels's argument, really means non-indifference, although von Ehrenfels does not think so. (For he expressly repudiates "unconscious" desires.) And non-indifference, as has been abundantly shown, is something far wider than

[1] *System der Werttheorie*, vol. I, pp. 35 *sqq.*

potential consciousness. While it may underlie all conscious desire, it may occur where desire and consciousness need not be supposed to exist at all. Natural election, in other words, need not suppose *any* capacity for being desired.

A second reason given by von Ehrenfels is more to the point. Indeed, unlike the former, it is, in its way, conclusive. We do not, he says, desire what we already possess, or what we possessed in the past. Yet certainly we may legitimately call past or present things "good". The goodness of anything, therefore, does not depend upon the accident of its futurity (as desire does). Further, it is legitimate to call a thing good if it is such that we *would* desire it under appropriate circumstances.[1]

In this sense, desirable means "capable of being desired", and the problem is frequently approached in this way. To paraphrase a celebrated but unfortunate saying of Mill's, "questions about ultimate values are questions about what is desirable"; and Mill went on to argue that just as "the only proof that a sound is audible is that people hear it" so the only proof that anything is desirable is "that people do actually desire it".[2]

The obvious rejoinder to this argument is that the word desirable is characteristically ambiguous. It may be doubted, indeed, whether the *only* proof that a thing is capable of being desired is that some man actually *has* desired it. At any rate, apart from definitive "proof", we may be permitted to hope that the human species will acquire finer capacities of this kind than have yet appeared in human history. Supposing, however, that the "proof" is what Mill said it was, it is evident that "desirable" may mean either "capable of being desired" or "worthy of being desired"—something that *ought* to be desired. A sound is audible (i.e. capable of being heard) if, in fact, someone has heard it. But it is not, therefore, worth hearing or the kind of sound that, in a better world, would be heard at all.

[1] *System der Werttheorie*, vol. I, pp. 52 *sq*.
[2] *Utilitarianism*, chap. iv.

This equivocation is so obvious, and at the same time so pertinent, that the marvel is how anyone should have failed to discern it. Perhaps, however, we may diminish the marvel by discovering some mitigating circumstances.

A reasonable-seeming interpretation would be that although it cannot be shown that anything *ought* to be desired on the simple ground that it *has* been desired, none the less nothing *ought* to be desired unless it *can* be desired. This is similar to Geulincx's principle, "Ubi nihil vales, ibi nihil velis". In other words, the capacity for being desired is a necessary, although not a sufficient, condition for desirability in the sense of worthiness.

This statement, if expressed with sharper precision, has the appearance of being true. In greater strictness, the statement should be that no one *ought* to desire anything that *he* cannot possibly desire. In greater strictness still, the time at which the man or animal has the capacity for desiring this or that should also be specified. A child, for example, ought not to desire anything beyond a child's capacity or comprehension.

Even so, however, if the argument is intended to show that what is good must, in some sense, be "desirable", a prior condition of its validity must be that everything good is the proper object of *someone's* desire. And this seems false. If "desire" be taken to imply even the tiniest hint of what Locke called "uneasiness", it seems plain that what we call good need have no trace of uneasiness but may be entirely peaceful, placid and serene for men as well as for the angels in heaven. If, on the contrary, we interpret desire in a broader sense, taking "desirable" to mean what the Stoics called "expetible" (that is to say, capable of being sought after), it still seems possible (and, indeed, not unlikely) that much may be good for men which is not expetible by mankind, and that much in the universe may be good which is not expetible by anything.

Anything that is good, we may say, ought to exist, supposing firstly that it could exist, and secondly that nothing better could take its place. Not everything that exists, however, is capable of being sought. Some good things, therefore, may be non-expetible; and in human experience many of the greatest values, especially those connected with religion and human affection, seem, *prima facie* at least, to belong to this class, or at any rate not to be obviously distinct from it.

I think we should conclude, therefore, that "good" need not mean "desirable". "Good" may not even be *capable* of being desired.

§ 5. *On an argument of Mr Ross's*

In an important paper read before the Sixth International Congress of Philosophy,[1] Mr W. D. Ross gives a brief outline of an argument which may suitably be considered here.

"It seems", he says, "to be characteristic of *all* objects of desire that they tend to satisfy the desire for *them*",[2] but such objects do not usually satisfy our desires for other things, and no particular thing satisfies all desires. Accordingly, if we say that anything is good which tends to satisfy desire, we have to make up our minds whether we hold that anything is good which satisfies *any* desire or that things are good in proportion as they satisfy the bent and substance of *all* our desiring. In the former case, we should be forced to include much that is commonly taken to be evil (e.g. the gratifications of spite or malevolence) under "good". In the latter case, we should have to say that no particular thing can be good. And neither alternative is inviting.

This criticism of the desire theory, I think, is very searching and very true; indeed, in all such theories "desire in general" and "particular desires" play a diverting game of hide-and-seek. Let us consider, however, some of the principal attempts that might be made to withstand the cogency of Mr Ross's dilemma.

It is frequently argued that no desire *as such* can be evil. Malevolence, for example, is a variety of hatred, and hatred need not be evil because we *ought* to hate, say, ugliness in art or unrighteousness in conduct. Envy is a complex in which

[1] Also published in *The International Journal of Ethics*, Jan. 1927.
[2] *Ibid.* p. 117.

emulation is the fundamental constituent; and emulation may be an excellent thing. Cruelty, again, is not a specific desire. Timid people may be cruel; unimaginative people may be cruel; curious people may be cruel. But although cruelty may characterise certain actions performed out of desperate timidity, or carelessly and unthinkingly, or from simple curiosity, cruelty itself is neither a specific appetence nor a specific desire.

These arguments, it must be conceded, have considerable weight in their proper place. They tend to show, if they do not convincingly prove, that none of our principal, original or uncomplicated hormic tendencies need be evil but that all may be good. To say this, however, is very different indeed from saying that *every* desire, *de facto*, defines what is good. A desire which *may* be good and also *may* be evil is not "as such" good; and the majority of our actual desires are neither primitive (for we have developed them) nor uncomplicated (for they are full of complications). In short, there *are* evil desires, whether or not there is any radical or immitigable evil in the fundamental or uncomplicated form of any specific type of desire.

It may be argued, however, that all this talk about good desires and bad desires is a peculiarly impudent way of begging the entire question, since if anything good is, as such, anything desired, it is nonsense to speak of "bad" desires. Indeed, it is fundamentally inconsistent to admit any qualitative distinction of any sort among desires.

As this is a large topic, it should be considered at some length.

§ 6. *The quality of desires*

In arguments of this species, where the charge of talking nonsense is freely made by all the disputants on the smallest provocation, there is some point in asking, first of all, where the nonsense lies; and I do not see what could conceivably be more nonsensical than the opinion that none of the desires, say, of Messalina or of Alexander VI, was thoroughly base.

THE VALUES OF DESIRE

In other words, there must be *something* significant in our discriminations between good desires and bad ones. On the other hand, it is entirely conceivable that the common way of describing what, in some sense, is an inevitable distinction, is egregiously mistaken; and, in particular, that the difference between what we call "good" desires and "bad" ones may be adequately explained in terms of the nature of actual desire without importing from the outside any other, or mystical, or mythological, idea of value.

It should further be remarked that the qualitative differentiation of desires is not necessarily opposed to the view that nothing is good except what is desired. It is quite consistent to maintain that desires alone are good but that some desires are better than others. If, however, it is contended, firstly, that anything is good simply because it is desired, but, secondly, that some desires are better than others, a double standard is implied, viz. desire *plus* excellence; and there would be an inconsistency if the first statement, as by some authors, were taken to deny the second.

Let us consider, then, how far it is possible to accept inevitable distinctions in this matter without frankly admitting, that some desires "as such" are nobler, more dignified or qualitatively superior to others.

In general, when we speak of "higher" or of "better" desires, we may be taken to mean any one of three different things. A "better" desire may be the name for the desire for a better thing, as when we say that spying for the sake of one's country is a nobler enterprise than spying to fill one's pocket. Again, and more strictly, we may mean that the desire itself is more excellent. To be sure, what is called a "better" desire usually has a nobler object than a "baser" desire, but it is possible at least that the same thing might be desired nobly in some instances, less nobly in others. When Socrates, for example, said that he meant to drink the hemlock and not to attempt to escape, partly because he was an old man who had little more to expect from life, and partly because he wished to demonstrate his loyalty to the Athenian community by abiding its legal sentence, however unjust that sentence might be, we seem to have a lower and a higher desire (under the circumstances) for the same thing. Thirdly, and more vaguely, we may mean that *something* may be higher or lower in processes which include desire, without specifying too minutely what precisely is higher and what is lower.

Accordingly, when the attempt is made to resolve all excellence into a function or derivative of qualityless desire, it is necessary to deny all three of the foregoing suggestions in their plain or ostensible meaning, and to interpret them all in some roundabout, or, as the modern jargon in philosophy has it, in some Pickwickian sense.

Among many such attempts, I shall select that of Mr I. A. Richards in his *Principles of Literary Criticism*, for special consideration. My reason for the choice is that Mr Richards's theory seems to me clearer, more succinct and better argued than most.

Correctly asserting that "appetence" is a better starting point than (too introspective) "desire", Mr Richards states (1) that "apart from consequences anyone will actually prefer to satisfy a greater number of equal appetencies rather than a less"[1] and relies upon "observation" to establish the point; (2) that the only *psychological* restraints upon appetencies are other appetencies,[2] but (3) that anything is valuable which will satisfy an appetency without involving the frustration of some equal or *more important* appetency; in other words the only reason which can be given for not satisfying a desire is that more important desires will thereby be thwarted. Hence it is necessary to define "importance";[3] and so he tells us (4) that "the importance of an impulse is the extent of the disturbance of other impulses in the individual's activities which the thwarting of the impulse involves".[4] The vagueness of this definition, he goes on to say, suits the hazy condition of our present knowledge on these matters;[5] and Mr Richards

---

[1] *Op. cit.* p. 47. [2] *Ibid.* p. 48. [3] *Ibid.*
[4] *Ibid.* p. 51.   [5] *Ibid.*

proceeds to examine the various ways in which our appetencies can be organised so as to attain a maximum of strength, tenacity, range and harmony.

These statements are hardly acceptable.

Regarding the first of them, it has to be said that every significant part of the statement is either doubtful or false. It is not true that observation establishes the contention, for, as we have seen, Epicurus (who counselled frugality in desiring) existed as well as Aristippus (who counselled opulence in it), and although consequences certainly determined part of the Epicurean prudence, there are a great many people who are content with little and disturbed by versatility and variety.

>   Me focus et nigros non indignantia fumos
>   tecta iuvant et fons vivus et herba rudis.
>   Sit mihi verna satur, sit non doctissima coniunx,
>   sit nox cum somno, sit sine lite dies.

Again the statement is dubious because it does not distinguish between number and variety of appetencies, and because it does not tell us what appetencies are "equal" or how we are to estimate their "equality". "Number" of appetencies would include repetition of the same appetency, but what Mr Richards has in mind is plainly the number of different appetencies, and these must differ qualitatively whether or not their qualitative difference is relevant to their value. There is probably a presumption that it is. Again, what *are* "equal" appetencies? Are they equally intense, or equally tenacious, or equal in their scope and range, or what? From the point of view of value-theory, what is essential is that they should be equally *valuable,* and unless Mr Richards can show that strength, tenacity and scope of appetency, either singly or in conjunction, define value, he would appear to have begged his own question by employing this little word "equal".

In the main, however, the point both of logical and of psychological momentum in his argument is in the neighbourhood of the fourth step (defining "importance"). Here the appetencies take in one another's washing and the importance of any one of them is said to be the extent by which the others are disturbed. Yet, as before, we should like to know whether number or variety is meant. Are the other disturbed appetencies of the same or of a different kind? And if the latter is meant (as it seems to be), is the former alternative altogether irrelevant to the issue? Supposing, however, that this ambiguity has been surmounted or ignored, we have still to ask whether all the disturbed instances are to count equally. If not, there is another sense of value than the sense Mr Richards supplies. If so, how do we know it and what right have we to suppose it?

I do not think it is necessary to proceed further. We might ask for an account of the relative importance or unimportance of disturbing *many* impulses in a small degree or of disturbing *few* in a great degree. We might raise questions about the importance or unimportance of impulses which, like the tadpole's tail, disappear without being obstructed, or of impulses which placidly incorporate others without disturbing them at all. And perhaps we might receive some sort of an answer. It is plain, however, that the proffered definition of "importance" is no definition at all.

§ 7. *Further on the same*

A deeper question remains. While, as I say, I do not think that Mr Richards has succeeded in explaining his conception of "importance", it is necessary also to consider whether, if he had succeeded, the "importance" and the "value" of desires are likely to be the same.

We should commonly say, I think, that an intense appetency is of greater "importance", that is to say, imports or matters more to us, than a more languid condition of the same appetency—and yet that it need not be more excellent. Indeed, if excellence lies in the mean, the starker intensities are probably not very excellent. Similarly, we should say that a more enduring or a more tenacious appetency is more important than a briefer one, but, despite certain notable authorities, not necessarily more excellent.[1] And thirdly, it might be maintained, although strictly (I think) with less confidence, that the richer the scope of an appetency the greater its chances in the way of "importance" and perhaps also of excellence. When it comes to weighing these different species of "importance" in comparative scales, we should not, I think, trust our estimates of "importance" very profoundly. This, however, is a problem of measurement, and perhaps something significant might be done.

In short, "importance" means primarily degrees of non-indifference, and the more we examine the matter, the less probable does it appear that excellence can be construed wholly in terms of non-indifference. Our present enquiries under this head tend to confirm the conclusions of § 6 in Chapter III.

A word should be added concerning the harmony of appetencies. The ideal of harmony is seductive, partly because disharmony is discouraging and exhausting, but principally because we assume a certain kind of harmony as our ideal. We assume, in effect, that the best or most excellent appetencies are conserved in the harmony, and united with as many appetencies as possible which, although not very good, are good enough. A harmony of appetencies, none of which are nobler or more excellent than any others, tells an entirely different story. If one man's interests revolved harmoniously round leeks, and another man's interests revolved harmoniously round cabbages, we really need not be expected to be greatly impressed. Let them have their harmonies, and let others improve the quality of very different aspirations even at the price of bitter self-communings and unconquerable discontent. Some kinds of harmony are attained very easily and are worth very little.

[1] Cf. Byron, *Don Juan*:
Now hatred is by far the longest pleasure:
Men love in haste, but they detest at leisure.

§ 8. *Desire and perfection*

It seems feasible, at this stage of our enquiry, to make certain more general reflections concerning the relation between desire and perfection.

According to the Platonic definition which Aristotle accepts at the beginning of his *Ethics*, "The good is what everything aims at". The difficulty here, as Aristotle was very well aware, is that there is no particular object at which everything aims, and that it is at least very doubtful whether there is any universal goal of everything's seeking. If the universal good is further supposed to be good in itself, self-authenticating and self-sufficient, it may turn out to be a pattern laid up in heaven. Such a good need not even be an inspiring mark to aim at,[1] since it may be beyond the range of all terrestrial and of all planetary ordnance. In any case it is not the truth that every finite thing, in all its doings, aims at this celestial target.

A very different conception emerges, however, when the statement is made that each particular thing aims at *its* good; and it is not unplausible to interpret this second statement as meaning that each particular thing desires *its own* perfection or excellence.

As we have seen, the term "desire" and even the term "appetency" are much too narrow for the opinion thus expressed. Only conscious things have desire. Only living things have appetency. Yet many things are neither conscious nor alive. It might be suggested, however, that whatever anything selects in the way of natural election is the perfection or excellence appropriate to the thing which makes the selection; and if it could be maintained further that no perfection is unselected, there would be a precise equivalence between what is selected and what is good.

Even so, I think, the assertion that everything selects its own excellence is significant and not pleonastic. It is intelligible to ask whether the selection might not, after all, be bad, although it would not be intelligible to ask whether the

[1] Plato, *Rep.* v, 472; Aristotle, *Ethics*, 1094 *a*.

THE VALUES OF DESIRE

selection was not a selection. In other words, the statement that everything selects its own excellence combines two different conceptions, viz. selecting and being excellent, although the domains of the two conceptions (in logical language their "extension") are held to be precisely identical.

It can easily be shown, I think, that the two conceptions really are different, whatever may be true of the facts to which they apply. Consider, for example, the common maxim of the schools *Quidquid petitur, petitur sub specie boni*, or, *anglice*, that, among conscious creatures, whatever is sought *appears* to be good. True or not, this statement has a meaning, and the meaning implies at least the logical possibility that a creature, acting in error, really does select what is not really its good but only appears to be good. If so, it is certainly conceivable that what is selected is *not* good.

Once the difference in the *conceptions* is firmly grasped, however, it becomes increasingly hard to believe that their domains are the same. As we have seen, when different species are compared, the ways of one species seem plainly to be more excellent than the ways of another, if indeed the ways of certain species can be said to have any excellence at all. And the same may be said of the ways of different men.

We commonly assert that these differences are qualitative, and that certain qualities are excellent, others not, while among the excellences some are vastly superior to others.

I have to maintain that this common opinion is also true. It has, however, been disputed (as we have seen), and although the dispute has already occupied us at some length, it may be advisable for us to review it once again.

As M. Goblot remarks,[1] it is preposterous to deny that there is an order of perfections and some sort of hierarchy of beings, or to suppose that these differences are wholly explicable in terms of utility to the human species. Granting that when we call the horse a noble animal we are apt to think, not impartially, of his services to *us*, we do not call sheep noble although, humanly speaking, they are more useful than horses;

[1] *La logique des jugements de valeur*, p. 26.

and in any case it was because the horse *had* his merits that man made use of horses. In short, "It is in themselves and by themselves that men, horses and dogs are superior to worms and molluscs, that animals, in general, are superior to plants, and men to animals".[1]

A certain kind of excellence, therefore, not merely relative or exclusively utilitarian, is, as M. Goblot says, "ni illusoire, ni métaphysique, ni mystique".[2] But he does not think it is qualitative. On the contrary, he regards it as a difference in perfection, "provided that by perfection is understood, as in the Cartesian tradition, quantity of being. The more perfect being is the being which *is* in a fuller way, which asserts its existence from a greater number of standpoints, which has a richer nature on account of its stronger and more varied potencies".[3] And M. Goblot goes on to argue that in this sense, and apart from utility, man's articulate speech is more perfect than animal cries, scientific thinking than prelogical mental excursions, and the like. What is more, the difference, besides being non-utilitarian, is also non-aesthetic. We need not think of beauty in describing it. For our proper criterion is the amount or quantity of hard, stubborn fact.

Thus, by a route slightly different from what has gone before, we arrive once more at the question which underlies what Mr Richards calls "importance" and others have called "completeness". The question is whether all existence is, as such, good or perfect, so that "degrees" of excellence simply mean amount of existence, or whether certain qualities are more excellent than others. It is not disputed, of course, that things actually do differ in quality. The problem is whether such qualitative differences are relevant to their value.

My contention is that when this question is squarely faced there can be but one answer, and that this answer is not M. Goblot's. Different species, as he rightly maintains, *may* differ in "perfection", not merely from their own standpoint (as on the theories of natural election, pleasure or desire) but

---

[1] *La logique des jugements de valeur*, p. 26.
[2] *Ibid.* p. 27.   [3] *Ibid.*

THE VALUES OF DESIRE

absolutely. This perfection, however, is *not* the amount or the extended character of their existence, but something quite *sui generis* which we call nobility, fineness, dignity or excellence.

SECTION II
OF CERTAIN HISTORICAL OPINIONS

§ 1. *Hobbes*

Thomas Hobbes of Malmesbury maintained that

whatsoever is the object of any man's appetite or desire; that is it, which he for his part calleth *good*: and the object of his hate and aversion *evil*: And of his contempt *vile* and *inconsiderable*. For these words of good, evil and contemptible, are ever used with relation to the person that useth them. There being nothing simply and absolutely so: nor any common rule of good and evil, to be taken from the nature of the objects themselves: but from the person of the man (where there is no commonwealth;) or, (in a commonwealth,) from the person that representeth it; or from an arbitrator or judge, whom men disagreeing shall by consent set up, and make his sentence the rule thereof.[1]

As he also explained, "That which men desire, they are also said to love; and to hate those things for which they have aversion. So that desire, and love, are the same thing; save that by desire, we always signify the absence of the object; by love, most commonly, the presence of the same. So also by aversion, we signify the absence, and by hate the presence of the object".[2]

He argued further that desire and aversion are actual motions, being either endeavour toward something or endeavour fromward something. There is nothing metaphorical, he said, about the notion in these endeavours. "For though words may be called metaphorical, bodies and motions cannot."[3]

[1] *Leviathan*, Part I, chap. vi.
[2] *Ibid.*
[3] *Ibid.*

§ 2. *Schopenhauer*

Hobbes's view has, of course, been frequently held. I have given his statement of the view, partly on account of Hobbes's historical influence, but principally because he stated the doctrine so admirably.

Among many who agree essentially with Hobbes in this particular, Schopenhauer may be mentioned. In the *Preisschrift* that was *not* crowned by the Royal Danish Academy, Schopenhauer says that he was forced to protest against those among his contemporaries who declared Good and Evil to be simple notions, incapable of explanation and requiring none, and who, consequently, endeavoured to found their ethical systems upon a mysterious Idea of Good.

In opposition to these philosophers, he was compelled, he said, to show that these conceptions of Good and of Evil are not at all simple (because they express a relation) and are not *à priori* intuitions (because they are fashioned out of everyday experience). "Everything conformable to the striving of an individual will", he continued, "is called good in relation to the will in question—good food, good roads, good portents—and the opposite bad or, in the case of animate creatures, evil."[1] He went on to argue that an unselfish man is called "good" by the public because he serves the public.

§ 3. *C. von Ehrenfels*

Among the moderns C. von Ehrenfels and A. Meinong are frequently (and not unjustly) supposed to have made the most effective contributions to the analysis of value-theory. Both of these authors were strongly influenced by the work of Franz Brentano, and by the Austrian economists, but both were themselves original and eminent.

In von Ehrenfels's view, *Begehren*, that is to say "desire" or "wish", had an evident priority in this analysis; and Meinong did not think so. It is von Ehrenfels, therefore, who has to be considered in the present section.

[1] *Werke* (Frauenstädt, 1874), vol. IV, p. 265.

THE VALUES OF DESIRE

It is affirmed on page 2 of his book[1] that "we do not desire things because we perceive a mystical and intangible essence called 'worth' in them, but on the contrary, we ascribe 'worth' to them because we desire them".[2]

The negative part of this thesis, so far as I can see, is not separately argued, but is regarded as established by the success of the positive part. In place of something "mystical and intangible", something positive is offered, and the undoing of the occult thing is accordingly presumed. Even when it might be thought impossible to forgo serious argument, as in this author's criticism of Brentano's view that worth is the object of a *right* kind of love just as truth is the object of a *right* kind of cogitation, we find, instead of argument, abuse of the plaintiff. We are told, in short, that Brentano was defending a prejudice.[3] The human race has an inveterate tendency to objectify and make absolute whatever affects it nearly, or, in some sense, constrains its allegiance. Spinning from their own substance, men's spidery minds take themselves to have fashioned some other substance.

In reality, it is declared, value expresses a relation between subject and object; and so we have the following elaborate, but sufficiently informative definition.

Value is a relation between some object and some subject, and expresses the fact either that the subject actually desires the object (or *would* desire it in the case in which he is doubtful of the object's existence) or that the object in question, being presented to the subject as a reality in the most concrete, liveliest and completest way, conditions in the subject an experience higher in the scale of pleasure and pain than the corresponding presentation of the non-existence of the object in question would do.[4]

Three points in this definition seem to be salient. These are (1) the relations between desire and pleasure-pain, (2) the insistence that desire is a conscious phenomenon, and (3) the relation between desire and existence. I shall deal with these points *seriatim*.

---

[1] *System der Werttheorie*, vol. I (1897).
[2] *Ibid.* pp. 42 *sqq.*   [3] *Ibid.* p. 43.   [4] *Ibid.* p. 65.

(1) The essence of von Ehrenfels's position here is that desire is moved not by pleasure as such, but by greater pleasure or lesser pain. In other words, desire is always *preference*—a transition to greater satisfaction, not the search for satisfaction taken simply and absolutely. To choose a physical analogue, desire has to do with accelerations, not with simple velocities. In this von Ehrenfels differs from the majority of hedonists who maintain (i) that in default of more than one pleasant alternative we choose pleasure *simpliciter*, and (ii) that among several pleasant alternatives we choose the most pleasurable. It does not appear, however, that von Ehrenfels supplies any effective refutation of the usual hedonistic view.

Von Ehrenfels maintained, however, that the "promotion of relative felicity" was a genuine psychological law; and he even invites us to believe that all sufferers from melancholia, although not absolutely happy, are happier in their preoccupation with their own misery than they could be in any other conceivable way. This seems absurd. Melancholy may sometimes be an interesting luxury, but the madhouse shows that von Ehrenfels's "law" is unbelievable in at least *some* cases; and it is most highly speculative in many others.[1] As in the parallel case of a supposed law of "forgetting the unpleasant" (although, as it happens, we remember what is unpleasant as readily and as firmly as what is pleasant),[2] we can only marvel at the way in which untested and quite false dogmas regarding pleasure have been greedily accepted by so many eminent men.

(2) In von Ehrenfels's opinion the conception of "unconscious desire" is self-contradictory, and, contradiction apart, thoroughly inadmissible.[3] Indeed, he maintains that the object of desire must necessarily be consciously accepted as a possible fact, and consciously included in the web of

---

[1] Cf. A. Meinong, *Über Annahmen*, chap. viii, §§ 48, 49.
[2] For experimental evidence see A. Wohlgemuth, *A Critical Examination of Psycho-Analysis*, pp. 34 *sqq.*
[3] *Ibid.* p. 257.

causes in which our lives are enmeshed.[1] It presupposes, in short, conscious self-acquaintance as well as the capacity for discriminating between real and imaginary,[2] although the information, in both cases, need not (of course) be very abstract, precise or philosophical. Desire, according to von Ehrenfels, is even, in its way, an intellectual thing, not to be found among the brutes, although possible to children despite their inferior powers of abstraction.[3]

Statements such as these certainly give precision to von Ehrenfels's account of desire, and, so far, are to be commended. He has to pay a price, however. For it is surely permissible to hold that animals may seek their good even if they cannot conceive it, or that we can infer from men's actions that they prize certain things, even if it is probable that they have no beliefs or opinions concerning such things. Beliefs and opinions seldom arise except in answer to some question; and many men's values seem to belong to the order of unquestioned things.

(3) When good is taken to mean the "expetible", or (as by von Ehrenfels) the "consciously expetible", it seems evident both that our seeking is an actual fact and that it is directed towards actuality. To be sure, at the conscious level, error may occur, and therefore we may seek what is not fact but illusion. Even here, however, it may be contended that the illusion is a fact *in ourselves*, although not what we take it to be, or, again, that when, in the grip of some error, we pursue what in fact is impossible, we at least do not *believe* that the thing is impossible. The latter point is confirmed by the circumstance that a man's desire ceases when he becomes convinced that its object is quite unattainable. This confirmation, it must be admitted, is lacking in precision, since "desire" in these cases may remain in the form of longing or wistful craving, or, again, since men, in these instances, may struggle against an intellectual conviction which they cannot withstand, or even stifle the conviction (as many have done on religious questions). Indeed, it might be said, that no one is

[1] *Ibid.*   [2] *Ibid.* p. 256.   [3] *Ibid.* p. 257.

really convinced of the impossibility of any of his desires until he has ceased to have them. On the whole, however, we must accept the general accuracy of arguments of this order.

In other words, granting that the relation between value and existence has been the subject of much philosophical dispute, there can be no occasion for the dispute if values express nothing but the fact of desire. For our seeking is a fact and is bent upon fact. On the other hand, if we stretch desire into desirable, and, like von Ehrenfels, are prepared to call a thing desirable if it would be desired under conditions which in fact do not occur (e.g. if it *might have* been desired in the past although it was *not* desired) it may be dubious whether the alleged connection between value and existence is really very close.

Finally, we should add the circumstance that followers of Brentano, and some who are not followers, appear to accept the connection in a sense that cannot be said to be at all obvious. Thus Mr Scheler states the following "axioms" of a "material" ethic or value-theory:[1]

1. The existence of a positive value is itself a positive value.

2. The non-existence of a positive value is itself a negative value.

3. The existence of a negative value is itself a negative value.

4. The non-existence of a negative value is itself a positive value.

If "value" and "desire" are the same, these statements would seem to be absurd. For what is the meaning of saying that the existence of a positive desire is itself a positive desire? In any other sense they are, to say the least, highly doubtful. The fourth of them, for example, would appear to countenance the silly occupation of congratulating ourselves upon our immunity from an infinity of fantastic evils.

---

[1] *Der Formalismus in der Ethik und die Materiale Wertethik*, pp. 21 *sq.*

§ 4. *T. H. Green*

During the present enquiry there has been frequent occasion to consider the infra-conscious analogues of desire in animal appetency or, still more generally, in natural election. While, however, so much has been said about the bottom and the lower reaches of this elective scale, comparatively little has been said about the top, except to point out that the principle of excellence cannot be identified with the principle of non-indifference.

In the opinion of certain philosophers, however, it is the top of the scale that should command our attention; and one of the most notable of them was T. H. Green. According to Green "the common characteristic of the good is that it satisfies some desire".[1] Yet Green differs from Hobbes, von Ehrenfels and others in a striking and trenchant way, because he means by "desire" something very different indeed from what they mean by it.

In Green's view, "desire" must be carefully distinguished both from animal wants and from our feeling of these wants. It is neither egence[2] nor sentience but of a spiritual, non-animal order, and the reason has to be explained with precision.

Green's explanation involves a detour along a path first charted in Königsberg—or, in other words, an extension of Kantian theory.

Let us consider the difference between sensing on the one hand, and the knowledge which we base upon the senses on the other. Suppose, in some subtropical country, that the sun, after being obscured for a time, comes forth in his strength; and suppose a lizard among the stones. Suppose also that the mentality of this tiny saurian is at the level sometimes called "attuition", that is to say that the animal is sentient but cannot think at all.

In this case, what happens in the lizard is (we may con-

---
[1] *Prolegomena to Ethics*, § 171.
[2] For the meaning of this term see pp. 109 *sq.* n.

jecture) that the animal feels, and sees, the warmth of the sun, and, later, feels the stones to be warm as he darts among them. This succession in the animal's feelings, however, is plainly very different indeed from the message which a human interpreter would elicit from similar sensations. The human interpreter would not only experience sensations which in fact were successive but would also know (or at least believe) that they were successive, and would probably go on to interpret this belief as testimony to the physical verity that the sun warmed the stone. In animal attuition nothing of the sort need be supposed.

If so, there is a difference of the greatest magnitude, and Kant, we may say, touched the very nerve of it. Green, generalising from Kant's distinction, argues as follows.[1] Animal feelings are natural events, but are not, properly speaking, conscious. For *con*sciousness in the strict sense it is necessary that a number of feelings or attuitions should be held together in the unity of a single mind (or spiritual agency), and *interpreted* (or referred to the order of nature) not merely *enjoyed* as they occur. Accordingly no form or degree of knowledge or of interpretation can be simply a natural event; or, in other words, whatever is spiritual must be *more* than natural.

If we assume that "natural" means attuitive and nothing else, Green's conclusion, I think, plainly follows. It is another question, however, whether the conclusion supports the construction that Green put upon it, viz. that the spiritual principle in knowledge, being not *merely* an event, is never an event at all (that is to say, is not in time or space); or again that, since truth is single, all the events in nature must be supposed to be held together and unified by a single divine consciousness in which, somehow, we participate. Kant never went so far, and his caution seems to have been sound. It is unnecessary for our purpose here, however, to pursue this further topic. For us it is sufficient to note what Kant and Green may be said to have established, viz. that knowledge is spiritual and not merely attuitive, at least in the sense that,

---

[1] *Prolegomena to Ethics*, Book I, chap. i.

in interpreting our sensations, several sensations may have to be present together in the unity of a single self.

In Kant's theory, for reasons which do not now concern us, the analysis of human practice or action differed notably from the analysis of knowledge or speculation. In Green's view, on the contrary, spiritual knowledge and spiritual action, although they were not the same, matched one another with the nicest precision. And so we come to Green's account of "desire".[1]

"Desire" to Green's mind was spiritual, not natural. Just as our knowledge of nature, although arising from sensations, is not a mere play of sensations but a holding of them together in the *con*sciousness of a single self (which thereby transcends them), so (he said) our spiritual acts are not animal wants, felt as they happen to occur (i.e. egences which provoke and disturb us), but are *adopted* and *unified* by a single spiritual self. "Desires", it is true, need not be completely "adopted" by the self since we may be tempted, drawn and beset by many desires and, in the end, choose or "adopt" but one. They are always, however (so to say), *candidates* for adoption, and therefore are never merely natural, but in potency and appearance are spiritual.

Another way of putting Green's contention is to distinguish between the experiencing of sensations at the attuitive level, and the reference, through sensations, to some *object* at the knowledgeable or interpreting level. In the parallel case of spiritual action, this means that (spiritual) desire is always for an *object*, while animal wants, even where there is sentience, are *objectless* and only a moving crowd.

According to Green's argument, therefore, "desire" differs characteristically both from appetition and from natural election; and, as we have seen, Green maintained very forcibly that nothing "spiritual" can be derived from what is "natural" but that the spiritual differs in principle and altogether from the natural.

How much, then, does Green's argument prove?

A dispute concerning the meaning of the word "desire" would of course remain a battle about a word. It could hardly

[1] *Ibid.* Book II, chap. ii.

be maintained, however, that the difference between attuition and knowledge is but a dictionary distinction, or that its implications are other than fundamental. If, therefore, the desire for an object differed from animal wants with the same trenchancy and finality as knowledge of an object differs from the play of the senses, it would be an unpardonable error to contend that spiritual desires differ only in degree from animal appetency and natural election.

It must be conceded to Green that action is fundamentally distinct from contemplation. To commit a theft is very different indeed from contemplating a theft, if only because, in the second case, nobody's pocket is emptied. It should also be conceded (as we have seen) that action at the reflective level is to be distinguished from the play of impulse at least as clearly as a higher physiological integration is from a lower, or a banking system from an old woman's stocking.

Despite these concessions, it may fairly be contended that the fundamental distinction between simple experience and the reference, through experience, to an *object* is counted twice over in Green's analysis. The distinction arises wherever knowledge arises. What Green calls "desire" is mixed with knowledge. Why, therefore, should he suppose a double root for the distinction? To be sure, the knowledge, in practical pursuits, does not remain mere knowledge—a speculative accompaniment of the action, like oil floating upon water. It is effectually incorporated into our actions and part of the stuff of our motives; but we need not suppose ourselves to have two co-ordinate sources of this distinction, if in reality there is only one.

Putting the point otherwise, we may say that *knowledge* cannot begin until there is reference to an object; but that *action* may. I do not think, even, that we have the right to say that all characteristically human action involves explicit reference to an object, although our responsible and intelligent actions do involve such reference. In action there may only be a difference of degree, between what does, and what does not, "refer to an object". In speculation the difference must be of kind.

The further development of Green's theory of desire and of "good" appears to be still more dubious. Granting that spiritual realities are not natural, and that natural events are temporal, it does not follow that spiritual realities cannot be temporal. And if they were non-temporal, they need not, in consequence, have any special affinity with permanence. For permanence is as temporal as transience. Similarly the unity of the self when it holds experiences together in a single act does not establish the changelessness of this unifying activity, much less the changelessness of the knowing self from its infancy to its second childhood. In short, the permanence of objects of "desire", and their contrast with the transience and the perishable nature of animal wants, however true it may be, does not, so far as I can see, follow logically from the spirituality of man's experience.

The same must be said of what is still more prominent in Green's philosophy—I mean his view of the common good.[1] When, like the lizard in our illustration, we do not merely feel warmth, but refer the warmth to the influence of the sun, we naturally interpret the circumstance as a reference beyond our private selves to a common order of nature which is public in the sense that we all, when referring to the sun or to its influence upon the stones which it warms, refer to the same thing. It may be doubted whether the Kantian principle truly yields this inference without several additional assumptions, but whether it does or does not, we have no right to maintain that a common or public good is part of the meaning of desiring an "object" in the same sense as a common or public world may perhaps be part of the meaning of the "reference to an object" in knowledge. A man may knowingly adopt as the object of his desire something which is at variance with the public benefit. If, on the other hand, he refers in his thoughts to a world which is nobody's world but his own, we have to say that he is mad. And madness and selfishness are not the same, even if it be true that selfishness is usually, or always, unwise.

[1] *Prolegomena to Ethics*, Book III, chap. iii.

CHAPTER V

BONUM JUCUNDUM

SECTION I. GENERAL

§ 1. *Nature of the subject*

THE subject of the present chapter, and of its immediate successor, is the extent to which good (or value) may be taken to be identical with, or wholly derived from, that feeling or pathic experience which, best and most simply, is called pleasure.

To be sure, the adequacy of "pleasure" to describe what here is meant, has often been doubted or gainsaid. According to T. H. Green and certain other authors, the life of pleasure, so far from being the good life, typifies the squandered existence of the rake or the voluptuary. For pleasures, it is held, are always fleeting and exciting, and so must be distinguished from the permanence and tranquillity that characterise what is better called happiness or contentment. Pleasures, it is also held, are in their essence sensory or animal, but our finer and our purer joys are of a nobler order.

Regarding these complaints, I can only say that lasting, tranquil or exalted pleasures seem to occur as well as brief, perturbing or earthy ones; and that it is difficult to find a better word than pleasure to describe the tone and flavour of all that is sweet in our pathic experience.

I mean, then, by pleasure, the sweetness of all we enjoy, and since I do not want to waste time over words, I am content to show that this usage of the term "pleasure" is permissible in English. For the proof, it is enough to refer, very briefly, to Shelley's *Defence of Poetry*. For Shelley was a master of English prose and he told us that "tragedy delights by affording a shadow of that pleasure which exists in pain. This is the source also of the melancholy which is inseparable from the sweetest melody. The pleasure that is in sorrow is sweeter than the pleasure of pleasure itself".

§ 2. *Pleasure and satisfaction*

The term "satisfaction", which certain authors oppose and prefer to "pleasure" in this connection, seems to me far less accurate.

Satisfaction, in its literal sense, means that we have enough. So regarded, the term seems to be dubiously expressive of our feelings, since we might have *no* feeling although we had enough of something or other; and, if we wanted too much of the thing, might even be distressed at not having more than enough.

Indeed, when we speak of satisfaction, either generally or as an experience, we may, and commonly do, employ the term in the schoolmaster's sense, which distinguishes, it is true, between *satis* and *vix* or plain *non satis*, but also distinguishes between *satis* and *bene*. If we do affirm that anything which is well enough is also well, we mean by "well" something that is not the best; as in the proverb *Le mieux est l'ennemi du bien.*

More importantly, we have to note that "satisfaction" is a term which applies to a process complete or fulfilled, rather than to any risk or adventure whose climax and outcome are hidden. It is the kind of term which is appropriate to one's retirement from business rather than to one's prosecution of business, and therefore, in strictness, applies to a certain class of feelings, and not to all. Most usually, the term means comparative complacency regarding what is over and done with, as when Mr Collins, in *Pride and Prejudice*, "reflected with augmented satisfaction" upon his rejection by Elizabeth Bennet after he came to hear of Lydia Bennet's elopement with Wickham.

§ 3. *Further on the same*

The truth is that most of the familiar arguments upon this topic, such as Bishop Butler's or T. H. Green's, are concerned with the sufficiency of the pleasure-theory *in ethics*, and so have to consider, on the one hand, whether pleasure can have authority or claim our loyalty, and, on the other hand, whether pleasure, as Bentham said, is our "master" and determines all our actions. In other words, the question is debated with explicit reference to what is expetible (in the main, directly and voluntarily). We have, however, no right to assume that whatever is good is expetible; and if, in fact, everything good is expetible (at least in a roundabout and semi-voluntary way) we should at least remember that many good things, in their primary incidence, are given rather than sought.

Among such goods, the joys of religion which are called peace, much in human affection, and most of the aesthetic values which are another name for beauty, should plainly be included. And something should here be said of joys such as these.

The Christian may indeed seek God's peace; and he need not be furtive in his search. Yet peace, when it comes, is bestowed, not earned, and it may come without being sought for. "O that thou hadst hearkened to my commandments! then had thy peace been as a river."[1] "As many as walk according to this rule, peace be on them, and mercy, and upon the Israel of God."[2] Even in passages such as these, the joy of this peace is taken to be supervenient upon righteousness or devotion and not to be the simple consequence or the natural fruit of these. It does not come by accident to the Israel of God, or to any unprepared to receive it; yet when it comes it is God's gift to His Israel. "Now the Lord of peace Himself give you peace always by all means."[3] "Peace I leave with you, my peace I give unto you; not as the world giveth, give I unto you."[4]

---

[1] Isaiah, xlviii. 18.   [2] Gal. vi. 16.
[3] 2 Thess. iii. 16.   [4] John xiv. 27.

Again, we may set ourselves to win the affection of others, even in the elaborate way which is often described as a siege; and (although the point is disputed) it would also appear that we may set ourselves to love our fellows and even our nearest neighbours. There are various ways of attempting to protect ourselves against the dislike of others (such as avoiding rudeness), and also many ways of trying to remove dislike and uncharity within ourselves. Such attempts may succeed, and it is unlikely that they are always negative and never positive. It is better, too, that they should be made. For love, left to itself, may be cruel, and even when it is not cruel, it may hurt because it is blind. The Augustinian *Ama et fac quod vis* should never be written of *all* love, magnificent though John's saying be that "love is of God; and every one that loveth is born of God, and knoweth God".[1]

Thus Kant was mistaken when he affirmed that love *could* not be commanded. Love is not entirely outside the range of man's will. In the main, however, love (as distinguished from lust) is not an appetite, and also is not to be obtained *expetendo*. Its sweetness comes to all lovers, and such knowledge as goes with it is glad with the light of joyful surprise.

The same is true of aesthetic joys; and here I propose to offer a less cursory survey.

§ 4. *Fine art and beauty*

Art is skilful production, and fine art is the production of something fine, that is to say, of something beautiful. In essentials, however, poems are made out of words, and paintings out of paint, in the same sense as shoes are made out of leather.

The difference between artists and other people lies primarily in the executive capacity of the former. To see anything with a painter's eye is to see it as something paintable. This is beauty, but not any species of beauty. It is the nuance and suggestion of a beautiful effect which the painter thinks he can put upon canvas. At least he can try.

[1] 1 John iv. 7.

And so in all the fine arts. When literary artists, like Hobbes or Samuel Butler, made a practice of jotting down elusive thoughts or phrases in order to keep them from darting away—the former with his ink-horn constantly ready, the latter with a little book sedulously retained in his waistcoat pocket—they were storing these words and phrases *for use*; and they built up their paragraphs round these words and phrases.

All the arts, therefore, are departments of practice, just as literally and as obviously as business or morality is. The aims of business or of morality may be different from the aims of fine art. But fine art is not less practical than morality or business. Are poets not busy with their pens or etchers with their burins?

It is no great matter whether the practice of artists is wholly voluntary or only semi-voluntary. In the experience of inspiration the artist may well be caught out of himself, and be a little mad. Very commonly, again, the artist, as he constructs, seems to perceive his symphony, painting or story growing, so to say, in front of him, rather than to see these things following his preordered plan.

Among artists, therefore, beauty is plainly expetible, and those who are not artists may also seek it. Lacking the skill to present anything beautiful to their fellows, they may, perhaps, dream beauty by themselves. Again, plainly, they may try to follow the beauties which others have created, visiting the Louvre or the Prado time and again, or that natural loveliness which is perhaps, as Sir Thomas Browne said it was, the art of God.

Nevertheless, although beauty may be sought, it may come without being sought; and often it does come unsought. What is more, if we distinguish (as we should), between aesthetic enjoyment and artistic creation, we have to conclude that beauty in its essence, like peace and human affection, is only subordinately expetible (when, indeed, it is expetible at all), and that in the main it is bestowed rather than sought or won.

With the object of confirming this opinion, I shall try, firstly, to remove certain objections that many readers may feel; and, secondly, shall attempt to analyse aesthetic experience in its broader outlines.

§ 5. *Discussion of objections*

(1) It is sometimes held, as by Hegel, that there is no such thing as "natural" beauty. For beauty, Hegel says,[1] must be born again of the spirit; and Croce adds that nature is stupid, not spiritual. This extreme paradox, however (even apart from the possibility of an interpretation like Sir Thomas Browne's), seems to have nothing to commend it. "Painted ships" upon "painted oceans" are just as stupid in their painted way as the "elms and hedgerows" in which the Vicar of Wakefield found "inexpressible beauty", and if the question be (as surely it should be) not whether natural objects have beautiful *minds*, but whether our minds can draw beauty from them or discover it in them, there seems no reason whatsoever why works of art alone should possess or impart this beauty. Indeed we may say that *because* there is natural beauty, the aesthetic experience of humanity cannot be the same thing as human art.

(2) Signor Croce's doctrine that art and aesthetics are instances of "expression" is another objection that has to be met.

In any ordinary sense, expression is *utterance*, and the importance of the utterance is that it communicates some meaning or idea to other people. In this sense, works of art are always uttered or published, and they do communicate to others than the artist. The aesthetic enjoyment of them, however, is a personal experience which need not (perhaps, strictly speaking, cannot) be uttered or published at all.

What is argued in terms of the expressive theory is something more subtle than this, and may be stated as follows.

[1] For these and further references see E. F. Carritt, *The Theory of Beauty*, p. 36.

A poet (let us say) begins with a certain vague impulsive experience,[1] and he proceeds to give form to the impulse in words. In the end he writes the words, either concurrently with the process of verbal formulation, or after, as we say, the poem has been composed "in his head". It is only when the words are written that his expression is conveyed to others.

From the poet's point of view the writing of the words need not greatly matter. He has expressed himself *to himself* before he records his expression. And as the words come to him, the expression itself comes. His initial vague impulse is a vague expression which gradually acquires form and clearness. Moreover, however excited the poet may be regarding the promise of his initial vague impulse, he is cheating himself if he supposes that there is any beauty except in proportion as his expression is successful. The proof of his poesy is the making of his poem.

Consider, now, the poet's readers. The mere reception of communicated sound is not the reception of poetry. For the sounds, in the extreme case, might even be in a foreign and unknown language. Communication, we are told, occurs only when the reader participates effectively, if indirectly, in the poet's experience. The words which are read enable the reader to express in his own mind what the poet expressed in *his* mind, to form for himself what the poet formed. In other words, no reader can appreciate a poem without *being* a poet. No reader understands Milton's *Lycidas* unless it is to him what it was to Milton when Milton wrote it, that is to say, unless *he* as well as Milton *is* the author of *Lycidas*, at any rate for a brief space.

This conclusion appears to me to imply the falsity of its premises. Two men who think of the same thing in the same way are no more identical than two horses which run the same course in the same way; and since the poet and the reader need not be supposed to be identical even in this particular, they need not be supposed to be identical at all. A poet does not

---

[1] Cf. L. Abercrombie, *Towards a Theory of Art*, Chap. iv.

only appreciate his poem, he also *makes* it; his readers may appreciate it, but do not make it. To suppose anything else is gratuitously to confuse the boundaries between creative capacity and critical taste. Poets must *have* taste in order to restrain and approve their work as it takes substance and shape. If any of them are poor critics in their own domain, the reason must be that they have little skill in *explaining* what they approve. And critics have perhaps rather too much of this special faculty. But even among artists it is necessary to distinguish clearly between production and appreciation, whether at the end of the work or as the work proceeds. In the onlooker the distinction is surely abundantly evident.

Accordingly, although art is the expetition of beauty, aesthetic experience need not be sought, and, even in art, yields a sweetness of glad surprise which effectually distinguishes it from the simple object of intended endeavour. In its finer essence beauty is free from all appetite, not only from lustful or everyday appetites. This *reception* of beauty on our part, this pathic flavour which clings to it, is the first thing to note about it, and the free and joyous activities which speedily supervene, even in those who are not artists and have little executive capacity, are the results of the reception of beauty, not the consequences of any aesthetic impulse. The pheasant's ruff and the proud peacock's magnificence at mating time may indeed suggest the possibility of exceptions; but even if such displays are authentically aesthetic they cannot overthrow the fundamental analysis of aesthetic experience.

And aesthetic experience is firmly and deeply planted in the human soul. If industrialists, some Puritans and some modern soldiers have no time for it, other people have; and children have something very like it. As Mr Dewey says,

The body is decked before it is clothed....Men make a game of their fishing and hunting, and turn to the periodic and disciplinary labour of agriculture only when inferiors, women and slaves, cannot be had to do the work. Useful labour is, whenever possible, transformed by ceremonial and ritual accompaniments, subordinated to art that yields immediate enjoyment.[1]

Men paint themselves and comb their hair before they drill. Art is not a parergon of civilisation, and the proof may be seen in Aurignacian caves even to-day. Yet the reason is not some primitive impulse but the universal appeal of pathic aesthetic emotion and the natural overflow from this emotion into the pools and the currents of man's entire existence.

Let us scan this question a little more narrowly.

§ 6. *The nature of aesthetic experience*

Mr Richards has recently called attention to the slipshod practice of critics and reviewers in appealing, whenever they choose, to "aesthetic emotion". He takes this practice to be the lively ghost of a defunct aesthetic philosophy—the philosophy, namely, which endeavoured to analyse "aesthetic experience" as a unique sort of mental process. Kant, he thinks, was the first, and Mr Bosanquet one of the last, to embrace this error.

With regard to the sense of aesthetic which "*is* confined to experiences of beauty and does imply value",[2] Mr Richards maintains that such experiences

are only a further development, a finer organisation of ordinary experiences, and not in the least a new and different kind of thing. When we look at a picture or read a poem, or listen to music, we are not doing something quite unlike what we were doing on our way to the Gallery or when we dressed in the morning. The fashion in which the experience is caused in us is different, and as a rule the experience is more complex and, if we are successful, more unified. But our activity is not of a fundamentally different kind.[3]

In considering arguments such as these, we must, I think, distinguish. We cannot hold (and Mr Richards does not seem to mean) that *nothing* distinctive occurs when there is experience of beauty. For surely we may walk *to* the Gallery

---

[1] *Experience and Nature*, pp. 78 sq.
[2] *Principles of Literary Criticism*, p. 16.
[3] *Ibid.* pp. 16 sq.

or *through* the Gallery in an utterly unaesthetic way. On the other hand, it is certainly true that a man who is looking at the Murillos in the Caridad at Seville is looking, in the same sense of looking, as if he were looking at his watch, or that the man who hears a nightingale with full aesthetic delight is hearing in the same sense of hearing as if he heard a cat on the tiles.

Is he not, however, experiencing a peculiar *emotion*? Here again we must distinguish. If he were, we should have to hold, I suppose, that *the same* specific emotion is felt wherever beauty is felt, so that those who respond emotionally to the beauty of Helen of Troy, T'ang masterpieces, Jenny Lind's voice, the corona of a solar eclipse, the velvet of Romanée Conti 1915 are (or were) experiencing what is literally and identically the same emotion. This is very hard to believe; and it is not very easy to suppose that art critics and other virtuosi possess this peculiar emotion in such a degree that "feeling they know", or, in the alternative that great and simple art makes everywhere the same catholic appeal to the hearts of all mankind.

To hold, however (as seems very likely indeed), that there is no single emotion called beauty (as different, say, from melancholy as melancholy is from fear) but, on the contrary, that aesthetic overtones may accompany and mingle with the widest range of experiences in very different ways, is very different indeed from holding that there is no such thing as aesthetic experience in a distinctive sense, or that aesthetic experience is not pathic or emotional in a way that is very pronounced. The first of these contentions has no greater cogency than the parallel argument that, because there is no single sensation called colour (but, on the contrary, *many* colours as different as yellow from purple), therefore it is nonsense to say that we see coloured things. The second contention enables us to affirm quite simply that although scarcely any of our experiences *may* not, on occasion, have the aesthetic quality, most of them, very often, have none of it. And this simple statement seems also to be true.

It is also, I think, plain to inspection, that this aesthetic quality in our experience is characteristically emotional, although I am not contending (and in fact do not believe) that it is *mere* emotion. When we attempt, however, to analyse the aesthetic quality more precisely, there seems no way of proceeding except the way of the late Mr Bosanquet and the other decried philosophers. This is not to say that these authors were right in detail. The point is that they adopted the only possible method.

Thus, when Mr Bosanquet declares that experienced beauty is not *simply* pleasing but also contains the character of permanence, relevance and community,[1] it is probable that his account is slightly misleading. It is true, as he says, that the sweetness of beauty does not easily pass into satiety (as many pleasures do), but this does not prove the experience of beauty to be essentially stable; for fleeting beauties may be much less stable than experiences like the dominance of ambition (which does tend to pass into satiety). Similarly, although (as language attests) we take beauty to be linked with certain objects, and so call *these objects* beautiful, the same is true of *any* object that we call attractive. Again, although it is true that the value of beauty "is not diminished by being shared",[2] there may easily be beauty in the solitary enjoyment of a solitary thing. Beauty is selfless rather than unselfish; and it may even be true, as Mr Collingwood says, that "the artist has no company, not even his own; and he does not feel lonely".[3]

Problems such as these will meet us later. For the moment, it is sufficient to observe that they are genuine problems, and that the analysis of aesthetic experience is the only conceivable way of attempting their solution.

[1] *Three Lectures on Aesthetic*, pp. 4 *sqq.* [2] *Ibid.* p. 5.
[3] *Speculum Mentis*, p. 69.

§ 7. *The quality of pleasures*

Aesthetic experience, like art, may possess the property of fineness—a noble gusto or a delicate flavour of beauty. We have therefore to ask whether this delicacy or nobility may belong to pleasure itself, or is only indirectly connected with pleasure. Do pleasures, in short, differ qualitatively?

As is well known, Mill held that they did, while Bentham, in his usual trenchant fashion, declared that "Quantity of pleasure being equal, pushpin is as good as poetry"—pushpin being a trivial game, something like spillikins.

> *Intense, long, certain, speedy, faithful, pure,*
> Such marks in *pleasures* and in *pains* endure.

These, Bentham maintained, were the only "*elements* or *dimensions of value* in a pleasure or a pain".[1] While there are pleasures of sense, pleasures of imagination and so forth, this difference, according to Bentham, lay only in the source of the pleasure. But pleasures of sense (e.g. "green fields, waving foliage, glistening water") and pleasures of sympathy (e.g. "the idea of the innocence and happiness of the birds, sheep, cattle, dogs, and other gentle or domestic animals")[2] differ only in their origin and not in their nature or value.

Bentham consistently applied his doctrine of pleasure to animals as well as to men.

"It may come one day to be recognised," he said, "that the number of the legs, the villosity of the skin, or the termination of the *os sacrum* are reasons insufficient for abandoning a sensitive being to the caprice of a tormentor. What else is it that should trace the insuperable line? Is it the faculty of reason or perhaps the faculty of discourse? But a full-grown horse or dog is beyond comparison a more rational, as well as a more conversable animal, than an infant of a day, a week, or even a month old. But suppose the case were otherwise, what would it avail? The question is not, can they reason? nor, can they speak? but, can they suffer?"[3]

---

[1] *Principles of Morals and Legislation*, chap. iv.
[2] *Ibid.* chap. v. Concluding note.
[3] Quoted by J. S. Mill, *Dissertations and Discussions*, vol. II, p. 483.

Mill, commenting on this passage, declared that the utilitarians were

perfectly willing to stake the whole question on this one issue. Granted that any practice causes more pain to animals than it gives pleasure to man; is that practice moral or immoral? And if, exactly in proportion as human beings raise their heads out of the slough of selfishness, they do not with one voice answer "immoral," let the morality of the principle of utility be for ever condemned.[1]

Anthony Trollope, defending his taste for fox-hunting, argued that the sole principle to be debated was whether the pleasures of hunters, hounds, and riders outweighed the misery of the foxes; and some may think that this is not the only question. There are not very many, for example, who would maintain that if a bully, tormenting a child or a woman, enjoys greater pleasure than his victims suffer pain, the bully is therefore morally admirable. Passing the point, however, we must at least concede that Bentham, Mill, and Trollope strongly affirm that the pleasure of any animal *counts* in the same authentic sense as the pleasure of any human being. Accordingly, if quantity of pleasure is the only circumstance that matters, there is nothing more to be said.

Mill, however, also maintained that the quality of pleasures counted as well as their quantity. For human beings, he held, had "faculties more elevated" than beasts; and their sense of dignity forbade them to be satisfied with the fullest possible allowance of a beast's pleasures.[2]

As in the similar instance of desires, this question of the

---

[1] *Dissertations and Discussions*, vol. II, p. 485. A very curious commentary on this passage may be found in Mr Edgeworth's *Mathematical Psychics*, p. 130: "It may be admitted", Mr Edgeworth says, "that there is a difference with respect to *capacity for happiness* between man and the more lowly evolved animals; and that *therefore*—among or above other considerations—the interests of the lower creatures are neglectible in comparison with humanity; the privilege of man is justified." Otherwise, Mr Edgeworth (speaking as a good utilitarian) proceeds to say, we have an unconscionable human oligarchy, man's *ipse dixitism*. Mr Edgeworth, however, makes no attempt to prove that animal sentience is so very slight that the sum of all animal happiness or misery is, in fact, "neglectible" in comparison with human sentience.

[2] *Utilitarianism*, chap. ii.

quality of pleasures is much more intricate than superficially it appears to be. A "noble" pleasure indeed may have three distinct meanings. For, firstly, a pleasure might be said to be noble if anyone felt it when he was concerned with a noble thing; secondly, the pleasure might be called noble if it accompanied, and was appropriate to, the exercise of some elevated faculty; and, thirdly, the pleasure itself might be noble.

The first two of these three possibilities, although they have to be distinguished, are allied very closely indeed. In general, we call a faculty noble, if it is capable of being nobly employed, and this, for the most part, means its capacity for dealing with noble things. If a man, in imagination so like a God, employs his potentially noble imagination over unworthy salacities, we should not call his pleasure noble, whatever the potentialities of his faculty might be.

It is only in the third sense, however, that *pleasures*, in strictness, could be said to differ qualitatively; and when the third sense is carefully distinguished from the first and from the second, it is surely most difficult, if not altogether impossible, to decide whether pleasures do, or do not, so differ.

The problem itself was disastrously confounded by Mill and by certain others who persisted in speaking of *a* pleasure when they meant any pleasant state, condition, or process. Evidently, pleasant states are themselves qualitied; and accordingly differ in quality. Intellect, fancy, mountain climbing, warm baths, ludo and literature, spillikins and sculpture, may all be enjoyed; and are very different in their qualities. If, however, as language suggests, we pretend to find a common element called pleasure in all these different pursuits, have we any sufficient reason either for asserting or for denying that this common element itself may differ in quality?

I do not think that we have. The most, I think, that we can do is to state the problem accurately; and in any statement that begins to be accurate we must explain, rather carefully, what may be meant by a common element or property.

Wherever there is pleasure there is liking, and there is a

quality of sweetness—I do not, of course, mean the taste of saccharine. We may, however, show and experience "liking" in very different ways, and it is improbable that we distil to ourselves literally and identically the same sweetness from sense and intellect, art and religion. If we did, this common distilled substance could not differ in quality because it would be always the same.

More probably, however, the "common" property of pleasure is similar to such other "common" properties as shape or colour. To have a shape is to be a bounded figure, but the boundaries may be as dissimilar as oval is from square; and colours, as we have seen, may be as different as yellow is from purple.

Yellow and purple differ in quality although both are colours; and straight lines differ in quality from curved lines, although both are lines. It is therefore possible that our pleasure in reading Shakespeare differs in quality from a duck's pleasure in diving into weeds—although both are pleasures. It is also possible, however, that the pleasure in such instances corresponds to the linearity of the straight and the curved lines, not to their straightness or curvedness. In other words, the difference between ourselves and the ducks in the example just stated may be not in the *pleasure* but in certain accompanying features of experience. And I do not see how we can be certain that it is not.

§ 8. *Pleasure and perfection*

It is natural to assume that there is a radical antithesis between all pleasure-theories of value and all perfection-theories. M. Goblot, for example, in the work we have already consulted, finds precisely at this point "perhaps the most profound and the most intricate of all the problems that lie at the root of ethics".[1]

"**The true question**," he continues, "is whether life, health and **normality**, which are the perfections of a living creature, are goods

[1] *La logique des jugements de valeur*, p. 89.

for him; if death, disease and abnormality, which in him are imperfections, are evils *for him* irrespective of his experience of these goods or these evils; or if, on the contrary, these goods, which are assuredly his ends as an organised being, are goods *for him* only if he enjoys them, and if these evils, which are constituted by the fact that his organisation misses its end, are evils *for him* only if he suffers from them."[1]

Stated in this form, M. Goblot's dilemma is not, perhaps, very formidable, since both its horns may be sawn across. Health and strength are not the only perfections, still less the only excellences, of a *man*, and what is good *for him*, even from his own point of view, need not be simply and altogether what pleases him. M. Goblot's statements, however, forcibly describe the *prima facie* distinction between pleasure-theories and perfection-theories. The former, we think, describe something completely subjective and the latter something completely objective.

And yet—are we right in this opinion?

§ 9. *The distinction in aesthetic theory*

It is at least significant that those who lay most stress upon the office of our private emotions in the domain of the beautiful very often do not disclaim, but on the contrary eagerly embrace, the doctrine of a profound affinity between such emotions and the formal perfection of things.

According to Mr Clive Bell, for instance, "the starting point for all systems of aesthetics must be the personal experience of a peculiar emotion",[2] and he conjoins this statement with the still more explicit assertion that "any system of aesthetics which pretends to be based on some objective truth is so palpably ridiculous as not to be worth discussing".[3]

Midway between these two assertions, however, we also find the following:

Either all works of visual art have some common quality, or when we speak of works of art we gibber....What quality is common to Sta. Sophia and the windows at Chartres, Mexican sculpture, a Persian bowl, Chinese carpets, Giotto's frescoes at

[1] *Ibid.*   [2] *Art*, p. 6.   [3] *Ibid.* p. 8.

Padua, and the masterpieces of Poussin, Piero della Francesca, and Cézanne? Only one answer seems possible—significant form.[1]

Mr Bell's theory accordingly implies that certain of the forms of visual objects—those, namely, which are significant —(always?) evoke an intensely private aesthetic emotion, at any rate in those gifted persons who are genuine aesthetes. And, according to the theory, we "gibber" if we deny either the emotional or the formal limb in this conjunction. The thing, to be sure, is very strange; but it is Mr Bell's theory. And it is implicit or explicit in a great many other theories upon this subject. For example, Mr E. V. Lucas writing of Cinquevalli's "miraculous" feats says that "with him we may use the word 'perfection' quite comfortably, without fear of molestation. And I know I am right by an infallible test. Anything perfect moves me in the way that anything pathetic ought to do".[2]

So far as I know, Mr Bell does not define the "significance" of "significant" form, or explain the non-significance of the forms which do not evoke "the aesthetic emotion". Indeed, it seems to be an essential part of his contention that all such explanations are false. Some forms evoke the emotion and some do not. This is all that should be said.

Even so, however, it is surely striking and peculiar (supposing it to be true) that the aesthetic emotion, in matters visual, should respond *only* to form, and that form should play so large a part in regions of beauty other than visual— for example, in music, where counterpoint can be evaded only at the musician's dire peril. If emotions, as the Germans say, give the *Anlage* of beauty, so also does form and proportion. To be sure, formalism in aesthetics may no more be sufficient than formalism elsewhere—and neither may formalism *plus* emotion. Yet form and beauty *are* intertwined. It may be a mistake to look for a mathematical passport to beauty, but it is something to be mistaken in Giotto's company, and

[1] Bell, *Art*, pp. 7 *sq.*
[2] "Dan and Paul" in *A Little of Everything*. Mr Lucas proceeds to quote Blake's "a tear is an intellectual thing".

artists who say they have followed the golden section[1]—
$a : b = b : (a + b)$—need not be supposed to be talking merely at random or wholly faddishly. Without necessarily endorsing Flaubert's conclusion, we cannot deny all force to his argument when he wrote to George Sand:

> I remember feeling my heart beating strangely, and quivering with vehement emotion, when I gazed on a wall of the Acropolis, a naked wall.... Well, then, I ask myself whether a book, independently of what it says, may not produce the same effect? In the precision of its groupings, the rarity of its elements, the polish of its surface, the harmony of the whole of it, is there not an intrinsic virtue, a kind of divine potency, something born of eternity like a principle?[2]

It is true that beauty, as Bacon said of poetry, deals with "the shows of things" (I wish he had not added "submitted to the desires of the mind"). The question, therefore, is not what rulers and compasses prove, but what proportions are revealed to us in the *shows* wherein beauty resides. These shows, however, *are* proportioned and their connection with the sweet savour of pleasure in beauty can scarcely be a thing of chance.

§ 10. *Leibniz and Locke*

We may now be the better prepared to find something of substance in certain abstract philosophical controversies. At any rate they have a substance.

The general point in these abstract controversies appears very clearly in the running comments that Leibniz, in his *Nouveaux Essais*, made upon Locke's *Essay*.

Locke, as we saw, was a complete subjectivist regarding pleasure, comparing it to the different relishes of apples and nuts. He also identified our pleasure with our good.[3] No one,

---

[1] Cf. Curt Hermann as quoted by M. Dessoir, *Aesthetik und allgemeine Kunstwissenschaft*, 2nd edn. p. 71 n.

[2] Quoted *op. cit.* pp. 126 *sq.*

[3] That is, in the general sense of good. Locke defined *moral* good and evil as "the conformity or disagreement of our voluntary actions to some law, whereby good or evil is drawn on us, from the will and power of the lawmaker" (*Essay*, Book II, chap. xxviii, § 5). He also believed in the possibility of a mathematical science of moral rectitude (*ibid.* Book IV, chap. iii, § 18).

he said, can be mistaken about his pleasure when he feels it; therefore no mistakes are possible concerning *present* good. Remote or fancied goods are different, and mistakes may be made concerning them.

Nevertheless, Locke did not regard pleasure and perfection as opposed.

"It is as much a perfection", he declared, "that desire, or the power of preferring, should be determined by good, as that the power of acting should be determined by the will.... And therefore every man is put under a necessity, by his constitution as an intelligent being, to be determined in willing by his own thought and judgment what is best for him to do."[1]

Locke also maintained that "the highest perfection of intellectual nature lies in a careful and constant pursuit of true and solid happiness".[2]

It seems evident that these statements involve a certain confusion between the expectation of pleasure (which may be an intellectual expectation) and the motivation of action by pleasure or uneasiness (which is not intellectual). Again, to say that the efficacy of pleasure as a motive is a "perfection" does not seem to be different from saying, quite simply, that it is a fact of our constitution.

Leibniz, therefore, very properly considered that if pleasure and perfection are really allied, something more must be meant by the alliance. His own position was as follows:

Locke's distinction between remote and present pleasures was not, Leibniz said, to the point. To most people, absent good is a vague and cloudy thing. Indeed, it is usually a thing of hearsay—a word repeated parrot-wise in the psittacism of conventional opinions.[3] Confused ideas of sense may therefore very easily overcome dim and misty ideas of good.

Yet pleasure *is* a confused sensory idea of perfection,[4] although it has a certain indefinable quality and flavour as

---

[1] *Essay*, Book II, chap. xxi, § 49.
[2] *Ibid.* § 52.
[3] *Nouveaux Essais*, Janet's edn. vol. I, pp. 148 *sqq*.
[4] *Ibid.* pp. 156 *sq*.

other confused ideas have—for example, colour, which is a confused idea of certain physical regularities.

There are, in fact, three stages of the same thing. At the lowest stage we have small insensible inclinations which draw us, as it were, in an occult fashion. At the second stage we experience pleasures and pains, being sensible of their existence and of that which they draw us towards or impel us fromwards—but of nothing else that is clear. At the third stage we have distinct cognoscible inclinations, which acknowledge the suzerainty of reason, order and harmony—in a word acknowledge the dominion of perfection proper. All these stages, however, are stages in the same fundamental process. We learn what the process means when we examine the clearest level of it—that is to say, when we reflect upon rational perfection. But we can also see, arguing downwards from the clearest level of the process, that the same search for perfection occurs confusedly in the sensation of pleasure, and that it occurs insensibly at the level of *petites perceptions*—or the sub-conscious.

That which is perfect is *le bonheur*, not pleasure. Pleasures are steps towards, or phases in, *le bonheur*; and every pleasure directly indicates the shortest, although not necessarily the best, way to perfection. Reason, therefore, takes long views and pleasure takes short views.

§ 11. *The metaphysics of felicity*

We may state the Leibnizian view briefly by saying that, according to it, pleasure attests, but does not constitute, perfection. Any such opinion makes an attempt to penetrate into the principle of pleasure, and so may be called a metaphysics of felicity, although, to be sure, many theories of this general sort do not go very deep.

These attempts to lay bare the basis of pleasure have an intricate task to perform, because "pleasure" has so many sources, conditions and developments. In particular we have to distinguish active from passive pleasures, sensory from mental pleasures, special from general pleasures; and there is some importance in considering the relation of the various divisions and sub-divisions thus arising to the (more or less) metaphysical theories designed to explain them.

I shall try to consider each division and sub-division.

1. It is very widely held that pleasure attests the fulfilment or completion of active process. In most statements it is added that there must be measure or proportion in the fulfilment, deficiency and excess tending alike to be unpleasant, although the latter is usually more unpleasant than the former.

1. 1. Pleasures of the senses, according to the active view, are usually interpreted biologically, and pleasure is said to testify to the restoration of organic equilibrium in what Avenarius[1] called the vital series. Spinoza and von Ehrenfels, as we have seen, held that pleasure is differentiating—a passage to *greater* fulness. There would seem, however, to be many pleasures of mere repose.

1. 1. 1. It is evident that special aptitudes or activities of the body may be highly pleasant without exhibiting any close correlation with bodily pleasure as a whole. The time factor in such pleasures, again, may be regarded as a specialising factor. Freshness and recurrent rhythm augment and sometimes create sensory pleasures, but constitute very special conditions in the case of many such pleasures.

1. 1. 2. What we call "fitness" and the tonic glow of health (when regarded from the active point of view) clearly are relevant to, and illustrate, this doctrine of the sources of pleasure. So also may Herbert Spencer's "quantity of life".

1. 2. The distinction between sensory and mental pleasures is itself a thing of difficulty. A natural way of looking at the problem is to hold with the Cartesians that *all* pleasures are mental, but that we call pleasures sensory when we refer them to any of the senses as their source, that is to say when we refer them either to the organs of the "external" senses, or to "internal" and organic senses. A plausible alternative to this view would be to say that all the pleasures and all the pains

[1] In *Der menschliche Weltbegriff.*

which we localise in our bodies are themselves sensations (or sensa), and are neither more nor less "mental" than colours or sounds. In this case the *feeling* that accompanies such sensations (and may accompany much else) is alone "mental".

Among the many difficulties connected with the Cartesian view may be mentioned the circumstance that pleasures and pains not visibly connected with any sense organ (according to the superficial anatomy of common experience) may well be connected with some organ in the brain, or again may be due to some bodily factor other than a sense organ. They may be due to the pressure or purity of the blood, let us say, or to the tone of our nerves, or to the presence or absence of toxins, endocrine supply and the like. Still more obviously, it would be a task of extreme delicacy to declare that *any* "mental" processes do not have a carnal source, or magisterially to set limits to the fineness or intellectuality that the flesh may attain to.

Difficulties not quite the same, but, very likely, quite as serious, beset the alternative opinion mentioned above. And, of course, there are other opinions still. It must be conceded, therefore, that the separation of bodily from mental, in this instance, is very hard to effect, without dogmatism and, at the same time, with clarity. Nevertheless, nearly every psychologist finds it convenient, if not essential, to distinguish between, let us say, "mental" discomfort and definite, localisable bodily pain; or, again, between organic titillation and "mental" charm. Even if the distinction is in many ways imprecise, it is unavoidable; and, with regard to our present topic, it is, as Sidgwick said, incontrovertible that while physiological theories may carry us a certain way towards a "deductive hedonism" of the senses they do not, at the present stage of our knowledge, appreciably clarify our understanding of intellectual pleasures or of the sweetness of personal affection.[1]

In general we may say that "desire" theories of pleasure,

[1] *The Methods of Ethics*, Book II, chap. vi, § 1.

interpreted in the psychological way adopted by von Ehrenfels and others, are typical of the class of theory here in question.

1. 2. 1. According to Dr Ward, who follows, he tells us, a tradition as old as Aristotle:

> There is pleasure in proportion as a maximum of subjective activity or attention is effectively exercised, and pain in proportion as such effective attention is frustrated by restraints, distractions, shocks or incomplete and faulty adaptations, or fails of exercise, owing to the narrowness of the field of consciousness or the slowness and smallness of its changes.[1]

If, in the ordinary way, we regarded attention as a special mode of mental activity, this theory would illustrate the sub-division now under review. Dr Ward, however, takes "attention" to be the general form of all mental activity (feeling or pleasure-pain being determined by it). His statement accordingly illustrates:—

1. 2. 2. as most such theories do. Pleasure, in short, is determined by economy of mental activity.

2. We have already seen that pleasure is essentially pathic and that its pathic character does not necessarily result from prior activity on our parts. It should not be necessary to pursue this topic further.

2. 1. The pathic pleasures of sense are easily illustrated. Lazy enjoyment of the sun, and nearly all the beauties of nature are sufficient examples. So also are most of the beauties of art. A doubtful case occurs when there is the suggestion of movement in such instances, as when the proudly poised Alcazar at Segovia seems like a ship unfurling its sails towards the westering sun. In *us*, however, these suggestions of motion (indeed any actual motion) on the part of the things we see are passive in the main. Even our "empathy" indicates that we are carried along.

2. 1. 1. These pathic enjoyments of sense are for the most part highly specialised—indeed, art is the purer in proportion as it keeps to hearing or vision or some other special sense and does not diffuse itself over many. "If I could tell you about

[1] *Psychological Principles*, p. 262.

it, why should I paint it" is the painter's very proper rebuke to chattering onlookers.

2. 1. 2. On the other hand, some such pleasures are diffused. Physical indolence, a warm bath, the exhilarating crispness of the days in early winter are examples.

2. 2. While the sensible shows of things in art or in nature give us the purest pleasures of their kind, there are also, as we say, purely mental pleasures. Such pleasures occur whenever meaning vanquishes sense.

2. 2. 1. These distinctively mental pleasures are for the most part special. Consider, for instance, the mathematician's pleasure in elegant formal demonstrations, his excitement over cosines and integrals, and the like.

2. 2. 2. The sources of such pleasures, however, may be more general, attesting as some think, the harmony of a man's whole soul. We shall see this when we come to treat of Kant's aesthetic theory.

While the members of these elaborate divisions are not necessarily mutually exclusive, enough (I think) has been said to show something of the variety of ideas which enter into all such metaphysical accounts of pleasure. I have taken, I fear, a very long road to prove a very simple conclusion, viz. that while pleasures depend upon many conditions, some of which may be so fundamental as properly to be called "metaphysical", there is no *single* "metaphysical" explanation of man's myriad-based felicity, no *one* principle in ultimate reality from which pleasure, of every species, can be logically deduced. The inferences and the principles of deductive hedonism, in a word, are much less certain that the fact of pleasure, and can at best express general tendencies easily overborne in a host of cases. We cannot probe very deep in this way.

§ 12. *Pleasure and excellence*

In theories of the metaphysics of felicity, a maximum of completeness or an optimum condition of efficiency, strength, vigour or the like, is usually supposed; and therefore perhaps a certain species of "excellence" is supposed also. This excellence, however, need not be fine or noble. It need not be that *praeclarum quid*, which, as we all know, is rare. For pleasures are not rare. It is in the latter sense, accordingly, that I am speaking of "excellence" now.

Such excellence, clearly, is not inconsistent with pleasure. The joys of human affection, and many of the joys of great art are, or testify to, authentic excellence and are also authentic pleasures. Even in morals we should *love* what is good; and the quality of love is strained if there is not joy in it.

On the other hand, it may be doubted whether pleasure is necessarily found in *all* human appreciation of excellence. If tragic art, as Shelley said, has its sweetness, it is pleasing in a way that is both subtle and obscure. Indeed, keen tension and high excitement rather than pleasure are what we feel when we see *Othello* acted, or respond to Rembrandt in his sombre vein, or to the gloom and horror in so many of Ribera's works. Grandeur, majesty and awe, rather than pleasure, mark the sublime.

The same holds of the experience of love. To say, as some do, that love cannot be a pleasant and comfortable thing, or again that it cannot be placid and serene, is quite insincere. Friendly, parental or conjugal affection may be all of these. But love may also become rapture or fierce torment. And in the torment there need not be sweetness. To be sure, many, even during this torment, would rather suffer it than continue in apathy. This circumstance, however, is evidence of nothing; for men are so constituted that many of them take pride, not merely in great experiences which may be their ruin, but even in miserable, furtive and shameful things.

The partisans of golden mediocrity, I suppose, would deny that either rapture or torment is excellent; and certainly love and its excellences are full of paradox to the student of values. Love is no evidence of the value of the person who is loved; for a father should love his worthless son, although he cannot respect him. Is it, then, evidence of value in ourselves? Many have said so. "Since I love, I have value", Dr McTaggart said—"supreme value, since I am possessing the highest good. And since I have value I shall regard myself with reverence."[1] Yet love and all its loyalties may be seen very often in those whom we call idiots and defectives. Reverence indeed may be their due. But there is pathos in such reverence.

For the moment, however, our theme is pleasure, not love, and enough has been said, I think, to show that our experience of excellence need not contain any marked or obvious pleasure. It is also plain that we may take pleasure in much that cannot be considered noble. This does not prove that pleasure itself may not be always an excellence. For, as we have seen, we may love worthless persons, and yet, in loving them, experience a very great value. Unworthiness in the object, therefore, need not imply unworthiness in the emotion. It is commonly held, however (and, I think rightly), that love is the only excellence which ought to be wholly catholic in this way, the only thing that should go forth from us irrespective of the merits or condition of the beings that are loved. And pleasure, we think, should never be taken in anything that is base.

In short, pleasure is neither necessarily an excellence nor an infallible indication of excellence; and this may be shown from simple examples of our experience of excellent things. What then of excellences not experienced?

There was a time before Shakespeare wrote and before El Greco painted. Consequently there was a time at which the excellence of *Hamlet* or of *The Burial of Count Orgaz* could not have been appreciated by anyone. Such instances do not trouble us because we think that books and pictures live only in the minds of authors and artists, readers and beholders. Without challenging this opinion, I should like to ask whether it is never possible for a poet to *discover* some exquisite verity, or some beautiful thing that no one had perceived before; whether musicians after Palestrina have not *discovered* a world of musical relationships that the Greeks never dreamed of; or whether Lorenz, Minkowski and Mr Einstein may not have *discovered* relationships which are as broad as Space-time and

[1] *The Nature of Existence*, vol. II, p. 164.

co-eternal with it. If so, and if there is any excellence in these discovered things, I should like the reader to ask himself whether these excellences depend upon the accident of their discovery, and whether there could not be excellences of this order that no one, in all probability, will ever find.

SECTION II. MEINONG'S THEORY OF VALUE

§ 1. *Preliminary*

The most notable, and, I think, the subtlest attempt to show that the very meaning of value is dependent upon feeling and sentiment was made by certain British moralists in the eighteenth century when they analysed what they called "approval". This attempt will be considered in our next chapter. In the present section a brief account will be given of some of the more important of the opinions set forth by the late Professor Alexius Meinong of Graz. If Meinong's doctrines were often perhaps rather complex than profoundly subtle, their importance, and their influence upon contemporary philosophy were, nevertheless, deservedly very great.

§ 2. *"Personal" value*

In German, as well as in so many other languages, the word value (Wert) may signify anything from equivalence to dignity, but in Meinong's view the "personal" significance of "value" is its authentic essence. Thus utility, he says, must be *personal* utility, need must be *personal* need, exchange and sacrifice must be of objects which have *personal* worth. In short, a review of the principal theories on this question (and more particularly of the contentions of the Austrian economists) settles the priority of "personal" value.

Personal worth is defined by Meinong as "the aptness of any object, in virtue of its constitution and position to become the source of value-experience in a subject", and to be treated accordingly.[1] In this definition "position" is made requisite

---

[1] *Zur Grundlegung der allgemeinen Wert-theorie*, p. 143. (This work will be referred to as *G*.)

in addition to the vaguer "constitution" in order to make it clear that authentic values must be available or feasible, not bare abstract potencies under conjectural or merely fanciful conditions.

This being understood, the essence of the definition is its double implication of subject and object. To treat values as absolute, or to ascribe them quite simply to "things", as common speech does, is declared to be wholly erroneous. What is more, all attempts to find any common characteristic in values things other than the property of being valued is declared to be as good as impossible (*G.* 33). In short, value without a valuing subject is an absurdity (*G.* 125). Every value has, in this sense, a spiritual component (*G.* 81).

On the other hand, Meinong contends with equal emphasis that value is never a spiritual state. It inheres, not in the ego, but in things-as-related-to-an-ego. One of his favourite examples is the grateful warmth that comes from a stove. We call the stove valuable, he says, because it yields these agreeable sensations; but the pleasant sensations are not themselves values (e.g. *G.* 50). We *feel* pleasure in ourselves, but we *attribute* worth to things other than ourselves. So far from being an immanent condition of the soul, value necessarily implies a transeunt reference of the soul to something else.

Such a view, since it denies all "intrinsic" as well as all "absolute" values, may well appear paradoxical. It is, however, Meinong's, and it implies a notable parallel between appreciations and ideas. In the theory of scientific knowledge, the fundamental problem is how our ideas refer to, and may be vindicated by, the world. In Value-theory the fundamental problem once again is the *reference* of Value-experience to objects.

§ 3. *The emotional basis of value*

In a word, value is *emotional significance* (*G.* 162), the transeunt reference of emotion to fact; and the truth of this contention, in Meinong's eyes, is so very evident that he seldom wastes many words in defending it. Value *must* be thoroughly emotional in the roots of it, he says (*G.* 35). Emotion is "subintelligiert" if not expressly stated (*G.* 130); and anyone who, like Mr Haering[1], attempts to delve underneath the visible emotions of the ego into psychical structures, tendencies, dispositions and so forth is really missing the point (*G.* 47). Haering's views would not even appear to be significant unless we understood him to be discussing that very emotional basis in which Value-experience has its being. This experience, however, can be observed introspectively, and it is spurious (never genuine) profundity to look for any other starting point.

Indeed, the only question which gives Meinong serious concern in this matter is the vogue of Appetency-theories (such as those of von Ehrenfels) as opposed to his own Emotion-theory.

Meinong's earliest papers on Value-theory were published before von Ehrenfels's, and his book *Psychologisch-ethische Untersuchungen zur Wert-theorie* (1894) appeared some three years before von Ehrenfels's *System*. The two authors, however, were near enough in time to find difficulty in avoiding the appearance of a certain rivalry between Graz and Prag. Accordingly they rebuked one another in love, although, for the truth's sake, with a certain asperity on occasion.

Meinong never abandoned his essential contention that Appetency-theories of value are plainly *insufficient*, and his criticism of von Ehrenfels in *Ueber Annahmen*[2] (1902, chap. viii) is thoroughly trenchant although somewhat modified in comparison with his earlier exposition. In the later *Grundlegung* (posthumously published in 1923), however, Meinong is prepared to admit that the Appetency-principle may be complementary, not antagonistic to, the Emotion-principle. Yet he insists that the former is subordinate and the latter fundamental.[3]

---

[1] Th. Haering, *Untersuchungen zur Psychologie der Wertung*. Leipzig, 1912.
[2] Hereafter referred to as *A*.
[3] *G.* chap. ii, § 3.

These later admissions were probably judicious, despite the reluctance with which they were made (*G.* 44); for some of Meinong's arguments appear to beg the question, and others to invite a *riposte*. While it may be true, as he suggests (*G.* 41), that things are sought because of their value and not conversely, the Prag school could scarcely be expected to agree. Again, Meinong's argument that a people proud of its history *does* ascribe value to the past (which cannot be an object of appetition because it is over and done with) may in part be met by the counter-assertion that a glorious history or a glorious pedigree *is* sought very actively indeed (say by patriots or by Americans who attempt to trace their ancestry to emigrants on the *Mayflower*). What is sought in these cases, to be sure, is the glory of the past; and the glory of past events survives their passing. Yet a necessary condition is that the past itself should be thought to vindicate the glory we ascribe to it.

In the main, however, Meinong's denial of the sufficiency of all Appetency-theories to answer this question is surely unassailable. When we are satisfied we seek no longer, but we should not cease to ascribe value to that which has satisfied us; and, as we have seen, many values, if they are not wholly non-expetible are at least only secondarily expetible. That is enough, and more than enough, to establish Meinong's case; and when the fact is admitted, there is surely no further difficulty in admitting that appetency, either potential or actual, always refers to the future (if the term is used with any accuracy) although emotion does not, and although value does not. Indeed, it seems abundantly plain that the Emotion-theories of value are enormously more plausible than the Appetency-theories, so long, at least, as the introspective basis common to Meinong and to von Ehrenfels is explicitly accepted. It is the *horme* of biology or of natural election which is the true basis of Appetency-theories. Von Ehrenfels *meant* this *horme*, although he *said* he was arguing from introspective experience.

§ 4. *The analysis of Value-experience*

The emotional or passional significance—which is value—has to be distinguished from the (supposedly) passionless exercise of the intellect (*G.* 35). Nevertheless, as we have seen, both kinds of significance involve (and indeed essentially are) reference to an object, and Meinong's chief concern is the analysis of what may be called *appreciative* reference.

Value, he maintains, would not occur without Value-experience (i.e. in the traditional English terminology, without "approval" or "appreciation"), and all tenable accounts of value must begin with the analysis of approval. It is vicious psychologism, however, not sane psychology, to suppose that value can ever be (or mean) the psychological state of approving. In fact, value is never Value-experience (*G.* 150); for the essence of such experience is to indicate something beyond its private character and existence. Our experiences come and go, dying almost as soon as they are born; but the values which we ascribe to things have a certain character of permanence (*G.* 124). Again, emotional significance cannot be treated as something self-subsistent, because emotions themselves cannot be treated so (*G.* 76). In sensory pleasure we are pleased *with* something sensory, and the pleasure is grounded upon sense-acquaintance. In aesthetic joys we are charmed *by* something, and the charm is grounded upon aesthetic acquaintance. And so in Value-experience.

This argument, to be sure, seems to invite the objections that since emotions themselves are grounded upon modes of experience which imply reference to an object, there seems no necessity to regard emotional significance (or value) as an *independent* species of objective reference. Meinong's view, however, is that this "reference to an object" is *not* counted twice over in his theory of value, *although* the emotional significance in value is grounded upon something which is itself semi-intellectual and entails objective reference. And of course the two might be different although closely connected.

Supposing, then, that appreciations must be our starting point, and that all appreciations refer to something beyond themselves, it remains to enquire what species of appreciation is of greatest moment in Value-theory and what, in detail, its objective reference implies.

According to Meinong, Werthaltung or "prizing" is the fundamental fact of valuation. The generic Werthung (or valuing), he maintains, is altogether too vague (*A.* 251 *sqq.*). "Prizing" is not a judgment of value or the conscious assigning of value—which is "Bewerten" (*A.* 251) or "für wert halten" (*G.* 68)—but is more than half way towards it. It is, so to say, a judgment of value without the *t*'s crossed or the *i*'s dotted. For normally it includes full practical conviction of the existence of that which is prized, even when we do not trouble to state the fact or explicitly to think about it. In this sense value-feeling (Wertgefühl) is vaguer; and therefore is more appropriate when we have to deal with dreamland poesy or fancy (*G.* 68 *sq.*).

§ 5. *The "objective" of prizing and of other valuations*

According to Meinong's general analysis, we have to distinguish act, content, and object in every instance of apprehension or acquaintance, and we usually find that the second of these repays attention more markedly than the first. For the acts of the mind evince great instability, and the content does not vary to the same extent. A parallel is to be expected in the case of approval; and Meinong finds it. He also commends Witasek for clarifying this conception in the domain of aesthetic theory (*G.* 62).

In other words, we have always to distinguish what Meinong calls the "objective" before our minds both from the acts of our minds and from the (non-mental) things which are signified by such "objectives". What, then, is an "objective"?

Some people have questioned whether Sir Philip Francis wrote the "Letters of Junius", others have asserted that he did, others denied it, others merely supposed it. These mental attitudes are very different, but all of them have a common content which may be called their common "objective", viz. the-writing-of-the-Letters-by-Francis or that-Francis-wrote the-Letters. Since the same objective might occur when the optative mood is used, we plainly come very close to a similar analysis in value-theory.

In short, the vehicle of significance in our appreciations is, in fact, an "objective". Is it possible, then, to define the "objectives" of appreciation more closely still?

A common opinion is that we ascribe value to existence and to existence only. If so the existence of this or that would be the objective that is sought. In reality, however, any such statement would be inadequate and misleading. It would be inadequate because, e.g. we prize not the existence of a knife but the sharpness of the knife, that is to say a character of existence, not bare existence (*G.* 53). Again, this common theory might mislead in various ways. When a mathematician, for example, sets value upon the elegance of a proof the only kind of existence that is relevant is the sort of existence that proofs may have; and Meinong does not think they exist as cups and saucers do (*G.* 56). Moreover, and more importantly, we may and do ascribe value to the non-existent —to the absence of pain, for example, or to the future, or to ideals and contingent possibilities. Actual existence, therefore, need not be supposed in all our valuations; and, in aesthetic valuations especially, the "objective" may be make-believe, or pure phantasy. The emotional significance of our experience does not suffer in any way from the simple circumstance of the non-existence of objects corresponding literally and precisely to the relevant objectives.

§ 6. *Value and excellence*

This summary and condensed account of certain of Meinong's principal views will have served its purpose if it indicates to the reader something of the fashion in which the general notion of emotional reference to an object may be developed in ways that attempt precision. The more important question, however, is whether the emotional theory itself is true; and this is the problem of the next two chapters. Accordingly, I do not think it would be politic to debate Meinong's special contentions in greater detail—at any rate at the present stage of our argument. There is, however, one important part of Meinong's general theory which ought to be considered here, and that is his account of the relations between value and dignity.

As we have seen, Meinong holds that value, in its proper sense, is distinctively personal. It is relative to personal emotion, and indeed is most explicitly appropriate to things which are, in some sense, our private property. At any rate Meinong's favourite examples are drawn from instances like that of the musician who has acquired an Amati, or lost it, or been persuaded that the instrument is not genuine, and from the musician's reactions to these "objectives" (e.g. *G.* 34 *sqq.*).

Any such conception, it is plain, lies nearer to the conceptions of economists than to the ideas of most philosophers; and Meinong is far too good a philosopher to be oblivious of the circumstance. When confronted with it, however (e.g. in *G.* 51), he employs what seems a peculiar expedient. The personal and proprietary sense of value, he says, is its common, its natural, and its proper sense. Any other interpretation is an extension of the natural significance of value, and should be designated by another name. It is "timological", not proprietary; and it is best called "dignity".

Manifestly, names are no great matter—unless they mark a distinction of principle. It is possible, no doubt (indeed, we may eventually be forced to conclude), that "value" has more than one meaning, and consequently that the timological and the proprietary senses of the term, although quite different, are both legitimate and natural. This, however, is not what Meinong holds; for although he regards timology as an addendum to value-theory, he also regards it as a consistent addendum. And he frames his timological theory accordingly. If these assumptions are retained, I wish to suggest that Meinong's analysis ought not, in principle, to stop short at what he calls "value" but demands what he calls "timology".

As we have seen, Meinong's contention is that while value implies and starts from appreciative experience, it never *is* the state of appreciating since the very meaning of appreciation is to signify, or refer to, something not itself.

Proceeding from this base, it is possible to go either a long way, or, comparatively speaking, a short way. In the main, Meinong goes the short way; for he is content, in the bulk of his argument, to defend his conception of emotional significance against, say, the appetency theories, and to describe its "objectives" in the sphere of proprietary and personal value.

It is also, however, an essential part of his theory that emotional significance has a function *similar* to the function of other significant experiences—similar, for example, to the function of the types of experience we call sensation or thought. To be sure, as he admits, emotional significance may lag a little behind the others in point of clarity (*G.* 157). Yet although tardy it has an analogous office.

As soon, however, as we take the objective reference or significance of sensations or conceptual ideas seriously, we perceive at once that the fact of reference is only a part of the problem. The reference may be clear or confused, erroneous or valid, in various degrees. *Because* ideas are not simply mental occurrences, they claim to express reality; but while some ideas implement their claim tolerably successfully others implement it very ill.

Accordingly, if emotional significance is really analogous to other species of significance, our appreciations also, in their own emotional way, must lay claim to truth and validity; and it would be odd if the claim in their case did not have to be striven for arduously with various degrees of clearness and success.

The fact appears very plainly in two of Meinong's examples. First, let us consider the case of children and defective persons. What a child prizes and what a changeling prizes are, in so far forth, genuine values to the child or to the changeling (*G.* 146 *sq.*); but they have a very minor validity as compared with the significance of the things that are prized by Socrates or by Aristides. The child's values are as childish as his ideas —not necessarily false, but seldom mature. Or, secondly, let us consider the value of a mascot or of an amulet (*G*. 148 *sq*.). To a superstitious person the emotional significance of the amulet is altogether beyond question; and yet this significance is mistaken. The amulet, in short, makes a claim which is not a good claim. Emotionally it is genuine, but its emotional *significance* is a sham, and its emotional *claim* is a bastard claim, begotten of pretence.

In short, once we grant that *all* our ideas signify something beyond themselves, we are logically bound to continue the investigation of this important matter. For some of them signify not inadequately and others very inadequately indeed. Consequently, we have to examine the adequacy, range and validity of their significance with the most scrupulous care. Why, then, should it not be so with emotional significance also? The same considerations seem to enter, as the example of children, or again of defectives, clearly reveals.

If so, may not a "personal" timology be as absurd as a "personal" truth? Meinong's answer to this question (*G*. 151 *sqq*.) is, in effect, *Nihil obstat*—except the crucial fact that our emotions have a closer union with our private personality than anything else in us that achieves significance. In the end he concludes that while absolute worth (that is to say, the worth of things irrespective of their relation to any personality) is a vulgar error, the greatest goods (that is to say, the things that are "dignified" as well as merely "valuable") need not vary from person to person, but may have complete objective validity in the sense that all such goods ought to be the same for everyone.

Meinong's timology, therefore, carries us far beyond his account of "personal" value; and yet, I think, it carries us along a course which the earlier part of the theory could not disclaim without coming to an abrupt and arbitrary halt. In the end, we have still to ask whether even his timology goes far enough. Truths, we concede, ought to be the same for all, but the reason, we think, is that there is just one truth for anyone to know. It therefore *has* to be the same for anyone who knows it. And some have thought that the same should be said of worth and of goodness. "Goodness", according to Dr McTaggart, "is a quality of the thing judged good, and a thing can no more be good for one man and bad for another, than twice four can be eight for one man and nine for another."[1] The man who takes it to be nine is, quite simply, wrong, because it *is* eight and is not nine. This could not hold of Meinong's "dignity", because, even if every man ought to prize the best things in the same way, Meinong has to maintain that all man's prizings must be based upon his personal emotions, and nothing, consequently, would *be* good unless someone felt about it in a certain way. On this theory, nothing at all would be good in the eyes of Omniscience, supposing, that is, that God, as in orthodox theory, is exempt from passions.

[1] *The Nature of Existence*, vol. II, p. 136.

CHAPTER VI

THE ANALYSIS OF APPROVAL IN THE BRITISH MORALISTS

§ 1. *Preliminary*

ANYTHING, we may say, is considered to be valuable when it is approved or esteemed. Accordingly, if we could determine the scope of esteem and its justification, we should, at the same time, have determined whatever is cardinal in the theory of value. Certainly, these statements might require qualification if it turned out to be convenient to interpret "approval" or "esteem" in some restricted sense (say emotional appreciation). For the moment, however, we may neglect this possible source of perplexity.

It is a fortunate circumstance, therefore, that a succession of British philosophers of the first rank should have debated this question in great detail, each beginning where the other left off; and this is precisely what Shaftesbury, Hutcheson, Hume and Adam Smith successively did. It is also fortunate that such eminent philosophers as Price and Reid should, at a later date, have supplied an effective criticism of the earlier movement.

The problem in debate was the relation between *bonum jucundum* and *bonum honestum*; and the topics principally discussed were aesthetics and morals. Since "morals", however, was a subject treated with the widest latitude and taken to include decorum, manners and good taste as well as duty and righteousness, and since utility was also present to the minds of all these authors, it is evident that they meant to discuss, and really did discuss, the greater part, if not the whole, of the domain of value.

Again, I do not think they can be charged with entertaining narrow conceptions or with employing pedantic methods.

Certainly, their principal theme was the relation between reason and sentiment in this affair. But whatever language we employ, this *is* a theme to which we must recur. Are all, or any, values, matters of taste, or liking, or our pleasure? If any are, can moral and aesthetic values really be of this order? Is there *no* excellence in things which rationally determines our approval? Can our approval never claim authentic validity? If it cannot, what becomes of duty? And if it can, how can the claim be reconciled with *bonum jucundum*, or with the prevalent view that values are matters of taste, and that tastes rest on feeling or emotion? Is there any road from pleasure or sentiment to dignity and worth? Can we justify our values by rational reflection, or have we to say, in the end, that we feel them strongly, and act upon them, but must renounce even the idea of finding any rational justification for them? These are questions essential to the issue; and they were precisely the questions discussed among the philosophers we are now about to consider.

I propose, therefore, to invite the reader to remember what these authors said with the object of showing, firstly, how much has to be admitted by those who would say that values, after all, are but matters of taste, and secondly, how impossible it is, when these questions are reviewed widely and thoroughly, to ascribe to sentiment pleasure or emotion, all or nearly all, that properly pertains to an adequate philosophy of value.

§ 2. *Shaftesbury*

That my Lord Shaftesbury was both an elegant and a judicious writer was the unanimous testimony of an acute and lettered society most admirably qualified to form an opinion on such matters, and there is no mystery in the prolonged and extensive influence which his writings wielded over literature and philosophy alike. Nevertheless, although he is easy and pleasant to read, he is not at all easy to follow—unless, indeed, one follows him apishly by way of paraphrase as Pope did in his *Essay on Man*. The virtue of orderly composition was but fitfully present in Shaftesbury's constitution, and he is notorious even among literary philosophers for trying to say half a dozen things at once. To refute Hobbes by solid argument and to rebuke enthusiasm by a "home-spun philosophy" of self-examination, to unite a most penetrating account of the sociability of man with panegyrics upon a universal system or economy in which the amiable duty of the species fly is to feed the species spider[1]—these and a swarm of other aims jostle persistently in his pages. This entanglement of serious designs is connected with a studied (if not a foppish) carelessness, and with an extreme fluidity in the use of terms which most philosophers take to be technical and are at pains to make precise. The last of these defects is vexatiously apparent in his treatment of our present theme, since that which he prefers to call "taste" or even "relish" he also calls "judgment" or "science". He is also prepared to unite it, in a sort of negligent aplomb, both with "opinion" and with "reason".

Among the many names by which Shaftesbury describes this faculty, he sometimes selects the word "Approval", and Approval is the name commonly employed by those later writers whom, directly or indirectly, he greatly influenced. Shaftesbury's principal aim, we may say (at least as a moralist), was to appeal to the good taste of men of sense regarding serious issues and to explore the fundamental affinity between serious taste and the realities of good and evil. He addresses himself, indeed, to those who "would try effectually to acquire the real science or taste of life".[2] The office of Taste in the domain of deportment or of manners, he says, is never disputed by gentlefolk. "There are few so unaffectedly clownish as absolutely to disown good-breeding, and renounce the notion of a beauty in outward manners and deportment."[3] Yet "who can admire the *outward* beauties and not recur instantly to the *inward*, which are the most real and essential,

[1] *Characteristicks*, vol. II (1723), p. 18.
[2] *Ibid.* vol. III, p. 168.
[3] *Ibid.* vol. III, p. 179.

the most naturally affecting and of the highest pleasure, as well as profit and advantage".[1]

In short, if a gentleman made himself as gentlemanly as he could, neither he nor anyone else could distinguish the product from a thoroughly virtuous man; and the very definition of goodness chimes in with this result. "That which, being present, can never leave the mind at rest, but must of necessity cause aversion, is its ill.... In the same manner, that which being *absent* can never leave the mind at rest, or without disturbance and regret is of necessity its good."[2]

The distinctive character of this gentlemanlike Approval is revealed most clearly in the contrast between *mere* goodness and *human* goodness. Into this contrast, utility (or the benefits of sunshine, rain and all serviceable commodities) does not enter at all, since things of this sort have no good or evil either *in* themselves or *for* themselves. Certain of the animals, however, may literally and with entire propriety be called good creatures. Hence the definition that "a good creature is such a one as by the natural temper or bent of his affections is carried primarily and immediately, and not secondarily and accidentally, to good and against ill".[3] Such *mere* goodness, however, is not enough for man, although man's goodness, like that of humbler good creatures, must also have its roots in the temper and bent of man's affections. A *man* is good, not simply because he serves the public interest with zeal and affection (as demented but faithful creatures have been known to do), but because he has a sense or conscience of right and wrong. It is too little for him to be moved by pity or gratitude or other kindly social emotion. He must also be able to perpend the bent and aim of these emotions or, in Locke's sense of the words, to exercise "reflexion" upon them—that is to say, to cast the emotions back upon themselves as in an ideal mirror.

This indispensable and entirely human propensity is the proper nerve and the specific office of Approval. In short it

[1] *Characteristicks*, vol. III, p. 185. [2] *Ibid.* vol. III, p. 195.
[3] *Ibid.* vol. II, p. 26.

is approval. Approval is "another kind of affection towards those very affections themselves, which have been already felt, and are now become the subject of a new liking or dislike".[1] Its reality, surely cannot be matter for dispute. We have a sense of beauty (have we not?), or in other words an immediate relish for the proportion and harmony of sensory apparitions. That is plain for any *man* to behold, yet the proportion or harmony of sensory apparitions (according to Shaftesbury) is not itself a sensory apparition, but implies an appreciative faculty of a higher order—"higher" because it takes stock of these sensory apparitions while they but minister to it. The same analysis holds of the proportion and harmony of our inward parts, or, in other words, of our moral character.

In these vagrant characters or pictures of manners, which the mind of necessity figures to itself, and carries still about with it, the heart cannot possibly remain neutral, but constantly takes part one way or other. However false or corrupt it be within itself, it finds the difference, as to beauty or comeliness, between one heart and another, one turn of affection, one behaviour, one sentiment and another; and accordingly, in all disinterested cases, must approve in some measure of what is natural and honest, and disapprove what is dishonest and corrupt.[2]

Virtue itself is what is done "through just, equal and good affection",[3] and we are so constituted as to be able, unquestionably, to admit or to enter into the circumstance—in other words to approve.

Shaftesbury believed firmly in the doctrine (surely it was the dogma) of the schools, that affections and passions are the sole springs of action.[4] For this reason alone, if what has already been said of him had not proved the point to demonstration, it is manifest that Approval, for him, must at least be based upon emotion and action. Despite this obvious necessity, however, he is prepared, as we have seen, to speak of it in the language appropriate to knowledge and to call it science, judgment and reason—partly to be sure because

[1] *Ibid.* vol. II, p. 28.   [2] *Ibid.* vol. II, p. 30.
[3] *Ibid.* vol. II, p. 31.   [4] Cf. e.g. *Ibid.* vol. II, p. 86.

Locke's term "reflexion", although in the context it signifies rather introspection or a kind of meditative self-posturing than the sedulous investigation of principles, leads by an easy ambiguity to this second and more usual interpretation. Indeed, Shaftesbury is even prepared to say that "whatsoever causes a misconception or misapprehension of the worth or value of any object...must necessarily be the occasion of wrong. Thus he who affects or loves a man for the sake of something which is reputed honourable, but which is in reality vicious, is himself vicious and ill".[1] What is more, he is ready to claim *authority* for his Taste or Approval in a way that Butler and other rationalists could not think consistent with his theory. Thus the passage we have just noticed is preceded by a paragraph to the effect that defects in the senses are morally negligible since in these cases a man's failure "is not in his principal or leading part", although "'tis otherwise in what relates to opinion, belief or speculation".

In short, Shaftesbury conjoined in the smoothest fashion, what his successors were at pains to separate. Perhaps he was right, perhaps he was careless, perhaps we should be content to regard him simply as a shrewd and polished pioneer and therefore decline to press any such question. In any case the fact remains that we have to look to his successors for intentionally nice and painstaking analysis of questions such as these. And therefore we should turn to them.

§ 3. *Francis Hutcheson*

Hutcheson's earlier and more important work is based so frankly upon Shaftesbury's writings—"they will be esteemed", he says, "while any reflection remains among men"[2]—that they can hardly be said to break new ground. Hutcheson set himself, in a word, to vindicate Shaftesbury's doctrine against the glittering insufficiency of Mandeville's *Fable of the Bees*. Unlike Shaftesbury, however, Hutcheson had an eminent

---

[1] *Characteristicks*, vol. II, p. 33.
[2] *An Inquiry into the Original of our Ideas of Beauty and Virtue*, 4th edn. (1738) p. xix.

capacity for taking one thing at a time and for setting forth everything in order.

The senses and the primitive emotions, he tells us, yield pleasure or pain directly. Interest or advantage, on the other hand, so far from determining these immediate pleasures or pains, is, on the contrary, based upon them, being for the most part the possession of commodities which are expected to yield the pleasure with as little attendant pain as may be. It is not true, however, that all direct or immediate pleasures are of the simple sort which may be illustrated by the perfume of a rose. Harmony, beauty or proportion strike the mind quite as agreeably and quite as immediately as the perfume does, and although this harmony, if we thought it out, could be shown to be unity in variety, the manifest verity remains that normally we do not think at all when we respond to the enticing and enchanted quality of beautiful objects. This immediate appreciation of beauty, moreover, is independent of self-interest and even of desire; for "our desire of beauty may be counterbalanced by rewards or threatenings, but never our sense of it".[1]

Consequently, once we are fairly launched upon these investigations, we are bound, in candour, to admit *all* the immediate susceptibilities of human nature in this affair, and dare not reject the aesthetic or the moral susceptibilities if we accept as realities the simple joys that come from sunshine or the hardships that are felt during a bitter night. If, as is true in fact, we *are* naturally susceptible to beauty and lovingkindness, nothing *more* is needed on this head, although it is, of course, entirely legitimate to show how education may build upon, or transform, the natural basis of such appreciations.

"This superior power of perception", Hutcheson goes on to tell us, "is justly called a *sense*, because of its affinity to the other senses in this, that the pleasure is different from any knowledge of principles, proportions, causes, or of the usefulness of the object; we are struck at first with the beauty; nor does the most accurate

[1] *Ibid.* p. 13.

knowledge increase this pleasure of beauty, however it may superadd a distinct rational pleasure from prospects of advantage, or may bring along that peculiar kind of pleasure, which attends the increase of knowledge."[1]

The word "superior" in this passage is introduced, perhaps, a trifle too abruptly, and when our author, following Shaftesbury, proceeds to call it an "internal" sense, although he has given us no reason for concluding that the beauty, say, of an olive grove is either more or less internal than the sheen of the olive leaves, we may justly deplore the precipitance of convinced disciples. These incidents, however, are at worst regrettable.

The moral portion of Hutcheson's *Inquiry* is more elaborate and more important than the aesthetic. Its dominant note may be found in the statement that "moral goodness denotes our idea of some quality apprehended in action which procures approbation attended with desire of the agent's happiness".[2]

Moral goodness is consequently distinct from natural good, i.e. from the simple capacity for conferring happiness which we find in such things as gardens or vineyards, health or strength. If we know that anything is a source of pleasure we desire to possess it. If we know that a man is morally good we *approve* him, or in other words have both a disinterested esteem for him and a kindly feeling towards him.

In this analysis, there is obviously an oversight respecting "natural" good, since, e.g. the beneficence of the sun (outside the tropics) need not raise any question of possession. As a consequence Hutcheson s contrast between the selfishness of natural and the selflessness of moral goodness is something too easily drawn. Neglecting (while admitting) the point, however, we may say, speaking broadly, that Hutcheson's account of virtue and of our sense of it lays stress upon four principal considerations, viz. (1) that moral good presupposes intention on the part of the agent accounted good, (2) that the moral sense is aroused by benevolence or, as we might say, by public spirit and social loyalty, (3) that the moral

---

[1] *An Inquiry into the Original of our Ideas of Beauty and Virtue*, 4th edn. (1738) p. 11.   [2] *Ibid.* p. 105.

sense refers or attaches to the object approved, and (4) that its approval is independent of self-interest.

Of these considerations, the second and third have the greatest importance for our present purpose, since the last has already been noted—it is in any case an imitative iteration of the anti-egoistic arguments characteristic of the age—and since the first is a very usual (if disputed) opinion connected rather indirectly with our principal theme.

Taking, then, the second and third points together, we may state and examine Hutcheson's theory, in its outlines, somewhat as follows:

"Approbation and disapprobation", he says, "are probably simple ideas which cannot be further explained."[1] All that can be done is to reveal these ideas clearly in their appropriate connections.

Since Hutcheson calls approbation a sense, we might be excused for supposing it to be, if not a species of knowing, at any rate the apprehension of something possibly true. As we have seen, however, Hutcheson's principal reason for calling it a sense is its *immediacy* (particularly the immediacy of the pleasure it arouses), and his principal aim is to distinguish it absolutely from mediate, discursive or argumentative knowledge. Pretty clearly, he does regard it as affording a certain kind and degree of insight, but he is more particularly anxious to show that this immediate sensitiveness to value and worth proceeds from a virtuous temper and is part of an active disposition. "Every action", he tells us, "which we apprehend as either morally good or evil, is always supposed to flow from some affection towards sensitive natures; and whatever we call virtue or vice, is either some such affection, or some action consequent upon it."[2] It follows, therefore, that our approbation not only goes out towards benevolence when we notice the benevolence, but that it actually proceeds *from* the benevolence in our own breasts.[3] In other words we

[1] *Ibid.* p. 105.   [2] *Ibid.* p. 132.
[3] Cf. Shakespeare, Sonnet 151:
> Love is too young to know what conscience is,
> But who knows not, conscience is born of love?

have always to look for "that approbation or perception of moral excellence *which benevolence excites towards the person in whom we observe it*".[1]

Indeed, moral approval, in the normal case, is doubly unselfish, doubly removed from egoism. Pleasant reflections on our own virtue may indeed occur[2] (and, we may add, might be disinterested when they do occur), but, for the most part, our approval takes its rise from our spontaneous tendencies towards the well-being of others, and is exercised upon the conduct and character of those others themselves. Plainly, this is *one* of the important senses of disinterestedness, although it is not the whole of that quality. The other usual senses, however, are allied with it. "Whence this love, compassion, indignation and hatred", he asks, "toward even feigned characters, in the most distant ages and nations, according as they appear kind, faithful, compassionate, or of the opposite dispositions, towards their imaginary contemporaries?"[3] Again, "we love even those" (the "even" is quaint, perhaps) "who are beneficent to others".[4] We show indignation against men who are dead and gone, or against persons so remote from us as to be wholly without possible influence upon our personal concerns. If ingenious artisans, in time of persecution, take refuge in our own country, our interest is served, yet we praise, not them, but the sturdy burgomasters who refuse to be intimidated and continue a competitive commerce not to the interest of our own country. Although traitors (of the foreign variety) are useful to us, we never admire them, but admire, instead, the actions of a valiant enemy who may have done us great hurt. Our approval, in a word, so far from being tutored simply by our own advantage (direct or indirect) may actually extend to some action or person inimical to our own profit.

In the last analysis, therefore, we approve that which excites "admiration and love and study of imitation";[5] and

---

[1] *An Inquiry into the Original of our Ideas of Beauty and Virtue*, 4th edn. (1738) p. 112.   [2] *Ibid*. p. 142.   [3] *Ibid*. p. 115.
[4] *Ibid*. p. 156.   [5] *Ibid*. p. 120.

approval, in consequence, although quasi-aesthetic, is immensely more active and busy than the enchantments of beauty. It is, indeed, the guide of life.

This moral sense diffuses itself through all conditions of life, and every part of it, and insinuates itself into all the more humane amusements and entertainments of mankind. Poetry and rhetoric depend almost entirely upon it; as do in a great measure the arts of the painter, statuary and player. In the choice of friends, wives, comrades it is all in all; and it even insinuates itself into our games and mirth.[1]

Clearly, a busy faculty and not offensively puritan.

§ 4. *David Hume*

The analysis of approbation occupies a prominent place both in Hume's earlier *Treatise* and in his later *Enquiry*. The second of these works, as most people know, is vastly superior to the first in point of literary form, and had much more general influence in the matters with which we have to deal. Nevertheless it will suit us best to pay the greater attention to the first book, the reason being that Hume in his youth had a passion for minute analysis (or as he says for "anatomy")[2] which abated rather too sensibly in the decade which separated this pair of books. Despite Sir L. A. Selby-Bigge's opinion to the contrary,[3] it is doubtful whether there is any substantial difference between the two volumes, but the point, of course, must be considered in the sequel.

Summarising his general argument, Hume writes as follows:

We have already observed, that moral distinctions depend entirely upon certain peculiar sentiments of pain and pleasure, and that whatever mental quality in ourselves or others gives us a satisfaction, by the survey or reflection, is of course virtuous; as everything of this nature, that gives uneasiness, is vicious. Now since every quality in ourselves or others, which gives pleasure, always causes pride or love; as every one, that produces uneasiness, excites humility or hatred. It follows that these two particulars are to be considered as equivalent, with regard to our mental

[1] *Introduction to Moral Philosophy* (1747), p. 20.
[2] Cf. Hume's letter to Hutcheson in Burton's *Life of Hume*, vol. I, p. 112.
[3] In his Introduction to the *Enquiries*.

qualities, *virtue* and the power of producing love or pride, *vice* and the power of producing humility or hatred. In every case, therefore, we must judge of the one by the other; and may pronounce any *quality* of the mind virtuous, which causes love or pride; and any one vicious which causes hatred or humility.[1]

According to Hume, good and evil are, respectively, the same things as pleasure and pain; and the mind, by an original instinct, tends to unite itself with the good and to avoid the evil, although revenge and well-wishing together with "hunger, lust and a few other bodily appetites" produce pleasure and pain instead of being produced by them.[2] This union with pleasure, in the simplest cases, yields the "direct" passions of desire and aversion, grief and joy. It also yields the direct passion of volition. *Approval* in moral matters, however (and the parallel with beauty is very close, since, in the end, we are dealing with admiration, esteem and the like), is a highly peculiar sort of pleasure. Yet this is no objection, for we comprehend a great variety of facts under the general title of pleasure and pain, and these varied facts, so far from being identical, may have only a very distant resemblance.[3] In a word, *every* species of pleasure is peculiar.

The peculiarity of the complacent emotion (or pleasure) which is approval arises, of course, from the circumstances which call it forth, the chief of these circumstances being that the complacency always arises from and is appropriate to a *general* survey. On the whole, if we consider, *firstly*, Hume's account of the object of approval (or in other words of the facts to which this sentiment is appropriate), *secondly*, the alternative to rationalistic theories which his theory is expressly framed to supply, and *thirdly*, the way in which the "moral sense" (as he still calls it) is, in his pages, designed to supplant other theories that go by that name, we shall have covered the ground in a way that seems not entirely inadequate to an involved and devious theme.

The objects of approval are beauty (or harmony or pro-

---

[1] *Treatise*, Selby-Bigge's edn. pp. 574 *sq.*
[2] *Ibid.* p. 439.   [3] *Ibid.* p. 472.

portion) and "qualities durable enough to affect our sentiments concerning the person",[1] i.e. qualities of personal or moral character (particular actions, from this standpoint being regarded only as the signs of character). This personal merit in ourselves is the proper subject of pride, while personal merit in others is the proper subject of love. In both cases we have to deal with certain "indirect" passions in which some pleasant experience is united with a complacent pleasure in the idea of ourselves, on the one hand, or of the idea of someone else upon the other. *Anything*, therefore, which is agreeable after this fashion partakes of the character of virtue, though it be but wit, or cheerfulness, or decorum, and again, everything "where this pleasure is severe and serious; or where its object is great, and makes a strong impression; or where it produces any degree of humility or awe"[2]—which Hume calls "esteem" and regards as a sufficient account of the majesty and austerity of righteousness. The fact that voluntary actions, in his opinion, neither are nor signify the whole of ethics, enables him, in Ciceronian fashion, to rank natural abilities along with the other virtues. They also pertain to personal merit. "It belongs to Grammarians to examine what qualities are entitled to the denomination of *virtue*; nor will they find, upon trial, that this is so easy a task, as at first sight they may be apt to imagine."[3]

The *generality* of approval in its proper exercise necessitates a rather prolonged investigation into the reasons which led Hume to reject all rationalistic accounts of the subject, and to offer what he considered an improved version of the facts upon which the rationalists relied.

There is no doubt that Hume took this question to be one of the most serious upon which the human mind could be engaged.

"I wish from my heart", he wrote to Hutcheson in the year when the third volume of the *Treatise* appeared, "I could avoid concluding, that since morality, according to your opinion, as well as mine, is determined merely by sentiment, it regards only human

---

[1] *Ibid.* p. 575.   [2] *Ibid.* p. 608 n.   [3] *Ibid.* p. 610.

nature and human life. This often has been urged against you, and the consequences are very momentous.... If morality were determined by reason, that is the same to all rational beings; but nothing but experience can assure us that the sentiments are the same. What experience have we with regard to superior beings? How can we ascribe to them any sentiments at all? They have implanted those sentiments in us for the conduct of life like our bodily sensations, which they possess not themselves."[1]

Theology, in short, hung in the balance as well as the rationalism of "the popular side",[2] and Hume conceived himself bound to deal with the problem massively.

His argument has three parts, (1) that reason cannot play the part in action that popular opinion and the theories of certain philosophers have ascribed to it, (2) that nevertheless it does play an important although subordinate part, but (3) that certain habits improperly called reason have a most considerable office in these affairs.

(1) The kernel of Hume's criticism here is that reason is merely speculative,[3] calm and indolent, roused by curiosity only, and consequently unfitted to be the spring of virtue. For virtue is amiable by nature, and prompt to act. These contentions are further enforced by elaborate demarcations of the province of speculative reason (in other words by an elaborate *petitio principii* for those who deny that "reason" *is* merely speculative) and by reiterated statements to the effect that when the end is indifferent all processes subservient to the end must be in themselves indifferent.

(2) The moving and quite unspeculative influences, however, which lie at the roots of action are compatible with a very extensive concurrence of rationality, both of the unphilosophical sort that we employ in the current affairs of life and of the more exact and penetrating kind that we expect from the sciences. Many of our passions are founded on false suppositions, and may entirely disappear when it is shown that the misconceptions which aroused hope or agony do not in fact exist.[4] Again, our choice of means to an end is ordinarily an affair of thinking, and to this must be added the importance

[1] Burton's *Life*, vol. I, pp. 119 *sq*. [2] *Ibid.* p. 119.
[3] *Treatise*, p. 457. [4] *Ibid.* p. 416.

of general rules. These latter, to be sure, are to be ascribed, in part, to "custom" which "carries us beyond the just bounds in our passions as well as in our reasonings",[1] and in part are but aspects of that *general* survey which, in Hume's opinion, is always required for approval. Despite this, a certain part of the generality of general rules must obviously be ascribed to analogical and inductive processes.

Still more important in this connection are Hume's elaborate arguments to the effect that a great portion of virtue is "artificial". In so far as these arguments are criticisms of the Moral Sense School and of its facile propensity for fleeing to "nature" as a city of refuge for theories in distress, they properly concern us later. What we have now to notice is that the artificiality of virtue in this connection means essentially the intelligent contrivance of regulations concerning property or government for the end of public utility. Here "the actions themselves are artificial, and are performed with a certain design and intention".[2] Indeed, mankind is an inventive species;[3] "Nothing is more vigilant and inventive than our passions"[4] or more stimulating to reflection. What is more, "nature provides a remedy in the judgment and understanding for what is irregular and incommodious in the affections".[5]

(3) We might even say that if feeling and sentiment are the ultimates of Hume's theory, reflection and judgment have proximately the greater importance in it. This handsome concession, however, has to be modified by his refusal to allow to the rationalists much that they commonly appropriate. For neither the "calm" passions nor what we may call a general perspective in these affairs is "reason" in the strict and proper sense. Yet "reason" is precisely the name that most rationalists give to these tranquil propensities.

According to Hume

reason exerts itself without producing any sensible emotion; and except in the more sublime disquisitions of philosophy, or in the frivolous subtleties of the schools, scarce ever conveys any pleasure

---

[1] *Ibid.* p. 293.   [2] *Ibid.* p. 475.   [3] *Ibid.* p. 484.
[4] *Ibid.* p. 526.   [5] *Ibid.* p. 489.

or uneasiness. Hence it proceeds, that every action of the mind, which operates with the same calmness and tranquillity, is confounded with reason by all those, who judge of things from the first view and appearance.[1]

In view of this very deliberate statement it is unfortunate, to say the least, that, according to Hume's own admission, the division of the passions into calm and violent is itself but vulgar and specious, the ground being that if beauty, say, is regarded as calm and love or hatred as violent, it sometimes happens, notwithstanding, that beauty may become rapture (and so not be calm) or love became tepid (and consequently in no way violent).[2] Similarly Hume tells us that a gust of passion may really be weak and a calm passion be strong, although in general it is more effective to work upon a man's tempestuous passions than upon the tranquil side of him, or "what is vulgarly called his reason".[3] Again he tells us that the calm passions "when corroborated by reflection and seconded by resolution" are frequently capable of controlling the tempestuous ones in their most furious movements.[4]

Indeed, this zealous anatomist might with advantage have dissected a little more deeply. It is the strength and steadiness of these passions that is in question, not their superficial and very misleading calm, if calm there be. "There is a calm ambition," we find him reminding Hutcheson, "a calm anger or hatred, which, though calm, may likewise be very strong, and have the absolute command over the mind. The more absolute they are, we find them to be commonly the calmer."[5] Yet we may also nurse them to keep them *warm*; and precisely the same is true of reflective resolution. Strength and calmness, therefore, are quite different characteristics which should never be confounded; but if it were true that there is a certain correlation between calmness and indolence (or manifest weakness) it would be legitimate, surely, to remember that "reason" in any ordinary sense is not even superficially calm,

---

[1] *Treatise*, p. 417.   [2] *Ibid.* p. 276.
[3] *Ibid.* p. 419.   [4] *Ibid.* p. 437.
[5] Burton's *Life*, vol. I, p. 147.

although some people believe that it ought to be. "The heat of argument", to be sure, may be a misleading expression, since the phrase may describe, not logic, but contumacious contentiousness. Nevertheless, when anyone reflects in earnest, he reflects with a glow; and even the driest writers have to be drunk with their ideas before their pens can move effectively. Contrariwise, nothing is more disturbing than to find that the foundations of our beliefs are tottering. In short, on the surface at least, "reason" very often is *not* "calm", and nothing but a vehement and blinding dogma would make us suppose that it was. "Reason" may and should be impartial, but if indolence and impartiality are equivalent, what becomes of Hume's Impartial Approval?

Another thing that most of us include under "reason", and that Hume says we should not include, is comprehensiveness, or the attempt to diminish momentary vicissitudes and casual vexations in some larger perspective; and it is true that width of vision without the employment of principle (which is reason proper) might have something of this emancipating effect. Hume, however, seems to strain this interpretation beyond all moderation.

When we consider any objects at a distance, he says, all their minute distinctions vanish, and we always give the preference to what is in itself preferable without considering its situation and circumstances. This gives rise to what in an improper sense we call *reason*, which is a principle, that is often contradictory to those propensities that display themselves upon the approach of the object. In reflecting on any action, which I am to perform a twelve-month hence, I always resolve to prefer the greater good, whether at that time it will be more contiguous or remote; nor does any difference in that particular make a difference in my present intentions and resolutions. My distance from the final determination makes all those minute differences vanish, nor am I affected by anything but the general and more discernible qualities of good and evil;[1]

and he goes on to say that "frequent meditation and repeated resolution"[2] may serve to establish this general perspective,

[1] *Treatise*, p. 536.   [2] *Ibid.*

and guard it against the seductions of momentary and merely proximate solicitations.

These doctrines are in themselves sufficiently remarkable, the more so when we remember that Hume also declares that "the present situation of the person is always that of the imagination"[1] and that Time is the great barrier to the freedom of the fancy. For Time is more disruptive than Space, since it ties us to the present. Yet even in Space, he had formerly admitted, "the different degrees of remoteness from ourselves are discovered more by reason than by the senses".[2]

The same crucial difficulty appears when we consider what Hume has to say concerning Comparison. At the first look, indeed, a neater example of a flat contradiction could scarcely be found than between the statements that "all kinds of reasoning consist in nothing but a comparison"[3] and that "so little are men governed by reason in their sentiments and opinions that they always judge more of objects by comparison than from their intrinsic worth and value".[4] This particular contradiction, we may admit, depends principally on a verbal ambiguity. In the first statement, comparison is regarded as the confronting of facts or ideas with a view to discerning their relations. In the second, what is meant is that we call those values absolute and intrinsic which in fact are relative or comparative. Despite this, the very idea that there *is* an intrinsic worth and value which may be discerned is quite peculiarly odd in the mouth of a Hume, and it is hard to distinguish meditation and resolution from what, in the strictest possible sense, is usually meant by a rational process. There is *no* passion of meditation to chasten any other passion or in any intelligible sense to look before and after. For meditation is not a passion, and no passion can *look* at all.

Having considered, then, Hume's account of the objects of approval, and the character of his alternative to rationalism, we come to the third of our principal topics, viz. the particular

[1] *Treatise*, p. 430. [2] *Ibid.* p. 56, cf. p. 191.
[3] *Ibid.* p. 73. [4] *Ibid.* p. 372, cf. p. 593.

form of the moral sense theory which he was anxious to expound.

Here again there seem to be three main sub-divisions of his argument, and these are the contentions (1) that the moral sense and taste in general take their place as part of a general scheme of the passions and are not to be regarded as isolated, if inexpugnable, phenomena.

(2) That the deliverances of the moral sense are not final pronouncements of "nature" to be swallowed like raw gobbets, but are to be regarded in principle as things which develop from a single seminal origin.

(3) That the connection between the moral sense and active goodness is not to be assumed but is a problem requiring explanation.

(1) The theory of the passions starts from the division into direct and indirect passions. The direct passions, examples of which have already been given in this narrative, arise immediately from pain or pleasure, and, in Hume's opinion, need no explaining. They are the effect of our constitution, or instinctive. The indirect ones contain a further complexity, because they are entangled either with the idea of ourselves or with the idea of other people. Thus they include, of the one part, pride, humility, ambition and vanity; and they include love, hatred, envy, pity, and malice, of the other part. They also include virtue and vice, beauty and deformity.

Taking pride and humility as examples, we find that anything which arouses pride calls forth an idea of ourselves.[1] Something delights us, and, if it is our property, we are proud. Some blemish offends us, and we are ashamed if we believe the blemish to be due to ourselves. In this way an unlimited number of things may touch one and the same idea of the self, but it is nonsense to suppose that an unlimited number of faculties is consequently required. "To invent without scruple a new principle to every new phenomenon" is a certain proof "that we only desire, by a number of falsehoods, to cover our ignorance of the truth".[2]

[1] Cf. Descartes, *Les passions de l'âme*, Part III, Art. CLI.   [2] *Treatise*, p. 282.

This principle must be pliable, not muscle-bound, and Hume offers us Association by resemblance, sympathy, and the artifice of inventive contrivance, as a sufficient explanation of the facts.

The first of these may again be illustrated by the instance of pride. Pride, he says, never looks beyond self but is, on the contrary, an agreeable idea of the self. What happens, then, is that something agreeable (an impression) is associated with the agreeable side of self (an idea), and this double agreeableness is *de facto* a resemblance in point of pleasure. Hume adds, however, that the relation to self must be close, relatively permanent, rather peculiar and decidedly obvious to all[1]—and therefore suggests that pride implies a social reference. When in the same fashion and with corresponding limitations we associate an agreeable impression with the idea of someone else, we have the emotional foundation of love.

In the *Treatise*, resemblance, in the form of sympathy, is asked to work prodigiously hard. Sympathy (which, by Hume's definitions, is strictly the mere fact of correspondence between one man's feelings and another's) is also regarded as an organ of communication.

"So close and intimate is the correspondence of human souls," we are told, "that no sooner any person approaches me, than he diffuses on me all his opinions, and draws along my judgment in a greater or lesser degree. And though, on many occasions, my sympathy with him goes not so far as entirely to change my sentiments, and way of thinking; yet it seldom is so weak as not to disturb the easy course of my thought, and give an authority to that opinion, which is recommended to me by his assent and approbation."[2]

To sympathy, again, must be ascribed that whole department of aesthetic approval which has utility for its foundation. "I know not but a plain overgrown with furze or broom, may be, in itself, as beautiful as a hill covered with vines or olive trees; though it will never appear so to one who is acquainted with the value of each."[3] Accordingly, this species of beauty

---

[1] *Treatise*, pp. 290 *sq.*   [2] *Ibid.* p. 592.   [3] *Ibid.* p. 364.

is derived from our fellow-feeling with the proprietor of the olive-grove. And so of the utilitarian moiety of ethics. Because we have sympathy for the interest of society, we approve all human contrivances devoted to that end.

Hume was no follower of the selfish theory. "So far from thinking that men have no affection for anything beyond themselves, I am of opinion, that though it be rare to meet with one, who loves any single person better than himself; yet 'tis as rare to meet with one, in whom all the kind affections, taken together, do not over-balance all the selfish."[1] On the other hand, although he forgets the point not infrequently,[2] his official doctrine is that natural or spontaneous benevolence, although relatively strong, is *not* a sufficient basis for human sociality, and that sympathy supplements it enormously. "The happiness of strangers affects us by sympathy alone."[3] Our benevolence is a *confined* impulse, sporadic in its incidence and limited to neighbours or to near relatives. It is sympathy which enlarges this confined predicament and gives us the generality presupposed in all genuine approbation. He who approves must be capable of approving distant ages and the denizens of remote places. In this sense his approbation is self-neglecting.

A man will be mortified if you tell him he has a stinking breath, though 'tis evidently no annoyance to himself. Our fancy easily changes its situation; and either surveying ourselves as we appear to others, or considering others as they feel themselves, we enter, by that means, into sentiments which no way belong to us, and in which nothing but sympathy is able to interest us. And this sympathy we sometimes carry so far, as even to be displeased with a commodity commodious to us, merely because it displeases others and makes us disagreeable in their eyes; though perhaps we never can have any interest in rendering ourselves agreeable to them.[4]

"Virtue", Hutcheson had said, "is called amiable or lovely, from its raising good will or love in spectators towards the agent, and not from the agent's perceiving the virtuous temper to be advantageous to him, or desiring to obtain it under that

[1] *Ibid.* p. 487. [2] Especially e.g. on pp. 603 *sq.*
[3] *Ibid.* p. 619. [4] *Ibid.* p. 589.

view."[1] According to Hume, it is sympathy that makes us, in this way, impartial spectators.

"'Tis impossible men could ever agree in their sentiments and judgments", he says, "unless they chose some common point of view, from which they might survey their object, and which might cause it to appear the same to all of them. Now, in judging of characters, the only interest or pleasure, which appears the same to every spectator, is that of the person himself, whose character is examined, or that of persons who have a connexion with him. And though such interests or pleasures touch us more faintly than our own, yet being more constant and universal, they counterbalance the latter even in practice, and are alone admitted in speculation as the standard of virtue and morality. They alone produce that particular feeling or sentiment on which moral distinctions depend."[2]

(2) Instead of appealing to nature, therefore (or to spontaneous benevolence), Hume appeals to association in the form of sympathy. His "moral sense", therefore, is rather derived than original. On this basis, artifice and contrivance may be built; and with the utmost elaborateness. It is possible, indeed, as Sir L. A. Selby-Bigge suggests,[3] that Hume meant to be offensive in laying such stress upon the artificial character of justice and of some other virtues; but if there was malice in his thoughts (though I see no reason for supposing so) there is the soundest of good sense in his arguments. Both in Shaftesbury and in Hutcheson the transition from public spirit to the appropriate governmental and other social regulations for the public welfare is made in the most casual fashion. They spoke as if goodwill could divine what a statesman or a Parliament ought to do, and this, in Hutcheson, is the more surprising, since he expressed the utilitarian formula with great precision, holding that public advantage is "in a compound ratio of the quantity of good and number of enjoyers", although he also held that "the dignity or moral importance of persons may

---

[1] *Beauty and Virtue*, p. 130. [2] *Treatise*, p. 591.
[3] *Enquiries*, Preface, p. xxviii. When Burke some forty years later said that society was an invention of human wisdom contrived for the purpose of providing for human needs (*Reflections*, vol. v, p. 122), he at least did not mean to be offensive. Was there then an entire change of popular attitude during this part of the century?

compensate numbers".[1] What Hume saw, and what he said, was that government, property, contract and the like could not be regarded as a mere appendage to benevolent emotion. Although they depend upon a sentimental basis (as he thought) these things are elaborate constructions to which the hardest of hard thinking must be given. The provision for men's needs, in a complex civilisation, cannot be left to nature or sentiment, but has to be won by artifice; and Hume was concerned to show the extent to which this requisite should not be hid.

(3) Hume did perhaps mean to be mischievous (one can hardly say offensive) although he may only have meant to be thorough, when he took pains to point out that the connection of approval with conduct was radically and implacably non-rational, however "natural" it might be. The most striking assertion of this kind (which I leave without comment) is to be found in the following passage:

> Benevolence and anger are passions different from love and hatred, and only conjoined with them by the original constitution of the mind....According as we are possessed with love or hatred, the correspondent desire of the happiness or misery of the person, who is the object of these passions, arises in the mind, and varies with each variation of these opposite passions. This order of things, abstractly considered, is not necessary. Love and hatred might have been unattended with any such desires, or their particular connexion might have been entirely reversed. If nature had so pleased, love might have had the same effect as hatred, and hatred as love. I see no contradiction in supposing a desire of producing misery annexed to love, and of happiness to hatred.[2]

As we have seen, the Oxford editor of Hume's *Enquiries* maintains that there is so considerable a change of tone or temper in the later work as to suggest very strongly that "the system of morals in the *Enquiry* is really and essentially different from that in the *Treatise*",[3] and it is evident that Hume had discarded much of his anatomising zeal in the graceful and orderly periods of his later work, and that, in his own language, "some particle of the dove" had entered

---
[1] *Op. cit.* p. 181. [2] *Treatise*, p. 368.
[3] Hume's *Enquiries* (Selby-Bigge), Preface, p. xxiii.

into his frame when he dealt with his opponents. He is soothing, not contentious. Instead of stropping Occam's razor, he is content to accept "the obvious appearance of things".[1] Regarding the concurrence of reason and sentiment, he would go along with the rationalists—except in the crucial matter of the final determination; and certainly he comes much nearer to Hutcheson's position by regarding benevolence, sympathy and humanity as one and the same thing.

The last point is undoubtedly of cardinal importance in the theory. Sympathy instead of being regarded as a relation between all sorts of different emotions, is now declared to be a single, though diffuse, emotion; and instead of being *required* to liberate benevolence or humanity from the "confined" domain where these principles hold sway according to the order of nature, it is now swallowed up in a "generous concern for our kind or species".[2]

With this notable exception, however, the argument of the *Enquiry* is very much what we might have expected to find if we suppose Hume to have set himself to expand the *concluding* chapters of the *Treatise* into a fresh presentation of the subject, to compel interest rather by urbanity and literary art than by straining after provocative or new-fangled ideas, and (discarding doubtful or tedious niceties) to concentrate attention upon the effective and acceptable statement of the points which seemed, after a decade of reflection, to be of the greatest significance. Thus the general division into "qualities either useful or immediately agreeable to ourselves or to others" provides the outline of the theme of the *Enquiry*, and this judicious blend of the *utile* with the *dulce* is confidently recommended to "men of sense" leaving "gloomy hair-brained enthusiasts" to the company of those who are as "delirious and dismal" as themselves.[3] To an audience of this kind, minute analysis and the pure flame of theory are something out of place and the careful distinction between nature and artifice apt to be wearisome. Yet in the latter respect, at least, there is no authentic change of opinion.

[1] *Enquiries*, p. 298.   [2] *Ibid.* p. 178.   [3] *Ibid.* p. 270.

"I have never called justice unnatural but only artificial", we find Hume writing in the year when the *Treatise* appeared "'*Atque ipsa utilitas, justi prope mater et aequi*', says one of the best moralists of antiquity."[1] The moralist was Horace, and if we take the *Enquiry* to be an attempt on Hume's part to become more Horatian than before, we shall not, perhaps, read it seriously amiss.

In any case the analysis of approval remains substantially what it was. "The hypothesis which we embrace is plain. It maintains that morality is determined by sentiment. It defines virtue to be whatever mental action or quality gives to a spectator the pleasing sentiment of approbation; and vice the contrary."[2] This approval is more than half aesthetic,[3] and it is general and disinterested. We approve in others what is immediately agreeable *to them*,[4] and approve in ourselves what *others* praise in us.[5]

> When a man denominates another his *enemy*, his *rival*, his *antagonist*, his *adversary*, he is understood to speak the language of self-love, and to express sentiments, peculiar to himself, and arising from his particular circumstances and situation. But when he bestows on any man the epithets of *vicious* or *odious* or *depraved*, he then speaks another language, and expresses sentiments, in which he expects all his audience are to concur with him. He must here, therefore, depart from his private and particular situation, and must choose a point of view, common to him with others; he must move some universal principle of the human frame, and touch a spring to which all mankind have an accord and sympathy.[6]

§ 5. *Adam Smith*

Superficially, and for some distance beneath the surface, Adam Smith's theory of the moral sentiments (according to which the moderate standpoint of an impartial spectator is generated by the give and take of humane fellow citizens) has obvious resemblances to the doctrine of the last quotation from Hume. In detail, however, and in an integral part of its

---
[1] Burton's *Life*, vol. I, p. 113.
[2] *Enquiries*, p. 289.   [3] *Ibid.* p. 173.   [4] *Ibid.* p. 234.
[5] *Ibid.* p. 273.   [6] *Ibid.* p. 272.

conception, Smith may properly be considered an innovator. Nevertheless, it is perhaps a little odd that Smith, Hume's friend and later his executor, should have referred to Hume's moral theory with such clipped and studied brevity. Apart from general compliments,[1] all he has to say is that Hume "places virtue in utility, and accounts for the pleasure with which the spectator surveys the utility of any quality from sympathy with the happiness of those who are affected by it".[2]

On the other hand, Smith does criticise Hutcheson at some length, and Hutcheson, as we have seen, mentioned the "spectator" and spoke of Sympathy in the first chapter of his *Introduction* (which contains the lectures Smith heard as a student) in a vein which was certainly not foreign to Smith's point of view. Smith's criticism of his teacher, however, is sufficiently trenchant. After some argument, over-long for its purpose, to the effect that approbation is not a "sense" comparable to the external senses, Smith goes on to maintain that it is not a distinctive sentiment or emotion at all. For if it were it would be discernibly the same in all its phases. "Anger against a man is, no doubt, somewhat different from anger against a woman, and that again from anger against a child."[3] Yet all are recognisably the same emotion. It is quite otherwise with approval and disapproval. "Thus the approbation with which we view a tender delicate and humane sentiment is quite different from that with which we are struck by one that appears great, daring and magnanimous.... The same thing holds true with regard to disapprobation. Our horror for cruelty has no sort of resemblance to our contempt for mean-spiritedness."[4] In short, the alleged moral sense, instead of being a single entity, must be understood to stand for a character or relationship common to many *different* sentiments or emotions. It is a species of *agreement* and is due to sympathy.[5]

[1] *The Theory of the Moral Sentiments*, 4th edn. 1774, p. 264.
[2] *Ibid.* p. 411.   [3] *Ibid.* p. 406.   [4] *Ibid.* p. 407.
[5] Smith's critique of Hutcheson is part of a general historical survey in which his attitude to British rationalism should also be noted. Cudworth, Smith says, pricked the bubble of Hobbes's egoism very

As he explains, Smith's own doctrine of approval consists of four parts:

First, we sympathise with the motives of the agent; secondly, we enter into the gratitude of those who receive the benefit of his actions; thirdly, we observe that his conduct has been agreeable to the general rules by which those two sympathies generally act; and last of all, when we consider such actions as making a part of a system of behaviour which tends to promote the happiness either of the individual or of the society, they appear to derive a beauty from this utility, not unlike that which we ascribe to any well-contrived machine.[1]

Of these four parts of the doctrine, the first has outstanding importance, although the second is also of moment.

The first part of Smith's book gives a theory of propriety which may be stated, in outline, thus:

Approval is really a social thing, and essentially means agreement. This is clear in the domain of opinion and argument. "To approve of another man's opinions is to adopt those opinions, and to adopt them is to approve of them."[2] The same analysis holds, however, of "our approbation or disapprobation of the sentiments or passions of others";[3] and in this case the agreement is just what we mean by sympathy. "To approve of the passions of another, therefore, as suitable to their objects, is the same thing as to observe that we entirely sympathise with them; and not to approve of them as such is the same thing as to observe that we do not entirely sympathise with them."[4] Sympathy, it is explained, means nothing but fellow-feeling; and it arises from putting ourselves imaginatively in the situation of others. It is different, therefore, from simple contagiousness of emotion, since a bystander

---

effectively when he pointed out that unless covenants are binding in themselves a social compact cannot make them so. According to the faulty psychology of Cudworth's day this obligatoriness had to be ascribed to "reason" (*ibid.* p. 396) and general maxims *are* essential to ethics. These generalisations, however, are the result of induction, and moral inductions themselves depend upon certain final perceptions of a sensory or emotional order. For "Reason cannot render any particular object either agreeable or disagreeable to the mind for its own sake" (*ibid.* p. 398).

[1] *Ibid.* p. 410.   [2] *Ibid.* p. 17.   [3] *Ibid.* p. 18.   [4] *Ibid.* p. 16.

may be moved in his imagination when the party principally concerned is not moved at all. "We blush for the impudence and rudeness of another, though he himself appears to have no sense of the impropriety of his own behaviour."[1] When we go along with him in our feelings, however, we must approve his attitude, since, *eo ipso*, we agree or are in sympathy with it.

Certain further explanations follow. Psychologically, to approve of anything "as right, as accurate, as agreeable to truth and reality"[2] is prior to approval on the score of utility. Again, our sympathy need not be actually felt. If we know from experience that another man's misfortune (let us say) "naturally" excites sorrow "we know that if we took time to consider his situation fully and in all its parts, we should, no doubt, most sincerely sympathise with him".[3] Furthermore, there may be admiration, not mere coincidence of feeling.

When the sentiments of our companion not only coincide with our own, but lead and direct our own, when in forming them he appears to have attended to many things which we had overlooked, and to have adjusted them to all the various circumstances of their objects, we not only approve of them, but wonder and are surprised at their uncommon and unexpected acuteness and comprehensiveness.[4]

Essentially, however, the correspondence of emotions determines propriety. This correspondence, if it does not arise of its own accord, must be brought about in one or other of two principal ways. Either the spectator must overcome his indifference by an active attempt to enter into the sentiments of the person principally concerned, or that person must endeavour to depress his emotions to the pitch which the spectator feels.[5] Hence the radical distinction between the amiable virtues and the great and awful ones. A bystander may not (and indeed cannot) feel my joy precisely as I feel it, yet he may rejoice with me when I rejoice, by an easy and

---

[1] *Moral Sentiments*, p. 7. [2] *Ibid.* p. 24.
[3] *Ibid.* p. 19. [4] *Ibid.* p. 23. [5] *Ibid.* p. 30.

appropriate extension of human emotion. In the same way, he may, and should, feel with me in my sorrow. This is the amiable side of virtue (which Hume and perhaps Hutcheson had taken to be the whole of it). On the other hand, when we consider the virtue of self-command, or the Stoic attitude to the greater misfortunes, another type of virtue is looked for, and another dimension of sympathy required. What is admirable here is the restraint of the sufferer or the fact that he puts on an armour of calmness that matches the spectator's mood.

A host of examples is supplied to illustrate and enforce this doctrine—but not enough to save it. For its insufficiency leaps to the eyes.

Even if the account of the amiable part of virtue be deemed satisfactory, the account of the "awful" virtues is not. Of the man who shows exemplary self-command, Smith even says that "his firmness enables him to keep time with our indifference and insensibility",[1] and this, surely, is one of the most heartless statements ever made. *Ex hypothesi* the situation of the sufferer is one of signal and most dreadful misery. Why then should the spectators be indifferent? They are not even asked to make an imaginative effort worth calling by that name; and if they were, the effort (as all melodrama shows) would be quite singularly slight. It is the Stoic who is calm while the audience exclaims; and Smith himself supplies the antidote to this absurdity in his theory. "It is often more mortifying", he suddenly remembers, "to appear in public, under small disasters, than under great misfortunes. The first excite no sympathy: but the second, though they may excite none that approaches to the anguish of the sufferer, call forth, however, a very lively compassion."[2]

Again, if *we* admire the Stoic, many human societies do not. The man who shows in public (not callousness but) iron self-control at the loss of a beloved companion may be admired by us, but in many societies propriety is shown by outstripping a great company of professional wailers and crooners in the

[1] *Ibid.* p. 45.   [2] *Ibid.* p. 105.

violence of lamentation. This matter calls for thought. What is repressed, in the instances where Smith admires the repression, is not the emotion, but its expression. The bereaved person controls the show of his grief, and is friendly, quiet and attentive to others. He refrains from distressing them further by revealing the naked anguish of his soul. Dignity and decorum, in short, are not emotions, but the masks that men wear in public.

The same principle is plainly apparent in the highly unconvincing account that Smith gives of the repression appropriate to bodily appetites. It is indecent, he tells us, to show a wolfish appetite in company, even if we are very, very hungry; and to be sure this lack of control *is* indecent among persons who call themselves civilised and are grown men and women, exception being made of beer-drinking competitions and the like. But why? Even in the case of stark ravening hunger, a well-fed spectator has no real difficulty in putting himself, imaginatively, into the position of the starving person. What he does not like is to *see* the famished man eating without restraint. In the similar instance of sexual appetites (which Smith mentions very gingerly) the same thing holds. A thousand Anglo-Saxons (or so) seeing "life"—or flesh—at a continental cabaret exhibit a wooden decorum, and restrain even their imaginations from entering into a situation not conspicuously decorous. The reason again is that there are the strictest limits (among ourselves) to what, in public, is void of offence.

In short, Smith has dropped the substance for the lure of the shadow. If we apply his doctrines to our emotions themselves (as, according to his theory, we ought to apply them) we find his philosophy almost wholly inept. The bereaved person who felt as any casual spectator might feel at the death of *any* human being is not to be set up as a model, and the lover who felt about his mistress just what *any* man might feel about *any* woman should expect to hear from the lady, with complete propriety, just what she thought of his attitude. If again it is maintained that a lover ought to feel *only* what the average man, by a moderate exercise of a commonplace imagination, could fancy concerning his situation, it is plain that something is wrong. The lover's raptures would be standardised according to a flat traditional level. And sentiments tutored in hearsay are not the best.

The analysis of merit and of demerit (which forms the second part of Smith's system) is stated to yield a distinct species of approbation and of disapprobation. Instead of the decency or ungracefulness of any proposed action, we have now to consider "the beneficial or hurtful effects which the affection proposes or tends to produce".[1]

In short, we have now to deal with beneficence on the one hand, and with punishment on the other. Yet these, in the end, depend also upon propriety, since the first is the fruit of a proper gratitude and the second of appropriate resentment. In regard to gratitude, if we cannot sympathise with the donor (thinking him foolish or merely whimsical in his gifts) or if we cannot sympathise with the recipient (thinking him to have acquired a windfall or mere largesse) we cannot approve the transaction. And similarly of punishment. To be satisfied here we must sympathise with the resentment of the man or the society that inflicts the punishment, and agree that the performance of the person punished is one to which the punishment is proper.

So many moralists have argued that the spring and essence of justifiable punishment is a collective and restrained resentment, and such eminent authority (e.g. Sidgwick's[2]) can be obtained for the correlative statement that justice, in the core of it, is gratitude universalised, that Smith's doctrine in this matter must be admitted to be a thing of substance. Even so, however, something important is lacking in it. Supposing that "three clear Sundays after sentence" are sufficient to transform rage into righteousness, it is plain, nevertheless, that we may sympathise with duellists, exponents of the unwritten law and participators in vendettas without denying that they should be punished according to law—and again that

[1] *Moral Sentiments*, p. 110. [2] *Methods of Ethics*, Book III, chap. v.

our horror, say, at the way in which the corpse of a murdered person has been treated should be irrelevant to the jury's grim concern with some accused person. Here, if anywhere, we should attend to Abraham Tucker's comment "Were we to give a full latitude to sympathy, we should whiffle about with every wind, nor could ever keep steadily to one tenor of conduct, because we should perpetually meet with somebody or other leading us by their example to swerve from it".[1]

Certainly, we must freely admit that it is always legitimate to use an unquestionably natural principle as presumably a solid basis for a pretty extensive superstructure; but the thing should be attempted with caution. If justice is verily but gratitude universalised, we cannot at any rate decide on this ground alone whether (let us say) a fair day's work for a fair day's pay, or the communist principle that each should receive according to his needs[2] (out of gratitude for his companionship) is the proper expression of this principle, or again whether flogging or capital punishment are legitimate forms of resentful action and, if so, when and for what offences. If, on the other hand, these primary roots of gratitude or of resentment require unlimited nourishment from other sources in order to be even approximately justifiable, we are compelled, like Hume, to pay at least as much attention to the artificial as to the primitive elements in this affair. It is not to be contended that any conceivable intelligence could deduce the proper social procedure from any such basis as Smith's.

Indeed, at the very beginning of this part of his argument, Smith appeals to the sentiments of "any reasonable man"[3] when his argument ought to refer to "every sympathetic breast"; and when he goes on to explain that "nature has implanted in the human breast that consciousness of ill-desert, those terrors of merited punishment which attend upon its

[1] *The Light of Nature*: Human Nature, chap. xix.
[2] Cf. Godwin, *Political Justice*, Book viii, chap. i. "To whom does any article of property, suppose a loaf of bread, justly belong? To him who wants it, or to whom the possession of it will be the most beneficial."
[3] *Moral Sentiments*, p. 114.

violation, as the great safeguards of the association of mankind, to protect the weak, to curb the violent and to chastise the guilty"[1] we may decline to be impressed. But let us proceed. Smith admits that we may have to go against the dictates of humanity in our punishments[2] (as in the penalty for the sentry who sleeps at his post), and that very often actual sympathisers with the hangman are not to be found. Surely, again, it is a very telling admission when he informs us that

> whether the person who has received the benefit conceives gratitude or not, cannot, it is evident, in any degree alter our sentiments with regard to the merit of him who has bestowed it. No actual correspondence of sentiments, therefore, is here required. It is sufficient that if he was grateful, they would correspond; and our sense of merit is often founded upon one of those illusive sympathies, by which, when we bring home to ourselves the case of another, we are often affected in a manner in which the person principally concerned is incapable of being affected.[3]

Indeed, even in the province of sympathy, it is ideal not actual sympathy that prompts the theory, the sympathy that *would* occur "if the sentiments of mankind were either altogether candid and equitable, or even perfectly consistent with themselves".[4]

If this is not downright inconsistency it is at least very like it. For if sympathy must be controlled by candour and equity, how can these, in their turn, be based upon sympathy? The same inconsistency, however, is repeated and made even more prominent in the analysis of conscience and of the sense of duty which forms the third part of Smith's book.

The beginning of his argument in this place, to be sure, is consistent enough. A solitary being, we are told, could no more think of the propriety of his sentiments than (without a mirror?) of the beauty of his own face. "Bring him into society, and he is immediately provided with the mirror which he wanted before."[5] "Our first moral criticisms are directed upon...other people....But we soon learn that others are

---

[1] *Ibid.* p. 148.   [2] *Ibid.* p. 152.   [3] *Ibid.* p. 131 n.
[4] *Ibid.* pp. 189 *sq.*   [5] *Ibid.* p. 199.

equally frank with regard to our own."[1] In some such way as this (although children perhaps might be inclined to reverse the last piece of reasoning) it is not unreasonable to regard collective opinion as determining our standards or as a midwife to bring the impartial spectator to the birth. It may even be legitimate to represent the conscientious man as a divided creature partly judge and partly, in the Scots phrase, panel.[2] Accountability does imply this psychological partition and the necessity for attempting to see ourselves as others see us.

According to Smith's own statements, however, it is speedily plain that this public standpoint does not carry us nearly far enough. "We address ourselves to individuals", he says, "and for some time fondly pursue the impossible and absurd project of gaining the good will and approbation of everybody. We are soon taught by experience, however, that this universal approbation is altogether unattainable."[3] Therefore "We conceive ourselves as acting in the presence of a person quite candid and equitable, of one who has no particular relation either to ourselves or to those whose interests are affected by our conduct, who is neither father nor brother nor friend either to them or to us but is merely a man in general, an impartial spectator who considers our conduct with the same indifference with which we regard that of other people."[4] "This inmate of the breast, this abstract man, this representative of mankind and substitute of the Deity"[5] has in the end supreme authority, and we are even told that "compared with this final decision the sentiments of all mankind, although not altogether indifferent, appear to be but of small moment".[6]

In short, that very Reason which had been driven out with a pitch-fork is now restored with literally divine honours. "Reason, principle, conscience, the inhabitant of the breast, the man within, the great judge and arbiter of our conduct"[7] *emerges*, as the moderns say, from a type of process from which the phenomenon could not conceivably be deduced. And

---

[1] *Moral Sentiments*, p. 201.   [2] *Ibid.* pp. 203 *sq.*   [3] *Ibid.* p. 207.
[4] *Ibid.* pp. 207 *sq.*   [5] *Ibid.* p. 208.
[6] *Ibid.* p. 209.   [7] *Ibid.* p. 213.

THE BRITISH MORALISTS

Reason's sovereignty is conceded in a fashion as handsome as Butler's.

> Love does not judge of resentment nor resentment of love. Those two passions may be opposite to one another, but cannot, with any propriety, be said to approve or disapprove of one another. But it is the peculiar office of those faculties now under our consideration to judge, to bestow censure or applause upon all the other principles of our nature.[1]

Evidently the wheel has turned full circle, and a rationalist, lying in wait for his adversaries and mindful of the adage *fas est et ab hoste doceri* could not look for more heartening munitions. It is useless to plead that respectability (which, at the best, is all Smith's doctrine could give us) might be attained by custom and fashion rather than properly by reason. Smith himself bars the way. In his considered opinion fashion is to be regarded as a cause of *irregularity* in manners,[2] a petty tyrant that for a little space lords it over nature. Something far more efficacious is needed in the present affair.[3]

§ 6. *Price and Reid*

The first edition of Richard Price's *Review of the Principal Questions in Morals* appeared in 1757—that is to say, two years before Smith's *Moral Sentiments*, and seven years before Reid's *Inquiry*. The book, as we might expect, is less urbane and more puritan (if we may call it so) than the other works we have been considering in this chapter, and it is also learned and more academic. Its learning, however, is strictly subordinated to the march of its argument. Criticisms of Hutcheson, Locke and Hume, encomia upon Butler,[4] improvements upon portions of Cudworth's arguments,[4] gentle corrections of Balguy[4] and agreement with Cumberland's editor rather than with Cumberland himself[4]—all take their place as the context indicates. In this respect Price is better than Reid whose learning was apt to run away with him, but in most other respects they are very similar. Although they

[1] *Ibid.* p. 235.   [2] *Ibid.* pp. 291 *sqq.*   [3] *Ibid.* p. 320.
[4] *Review* (3rd edn. 1787), e.g. pp. 195, 147, 98, 187.

arrived at their conclusions independently, each, as time went on, made his bow to the other. Dr Reid, in his later work, found himself "apt to think with Dr Price",[1] and Dr Price, in the third edition of his book finds in Dr Reid "a writer of deep reflexion".[2]

Proceeding directly to the moral problem in its strictest sense, Price sets about enquiring "whether right and wrong are real characters of actions or only qualities of our minds, whether, in short, they denote what actions are, or only sensations derived from the particular frame and structure of our natures".[3] His answer is that moral ideas are derived from the *understanding*. For, by their means, we discern and distinguish what is real from what is only apparent, we view and compare the objects of all the senses as no single particular sense can even attempt to do, and we rise to general ideas or universals (as also to abstract ideas)[4] where sense is incapable of following.[5] A criticism of Mr Locke's "way of ideas", the burden of the criticism being the familiar doctrine of later philosophers that ideas of sense cannot furnish those conceptions of space, cause, or matter which are fundamental to Lockian and other conceptions of the material world, shows the range and potency of these general arguments.

The intellectual ideas at the basis of morals, Price goes on to say, are "simple ideas" and must therefore be ascribed to "some power of *immediate* perception in the human mind".[6] Hutcheson and others confounded this immediacy and ultimacy with the frank underivative character of sensation; but intuition, "by which I mean the mind's survey of its own ideas, and the relations between them and the notice it takes of what is, or is not, true and false, consistent and inconsistent, possible and impossible in the natures of things",[7] is the true and ultimate mentor. No one can deny that this *may* be so, or that this answer seems very rational to common sense. "Is there nothing truly wrong in the absolute and eternal misery

---

[1] *Active Powers*, Hamilton's *Reid*, p. 581.
[2] *Review*, p. 55.   [3] *Ibid.* pp. 11 *sq.*   [4] *Ibid.* p. 37.
[5] *Ibid.* pp. 18 *sq.*   [6] *Ibid.* pp. 57 *sq.*   [7] *Ibid.* p. 158.

of an innocent being?"[1] "Is there a greater absurdity than to suppose that the moral rectitude of an action is nothing absolute and unvarying?"[2] *Some* character certainly belongs to all actions. "This may be that some of them are right, others wrong."[3] And therefore (it would seem) we are entitled to conclude forthwith (as Cudworth and other Cambridge Platonists did) that since moral essences *are* essences, morality must be eternal and immutable.

The beauty of virtue, again, need not be taken to be *only* a pleasing emotion, since this pleasing emotion may signify and seal some congruity in the nature of things.[4] For beauty, though we cannot call it knowledge, occurs only in knowledgeable natures, being absent from the brutes; and if the high and rare pleasure which is beauty is truly unity in variety, the congruity between aesthete and aesthetic object implies at least the easy and comprehensive sweep of our minds, proportion or symmetry in the things we call beautiful, and, in a word, some *aptness* to charm us.

Similarly there may be rationality in desire. If we say that "happiness is better than misery" we do say something about what is reasonable in our preferences and "a mind that should think happiness not to be better than misery would mistake as grossly as a mind that should believe the whole not to be greater than a part".[5] The love and desire of happiness are both natural and reasonable; and in the same way "intelligence lays the foundation of fame and honour".[6] The analysis of merit, too, demands the same general assumption. "When we say a man deserves well we mean that his character is such that we approve of showing him favour. Reason determines at once that he *ought* to be the better for his virtue." "The virtuous person, every one would think, is *worthy* of the benefit, the other *unworthy*."[7] This also is a rational intuition.

Such doctrines conform wholly with religion, for truth and intelligibility, not arbitrary good pleasure, are the marks of

---

[1] *Ibid.* p. 70.   [2] *Ibid.* pp. 66 *sq.*   [3] *Ibid.* p. 70.
[4] *Ibid.* pp. 90 *sq.*   [5] *Ibid.* p. 112.   [6] *Ibid.* p. 115.
[7] *Ibid.* pp. 126 *sq.*

deity. Indeed, "infinite truth supposes and infers the existence of one infinite essence as its substratum and but one".[1] They also afford the only proper basis of obligation. "Obligation to action and rightness of action are plainly coincident and identical."[2] To be sure "it is not exactly the same to say it is our duty to do a thing and to say we approve of doing it. The one is the quality of the action, the other the *discernment* of that quality".[3] Nevertheless, rectitude "not only directs, but binds all, as far as it is perceived".[4] "When we are conscious that an action is fit to be done, or that it ought to be done, it is not conceivable that we can remain uninfluenced or want a motive to action."[5] "The intellectual nature is its own law. It has within itself a spring and guide of action which it cannot suppress or reject. Rectitude is itself an end, an ultimate end, an end superior to all other ends, governing, directing and limiting them, and whose existence and influence depend on nothing arbitrary."[6] Or as Price otherwise puts the point, "Understanding is, in the nature of it before will, knowledge before power, it being necessary that every intelligent agent, in exerting his power, should know what he does, or design some effect which he understands to be possible".[7]

It is frequently supposed that the British moralists of the eighteenth century, by the very act of their becoming, as we should say, psychological, could not retain the scientific rigour of an earlier period; and certainly in so far as Price retains the conceptions of his opponents, regarding sense and emotion as animal and blind, and believing reason, if it could show itself in its purity, to be something divine and coming from out of doors, he is bound to use assertion rather than argument when he maintains that our mixed human nature is, after all, not really mixed, but governed and everywhere permeated by a clear intellectual essence. In the last analysis, however, what Price had to show, and what (with rather unpliable assump-

---

[1] *Review*, p. 142.   [2] *Ibid*. p. 170.   [3] *Ibid*. p. 191.
[4] *Ibid*. p. 176.   [5] *Ibid*. p. 315.   [6] *Ibid*. p. 317.
[7] *Ibid*. p. 247.

tions and an obvious confusion between what is "natural" and what is clear) he went a long way towards suggesting, is the simple but profound reflection that the human psyche, when it achieves the dignity of a rational creature, achieves this dignity with the *whole* soul. However "mixed" we may be, we do not, in fact, combine unaltered brutal passions or inflexibly brutish instincts with a foreign (if sublime) intelligence, still less with an intelligence that is merely speculative. At the intellectual level there is a *general* psychic transformation, and this organisation, in action, desire and pleasure as well as in the things of thought, is not simply brutish, but profoundly different. To argue directly from these premises to the autonomy of ethics "self-valid and self-originated"[1] is at the best very hasty; and on any definition (wide or narrow) of the good in conduct and human life there is always far more to be shown than simply that our lives have conformed, of their own motion, to some intellectual pattern. Yet it is much (and more than many psychologies) to have shown even this.

Reid's account of Taste in his *Intellectual Powers*, and his account of Morals in his *Active Powers* owe something, no doubt, to his general philosophy, that is to say, to his tireless and persistent denial of the "modern" view that Ideas or Images of things in the mind are the only objects of thought. "I think there is hardly anything that can be called *mine* in the philosophy of the mind which does not follow with ease from the detection of this prejudice",[2] we find him writing to Dr Gregory in 1790 when his work was over and his faculties unimpaired. The nature of what he took to be his discovery, however, necessitated an independent revision of the main questions in philosophy; and this is what we find in the present instance.

Even what we call the *sense* of taste (or of relish), he argues, is something more than a mental event.[3] There is a sensation in my mind when I taste any sapid body, but there is also a

[1] *Review*, p. 179. [2] Hamilton's *Reid*, p. 22.
[3] *Ibid.* p. 490.

belief or judgment on my part that there is some corresponding quality in the physical thing that is tasted. This physical property may indeed be occult, since we do not know what it is, but we do not doubt its existence.

The same is true of Taste in the metaphorical sense which Shaftesbury, and those who learnt from him, had in mind. "When a man pronounces a poem or a palace to be beautiful, he affirms something of that poem or that palace; and every affirmation or denial expresses judgment."[1] This quality of beauty in the thing is also sometimes occult to us. For we know too little. But often it is more enlightened. When the judgment is enlightened, we apprehend some real excellence in the thing, and this is the quality of its beauty. Consequently there are at least as many species of beauty as there are discernible species of real excellence.

Analysis of the objects of aesthetic Taste supports this conclusion. Is it freshness and novelty that appeal to us? Then this novelty is a temporal relation between mind and thing, not in any way a mental sensation. Is it grandeur? The sublime is not (as Burke thought) only a product of dread. It is grave and solemn because the emotions appropriate to it are determined by a certain exalted excellence or perfection. In the *Iliad*, for example, it is Hector, or Achilles and the other great personages, human or divine, that are sublime—or else the conceptions in the mind of Homer.[2] Is it beauty? We have reason to believe, not only that the beauties we see in nature are real and not fanciful but that there are thousands of other beauties which our faculties are too dull to perceive.[3] Even "occult" beauty arises from perfection although in an oblique fashion. "The only perfection of dead matter is its being by its various forms and qualities so admirably fitted for the purposes of animal life and chiefly that of man."[4] This congruence with our vital faculties *is* the "occult" quality. Musical harmony is the way in which sounds are amicable and friendly to us—concordant not quarrelsome

---

[1] Hamilton's *Reid*, p. 492. [2] *Ibid.* p. 496.
[3] *Ibid.* p. 500. [4] *Ibid.* p. 503.

voices.[1] And so of the beauty of the human form in male or female:

> For contemplation he and valour formed,
> For softness she and sweet attractive grace.

Beauty, in short, is not irrational; for the emotions pertaining to it are appropriate to real excellence and may often be seen to depend upon some perfection in beautiful things. The same truth is still more evident when we turn to moral worth, and consider either of the two fundamental questions arising from it, to wit, the question what is good for us upon the whole and the question what appears to be our duty.

Regarding the former "whatever makes a man more happy or more perfect is good and is an object of desire as soon as we are capable of forming the conception of it".[2] While every animal and every child pursues goods or enjoyments "of short duration and soon forgot", the conception of our good on the whole "is one of the most general and abstract notions we form".[3] Yet once it is formed, it becomes a leading or governing principle. "To pursue what is good upon the whole, and to avoid what is ill upon the whole, is a rational principle of action grounded upon our constitution as reasonable creatures."[4]

"Moral conduct", however, "is the business of every man; and therefore the knowledge of it ought to be within the reach of all."[5] The general and abstract notion of good on the whole is much too puzzling to fulfil this requirement. "Men stand in need of a sharper monitor to their duty than a dubious view of distant good."[6] This monitor is our regard for duty itself. "Men of rank call it honour....The vulgar call it... conscience. Philosophers have given it the name of the moral sense."[7]

The notion of duty, Reid thinks, is "too simple to permit of a logical definition",[8] though it may be described in several different ways. Nevertheless it is very well understood.

[1] *Ibid.* p. 504.
[2] *Ibid.* p. 580.
[3] *Ibid.*
[4] *Ibid.* p. 581.
[5] *Ibid.* p. 594.
[6] *Ibid.* p. 584.
[7] *Ibid.* p. 587.
[8] *Ibid.*

Accordingly, Reid arrives at the conclusion that, "by an original power of the mind when we come to years of understanding and reflection we not only have the notions of right and wrong in conduct, but perceive certain things to be right, and others to be wrong".[1]

This conclusion, however, is not, as so many have supposed, a dogmatic assertion of Presbyterian morality under the nominal aegis of nature and common sense. Reid distinguishes the general axioms of morals from particular derivative maxims—the Golden Rule, for example, from an injunction to monogamy.[2] He insists that "ripeness of judgment" is required for all moral intuitions. "I am far from thinking instruction in morals unnecessary. Men may, to the end of life, be ignorant of self-evident truths. They may, to the end of life, entertain gross absurdities."[3] Again, although conscience, that pragmatical faculty, has, when men reach maturity, the office of guiding life and of showing what is good, what bad, and what indifferent in human conduct, Reid never maintains that this office is simple. "He must indeed be a great stranger to his own heart, and to the state of human nature, who does not see that he has need of all the aid which his situation affords him, in order to know how he ought to act in many cases that occur."[4] And although Reid, unlike the authors we have considered in the greater part of this chapter, separates moral rectitude very sharply from other laudable qualities (suppose good breeding) he at least gives reasons for his opinion.[5]

One of his favourite arguments—the "dictionary argument" we may call it—certainly seems overstated. It may, indeed, be true that "the meaning of a common word is not to be ascertained by philosophical theory, but by common usage",[6] and it is certainly true that the plain man, although he may be unable to defend his use of words, commonly means something intelligible by them. A certain weight should therefore be attached to the fact that language uses "good" and

---

[1] Hamilton's *Reid*, p. 589.   [2] *Ibid.* pp. 590 *sq.*, cf. 637 *sqq.*
[3] *Ibid.* p. 641.   [4] *Ibid.* p. 596.   [5] *Ibid.* p. 652.   [6] *Ibid.* p. 674.

"worth" as logical predicates qualifying logical substantives directly and immediately, but it is monstrous to assert that "an opinion, which makes the language of all ages and nations, upon this subject, to be improper, contrary to all rules of language, and fit to be discarded, needs no other refutation".[1]

Unlike Price, Reid did not object to the use of the phrases "moral sense" or "moral sentiment" to describe the character of moral intuition. In his view "Philosophers" (i.e. those who *of late* have followed the "new way of ideas") "have degraded the senses too much, and deprived them of the most important part of their office".[2] We *judge* by sense as well as feel; we rely on it as a vehicle of belief, and never use it without believing; and therefore even a sense may rise to first principles without absurdity. As for the term "sentiment", this, "in the English language, never, as I conceive, signifies mere feeling, but judgment accompanied with feeling".[3]

Language apart, however, there is no essential difference between the intuitionism of these two doctors of divinity. Like Price, Reid holds that "our moral judgments are not like those we form in speculative matters, dry and unaffecting, but, from their nature, are necessarily accompanied with affections and feelings".[4] Similarly he maintains "that esteem and benevolent regard, not only accompany real worth by the constitution of our nature, but are perceived to be really and properly due to it".[5] Reid also maintains that there is an aesthetic quality in esteem or regard. "The view of a vicious character, like that of an ugly and deformed object, is disagreeable. It gives disgust and abhorrence."[6]

---

[1] *Ibid.* pp. 675 *sq.*   [2] *Ibid.* p. 590.

[3] *Ibid.* p. 674. Cf. Buffon's *Essai d'arithmétique morale*, "Le sentiment n'est en général qu'un raisonnement implicite moins clair, mais souvent plus fin et toujours plus sûr, que le produit direct de la raison". Quoted by Edgeworth, *Mathematical Psychics*, p. 77.

[4] *Ibid.* p. 592.   [5] *Ibid.*   [6] *Ibid.* p. 593.

CHAPTER VII

THE OBJECTIVITY OF VALUES

§ 1. *Preliminary*

HITHERTO I have avoided those pestilent adjectives "objective" and "subjective" so far as I could, although sometimes they were not to be evaded. And now we must face them squarely, because the present stage of the argument plainly requires us to do so. May approval be valid or rational? Is there ever a right and a wrong in it, either in aesthetics, or in morals, or in some other department of value? These are the questions which have occupied us, now, for a great many pages. An affirmative answer implies a certain kind of objectivity; and even a negative answer does not sufficiently define the kind and degree of subjectivity which it permits or, perhaps, indicates.

It seems best, therefore, to attempt a general survey of this entire problem.

§ 2. *Values and physical objects*

One sense of the term "objective", as appears in the phrase "the objective world", is neither more nor less than "characterising physical existence". If we assume further (as common opinion does) that physical things may exist without any mind to know or to prize them, we should have to maintain that objective value, in this sense of "objective", may be radically and utterly non-mental.

Manifestly, not every value could conceivably be of this kind. For there *are* mental values, such as the values of knowledge or of pleasure or of human affection. And these values, very likely, are by far the greatest we have to do with. Nevertheless, even if purely physical values must in any case be of quite minor importance, it is worth while asking whether

CH. VII] THE OBJECTIVITY OF VALUES

there is either contradiction or absurdity in supposing that there might be some such values.

It is generally agreed, of course—indeed, as we have seen, it is agreed rather too readily—that physical things may be the means or instruments of values. Here, however, the rejoinder seems peculiarly easy. Physical things themselves (we are told) are *not* objectively valuable, but they *are* the causes of valuable effects in something not themselves. To avoid repetition we may let this rejoinder pass.

It is agreed, again, that "perfection" in many of its senses might pertain to (non-mental) physical existence. Completeness, totality, quantity of existence and the like might characterise physical things as definitely and as clearly as they could conceivably characterise anything else. The obvious rejoinder, however, that perfection in these senses need not be, properly speaking, a value at all (or again that it may be a value only when some mind rejoices in it) is also, perhaps, sufficient.

To be sure, there is a genuine difficulty here regarding, say, proportion in the objects called beautiful, or regarding the ideal of "nature" in ethics. The "golden section" and other formal proportions may be as obviously physical as the proportion of oil to vinegar in a salad, and it is quite beyond doubt that there is *some* correspondence between formal physical proportion and aesthetic value. While Leibniz or Reid, however, might be taken to have meant that the experience called charm really attests an authentic value (which is form or proportion) in charming objects, it may be more prudent, like Hume,[1] to admit the correspondence but to deny that physical proportion itself is a value.

Similarly, in the sphere of ethics, while a great many moralists maintain that moral values would be moral madness if the voice of duty cried in the wilderness—or, in other words, if the nature of things did not respond to moral aspiration—they would also probably hold that the "nature" to which rational morality must conform is spiritual and not "matter"

[1] *Essays*, Part I, xxiii, "Of the Standard of Taste".

(or despiritualised inertia), and they would argue that it is the soul of nature and not its body which shows forth the moral standard.

So probably it is best to refrain from disputing these explanations.

On the other hand, as has been abundantly shown, there is at least one species of value which might as readily be physical as mental. This class consists of the values of natural election. Filings are no more indifferent to magnets than hungry men are to loaves. Therefore, once more to avoid repetition of what has already been sufficiently discussed, we must admit the existence of at least one variety of "values" which may be purely physical.

§ 3. *The values of sensible appearance*

We saw in an earlier chapter that beauty, if it resides in things at all, resides in the shows of them, and chiefly in their sensible shows, although there may also be beauty in the intellectual show of an argument, or of a demonstration in geometry, or of metaphysical poetry. We also saw that this circumstance sometimes entails a certain qualification of the sense in which proportion characterises physical objects in a way that is relevant to aesthetic theory.

A question much more sericus, however, is further implied. Are the shows of things, and particularly their sensible shows, the things themselves (revealed partially and superficially but authentically) or are they altogether different from the things, a kind of veil or atmosphere around or about the things but not *of* them?

This question is peculiarly urgent in the present enquiry because colour and sound, to mention no other instances, do not enter into the definition of physical objects as defined by classical physics, and have frequently been held to be something with which our minds invest physical things instead of a character of physical things themselves. And colour, plainly, is a principal part of the show which is natural beauty (or,

THE OBJECTIVITY OF VALUES

again, of the beauty of paintings), while sound is the whole of the show which is beautiful music.

Without entering into details it may fairly be stated, I think, that competent opinion to-day is divided upon the question of fact that presents itself in these instances. For some good authorities maintain that colour and sound may be properties of physical objects, and others deny that they can. This being so, it is advisable to argue hypothetically, and consider the relevant consequences of these alternative opinions.

If colour, sound and similar properties really do belong to physical things, it seems unnecessary to deny that beauty may also exist in the things themselves. If so, many, though not all, beauties (not, for instance, most of the beauties of poetry) would be "objective" in the sense of being non-mental. And beauties, we say, are values. It might, however, be contended, and perhaps with justice, that such beauties are not values unless and until they appeal to a mind.

If, on the other hand, these sensible shows cannot literally be found in physical things, but are caused in part by the play of our minds upon the things, it follows that the shows are in part mentally conditioned. Since the shows could not exist apart from any mind, their beauty also could not so exist. On the other hand, if this statement were taken to mean, quite simply, that these sensible shows are, in part, *produced* by our minds, such products, although they have mental causes, need not contain any mental constituents or properties. Even if smells and colours are partially manufactured by our minds, we do not commonly think that minds have the properties of odours or of colours, i.e. that *minds* are red, or mauve, or fragrant.

According to this alternative hypothesis, therefore (interpreted as above), we ought to hold that the beauty of such sensible shows resides neither in minds nor in physical objects, but in a certain joint-product of both (which itself is neither mental nor physical). The second alternative, therefore, would not, any more than the first, properly suggest that beauty resides in the mind of the beholder. And the inference concerning the value of such beauty would be the same on either alternative.

Since, in classical philosophy, our physical emotions were always taken to be of the same order as our physical sensations, it seems plain that the argument we have just considered might cut pretty deep. I do not propose, however, to say any more about it, being content to suggest to the reader that it is at least highly disputable whether certain beauties may not be strictly non-mental. If so, a possible, although not a necessary inference is that their values may be non-mental also.

§ 4. *The objectivity of mental facts*

It is time, however, to turn to facts which certainly are mental. For, as we have seen, many, indeed most, of the qualities we esteem are indubitably mental—for example, courage, generosity, love and much else that is spiritual.

All mental facts are, in one sense, "subjective" because they are states or phases of some self, subject or ego. In another, and in a much more important sense, however, they are "objective", because they really are facts which may be known through observation, judgment, inference and other such processes. If, for example, we came to know that Jones's depression at the fall in his railway stock lasted fully half an hour after he took up the morning's newspaper we should be giving an objective description of Jones's (subjective) depression, comparable in every significant respect with any similar statement about physical things—for example, with the statement that the newspaper was in Jones's hands for half an hour. In other words, our thoughts may refer to minds or other thoughts in the same fundamental way as they may refer to things that are not minds at all. In every such instance there is reference to an object, and every property so referred to is, in the same sense and for the same reason, an objective property.

There should be neither hesitation nor dubiety on this

matter, for it is sun-clear. And when we esteem anyone, we certainly appear to ascribe value to him. Accordingly, the important question is whether when we ascribe value, say, to a generous impulse, the value *characterises* the impulse in the same sense as its duration, or its intensity, or any other such property does.

Before addressing ourselves, however, to this (which is the critical) question, it is convenient to consider yet another ambiguity in the vulgar employment of the term "subjective".

§ 5. *"Subjective" variations*

When any property appears to vary with the observer (i.e. with the observing subject) and not on its own account, we usually call it "subjective". Thus we are inclined to say that sounds are "subjective" because the same blast from the horn of a motor car normally appears of different pitch to observers at different distances, and we contrast all such variations with variations *in the physical object*, such as a fickle wind or a fitful flame.

As we have noted already, the inference, in all such cases, may be more doubtful than it seems. Let us suppose, however, that it is not doubtful at all, and examine the consequences for our present subject.

Clearly, what we call taste, or pleasure, or likings and dislikings, vary with respect to their conditions even more than our experience of colour or of sound. Some people are fond of Brussels sprouts, and others consider them odious little vegetables. Some people admire Tennyson's poems or the late Mr Bryan's oratory, and others abominate them. Accordingly, it would seem very unlikely that any single property in the things which, as we say, we relish or dislike corresponds to the variable and capricious pleasure which we take in them.

Yet, after all, what is it that is liked when one man likes Brussels sprouts and another man detests them? The proof is not in the vegetables themselves, but in the character of our experience when we eat them. One man, in eating them, has an experience which he relishes. Another man has an experience which he dislikes. Even if these experiences have something, perhaps a good deal, in common, the presumption surely is that the experiences, taken as a whole, are significantly *different* in the two cases. If the two men really had the same experience, is it not overwhelmingly probable that they would agree in their likings and dislikings? And is there not a certain likelihood that they would agree about the *value*, which, after critical reflection, each would attach to the common experience?

In short, the same thing, very often, may affect different people differently. And different affections have no doubt different values. But this is no proof that the same affection can have different values.

Strenuously pursued, these considerations imply very significant consequences. It is not merely a question of our affections, but of the actual objects to which, or in the light of which, values are actually assigned. Consider, for instance, our appreciation of poetry. The rhythm and cadence of a poem, the images it suggests, the nuances of its theme, the associations of much of its diction—all these and much more are relevant to our aesthetic approbation. Is it even remotely plausible to hold that different readers, all of whom are stimulated by what we call the same black marks upon the same white paper, catch the same rhythm, the same associations, the same images? Is not each of them appreciating, or depreciating, something different? If they are, they are *not* setting a different value upon the same thing.

The same is true of moral values. There could hardly be a greater difference than the conduct and ideals, say, of Torquemada regarding toleration, and the conduct and ideals of Spinoza. And yet we may reasonably ask whether the two were thinking of the same thing. Torquemada saw, as he supposed, the confusion and impotence of Spain through an unholy alliance between Christians and infidels for the purposes of mere commercial gain. The remedy, as he saw it, was to unite Church and State by force. Hence the *auto-da-fé*,

THE OBJECTIVITY OF VALUES

the prohibition laid upon Christians to supply any Jew with even the necessaries of life—and the conquest of the Moors. What was nationality to Spinoza, whose ancestors had been driven into exile from this very Spain? And what could he think of institutional religion, when this exiled community had expelled him with contumely from their own synagogue for holding what he could not but believe? Surely he and Torquemada thought of very different things.

I do not suggest that the whole of the difference in any such instance should be ascribed to some difference in the objects actually before the mind. If Torquemada had seen and understood all that Spinoza saw and understood it is probable that the two would still have assigned quite different values to nationality and to freedom of thought. If so, Spinoza would have been more nearly right than Torquemada, and might be shown by argument to have been so. All that I mean is that the difference in the objects which are actually approved explains, in most of us, a great part of our most crucial ethical differences.

And it is well for us that it should be so. If ethical distinctions, concerning the same things, were really a jumble of ultimate differences, then although, in the abstract, some opinions might be ultimately right and others ultimately wrong, we might well despair of even attempting to discriminate between the right and the wrong opinions. It is therefore comforting to observe that any really careful enquiry into such matters, for example Dr Westermarck's,[1] clearly shows a substantial agreement, and the possibility, at least, of authentic development, in these affairs. Hospitality, care of children, fidelity, a certain respect for life and liberty—in short all the major virtues have been practised, as we should say conscientiously, by every people at every time, imperfectly, to be sure, but very manifestly. What has to be set on the other side, the different rules concerning what constitutes incest or adultery, the exposure, for economic reasons, of defective children or of supposedly superfluous female

[1] *The Origin and Development of the Moral Ideas.*

infants, the judicial removal of the aged and infirm in certain primitive communities, and the like—all these are vastly important. But they are of minor importance in comparison with man's general agreement concerning what the virtues essentially are.

Indeed, I think it may well be doubted whether our approbation of our minds, of their states, and of objects in so far as we see and understand them—in technical language, of objects *as presented*—is actually more variable than any other employment of our minds concerning ourselves, their states or presented objects. Even the fundamentals of mathematics or of physics have been disputed quite as fiercely as the fundamentals of value.

§ 6. *Recessive and non-recessive approval*

We may now return to the essential problem which we reached at the end of § 5, and we may state the issue thus: In common speech we say both that a primrose is yellow, and that love is valuable, good, or excellent. In the first case we mean (I am supposing a naïve belief in the authenticity of perception) that the primrose really has the characteristic "yellow". May we, or cannot we hold, in the second instance also, that we really mean to assert that love has the character of value?

In examining this problem it will be convenient to employ a pair of terms which I have borrowed from Meinong's *Grundlegung*,[1] although I myself must be responsible for the interpretation I am about to put upon them. The terms in question are "recessive" and "non-recessive", and their meaning is easily explained. A non-recessive judgment is a straightforward judgment whose subject is just what it is stated to be. In a recessive judgment, on the other hand, the apparent or nominal subject is, in fact, a deputy, and the characteristics which, *prima facie*, we assign to it might be seen, if we thought more clearly, to be really assigned to something else—not to the deputy but to its constituency.

[1] p. 116.

THE OBJECTIVITY OF VALUES

What philosophers usually mean when they say that values are "subjective" is that values are *recessive* in a certain way. Thus, they say, an aurora borealis cannot really be beautiful in the same sense as it is bright. What is truly meant, although not what is said, in any such statement, is that the beholder, in seeing the northern lights, also experiences a lively titillation or vivid delight. Beauty therefore is in the beholder and applies only recessively to nature. In the same way, when we admire a mother's devotion or have moral respect for Luther's courage at Worms, we are told that neither the mother nor Luther is really esteemed, but that the esteem expresses a certain condition of emotion on the part of the persons who feel the esteem when they contemplate the mother or Luther. In our own case, to be sure, the matter is a little more subtle, but not at all different in its principle. Suppose that we do ascribe value to our own state of love, or reverence ourselves as lovers. In that case also the excellence, according to this doctrine, is not in the love, but is attached to, or accompanies, our admiring contemplation of our love.

It is possible, of course, that if we tracked a recessive judgment to its recesses we should run upon a non-recessive judgment, and this would be the natural interpretation of the argument I have just stated. If beauty, we say, is not in the aurora, it must be somewhere, and therefore it is in the beholder's mind. That is to say, the beholder is the genuine or non-recessive subject of the judgment, although grammar speaks recessively of the aurora.

In this case the effect of the argument would be to limit the number and probably the kind of subjects to which value could be ascribed directly or non-recessively; but to *affirm*, and not to deny, that there are certain subjects which do, non-recessively, possess the character of value. For whenever we find the non-recessive subject of a recessive statement, and ascribe value to *it*, that particular subject must literally *be* valuable.

It may be doubted, however, whether this is often meant, for, if it were, we should have reached a condition of extreme paradox. Let us consider the argument. Beauty is not in the aurora. Therefore it is in the beholder's mind. Therefore the beholder's mind is beautiful. A few philosophers, perhaps, really mean to say this. The aurora, they think, is not beautiful and the beholder's ideas are. In that case something actually *is* beautiful, viz. the beholder's ideas. But most philosophers, I am confident, really mean something quite different. They do not believe that *anything* is (non-recessively) beautiful, not even the beholder's mind; and they do not believe that *anything* has moral value (non-recessively), not even Luther's conscience.

In a word, their view is that *nothing* has value non-recessively. The aurora itself, they say, is not beautiful; the beholder's mind is not beautiful and the complex object "the-aurora-in-relation-to-the-beholder's-mind" is not beautiful either. In other words, nothing *is* beautiful in the non-recessive sense. When we say anything is beautiful we mean that a certain kind of admiration accompanies our thoughts of the thing. The admiration itself is not beautiful, but beauty is a way of saying that the admiration occurs.

Indeed, I think we may say that theories of this order are ultra-recessive because, after analysis, the nominal subject of which beauty (or some other value) is ostensibly the predicate recedes altogether. Such theories also are "subjective" because the critical element in their analysis of value is (not only mental but) a feature of the process of valuation.

§ 7. *The insufficiency of ultra-recessive theories*

These ultra-recessive theories may certainly be internally consistent. The simplest form of them, which we have already encountered pretty often, states that what we call a value really expresses the circumstance that *we* are in an agreeable condition. And this theory, at a price, may be consistently maintained. The price, however, is prohibitive in the simpler forms of the theory; for it implies a final and intransigent denial of all the more significant claims that are contained in dignity or excellence, nobility or esteem. Perceiving this, all

THE OBJECTIVITY OF VALUES

who have given themselves seriously to the analysis of approval, from Shaftesbury to Meinong, have attempted so to interpret the feelings and sentiments implied in the ultra-recessive theory as to yield a conditional and qualified but genuine acceptance of those claims without which the values of aesthetics, or ethics, or religious devotion would be the sorriest sort of sham. These qualified and sophisticated theories are, of course, less flagrantly insufficient than the simpler ones, but, as the last chapter showed, they *are* insufficient, and have to shelter themselves, in the end, under the aegis of the "impartial spectator" or of some other picturesque nonentity. What is more, the mere consistency of the theories, when they are stretched so far as to include what they have to include, partakes of the character of a dubious adventure.

The object of the last chapter was to show that the best of such theories, left to themselves, achieve their own undoing. If this object was achieved, no more need be said. As an added precaution, however, it may be well briefly to recount the reasons which reveal the inadequacy of these theories.

Since the dignity of great tragedy and of the sublime, or again the nobility of many moral values and of the pursuit of truth cannot be described as "agreeable" without forfeiting every pretence to accuracy, it is clear that something less wantonly trivial must be proposed; and the most promising candidates for the position would appear to be value-feelings for the general class, aesthetic emotions for beauty, and conscience (interpreted as an emotion) for moral values.

I shall not even enquire whether there is a distinct class of value-feelings, as different, say, from wonder as wonder is different from *ennui*. For it is clear that there is no single value-emotion; and that values, in so far as they apply to emotions at all, apply to the functions of emotions instead of describing a specific emotional class. If there were any point at all in the general contention, the truth would be clearer in the more specialised instances of moral or aesthetic emotion; and the discussion of these should therefore suffice.

Even if we grant that there is pronounced emotional quality in moral or in aesthetic determinations, it is clear that there is no specific moral emotion and no specific aesthetic emotion. Shame, anxiety and despair on the one hand, pride and joy on the other hand, to say nothing of hope, confidence and the like, are all of them allied and united with morals according to circumstances; and moral shame differs from any other shame only because it arises in connection with moral matters. Similarly, although aesthetics may not, like morals, call upon the whole gamut of the emotions on different occasions, there is no single emotion present whenever we admire the majesty of great events or savour the sweetness of a lyric. Appreciations or approvals, therefore, are *not* a distinct class of emotions.

Secondly, in any theory worth the name, the emotions in question must be appropriate to their *theme*. It is madness or superstition to feel ineffable emotions about trivial subjects; and levity is incongruous in the presence of anything serious or sombre. It is necessary, therefore, to examine what is meant by the appropriateness of the emotions; and although much in this subject is obscure, it is clear, at least, that the character of the emotion does not make objects appropriate, but, on the contrary, that the character of the object determines which emotions are appropriate. This subordination of the emotions is obviously connected with what we call truth, insight and vision. We have all, I suppose, jested when jesting was not appropriate; but have seldom persisted when we came to see that we were confronted with something that was not a jesting matter. We have all condemned actions in ignorance and have ceased to condemn when we found that the actions were not what we had supposed. And what is this but the dependence of our feelings upon insight?

In short, of two things one. Either our appreciative emotions themselves possess a certain discriminating and critical quality of rightness and appropriateness (as on Meinong's or Brentano's theory) or they depend upon, and should be conformable to, an intellectual insight into the quality of value.

THE OBJECTIVITY OF VALUES

In the former case they are not simply subjective or simply personal. In the latter case, *cadit questio*.

In the third place the quality of fair-mindedness or impartiality, so essential to moral and aesthetic determinations, implies logic and insight. It cannot therefore be the consequence of a special sort of feeling—even if there were such a feeling.

We have seen the inadequacy of Hume's "calm" passions to perform this office, or of Adam Smith's attempt to show that the equity of such passions is their respectability—the degree to which they are attuned to the prevailing sentiments of persons not specially concerned. The important question, therefore, is whether any better suggestion can be made in terms of the ultra-recessive theory. And it is very unlikely that there is any better suggestion.

Something like sympathetic insight or penetrative love seems the only possibility that could be even approximately adequate; and what is the sympathy without the insight, or the penetration except the insight? Moreover, whatever moral values may be, they must at least include and render possible the value of justice. In other words, we must be capable of approving *equally* actions or persons that are equal in *relevant* moral respects. Is there any emotion, even love or sympathy, in any way adequate to determine either the relevance or the equality?

A forlorn attempt is sometimes made to show that a contemplative emotion might perform these functions—at any rate as adequately as the functions are in fact performed. It is not at all clear what a contemplative emotion is unless it be the emotion appropriate to insight and intellectual contemplation. Nevertheless, however that may be, we must certainly admit that there *are* emotions of this "higher"[1] order —being in love with love, instead of simple loving, being pleased with pleasure, instead of simply being pleased, being pleased with love or loving pleasure. The trouble is that we know too much about these complicated emotions to believe

[1] "Higher" in Meinong's sense of "Gegenstände höherer Ordnung".

for a moment that they are likely to have the quality required. For pleasure-lovers, and people in love with love are not in fact less capricious or more impartial than others whose emotions are less subtle and more direct. On the contrary, they are far more crotchety and finicking.

§ 8. *Further concerning subjectivity*

It will be necessary for us to consider certain senses of objectivity other than those we have discussed hitherto. Before doing so, however, it is advisable to make an end of examining the current meanings of subjectivity.

In a loose way of speaking, whatever is relative, and, again, whatever is comparative, is sometimes called subjective.

Anything that is relative to some ego or person in such a way as to imply, and be permeated by, that ego (either recessively or ultra-recessively) is indeed subjective. Otherwise it need not be. And, regarding relativity, it is important to remember a very commonplace piece of logic that is far too frequently overlooked. Any single correlative term like "father" or "husband" is logically incomplete. For "father" is correlative with "child" and "husband" with "wife". On the other hand, "the-father-of-a-certain-child" or "the-husband-of-a-certain-wife" is logically complete. Logically speaking each of these complex terms is as absolute as "the ingenious Mr Locke" or "the incomparable Mr Newton".

Supposing, then, that certain values—let us say, the values of natural election—occur only when specific terms are in a certain specific relation, it is thoroughly permissible to ascribe value absolutely to the complete and complex fact which is constituted by these terms in this relation, although it is not permissible to ascribe value absolutely to the separate members of the complex. The separate terms are complementary to one another; and each of them, thus regarded, is logically incomplete. Together, however, they form a whole which is logically complete.

Thus carrots-in-relation-to-a-donkey might very well have absolute value, even if the donkey, on the one hand, and the carrots on the other hand, had only relative value. If value, as Meinong suggests, resides in the related complex of persons and the things they possess or enjoy, the consequence is not to make all statements concerning value "relative", but only to show that any fact which has value has this kind of complexity.

Comparison, again, implies a related series, but there is nothing in the least subjective about this circumstance. For example, the statement that a league is longer than a mile, although comparative, is as thoroughly objective as any statement could be. The same is true of superlatives. To speak of the oldest rabbit in Australia, or to say that the motion of light is the fastest in the physical universe is to express what is completely objective. There is never a hint of subjectivity here.

Accordingly, if any philosopher says (and some have said it) that values must be subjective because they are "only comparative", there is nothing in his "comparative" or in his "only" to imply subjectivity; and we must suppose him to mean a special sort of comparison. He means, in fact, relativity to a variable personal standard, as when the first game of golf during a holiday is delightful and the last a weariness. In short, unless the standard or "control" of the comparison is subjective, there is no road at all towards any proof of subjectivity along these lines.

§ 9. *Further concerning objectivity*

Up to the present, the substance of the argument of this chapter has been that value or worth may be a character of certain things, and therefore may be objective. The case for the subjectivity of all values, in so far as "subjective" is opposed to the possession of such a character, has not been proved.

A very slight acquaintance with philosophical literature, however, is sufficient to show that the word "objective" is frequently understood in a different sense from this one. For "objectivity" is often said to attach not to facts, but to our ideas about facts, with the striking consequence that although facts are just what they are, objectivity may vary in degree. Our ideas are *more or less* objective, although it is nonsense to speak of facts or things being "more or less" what they are.

Obviously, if any such view could be sustained, it would be necessary to enquire very closely into what is meant by an *idea*; and the result of the enquiry, I think, might be very damaging to the theory. A debate on this question, however, would involve an unconscionable digression, and so I mean to take the *prima facie* distinction between ideas and facts (or things) at its surface-value for purposes of discussion. Anyone, we think, must admit that there may be a very palpable difference between John Smith and his ideas about John Smith or, for that matter, between John Smith and John Smith's ideas about John Smith. Again, in the sciences, it seems necessary to distinguish between the cobwebby conjectures men spin in their minds (or even what we call instructive ideas) and the solid earth of reality.

Approaching the problem from this angle, we obtain a preliminary result which may be stated somewhat as follows: Our ideas, in the first instance, are private mental occurrences. They are "in our minds" if they are not even "in our heads" or "under our hats". The private character of the ideas, however, does not exhaust their essence and function. If indeed they are under our hats, as the pea is under the thimble, their business is to signify or indicate what need not be "under anyone's hat", or "under" anything at all. In short, these private occurrences are characteristically self-transcendent. Although they are private they may refer to something which is not private. And in any case they refer beyond themselves.

The natural and, I think, the correct interpretation of these considerations is to say that significant ideas refer to some object other than themselves, and that we endeavour to *know* this object. The ideas have objective reference because they refer to objects, and they attain objective truth when they grasp the character of their objects. Thus if I think in 1928 of the fluctuations of the franc in 1926, my present ideas must be distinguished from the former condition of the franc. Nevertheless, what I am thinking about is the franc, and it was the franc, not my ideas, that had a value in international exchange. Nothing that was under my hat was so much as considered in the Bourse.

This natural interpretation, however, is repugnant to many philosophers; for they obstinately maintain that we are "given" nothing but our ideas and so have to remain content with our ideas in the end. According to some of them, anything that is not a property, or a proper function, of the ideas is nothing but animal faith—that is to say, an irrational conviction. According to others, we should speak of "natural piety" instead—that is to say, we should invoke superstitious devotion. A third party simply asserts that although we are restricted to what is under our hats there is a correspondence between this cramped and obscure area and a world of fact. But none of the three is prepared to accept the simple truth that either we know nothing or else must be capable of signifying and knowing, through some idea, what is not that idea at all. What is more, none of the three can explain the first step in his own theory. They all believe that we can know our own ideas. But if knowledge consists in the transcendent reference of ideas, the knowledge of ideas must consist in the transcendent reference of *other* ideas to the ideas alleged to be known; and we need the same animal faith (or the like) in knowing our own ideas as in knowing anything else.

There is, however, a bolder expedient than any of the three I have mentioned. For it may be maintained that there should be no question of any reference beyond the sphere of ideas, and yet that ideas need not be mere private occurrences.

The bolder view has two principal forms. The first (which is Kant's) states that an idea may acquire the function of universality and necessity, and that when an idea becomes universal and necessary it has achieved full objectivity in the only possible sense in which there can *be* objectivity. And the universality of such ideas implies agreement among all right-thinking beings—that is to say, among all whose ideas have achieved the universal function, although not, of course, among those who have failed to achieve it.

The second form of the bolder expedient gives us some one of the varieties of the Coherence view, or of Absolute Idealism. According to this doctrine the circle of ideas is self-sufficient and self-nourishing, like the serpent consuming its own tail. This is an absurd diet for a serpent, but if the serpent is big enough, we are told, the absurdity disappears. In fact, reality consists of ideas, and therefore the serpent consists of *everything*. Consequently it could not feed upon anything except itself. When all ideas become coherent they cease to be private, and they are true or objective because they are the whole of truth and fact.

To the Kantian theory we must object that the universality or necessity of our thoughts cannot possibly *be* what we mean by fact and existence. Suppose that by reflecting upon human experience all right-thinking men are necessarily driven to the conclusion that there are successions, substances and causes in nature. The very meaning of this statement is that we are driven to the conclusion that there *is* succession in nature whether we think about it or not. Therefore the succession in nature cannot possibly be the rightness of anyone's thought about succession.

The coherence theory implies the same initial oversight. Succession, for example, is not the idea of succession, unless "ideas" are interpreted in a way wholly foreign to all these arguments. Hence reality cannot entirely consist of ideas. The serpent is a smallish serpent after all.

Certainly, we believe that reality must be internally consistent and coherent. Therefore our ideas cannot *all* be true if they do not cohere; and the coherence of our ideas is a very important test of their truth. In the actual state of our knowledge, however, it is only one of the tests we apply. There are some things, we hold, so certain that no reasonable man would doubt them; others very nearly as certain; and we attempt to make our weaker opinions cohere with these solid ones. Such prior certainties are not (in general) accepted on grounds of coherence, but on grounds of specific insight or definite observation. When we modify our views concerning what we took to be a prior certainty, we do so, again, on the ground of a finer and more circumspect insight. Apart from that, the coherence of any science is built upon a foundation of acceptance, not coherence. Observation and experiment yield certain data which it is the business of theory to explain in a coherent way. The data themselves, unless a mistake about them can be proved, have simply to be admitted. They do not have to wait upon our scientific systems in order to be accepted. On the contrary, our scientific systems wait upon *them*.

§ 10. *The consequence for value-theory*

If value predicates were generally agreed to have the same status as any other predicates, it might not have been necessary to consider these particular attempts to explain objectivity. The importance of this topic to our theme is precisely that many authors deny any possible identity in the status, and yet contend that values may (and do) have a certain kind of objectivity.

Obviously it is possible to have a certain faith in values—whether the faith be animal or spiritual—or again to regard values as angels or messengers—either with natural or with unnatural piety. And anyone may assert the reality of some vague kind of correspondence between values and fact. Again, anyone who cares to do so, may of course employ, in the instance of values, the type of (so-called) argument with which we are familiar in many debates concerning religion—that is to say, he may maintain that because science is not quite certain we should put our trust in values or in Christianity without hesitation or reserve.

It is needless for us to linger over these contentions, but necessary to dwell upon those developments of value-theory which are variations, respectively, of the Kantian or of the coherence views of objectivity. Thus Brentano's view that values are what is loved with a right kind of love (thereby achieving validity and permanence),[1] or Meinong's account of impersonal values, are theories of the first kind. And theories of the second kind are very common indeed, for it is a usual opinion that the coherence of willing or of feeling determines all that is properly meant by goodness or value.

Let us address ourselves, therefore, to these several views.

§ 11. *The "right" kind of emotion*

Perhaps love is always of the "right" kind although sometimes unwise. Regarding most emotions, however, if there is any validity in the arguments of § 7, it is necessary to maintain that the rightness of emotion is subordinate to insight, and that the relevant insight must be insight into values. This is not to say that there is nothing distinctive in the organisation of our emotions into sentiments; for Mr Shand has shown that there is. It is, however, an assertion that any such organisation is not self-sufficient, but allied with, and guided by, our knowledge of value, dignity and worth.

The same arguments apply to Meinong's theory. If objectivity were only a function of certain ideas, yielding at the best an ideal of agreement among right-thinking persons, it might indeed be argued that there is a *nisus* towards objectivity and an obligatory ideal of agreement in the reference of our emotions beyond their private character. Even so, however, it might reasonably be contended (as we have seen) that this reference of emotions to "their" objects means nothing more than the circumstance that the emotions are felt in connection with our ideas of such objects. There need not be two independent modes of reference. And in any case, on this theory also, the objectivity of reference which claims the validity of truth and of insight ought to control (although not completely to dominate) any emotional objectivity that might be signified.

[1] *The Origin of the Knowledge of Right and Wrong*, § 12 and *passim*.

In reality, however, this "right" kind of thinking does not constitute objectivity, but, on the contrary, is right because it attests what is objective in a fuller sense, and it would not appear that our emotions, when distinguished from the insight that may go along with them, could possibly, in the fuller sense, have objective validity. In other words, the plausibility of Meinong's theory (if, indeed, it has plausibility) depends upon its arbitrary and unjustifiable limitation of the objectivity of knowledge to something that is *not* value at any rate in those passages in which emotional validity is compared with cogitative.

§ 12. *"Coherence" and value*

"Coherence itself is a form of the perfection theory. It implies consistency but also comprehensiveness. As the cinema promoter said, "Why not be on the safe side and make it full of everything?"

In general, then, what is held is that the comprehensive consistency of our thinking is truth, the comprehensive consistency of our emotions is beauty (or something like it) and the comprehensive consistency of our volitions is goodness (usually with a moral implication). All these may be called values, but the emphasis in most discussions is upon the second and third—indeed principally upon the third. The three types of comprehensive consistency, again, are usually contrasted with one another. "Men adopt different policies", Mr Paton says, "not because they argue from different premises, but because they happen to be different sorts of persons and to want different sorts of things."[1] Again, although Mr Paton admits that "the will works differently when illumined by judgments of value", he also holds that these judgments "would mean little or nothing unless the will were already present".[2]

For the purposes of this discussion, then, I propose to choose

[1] H. J. Paton, *The Good Will*, p. 159.
[2] *Op. cit.* p. 209.

the third of these supposed species of value, viz. what is here said to be "goodness".

The coherence of a man's willing has to show itself in at least three directions. Firstly, a man's will must be harmonious within itself. Secondly, it must be harmonious with its environment, that is to say, it must be efficient and even, in a measure, successful. Thirdly, it must be harmonious with the wills of his fellow men.

Obviously these three varieties may be very friendly to one another. But they need not be. And, when they differ, it is not at all clear what sort of verdict or compromise "coherence" indicates. If anyone, like the proverbial juryman, finds himself at odds with the eleven other obstinate fellows, what then? And is it clear that value, even great value, cannot be present when the times are out of joint, our compatriots at odds with us, and we ourselves profoundly conscious of inner conflicts?

As soon as objections of this order are raised, we usually find that the level of the discussion is instantly raised. Actual coherence, the objector urges, neither *is* goodness nor a proper test of goodness. In action, as well as in theoretical speculations, the better, finer and more fertile minds contradict themselves "at least once a day", and the well-laid schemes of bootleggers, filibusters and expert log-rollers may be admirable examples of a coherence which itself is not admirable at all.

These thrusts are parried, not altogether easily, by the reminder that honour among thieves is rare, that buccaneers have to swing for it, or succumb to fiery waters, or are converted into skeletons which point the way to their captain's buried hoard; and that swindlers, however elaborate their schemes, are only parasites upon a credit system which, as a whole, is enormously stronger than they are. In the main, however, we are hurriedly introduced to the Ideal, and are then expected to be silent. In the Ideal, coherence is value, and the same is true in so far as the Ideal is realised.

It seems difficult, however, even to conjecture what an ideal

vii] **THE OBJECTIVITY OF VALUES** 249

or perfect state of society would be like except on the basis of values which are found in the imperfect conditions under which we live, or of aspirations which move a little in front of our present imperfect courses. Our standard, in short, is not the whole, but particular excellences which, so far as we can see, *any* valuable whole must possess—and the more the better. What is more, harmony is not particularly valuable unless it sustains and revolves around these excellences. In other words, coherence is neither the meaning nor the essence of value.

Other tactics, therefore, have to be employed—and commonly are employed. Instead of a pale ideal, social realities are invoked, and goodness is said to be a question of our actual station in the organised community into which we are born.

"Here, if anywhere", Mr Bradley says, "the idea of universal and impersonal morality is realised....Men's private peculiarities neutralize each other, and the result is an intuition which does not belong merely to this or that man or collection of men....This intuition tells you that, if you could be as good as your world, you would be better than most likely you are."[1]

The passage I have quoted occurs in the essay on "My Station and its Duties", which is the most eloquent, and, in many ways, the best expression in English of the view we are now considering. If these statements stood alone it would be necessary to protest against them in order both to rescue morality from mere respectability, and to give respectability its proper due. The passage, however, does not stand alone but, as is too often forgotten, is succeeded, in this very essay, by a critical addendum[2] which supplies a most penetrating qualification. Perfection, Bradley says, resides in the whole of things, and historical communities are but fragments of that whole. Particular communities may be most unworthily occupied, and our station in them may be indelibly smirched by their very sorry plight. Again, unless we take a fundamentally utilitarian view of the values of art and of "culture",

[1] *Ethical Studies*, 2nd edn. p. 199 (with slight verbal modifications).
[2] *Op. cit.* pp. 202 *sqq.*

it is not at all obvious, or even likely, that such values are directly or predominantly controlled by social requirements, or that they may not be authentic in spite of society.

As it seems to me, these qualifications of the "social" view of goodness are quite as essential as any truth that the social theory may possess; and they are fatal to the sufficiency of the social theory. It should not be necessary to say more, but for better measure, I propose to advance two considerations. The first may be briefly expressed by saying that a bad thing is seldom, if ever, made better by being socialised. The second is that the truth of the social theory (in so far as it possesses truth) is a consequence of more fundamental principles and not the premiss of them.

There is no doubt whatever that human societies are particularly prone to collective obscenity and to collective panic, and I think we may accept the conventional opinion that panic and obscenity should be numbered among the bad and ugly things. It is nonsense to say that these things are redeemed by being practised in a large social way. If anything, they are worse when they are magnified by contagion; and nearly everyone is agreed that mob psychology is often a very low psychology which may become almost bestial—or worse than bestial.

But a rabble, it is said, is very different indeed from an organised community; and social values are determined by integrated not by casual conjunctions.

Have there not then been integrated and organised obscenities among human communities both before and after the days of the Golden Calf, and do not the walls of many temples—and not the walls only—testify to the same at this very time? And does this mend the matter?

It may be argued, no doubt, that the deliberate practice of certain communities in these matters does in the end weaken the people, and that the badness and ugliness of the practices consist in this alone. One gathers, however, that the nature of the effect is doubtful, and at any rate that the worst consequential evils could be avoided by a little prudence. It seems evident, therefore, that what is evil and ugly in these practices is, in the main, independent of any social consequences other than the consequence that the evil continues.

Let us pass, then, to the second point.

Life in society is a corporate exercise, in which very few actions do not have, directly or indirectly, an effect upon the agent's companions as well as upon the agent. Even if we do not assume that every human agent, as such, has value, the possibility of attaining the simpler and also the greater values is, if not pretty evenly distributed, at any rate sufficiently nearly so to make it imprudent to deny that it is approximately the same for all. Therefore, he who seeks values dare not disregard the values of others, that is to say, his outlook must be sociable and companionable.

It does not follow from this that he should not sometimes go along a road that in the main is solitary, whether or not his companions disapprove; or again that he should never regard his family more than his club, his university more than his country, his country more than humanity at large, the future of any of these rather than their present condition. And these things should not follow because they depend upon the relevant values attainable under different circumstances and are not to be determined by a Sociality that is printed in capitals. What does follow is that the value of others is seldom, if ever, irrelevant to any action, and that, since nearly everyone, as we say, owes more to his fellows than to himself in particular (although he may be less concerned with any other single person), a social outlook *of some sort* is prescribed by the conditions of any normal human search for value.

An effective social organisation, to be sure, may create duties which would not be duties apart from the organisation. For it involves a machinery which must be sustained. Indeed, social laws create offences (including contempt of court or the obstruction of the machinery) as well as duties. This, however, is a necessary instrument of organisation, and, although it is inevitable, it is rather to be deplored than admired. If the machinery incident to any piece of organisation is more important than the purpose of the organisation, the result is, so far, a loss in value and not a gain.

In the end, social enterprises need to be justified quite as much as individual enterprises. It is no justification to say that they are social; and, as we have seen, a greater social solidarity (for a bad purpose) may very well be worse than a lesser social solidarity.

§ 13. *Summing up*

In the course of our review, in this chapter, of the principal senses of "subjectivity" and of "objectivity" which seemed relevant to our theme, the discussion, once it had gathered way, edged gradually, but with increasing momentum, towards a vindication of the objectivity of the character of excellence. To invert a famous phrase *Posse videntur quia possunt*. Values *seem* to do what they *truly* do.

Both for logical and for historical reasons, this course seemed plainly to be indicated. Logically speaking, the objectivity of excellence is the kernel of value-theory, where the greater values are concerned. Historically speaking, as we saw when we considered "approval" in the last chapter, or again when we examined Meinong's theory, the customary method of those who deny or of those who would qualify the objectivity of excellence, is to assume, in the first instance, that the values of natural election or of emotional approval are plainly subjective, and, in the second instance, to endeavour to establish some sort of quasi-objectivity in Approval in order to account for the obstinate and undeniable *appearance* of objectivity in so many human valuations.

Our conclusion, then, is that excellence is objective. Incidentally, we have attempted to examine "objectivity" with some precision, and to reject, for sufficient reasons, some of the things that should *not* be meant by the "objectivity of excellence".

We must, however, also take account of the possibility that "value" is an equivocal not a univocal term, and that the relative "values" of natural election or of emotional prizing

VII] **THE OBJECTIVITY OF VALUES** 253

cannot properly be assigned to the domain of excellence. If so, "value" in one sense may very well be objective, and value, in some other sense or senses, not be objective. Indeed, if any "values" are relative they must be "subjective" in one of the relevant senses of subjectivity, if the term to which they are relative is a "subject" or "ego".

Attention should therefore be called to the earlier stages in the argument of this chapter, where the "objectivity" or "subjectivity" of natural election was discussed. For emotional appreciation is natural election at the psychological level—that is to say, it is our sense or feeling of our natural elections.

§ 14. *Judgment and principle in these affairs*

Let us return, however, to the objective character which is absolute value.

To speak of "value" as a predicate or character is, of course, to speak in terms of judgment and of propositions. It may reasonably be asked, therefore, whether "valuing" and "judging to be valuable" are the same, and, if not, whether a further perplexity does not await us. For surely there may *be* excellences which no one has formulated in any judgment; and surely we may prize many excellent things without so much as thinking of what we are doing.

In all this (I should like to suggest) there seems to be no theoretical difficulty at all. The essential function of judgment is never to create a new character, but always to recognise a character already present. In judging, we know and assert the character; but we may pursue, or be affected by, valuable things, on account of their value, without understanding the rationale of the circumstance.

Anything that may be truly judged comes under the jurisdiction of reason—that is to say, it may be reflected on in terms of principle; and inference, comparison and other such processes are appropriate to it. Standards and principles of value, therefore, have the same objectivity as value itself has.

The character of value or excellence, in short, is amenable

to the laws of logic, but its rationality does not end with these formal laws. For rational insight discriminates any relevant connection or relation which it perceives; and these relevant connections, in any given field, need not be restricted to the general logical relations which hold of everything that is thinkable.

Let us, for example, consider once again those relations of equity which are essential to moral values. Equity, if you will, is a species of moral logic, but it is something more than logic in general. For equity is the systematic development of a distinct kind of insight. It is not unfair in a parent to treat his own children differently from other people's children, but it would be unfair in him to discriminate in favour of his own children, on the ground of affection alone, if he were the adjudicator in a supposedly open competition. It is consistent but unjust to conscript everyone on whom the press-gang can lay hands, just to exempt old men and boys, unjust and dubiously consistent to exempt property from conscription if money is needed as well as men. In short, right principles cannot be inconsistent, but the rightness and reasonableness of them cannot be determined by consistency alone.

CHAPTER VIII

BONUM HONESTUM

SECTION I. GENERAL

§ 1. *A retrospect concerning perfection and excellence*

THE notions of perfection and of excellence have been discussed very frequently indeed in the earlier parts of this narrative. A brief recapitulation concerning them, therefore, is all that should be necessary now.

For Spinoza, as we saw, perfection means strength, or power, or reality. Therefore, since everything is real, everything in that sense is perfect; and nature contains no imperfections. On the other hand, when the strength of any particular thing is compared with the strength of other things of the same kind, certain particular things have less perfection than others of the same sort. It would seem also that different kinds of things, in Spinoza's opinion, may be compared in this matter. For the kinds of things differ in their capacity to play a strong and varied part in the drama of nature. In particular, man (who has rational capacity) is, in virtue of his reason, incomparably more powerful and more perfect than any non-rational thing. And in the end we are told that man's reason unites him with Totality or with Deity who is the fountain and the whole of perfection, strength, and reality. From this standpoint *every* finite thing is weak, dependent and imperfect. Its finitude, as Leibniz afterwards said, implies its "metaphysical evil".

Pursuing separately the several parts of this majestic philosophy, we decided that what Spinoza called the *conatus* of finite things is in fact the principle of natural election, and that, in terms of this principle, specific things may be said to seek their own specific complement, completion or perfection. Such perfections, however, are differentiating or selective—

each thing's special bent or peculiar bias. If each thing seeks *its own* special perfection, it is difficult, for that very reason, to suppose that nature as a whole seeks *any* special perfection. We may speak, of course, of putting central things in the centre or in other such ways. And nature, to be sure, is always complete. But nature, as Goethe said, has neither kernel nor shell, being centre (if it has a centre) and circumference all at once. As in Peter's vision, there is nothing common or unclean; for God has cleansed all. Axiological neutrality, therefore, not differentiating selection, seems the proper inference from this line of thought.

We also saw that it is entirely possible for worthless things to seek their own worthless completion. Perfection, in the sense of completion, must therefore be distinguished from excellence. And excellence, so far from being universal, is rare.

Turning from natural election to psychological interest we found the same considerations reappearing. Our conscious appetency may be said to seek fulfilment, satisfaction or "perfection", and it is conceivable that every experience of this order has a certain value. But these experiences need not be fine or excellent. And the existence of what we call perverted fulfilments and satisfactions is sufficient to clinch the matter.

Similar accounts may be given of the nature of pleasure, especially by theories which attempt to expound a certain metaphysics of felicity. And the same distinction between any such (dubious) account of the "perfection" of pleasure, on the one hand, and excellence or fineness, on the other, must again be drawn.

It is possible that certain accounts of metaphysical perfection do mean something quite different from completeness; for example, those special proportions which, according to Reid and to others, are the specific counterparts of that special experience which we call the sense of beauty. And it is likely, even, that perfection, in most metaphysical theories, is regarded rather as a property or consequence of completeness than as the simple fact of completeness. What is meant, very possibly, is that harmony, organisation or mutual adaptation has, of itself, a genuine and overmastering excellence, and that this excellence is the greater in proportion as its range is greater, reaching its maximum in the (supposedly) "perfect" whole.

If so, the essence of all such theories is the *special* intuition that Order is the greatest of all conceivable values. Yet if this be what is *meant*, completeness is what is *said*. The theories differ, indeed, according to the sort of completeness which the theorists have in mind. Some think of the unity of an organism, some of the development of personality (or "self-realisation"), some of the coherence of a nation or other social community, some of the "individuality" (i.e. the undivided character) of the Whole or the Absolute. But the principle, however employed, is the same in all these cases.

This is also so when Time (as with Plotinus or Spinoza) is one of the determining considerations. For Time, the great divider, is (they think) the complete enemy of all completeness, the only perfect example of radical imperfection. Even the Devil, Spinoza suggested, would be too weak to exist,[1] being the embodiment of supreme infirmity or of the absence of perfection and reality; and so need not be helped to perish. But Time must be buried at the cross-roads and a stake driven through his heart. Therefore Time, in the first instance, is confounded with random vicissitude (although orderly change, abstractly considered, is as perfect an illustration of Order as the wit of man could devise). In the second instance, completeness or totality is taken to imply permanence in the sense of *unchanging* stability. And in the third instance, Time is said to be swallowed up in Eternity.

§ 2. *Further concerning excellence*

"Perfection", therefore, in so far as the term is taken to signify either completeness in general, some determinate sort of completeness, or as signifying that which is per-

[1] *Short Treatise*, Book II, ch. xxv.

manent and orderly, must be distinguished from the rare excellence which may very well be fugitive. It may reasonably be objected, however, that excellence is just a superlative, and is rare because superlatives are rare. Excellence marks the peaks; but why should we not maintain that everything, even the plains, has a certain elevation? Why should not "fineness" or "nobility" themselves (which we have taken to be synonymous with "excellence") express only the maximum or optimum degree of a quality which everything has?

If value were indeed strength or fulness or varied capacity, the above would be the only possible interpretation. For a weak thing has a little strength, although not very much; and patently not enough. Similarly the most fragmentary or transient of things has a certain fulness and a certain endurance.

It is not true, however, that sin is goodish conduct from which saintliness is merely absent; or that pain is rather agreeable although not superlatively so; or that ugliness is rather pretty although less beautiful than beauty. On the contrary, sin and virtue, ugliness and beauty, pain and pleasure are *opposites* in their several scales, not different degrees of the same quality. And fineness or nobility are the polar opposites of what is contemptible and vile.

There might be a universe in which all was vile, and there might be another in which nothing was vile. Similarly there might be a universe in which nothing was noble, or another in which everything was noble. In the actual universe certain things are vile, others noble, and many things neither the one nor the other.

§ 3. *Perfection and reason*

"Perfection" is always regarded as an objective quality, and therefore as a suitable field for the exercise of reason and reflection.

Again, the completeness usually connoted by "perfection" seems eminently congruent with "reason". For the rational man looks before and after, and also looks towards eternity.

In the third place, a man is said to be most fully or most perfectly himself when he is sane and not mad; and his reason or his sanity, according to an ancient saying, makes him the only rational animal. Hence human perfection is said to be "reason" and yet to reveal itself, after enquiry, as the authentic perfection of the universe itself. It has even been contended that a man's reason *is* his mind, anything short of it (and yet mental) being a sort of muddied or watered "reason".

I shall try to illustrate the interplay of these conceptions in the second section of this chapter where I shall consider the doctrine of value and of perfection in Descartes, Malebranche, and Geulincx. These, along with Spinoza and Leibniz, were the great metaphysical rationalists.

§ 4. *Reason, perfection and moral good*

Moral values are not the only values, yet all the rationalistic theories of value which we are about to consider are in effect prevailingly ethical. While they deal with the *summum bonum*, their main concern is with *bonum honestum*.

For this there were many reasons. Virtue, the rationalists held, was the primary if not the sole expetible good; and grace or peace are given to the virtuous only. Again, they held that man is free (or himself) only when he is acting rationally. To be rational or most perfectly human, therefore, is to exercise one's "good" or "free" will. And the exercise of good will is ethics.

This last consideration weighed profoundly both with Descartes (whom Kant considered a "dogmatist") and with Kant (who believed himself the destroyer of dogmatism). Kant's own theory of value will be the subject of the third Section of this chapter, and appropriately so. Tutored in the perfection-theories of the metaphysical rationalists, Kant was profoundly impressed, in manhood, by the ideas of Rousseau and those British moralists whom we considered in a former chapter. In the result, whether we agree with him or not, we cannot but be impressed by the range and sweep of his views especially with regard to the relations between moral, aesthetic and religious values.

Apart from these special philosophies, however, it must be noted that any rationalistic theory of value is likely to accord a special prominence to *bonum honestum*. For it is always a man's duty to do the best that he can; and no one could have rational knowledge of this duty unless he had made a critical and comprehensive survey of the whole domain of expetible values. This truth does not imply that all values are moral, for it may be a moral duty to seek something that is not itself moral. As we saw in an earlier chapter, it is our duty not to cause needless suffering among animals, and this would not be less of a duty if, as we commonly believe, these animals are not moral creatures.

SECTION II. OF VALUE ACCORDING TO METAPHYSICAL RATIONALISM

§ 1. *Descartes*

Like the Greeks, Descartes took the love of wisdom (which is philosophy) to connote a practice and way of life as well as a speculative attitude. This view of the subject appears very clearly in the title even of the *Studium bonae mentis* which was his first draft of the later *Discours de la méthode*. As he says in the *Regulae*, he numbered himself among those *qui serio student ad bonam mentem pervenire*.[1] Good sense, he thought, was man's prerogative, fairly evenly distributed among the human race. By cultivating good sense man may achieve a good mind, and so attain the greatest perfection, as well as the sweetest and most dependable felicity that is possible to him.

Indeed, Descartes went so far as to hold that the pursuit of reason was the prime rule of physical health. He told the Princess Elizabeth that his own mother had been *poitrinaire*, and had died shortly after his birth; that in his childhood the doctors had thought that he would die young of the same

[1] *Œuvres*, Adam et Tannery (hereafter called *A.T.*), vol. x, p. 395.

malady; but that he had lived to some effect by continuously following his self-imposed regimen of reason.[1]

In the *Discourse on Method* itself—that historical manifesto of the birth of modern philosophy—the ethical standpoint of the Cartesian philosophy is clearly, although briefly, set forth in the provisional rules of conduct which appear at the beginning of Part III. Of these rules, the first two are very definitely provisional, for the first counsels obedience to the most judicious among prevalent customs and opinions, pending fuller enquiry, and the second enjoins resolution in pursuing a course that has been deliberately adopted, even if the course itself is only probably right. The third and fourth rules, however, are something more than provisional. The third maxim is "to endeavour always to conquer myself rather than fortune and change my desires rather than the order of the world, and in general accustom myself to the persuasion that, except our own thoughts, there is nothing absolutely in our power"[2]—in short *Abstine et sustine*; and Descartes adds, "I believe that in this chiefly consisted the secret of the power of such philosophers as in former times were enabled to rise superior to the influence of fortune, and, amid suffering and poverty, enjoy a happiness which their gods might have envied".[3] The fourth rule again is only nominally provisional; and it is the greatest of the four. "I thought of reviewing the different occupations of men in this life," Descartes said, "with the view of making choice of the best";[4] but he proceeds at once to inform us that nothing can approach the cultivation of reason, in excellence, satisfaction or innocence. He concludes:

Inasmuch as we neither seek nor shun any object except in so far as our understanding represents it as good or bad, all that is necessary to right action is right judgment, and to the best action the most correct judgment—that is, to the acquisition of all the virtues with all else that is truly valuable and within our reach;

[1] *A.T.* vol. IV, pp. 220 *sq.*
[2] *A.T.* vol. VI, p. 25, Veitch's translation, p. 26.
[3] *Ibid.* p. 26, Veitch, pp. 26 *sq.*
[4] *Ibid.* p. 27, Veitch, p. 27.

and the assurance of such an acquisition cannot fail to render us contented.[1]

These opinions concerning value, wisdom and the best life are further developed in the *Letters to the Princess Elizabeth*, and in the treatise *The Passions of the Soul*. Chronologically the *Letters* come first and should now be considered.

The Princess Palatine Elizabeth was the daughter of the luckless Frederick of Bohemia, and of Elizabeth, daughter of James I of England. At the time of the correspondence (1645 and onwards) the Princess, living in exile and in comparative poverty, had to bear the accumulating misfortunes of her father's house and of the house of Stuart. Being, like so many women of her age, enlightened, acute, and studious, she was eager to obtain the consolations of philosophy, although she was very doubtful whether they really could console her.

It is on this chastened and sombre note that the correspondence begins and ends. "I think that since there is nothing good in the world, save good sense, that can be called good quite absolutely", Descartes says, "there is also no evil from which some advantage may not be drawn by anyone possessing good sense."[2]

The above is an assertion of the value of reason, but Descartes's assertion of the reasonableness of values is equally important and equally unqualified.

"The true use of our reason for the conduct of life", he says, "consists only in examining, and considering without passion the value of all the perfections, whether of the body or of the mind, which may be acquired in the course of conduct, in order that, being usually obliged to relinquish some of them in order to have others, we may always choose those which are best."[3]

Rational axiology, in short, is the Ariadne thread in these intricate and perplexing affairs; and Descartes elaborates and defends his theme in many notable ways.

Zeno and Epicurus as well as Aristotle, he maintains, all believed that contentment, felicity or beatitude presupposed

---

[1] *A.T.* vol. VI, p. 28, Veitch, p. 28.   [2] *A.T.* vol. IV, p. 237.
[3] *Ibid.* pp. 286 *sq.*; cf. p. 284, "la juste valeur".

the sovereign good.¹ If, therefore, anyone pretends to exalt mere happiness above what reason attests to be good, he has authority as well as clear fact against him. Certainly there are times when we all must wonder whether it might not be better to be ignorantly content with superficial and vulgar joys than to understand them with greater seriousness and so to be the sadder.² The ancients, however, were right; for contentment and serenity is but a witness within our breasts to the possession of some authentic perfection. Rationally speaking, every pleasure ought to be measured by the degree of the perfection from which it springs. This is what we do when we have clear knowledge of the source of any pleasure. Our ideas of virtue, and generally our ideas about what concerns our own spirits, although not infallible, are likely to be very nearly correct. It is otherwise, however, with carnal pleasures. Thus anger appears to give evidence of the sweetness of revenge, but the only possible perfection in accomplished revenge is a certain superiority in point of bodily strength, and *this* excellence is far inferior to the value of restraining vengeful feelings.³

Again, replying to the Princess, Descartes maintains that a nice calculation of values (especially the relative values of ourselves as compared with others) although very hard, is not usually required. In general, the public good is a higher and a more glorious thing than our own good; and it appeals as such to all nobler minds.⁴ Charity and virtue go together. The contrast, therefore, between our own advantage and the welfare of others is indefinitely smaller than many suppose. In any case if, having judged as well as we can, we are nevertheless mistaken, we should not grieve. It is not in man's nature to know everything. We should rather grieve if, acting against our conscience and our knowledge, the event should be more fortunate than we had any right to anticipate.⁵

From a broad philosophical standpoint there are four pieces of knowledge specially relevant to this matter.⁶ The

[1] *A.T.* vol. IV, pp. 275 *sqq.*   [2] *Ibid.* p. 305.   [3] *Ibid.* p. 285.
[4] *Ibid.* p. 317.   [5] *Ibid.* p. 307.   [6] *Ibid.* pp. 291 *sqq.*

first is the existence of God in His infinite perfection and power. For perfection is the true object of love, and if we love God we may rejoice even in our afflictions because we know they come from Him. The second is the superiority of our minds to our bodies as being nobler and capable of an infinity of joys not bodily. The third is a proper understanding of the magnitude of God's universe.

For if we imagine that there is nothing beyond the heavens but imaginary spaces, and that the skies are made only for the service of earth, and earth for man, the result is that we are inclined to believe that the earth is our principal dwelling place, and the present life our best, so that instead of understanding the perfections that are truly within us, we attribute to other creatures imperfections that they do not have, in order to raise ourselves above them, and attaining an impertinent presumption, we would arrogate a place to ourselves among God's counsels, and undertake the task of governing His world along with Him, the result of which is an infinity of vain inquietudes and distractions.

The fourth piece of knowledge is that although each of us is in a manner separate from all others, we do not exist alone, but are parts of the same universe, state, society and family.

These explanations exhibit the substance of Cartesian axiology. It remains to consider their application, and this application has two principal features. The first of these is that any man's sovereign good must depend upon himself, and this is taken to mean that it must depend upon a man's free or rational judgment and volition. The second is determined by Descartes's views of the relation between mind and body.

While both these cardinal applications are abundantly illustrated in the correspondence with the Princess, they are, for the most part, discussed even more adequately in *Les passions de l'âme*. To it therefore we should now proceed.

What is a passion (or suffering) in the soul may be caused by an action (or activity) in the body.[1] We may, however,

---

[1] *Les passions de l'âme*, Art. II. Reference to this treatise will specify the Article and will employ for the most part Haldane and Ross's translation. (Cambridge Univ. Press.)

distinguish by inspection between passions so caused in the soul, and the soul's proper desires which are its own activity (Art. XXIX). Since the body is a mere machine, whatever happens in it might happen in the absence of any soul. Nevertheless these mechanical motions may affect the soul through the pineal gland and so may nourish and sustain our passions. Conversely the soul (or the will) may indirectly affect the passions by arousing representations whose natural function is to guide our movements. Direct or immediate control of the passions which spring from the body is, however, impossible (Art. XLVI).

Judgment and resolution are the proper arms of the soul, and show themselves forceful even when opinions are false. But true opinions are stronger than false ones (Arts. XLVIII and XLIX).

There are six primitive passions, wonder, love, hatred, desire, joy and sadness. All of these arise from the consideration of Good and Evil. A thing that is agreeable is presented as relatively to us good (Art. LVI).

The utility of all the passions consists only in their capacity for fortifying and perpetuating in the soul thoughts which it is good it should preserve (Art. LXXIV).

Descartes was fully prepared to admit that even bodily movements may assist the soul in performing its proper functions. "I see no reason", he says (Art. CLX), "preventing the same movement of the spirits that serves to strengthen a thought when it has a foundation which is bad from also fortifying it when it has one which is just." In the main, however, he regarded his theory as an immense simplification of former views. It did away, he thought, with the traditional opposition between reason and sense, higher and lower principles in the soul, and the like. "For there is within us only one soul, and this soul has not itself any diversity of parts" (Art. XLVII). There is only *one* relevant distinction, viz. that which is truly our soul, and that in the soul which is a passion due to the body. We *in ourselves* are free and rational, and therefore our main business is to distinguish that in ourselves which is due to our own spontaneity, rationality and freedom.

As we saw, the desires of our souls are to be distinguished from their passions. Now "desire is always good when it follows a true knowledge" (Art. CXLIV). Our usual error is that

of not distinguishing the things that entirely depend on us from those that do not so depend. For as to those that only depend on us, i.e. on our own free will, it is sufficient to know that they are good, in order to avoid the possibility of desiring them with too much vehemence, because it is following virtue to bring goodness into the things that depend upon ourselves, and it is certain that we cannot have too ardent a desire for virtue. Besides which, since the things that we desire in this way are bound to succeed, as it is on ourselves alone that they depend, we shall always receive from them all the satisfaction that we have expected. (*Ibid.*)

In short, virtue and the sovereign good consist essentially in purity and in self-reliance. The good man strengthens his soul and learns to dispense with anything that comes from outside his soul, either from his body or from its surroundings. And he will respect and salute this rational soul in every other man. Being masters of themselves, good men are easily the masters of jealousy, anger and hatred; for these passions depend upon what, although seekable, is not worth seeking (Art. CLVI). Again, good men never despise any one,

and although they often see that others commit faults that make their feebleness apparent, they are at the same time more inclined to excuse than to blame them, and to believe that it is rather by lack of knowledge than by lack of good will that they commit them. And as they do not think of themselves as being much inferior to those who have more goods or honours or even who have more mental gifts, more knowledge, more beauty or, generally speaking, who surpass them in some other perfections, they do not at the same time esteem themselves much above those whom they surpass, because all these things seem to them to be of very small account as compared with the good will for which they alone esteem themselves and which they also suppose to exist, or at least to be capable of existing, in all other men. (Art. CLIV.)

Despite the dignity and, so to say, the more than Kantian democracy of passages such as these, it is difficult to avoid the conclusion that Descartes's theory, in the end, suffers an unenviable contraction. Spiritual values, at his hand, have shrunk to the moralist's mere good will, the rationality of values tends to be reduced to the exclusive value of pure rationality, and the human mind itself appears in the end to be something hard, impenetrable (though very precious) like a diamond in the midst of rubble. The ancient ideal of self-sufficiency has dwindled into a naked asceticism, and the prudence of avoiding reliance upon success or good fortune seems to become the plain absurdity of turning one's back upon fortune altogether.

On the latter point at least, Descartes was very shrewdly criticised by the Princess Elizabeth, and was forced to admit that disease may impair our rational powers as well as our other faculties. All he could plead in effect was that our reason (that is to say, in the context, "keeping one's head" or "remaining in one's senses") is less pervious to such impairment than bodily humours are.[1] If so, the difference is of degree and not of kind; and it might be argued that our arteries must be at least as hardy as our reason if the impairment is to be avoided. The Cartesian philosophy of mind and body *ought*, no doubt, to establish a distinction of degree, even if it failed to establish a difference in kind; but the question is whether, in the face of such admissions, it really succeeded in doing so.

Again it is plain that a thing need not be good because it depends upon ourselves. This would follow (on Cartesian principles) only if *we* (that is our soul or reason) are good; and Descartes, to be sure, maintained that all men, in this general sense, were good. Even granting this doctrine, however, it surely does not follow that the good of each man should depend upon himself individually and upon no one else. Love does not depend upon ourselves either in the sense that we can command it freely when we wish, or that we can compel others to bestow it upon us. And yet it is neither mad nor absurd for a man to say that he would rather love and be

[1] *A.T.* vol. IV, p. 282.

loved than attain anything whatsoever that depended upon his solitary will. In short, the ideal of self-sufficiency is not only impracticable; it may be, and often is, the height of unwisdom.

§ 2. *Geulincx*

In Geulincx's once celebrated system of ethics, the two principles that a man's reason is his very self, and that excellence is completely derived from man's good or rational will are developed with such transparent sincerity and ostensible consistency that, for this reason alone, they compel consideration at the present stage of our discussion.

Geulincx was indeed the complete ethical rationalist. "Ethics", he says, "is the very hearth and home of reason. In questions of physics, reason is turned upon the facts, and so to say journeys among them. In ethical matters reason is at home and pours itself out, developing its precepts and obligations from its own intrinsic nature."[1] In short, virtue is the proper domain of reason.

Virtue itself is Love—the undivided love of right reason. The vulgar think of love as a passion and include in it the sweetness of joy and the attractions of desire, hope and trust. This is the love of affection, and is not virtue.

Again, there is a love of business which is not virtue either. For virtue is different both from benevolence and from concupiscence, which are respectively the unselfish and the selfish forms of this love of doing. In opposition to both of these, virtue is the firm determination to do that, and that only, which reason decrees.

This virtue is one and single. For reason is one. It has, however, the cardinal features of diligentia, obedientia, justitia and humilitas. He who loves reason must hearken to reason and perceive what it decrees. Hence obedience, exactitude (or justice) and obligation (which is the essence of humilitas).[2]

---

[1] *Opera* (Hague 1893), vol. III, p. 183 (freely translated).
[2] E.g. *ibid.* p. 174.

What has to be asked, therefore, is firstly, What *is* right reason, and how do we know it? and secondly, What is the kind and degree of guidance that right reason affords?

The answer to the first question is that we know what reason is because we *are* rational. It is no matter if sometimes we are doubtful; for no one would deny that the son of a house knows his father on the ground that he may sometimes be perplexed or doubtful if the father is at a distance, or standing in the dusk, or masquerading in a woman's habit.[1]

In a word, the principle is "Know thyself". When we examine ourselves with sufficient perspicacity, we learn to neglect all that is not ourselves;[2] and we find that we consist wholly of knowing and willing.[3]

To *know*, in this sense, is *not* to be a mere spectator. We are but spectators of the machine of the world and of the smaller machine which is our own body. *Numen est*, or God's signal.[4] Genuine knowledge implies unity between knower and known; and there can be no unity between minds and matter. Therefore we may exclude everything that goes by the name experience and is commonly said to be "explained" by the action of nerves upon the mind.[5] Experience is the alleged knowledge of a mere spectator. Genuine knowledge is the knowledge of an author knowing his work.

In other words we must be more resolute than Descartes was in excluding from self-knowledge all that is not ourselves; and when we do so our rational selves, in their ultimate authorship, clearly stand forth. More in detail, we may thus learn precisely what our wills are and do. "Quod nescis quomodo fiat, non facis."[6] We are not genuine authors unless we know precisely what we are doing; and therefore when we are said to act in passion we are not genuine authors because the nature of such processes is always obscure.

This genuine authorship is at the same time our freedom. To be free is to do what we *will*, that is to say, to do that of

[1] *Opera*, vol. III, p. 14.
[2] *Ibid.* p. 214.
[3] *Ibid.* p. 203.
[4] *Ibid.* p. 35.
[5] *Ibid.* p. 208.
[6] *Ibid.* p. 207.

which we clearly know ourselves to be the authors—although not, of course, to do what we *like* (when liking is obscure or passionate) still less to do as we chance to have begun.[1]

Accordingly what appears to be a negative path, the separation of mind from body, is held, in the end, to have a most positive and determinate message. And when we interpret the message we find that something very great indeed is revealed. For we find that our rational selves do not stand alone. *Meum* and *tuum*, indeed, do not apply to them at all. When we behold ourselves, we behold the Word in us. We are altogether creatures of deity, understanding, that is, that deity is nothing fabulous or beyond rational divining, but the deity of "natural" religion or of reason. In other words the good man does not act *quia ipse vult*, but *quia Deus vult* or *quia Ratio praecipit*.[2] God is not an Other to him, but is the good man himself accepting and obeying his reason.

Such, then, is the answer to the first question concerning the nature of reason, and our knowledge of it.

Regarding the second question, Geulincx professes to deduce no fewer than nine sets of obligations.

The first two of these obligations are to accept death cheerfully when God recalls us from among the living, and yet not to anticipate God's decree in this matter.

The argument here depends on the maxim *Ubi nihil vales ibi nihil velis*. This is the logical contrapositive of the proverb, where there's a will there's a way, i.e. the Geulincxian principle is, Where there's no way, there can be no will. What is alleged, then, is that we have no power over the term of our existence, and so cannot clearly will our own deaths. We can only pretend, knowing not how, to act upon the machine of our bodies.

The conclusion therefore is that we should not interfere in these matters because we cannot do so.

The third, fourth, fifth and sixth obligations are, respectively, to eat, drink and otherwise supply the needs (not the superfluities) of the body, to perform the offices of one's

---

[1] *Opera*, vol. III, pp. 187 *sq*. [2] *Ibid.* p. 189.

station in life, to do and suffer many things in consequence, and to seek all proper repose and relaxation.

According to Geulincx's theory of the relation between mind and body (usually called Occasionalism), none of these things is within our power. For they have to do with the machine we call our body; and of this machine we are mere spectators, not authors. Consequently, we must object to him, if it is not in our power to end our days by drinking laudanum, it is equally not in our power to continue our days by drinking milk. And if "experience" is irrelevant to rational action, the experience implied in duties of this kind must also be irrelevant.

Faced with objections of this type, Geulincx replies lamely that although we do not strictly have the power to eat or to drink, we know, as spectators of the bodily machine, that the machine cannot survive without sufficient nourishment.[1] He therefore endeavours to deduce the third obligation from the first pair. But vainly. If we do not have this power, we do not have it. If we do have it, we have the power of suicide also.

His only remaining argument is that God tells us to eat and to drink.[2]

Consequently the alleged deduction collapses, and it is needless to pursue the point in further instances. This collapse of the argument is in no way accidental. For Geulincx the bodily machine is *not* the mind and cannot be influenced by the mind. Hence it is nonsense to seek to guide or control it. In other words the moral rules which concern, say, murder, or rape, or suicide can have nothing to do with the good will. The surprising feature of Geulincx's ethics is that he should ever have attempted to deduce what is so plainly beyond all deducing.

In detail, Geulincx was one of the sanest of rationalists. It is possible he says to act *ex passione*.[3] This the vulgar do, whether they profess to be pious and follow the sentiments they call their conscience, or are prudent for the sake of mere enjoyment, or are the slaves of greed and lust. And all such

[1] *Opera*, vol. III, pp. 243 *sq*. [2] *Ibid*. [3] *Ibid*. pp. 106 *sqq*.

action is wrong. It is also possible, like the Stoics, to profess to act *contra passionem*; and this is a mistaken enterprise. The truth is that we should act *praeter passionem*, not attempting to extirpate the passions, not refusing the joys they may bring, yet in no way truckling to them. They are irrelevances (sometimes grateful irrelevances) to the good life itself.

The trouble is, as we have seen, that the ideal of reason, interpreted as Geulincx interpreted it, cannot yield the determinate guidance which he professed to extract from it.

It remains to mention briefly what Geulincx had to say concerning the nature of Good and of Evil.

Good (he says) is what we love and evil what we shun.[1] They are therefore extrinsic denominations, applying not to things but to our attitude towards things. Again what is good (in some sense) to one man may be bad (in some sense) to another man.

The three species of good are *bonum utile*, *bonum jucundum* and *bonum honestum*. The first is but a means to good. The second defines what we love with passion or sentiment of any sort whatsoever. The third is what we love because reason so decrees.

In the third case (which is the true good) Geulincx explains that we do not love what proceeds from reason, but the rational mind of God from which all rational commands emanate. It seems plain from this explanation (if it were not already plain in itself) that *bonum honestum* is not an extrinsic denomination, and that on Geulincxian principles it should not vary from man to man.

§ 3. *Malebranche*

Malebranche is a signal example of the way in which individual genius, although conforming to a general pattern of ideas, weaves a fabric of its own. Although a Cartesian and an occasionalist, he was, nevertheless, one of the most original of philosophers; and if his views concerning ethics and the

[1] *Opera*, vol. III, p. 99.

nature of perfection are somewhat less noteworthy than certain of his other ideas, they indicate the possibility at least of an application of Cartesian notions widely different from what is usual. I shall therefore give a brief account of these views, confining myself, almost entirely, to what is said in Malebranche's *Traité de morale*.

Summarising the argument of the first, and most considerable, part of this work, Malebranche says that he has endeavoured, in the first place, to show that virtue consists, quite precisely, in the dominant and habitual love of the immutable order of the universe; in the second place, to treat of the two qualities principally requisite to the acquisition of virtue, viz. the strength and the liberty of the mind; in the third place, to examine the accompanying (mainly physical) occasions of understanding and sentiment without which this essential love of order could neither be won nor kept.[1]

The "order" here in question is the order of perfections in the universe. "I am able to discover", he says, "at any rate confusedly the *relations in the way of perfection* which occur between our ideas;...and these relations are the immutable order to which God has regard in His actions, an order which should also govern the approval and affection of every intelligence."[2]

It is currently maintained by historians of philosophy that two Augustinian tendencies achieve harmonious fusion in Malebranche's theory. These are the ontological status of rational truth, evidenced by Descartes, and the experimental testimony of religious experience, so notable in the writings of Pascal.[3] And certainly Malebranche's account of the *rapports de perfection* is saturated by both these influences. On the one hand, Malebranche strenuously maintains that intelligence is essential to these affairs. Reason, he says, is consubstantial with God;[4] and again, "Neminem enim diligit Deus nisi eum qui cum sapientia habitat",[5] or, still more

[1] *Traité de morale*, I, Part I, chap. XIII, § xiii.   [2] *Ibid.* I, I, § vi.
[3] Cf. J. Sirven, *Les années d'apprentissage de Descartes*, p. 318.
[4] *Traité de morale*, I, I, § x.   [5] *Ibid.* II, III, § viii.

explicitly, "Faith without intelligence—I do not speak here of the mysteries concerning which clear ideas are impossible—faith, I say, without the light of reason, if it is possible, cannot achieve solid virtue".[1] The grace that comes from feeling, or *la délectation prévenante*, is but a makeshift for it.

Similarly, the love that is here in question is the love of union—*amor unionis*. We become more perfect by uniting ourselves with that divine perfection which is God. And differences in perfection are wholly objective. A brute has more perfection than a stone and less than a man.[2] We are capable of knowing the true good as well as of loving it.[3] Indeed, the light of reason reveals the good that we love with all the impetus of an invincible impression.[4]

In short, this rational love implies the commingling of essences. He who has it therefore must have his whole being controlled by it. Seeing perfection in love, he is, in so far forth, perfect, virtuous, united with the good. And God, who loves His creatures in proportion to their affinity with His perfections, may be said to love what is authentically lovable.[5] To be lovable in this sense is to be, in that measure, perfect or estimable. This is the law of God's being, the law which God Himself loves invincibly, because it expresses, and indeed *is*, His proper being.

At the same time it is evident that this equation of the perfect or excellent with the lovable, if it softens the dry light of intellect with a hint of tenderness and also induces a warm glow of loyalty, needs to be interpreted with great circumspection in order to avoid the vapours and enthusiasms usually (although, very likely, unjustly) associated with Pascal's *raisons de cœur*. Indeed, since God loves sinners as well as the righteous, and since His Son lived in charity with publicans and erring women, it is hard to see how a love strictly proportional to perfection can be consistently united with love in these other senses. If Malebranche, however, could not altogether succeed in his enterprise—any more than the others

---

[1] *Traité de morale*, I, II, § xi.   [2] *Ibid.* I, I, § xiii.
[3] *Ibid.* I, I, § xviii.   [4] *Ibid.* I, IV, § xvii.   [5] *Entretiens*, XI.

who have tried to solve the mystery of evil—he tried very hard to explain the distinction and the relation between *amor unionis* and tender or benevolent emotion.

The principal meanings of love, he says, are firstly, voluntary union with some object as one's good or as the cause of felicity, and, secondly, facilitating in some one else the advent of a good which the other needs.[1] These two senses show us, respectively, what should be the love of God and what should be the love of our neighbour. In all cases, esteem and love should conform to perfection and order; and because there is this proportion, love of God's infinite perfection should immeasurably out-distance all other love.[2] Since we have the strength to enter within ourselves, and to attend to what is clear and rational, and have freedom to suspend our judgment in order so to attend,[3] we may do much towards stilling the clamour of the body, and cultivating this rational love. In addition to this we must have "exact obedience to the law of God, a scrupulous and catholic discrimination of all our duties, a stable and governing disposition to regulate all movements of the heart and all the gait of our conduct in conformity with the rational order that we know. For this is the love of order".[4]

The enemy of *l'amour de l'ordre* is *l'amour propre*,[5] or a selfish regard for our own pleasure; and it is also forbidden to love either oneself or any other creature as an ultimate end, or as the cause of its own perfection or happiness.[6] For these things (including all happiness) come from God alone.

Nevertheless, it is not forbidden to seek happiness; and indeed any such command would be senseless as well as cruel. Again, although bodily pleasures are deceitful, seductive and corrupting; and although, the more carnal-minded we are, the less we are fitted to love our Maker, God does give us happiness even on a bodily occasion, and pleasure itself testifies to the actual presence of some perfection.

---

[1] *Traité de morale*, I, III, § ii.
[2] *Ibid.* I, III, § vii.
[3] *Ibid.* I, V, and I, VII.
[4] *Ibid*, I, VII, § i.
[5] *Ibid.* I, III, § xii.
[6] *Ibid.* I, XII, § xv.

We should act therefore as towards God and as towards the city of His saints. Yet, in a minor way, custom, habit, and sentiment may give a certain unity and graciousness to our lives—or a reproach of conscience passably similar to rational admonition.[1] On the other hand, the mere fact of social unity may be of very little ethical importance. In the bibulous societies across the Rhine, "it is wine, not reason, that unites societies, seals their mutual services and determines their contracts".[2]

SECTION III. KANT'S THEORY OF VALUE

§ 1. *Introductory*

The essence of Kant's theory of value is to be found in his analysis of what he sometimes calls dignity and sometimes intrinsic worth. Such dignity, he thinks, is moral and exclusively so; and yet there are advantages in approaching his account of dignity through its contrast with his aesthetic theory.

These advantages are partly general and partly more specific. The general advantage is that most theories of value bring beauty and moral worth into the same large perspective; and Kant's denial of the legitimacy of this procedure is accordingly the more noteworthy. The special advantage is that Kant's account of this contrast in the *Critique of Judgment* is in many ways the most interesting presentation of his theory of dignity.

§ 2. *Kant's aesthetic theory*

Kant's aesthetic theory is dependent upon his analysis of the judgment of beauty—as is appropriate in a "critical" philosophy.

The first point to note is that beauty, for Kant, *is* an affair of judgment and is *not* an affair of pleasure or of emotion.[3]

---

[1] *Traité de morale*, I, v, § xx.   [2] *Ibid.* I, II, § vii.
[3] *Critique of Judgment* (Bernard's translation), pp. 45 *sqq.*

This, then, is not in dispute—that is to say, Kant does not question it. What he does make a question of is the character of the aesthetic judgment. In his view, any such judgment is highly distinctive and entirely peculiar; for it is in one sense *à priori* and in another sense subjective.

It is *à priori* because it lays claim to strict universality.[1] He who asserts that anything is beautiful asserts something that is meant to be necessary, not accidental; something that should hold in principle for all who judge, not something that varies with private biographies. To be sure, men may differ in their judgments about beauty; but that is not the point. Some or many of them may be wrong. The question is: What do they *mean*?

Accordingly, the judgment of beauty is not subjective in the sense of being an affair of a man's private and variable constitution. On the other hand, if we mean by "objective" some knowledge of objects by means of assignable and intelligible conceptions, aesthetic judgments are not in this sense "objective" at all.

In Kant's view, the appreciation of a thing's beauty does not imply any knowledge whatsoever of the properties which make the thing what it is.[2] On the contrary, beauty comes about when there is a general harmony between the powers of the human mind and the form and features of the thing whose beauty we take ourselves to grasp. This harmony, however, need not be known, and, if it is known, is irrelevant. Beauty is the joyful poise, the free play, the untrammelled equilibrium of the mind, *à priori* because it is the free play of mind as such, not the expression of some private constitution; but subjective in the sense that it is neither a way of knowing things nor of acting upon them. This is what Kant means by the moment of disinterestedness in beauty.

A consequence of this opinion is Kant's emphatic distinction between what he calls *pulchritudo vaga* and *pulchritudo adhaerens*.[3] In essentials, this resembles the familiar aesthetic

---

[1] *Ibid.* p. 70.   [2] E.g. *ibid.* p. 66.
[3] *Ibid.* p. 81.

doctrine of the necessity for a certain species of purity or asceticism in art. Knowledge of fact or knowledge of purpose pertain to *pulchritudo adhaerens*, and are to be eschewed. Kant's own argument, however, is peculiar. He seems almost to regard anything beautiful as a brilliant natural spectacle, as Sir Edmund Gosse says he did when he went with his father to see a picture of Holman Hunt's.[1] At any rate, Kant regards flowers or "delineations *à la grecque*, foliage for borders or wall papers" as the best examples of free or vague beauty because "they mean nothing in themselves";[2] and he appends the astonishing comment, "We could add much to a building that would immediately please the eye, if only it were not to be a church".[3]

Hence beauty, Kant says, is wholly distinct from perfection. "Perfection gains nothing by beauty or beauty by perfection."[4] "To seek for a principle of taste which shall furnish, by means of definite concepts, a universal criterion of the beautiful, is fruitless trouble; because what is sought is impossible and self-contradictory."[5] In other words, "the aesthetical idea is always an *inexponible* representation of the imagination".[6]

In short, Kant maintains that the aesthetic judgment is unique and not to be confounded with anything else in the world. It is therefore distinct from pleasure. For pleasure is simply the agreeable quality of all our private sensations.

Nevertheless, Kant's doctrine is curiously balanced. Despite all he says about the freedom of *pulchritudo vaga*, he also maintains that the *necessity* contained in the aesthetic judgment is conditioned, in a general way, by the very nature of our imagination, and that it presupposes a certain bent and aim of human faculty.[7] Again there are further qualifications concerning the sublime, and the sense in which beauty, after all, is a symbol of moral worth. It will be expedient, however, to postpone discussion of these points for the moment, and

---

[1] *Father and Son*, p. 271.
[2] *Critique of Judgment*, p. 81.
[3] *Ibid*. p. 82.
[4] *Ibid*. p. 83.
[5] *Ibid*. p. 84.
[6] *Ibid*. p. 236.
[7] *Ibid*. pp. 92 *sqq*.

§ 3. *Beauty and goodness*

Unlike the beautiful, the good, according to Kant, is intrinsically and expressly conceptual. Indeed, it is causality according to concepts. Appetite (Kant even says Life[1]) is the faculty of making actual what initially is but an idea. When the pleasantness, or promise of pleasantness, in such ideas determines our action, we have animal or sensory desire; but when our concepts themselves, on account of their rationality, determine our action, we have the good or the rational will. Instead of the free play of imagination which characterises beauty, we have in goodness nothing but rational self-determination as the basis of the process. And the autonomous freedom of the will must be distinguished from the freedom of imagination which, as we have seen, is conditioned by the general conformity of beautiful things to our faculties.

Accordingly, there are many sides to this contrast. Properly speaking, the beautiful is not purposive, although it presupposes a harmony between our faculties and their objects. Goodness, *per contra*, is purposive and practical to the core. Again, what Kant calls the "interest" of the two is disparate both in principle and in quality. The satisfaction of beauty is a joyful freedom, but the interest or satisfaction of practical good is stringently determined and conditioned. For the moral law, itself unconditioned, generates a submissive glow of feeling which Kant calls "respect", and "respect" is esteem, not enchantment, an appropriate consequence and not, as it were, a free gift from nature's horn of plenty.[2]

Whatever is good must be capable of being rationally willed, and the only pleasure that can be rationally willed is pleasure consequent upon, and appropriate to, rational dignity or

---

[1] *Introduction to the Metaphysic of Morals*, i (Abbott, *Kant's Theory of Ethics*, p. 265).
[2] *Critique of Judgment*, p. 52.

worth. Hence pleasure, *in se*, is not good. Only a conditioned pleasure is good. And beauty, being exempt from concepts, is also, in that sense, not rational. Accordingly, value or dignity has not, for Kant, that general significance which it had for the British moralists.

Our principal task in this chapter is therefore to attempt to understand how Kant developed his theory of (moral) worth or dignity. Before doing so, however, it is necessary to consider what he says concerning the sublime, and concerning the way in which beauty is the symbol of morality.

§ 4. *The sublime and the ideal of beauty*

Beauty is the play, but the sublime is the earnest of imagination.[1] Again beauty is restful, the sublime in nature profoundly disturbing.[2] Properly speaking, indeed, nothing in nature is adequate to the emotion of sublimity.[3] The sublime is the unattainable, our sorrow in our own littleness when we are in the presence of something we divine to be (not simply great) but majestic and ineffable.[4] This is followed by an experience of exaltation. In such an experience, reason, although with some vagueness, admonishes and chastens us. The sublime has authority although it exercises this authority only on those whose culture has prepared them for it. What is only terrible to a savage may be sublime to a man whose soul has been nurtured.[5]

Indeed, the majesty of the sublime is at least three parts moral or religious, and the sublime awakens feelings in us so similar to *respect* for the moral law that there is very little difference except in point of vagueness. This genuine similitude is absent in the case of beauty,[6] and yet we find Kant (in a tortuous and hesitating way) suggesting a certain affinity between beauty and morality. This is his doctrine of the Ideal of Beauty.[7]

---

[1] *Critique of Judgment*, p. 102. [2] *Ibid*. pp. 105 *sq*.
[3] Kant discusses the sublime in art as well as the sublime in nature.
[4] *Critique of Judgment*, p. 122. [5] *Ibid*. p. 130.
[6] *Ibid*. p. 177. [7] *Ibid*. pp. 84 *sqq*.

An Ideal, Kant explains, is the presentation of an idea in sensible show, and beauty, as we have seen, cannot be a specimen of any idea whatsoever. In another way, however, beauty may be said to express the conformity between sense and the intelligible. In its own way, therefore, it does embody a certain ideal; and Kant even suggests that the human form expresses a moral ideal since it is the sensible form of man, and since man, alone among creatures, has the reason for his existence (i.e. his intrinsic worth) within himself.[1] Similarly, it is significant that man alone should be susceptible of an ideal of beauty.[2]

Again, there is something intellectual in beauty; for its *raison d'être* is the peace and harmony of an intellectual being brought face to face with something appropriate to his powers. Consequently, the mind that ponders over beauty ponders over something akin to the rule of reason over nature, i.e. akin to the principle of morality. Thus man's aesthetic interest in nature is at least an interest congruent with a truly moral disposition.[3] Beauty, indeed, implies the urbanity of the higher cognitive powers;[4] and Kant, proceeding in this vein, roundly declares that beauty is the symbol of morality. "By this the mind is made conscious of a certain ennoblement and elevation above the mere sensibility to pleasure received through sense, and the worth of others is estimated in accordance with a like maxim of their judgment."[5] The universality and freedom of the aesthetic judgment is also cited as well as its superiority to the thraldom of sense.

§ 5. *The nature of value or dignity*

It is time, however, to pass from these symbols, intimations or analogies to value or dignity itself.

The obvious starting point here is the passage in which Kant distinguishes market or fancy value from intrinsic worth or dignity.[6] That which has market value, he says, depends

---

[1] *Ibid.* p. 86.   [2] *Ibid.*   [3] *Ibid.* pp. 179 *sq.*
[4] *Ibid.* p. 219.   [5] *Ibid.* p. 251.
[6] *Fundamental Principles* (Abbott), p. 53.

upon the inclinations and wants of mankind. It is, in a word, economic good. That which has fancy value is regarded as independent of wants but as satisfying the free play of our faculties. It is illustrated by wit, lively imagination and humour. And intrinsic worth is opposed to both of these.

The distinction is buttressed by the argument that market and fancy value permit of substitution, while intrinsic value does not. This dubious support, however, is of no real moment. The essential point is the connection between value or dignity and rational humanity as an end in itself.

§ 6. *Reason as an end*

Both in the *Fundamental Principles* and in the *Critique of Practical Reason*, Kant's mode of exposition partially excuses those of his critics[1] who take the essence of his ethic to lie in formal consistency, and therefore maintain that the conception of reason as an end is a furtive and backstairs effort to introduce something very thoroughly different. The excuse for such critics, however, if real, is very slight indeed. From the outset and all the time Kant is referring to that which is practical; and practice with him is always an attempt to accomplish some end.

In short, Kant never doubted the plain fact that every volition has an end, purpose or object. The question he debated was whether this purpose comes from outside (so to say) or from within the rational will.

If it came from outside, he thought, reason either became a slave to our animal inclinations, or to an empty idea of perfection, or to a "courtly" standard of arbitrary theology.[2] The rational will must therefore be actuated from the inside, that is to say, from its own spontaneity. It cannot be contingent upon circumstances and it dare not wait for success. It must impress and indeed force its own ends upon the circumstances it encounters.

---

[1] Cf. Rashdall, *The Theory of Good and Evil*, vol. I, pp. 109 *sq.* n.
[2] *Practical Reason*, Analytic, Theorem IV, Remarks on § viii (Abbott, pp. 122 *sqq.*).

The same result follows if we consider Kant's alternative term "interest". To have an interest and to be practical are for him one and the same. Therefore the will always has an interest;[1] but it should never, if it is moral, be subservient to a foreign interest. It has "pure practical interest", i.e. it impresses itself upon the world or makes a difference to the world. Again, by striking down self-conceit, it induces "respect" or the sentiment of awe or reverence within our breasts.[2]

We may state Kant's position briefly as follows:

1. Man is both a part of nature (homo phenomenon) and a rational being belonging to a rational order superior to nature (homo noumenon).

2. As homo noumenon he is in no way beholden to nature or to the facts of his animal or sensory constitution.

3. As homo noumenon he is entirely autonomous, and therefore not beholden as such to God or to other rational beings.

4. His rational will is his autonomous self-legislation, and this, by right, is dominant over nature (including his own sensory nature).

5. Accordingly his action, so far as it is rational, springs from the pure spontaneity of his own person and has no other determinant.

6. The test of universality is sufficient to show whether any proposed plan of action is truly rational or not.

7. But this universality has the alternative form of setting laws to nature, i.e. of acting as a righteous governor of nature should.

8. And since the question always is that of dominance by reason, the only question is whether pure reason is at work or not.

9. Hence pure reason respects itself wherever it appears, i.e. in any person.

---

[1] *Fundamental Principles*, Third Section, Abbott, pp. 67 *sqq.*, especially p. 80 n.
[2] *Practical Reason*, Book I, chap. iii (Abbott, pp. 164 *sqq.*).

10. Therefore any "end in itself" should be treated as a thing that has dignity.

§ 7. *The good will*

Kant begins his argument in the *Fundamental Principles* by stating that nothing in the world, or out of it, is good without qualification except the good will. Other goods may be abused and therefore are good only under a certain qualification or condition. Even in this passage, however, more is meant than meets the eye; for it has to be remembered what a will *is*. The will is always an efficacy, since it is causality through concepts; and it always acts for an end. Good is substantive, not adjectival, existential, not merely ideal; for that which alone has worth or intrinsic dignity is a substance whose actions spring from its own rational nature and are directed towards ends which are derived exclusively from this rational nature.

The subsequent argument is the unveiling of these concealed premisses. To prove the rationality of the will, it is necessary only to show that it expresses a logically universal law. But this is the law of a will or autonomous lawgiver. And the lawgiver in question rules *de jure* over nature. *In the case of a rational will*, to be universal and to prescribe universal law to nature are one and the same. For, in the end, the whole sensible realm has a supersensible foundation. Nature is the sensible appearance of a supersensible foundation. It is the similitude of a *corpus mysticum* of productive rational wills.

For the same reason, *all* the ends of authentic rationality must be accepted by pure reason wheresoever they occur. Whatever has dignity should be accorded dignity. And dignity or intrinsic worth gives the sole sufficient reason for *any* existence. In the world, man is the only being who, having dignity, justifies his own existence, and then only so far as he is rational. Metaphysically, indeed, we must hold that all existence is similarly justified; but ethically our plain duty is to respect all justifying reasons for existence wherever we find them, that is to say, to treat every rational man as an ultimate end, and to treat humanity, whether in our own person or in any other person, always as an end, never merely as a means.[1]

Kant puts the same point otherwise when he says, in highly technical language, that moral action is *synthetic*. The mere conception of a will never contains the injunctions of moral conduct. On the contrary, the will ensues ends towards which it reaches out. It creates its duties, and does not already contain them within itself, although it does not accept them from some outside source. According to Kant, freedom is the key to this synthetic action of the will.

§ 8. *Value and freedom*

Kant himself admitted, very candidly, that his doctrine of freedom involved grave difficulties, and was scarcely susceptible of a lucid definition. It was his business, he thought, to lay bare these difficulties.[2]

The first step is tolerably plain. Value, dignity, or intrinsic worth alone justifies existence, and unless the contrary can be shown, we have the right to believe that all existence, including the whole realm of nature, is so justified.

The outstanding *prima facie* objection is, of course, the *inevitability* of natural events (interpreted, as they should be interpreted, according to the laws of physics) combined with what is sometimes called the *ethical neutrality* of physics, that is to say, with the plain circumstance that neither purpose nor value is a scientific or descriptive conception. Rational value, therefore, can never yield a natural or scientific explanation of the ways of the universe. But if nature itself, as we have reason to believe, is not self-explanatory but depends upon an invisible, noumenal or supersensible order, it must, as a whole, have a supernatural (although not a superstitious) foundation. Natural science, which *ex hypothesi* is

---

[1] For this entire argument see *Fundamental Principles*, the second section.

[2] *Practical Reason*, Book I. Concluding critical examination (Abbott, p. 197).

concerned with nature and with nature's ways, has not the right and should not have the desire, to interpose any obstacle whatsoever in the path of any such metaphysics. What it rightly protests against is the attempt to employ these supersensible, non-natural conceptions as scientific explanations, or in other words, to regard freedom, value or even purpose as particular physical causes among other physical causes.

It is therefore entirely possible that nature as a whole should be an emanation from, or an appearance of, a supersensible determination by invisible but purely rational agents; and although this determination cannot be physical causality, there is more danger of verbal than of real ambiguity in the circumstance. Again, in the case of humanity, if we can distinguish clearly, as Kant thinks we can, between man's rationality (which is not a part of nature) and his sensory character (which is such a part), there should be no fundamental obscurity.

Thus nature as a whole may have a rational justification, although natural science cannot employ this type of explanation as a particular scientific hypothesis in any particular case. And if moral worth is the only unconditioned worth, the rational justification in question is a moral justification of nature as a whole. Nature is the free or created product of a rational order which exists, and justifies its existence, in and through its intrinsic worth.

It is not to be contended that this metaphysic is free from difficulty, or that Kant, in most of his writings, does not tend to accept it rather too easily owing to the influence Leibnizian theory had had upon him. (For Leibniz, nature was only a *phenomenon bene fundatum*, and the reality was the intelligible harmony of monads.) The greatest difficulty of all, however, is the way in which Kant, with his strong ethical convictions, attempted to use his doctrine, not merely as a general account of the supersensible foundation of all sensible phenomena, but also as (up to a certain point) an explanation of particular moral actions on the part of particular human beings at definite times.

The human will, he says, is an elective will,[1] that is to say, it may either be determined by reason or by sensible inclination, and there can be no doubt that he frequently regarded moral principles as making a special and noticeable difference to the course of nature, at least in our own persons, at some particular moment.

Thus, to choose one typical example among many, he argues to the following effect in the *Practical Reason*. A man who says he cannot control his lusts is talking nonsense. Put a gallows before him as the necessary consequence of his act, and the fear of death will straightway stop him. Yet if he were ordered, under threat of immediate execution, to testify falsely, say, against an innocent man, he knows that he *could* tell the truth, and suffer the penalty.[2] Moral determination is therefore a fact in our experience; and experience also attests that our free and rational will is strong enough to prevail against any sensible inclination whatsoever.

Whatever may be thought of this argument (and it does not seem to be strong) it is at least apparent that the moral motive is here regarded as a particular operative force, comparable to, although stronger than, such special facts in nature as the fear of death or a lustful appetite. In other words, moral determination, although never a "natural" cause, is said to produce quite special natural effects (which would not have occurred otherwise in the course of nature), thus interfering with some particular part of the course of nature as well as determining the entire course of nature.

Any such philosophy appears to contain the same inconsistency as those theologies which point to the general regularity of nature as a signal proof of God's goodness and power, and at the same time approve God's special interference with His own orderly work in what is called His particular providence. Kant might, perhaps, have consistently maintained that the sun of reason, so to say, shines through the clouds of

---

[1] E.g. *Practical Reason*, Book I, chap. I, § vii. Cor. Remark (Abbott, p. 121).

[2] *Ibid.* § vi, Prob. II. Remark (Abbott, pp. 118 *sq.*).

nature (which it itself has created) in particular patches of moral action. In that case, however, he would have to have held that the man who goes to the scaffold rather than bear false witness is determined wholly by his antecedent sensible inclinations, just as much as the craven who prefers his own security. The only difference would be that the general moral order which determines both sets of actions (because it determines everything in nature) is seen very darkly in the second instance and almost translucently in the first. But that is not what Kant says.

§ 9. *The ego or subject of dignity*

It is small wonder that we cannot use our knowledge of the efficacy of our own reason as a clue to discoveries in the natural sciences. Reason, perhaps, makes nature; but a man does *not* make his body, his instincts or his passions, and his moral worth is *not* the ground of his own physical existence.

It may be replied, and very justly, that this way of regarding the question is foreign to Kant's point of view. Kant expressly repudiated the traditional distinction between soul and body. The "soul" of traditional metaphysics, he said, was but a psychological phenomenon, falsely, although very naturally, taken to be a substantial thing. What is free then is not the soul, but homo noumenon.

And yet the reply seems inadequate. We learn from certain of Kant's manuscript notes how profoundly he believed himself, at a certain stage of his career, to be indebted to Rousseau. Rousseau, he there declared, did for human nature what Newton did for physical nature—he discovered its simple essence despite the bewildering multiplicity of experiences. He also declared that it was Rousseau who taught him to honour humanity as such; and to make the rights of humanity stand forth.[1]

What Kant took from Rousseau he transformed. Kant's infallible conscience is not Rousseau's infallible conscience.

---

[1] For the evidence here see V. Delbos, *La philosophie pratique de Kant*, 2nd edn. pp. 115 *sqq.*

Indeed Kant gives us an inverted Rousseauism, in which all of man's dignity is reason and none of it sentimental or romantic. And yet one must ask whether he had the same right to appeal to individual moral experience as Rousseau had. Rousseau's men were visible men. The humanity he honoured was a humanity to be distinguished in the usual phenomenal ways. We can all make a shift, at least, to distinguish one phenomenal man from another, and our own phenomenal selves from the rest of mankind. When men's bodies and souls, however, are expressly denied to be the persons we honour, what grounds can we have for distinguishing one homo noumenon from another? Why should each phenomenal self have a single noumenal ego corresponding to it? How do we know that there is a plurality of noumenal egos at all?

If what Kant says is true, we know that the voice of reason may be heard by each of us; but with what right does he tell us that each of us is a specific centre of reason, distinct from all other centres in the way one man's mind or body is distinct from another man's mind or body? For all Kant has shown the noumenal realm might perfectly well be *a single* rational order actuating *all* the phenomenal selves. If there were only one rational subject of value, instead of a kingdom or society of rational ends, no essential part of Kant's contentions would appear to be in jeopardy.

§ 10. *The restriction of dignity to reason*

Provided, however, that reason somehow operates among men, and that the worth of its operation may be recognised, it is perhaps of lesser moment than we might carelessly suppose, what precise relation reason has to the animal organisations that we call our bodies or to the whimsical, fluctuating integrations of consciousness that tradition calls our minds. On the other hand, it is of the greatest consequence whether reason, in fact, is the *fons et origo* of all value.

In considering this question it is necessary, first of all, to be quite clear about the precise meaning of Kant's contention. He does *not* hold that reason (i.e. the good will) is the sole or complete good, but only that it is the supreme unconditional and only intrinsic good.[1] In the *Practical Reason* he maintains that the complete good for man is a union of moral good with happiness. He who is morally good is alone worthy of happiness, and ought to achieve (indeed will achieve) that fuller good in which happiness is added to moral worth. Happiness, which we commonly regard as the gift of fortune, is a genuine part of the complete good when, instead of fortune, we rightly postulate the providence of God.[2] Again, the gifts of fortune are only one species of what Kant calls the gifts of nature. Another species is the gifts of personality such as courage, resolution or other gifts of temperament.[3] These, in Kant's view, should be made subordinate to character or to the moral will; but when the good will is supreme they add to the goodness of a man.

The essential part of this contention is that the good will is not a "gift" but the substance of homo noumenon, and that all gifts, if they are good gifts, are conditionally so. Intrinsic worth belongs solely to the principle of expetition, and anything good that is added to the principle of expetition has a subordinate, although real, status.

The foundation of this contention seems peculiarly insecure. Is our reason either more or less of a gift than our courage or intelligence? And may not peace or love, even if they are not directly expetible, be as great goods as any?

Again, even if reason were the sole intrinsic or unconditional good, is it at all evident that conditioned goods may not, nevertheless, be greater goods than unconditioned ones? If love is conditioned and reason unconditioned, may not love, all the same, be better than reason?

Considerations of this type have been discussed so frequently in the present enquiry that it should be needless to repeat our

[1] E.g. *Fundamental Principles*, Section I (Abbott, p. 12).
[2] See the entire arguments of the *Dialectic*.
[3] *Fundamental Principles*, Section I (Abbott, p. 9).

findings concerning them. Even if we have been mistaken in our attitude, however, Kant's position would seem to be vulnerable from another quarter. His proof that the gifts of temperament are conditioned is that they may be misapplied —that is to say, that they are good, sometimes only, and for special reasons, and that they are not good absolutely or in themselves. But is it really so? May not courage, love and loyalty always be good wherever they occur? May not a courageous piece of villainy, even, be redeemed by its courage, having thereby worse effects, to be sure, than if it had been craven or spineless, but being intrinsically nobler and finer?

In short, if Kant had not supposed from the first that the choir of noumena or of things invisible is necessarily and always a perfect choir; and that all the "gifts" of nature, although not vile, are of the earth earthy and of little genuine worth, it may be doubted whether the austere and even grim outlines of his general theory of value would ever have appeared plausible to himself or to others. It is not surprising, therefore, that a phalanx of critics should have constituted themselves the defenders of empirical values—the protagonists of beauty, benevolence, sympathy and hope. The nature of this criticism, I suppose, is sufficiently widely known, and I do not intend to beat a small drum at the rear of this huge procession. Instead, I mean to ask whether Kant himself consistently adhered to his declared doctrine that dignity or intrinsic worth is wholly noumenal. If he did not, the rationality of values need not be denied, but the restriction of intrinsic or unconditional value to *mere* reason must be regarded as very hard to sustain.

§ 11. *The rights of man*

In Kant's Introduction to the *Metaphysic of Morals* we learn (as we might have suspected) that responsibility is the essential attribute of moral personality. The moral agent is the author of his deeds, and these may be imputed to him if he knows the law on which the obligation rests. Hence a *person* is the subject whose actions may thus be imputed.[1]

Both legal and moral obligations imply constraint, but the law imposes external constraints. Juridically, a compulsion is imposed upon men so to act that the use of one man's freedom may not circumscribe the freedom of any other man. Ethics, on the other hand, yields internal constraint. Its peculiar essence is shown quite precisely in the way in which the moral will constrains itself to attain ends which are also duties. No one can be forced to have an end, but a rational being forces itself to make rationality (or intrinsic worth) its own end. As Kant says paradoxically, "the less a man can be physically forced, and the more he can be morally forced by the mere idea of duty, so much the freer he is".[2]

Even from the legal point of view, Kant maintains, the autonomy of man's rational will entails many remarkable consequences. Freedom is the unoriginated birthright of every man. Hence, by law, each man must be held to be his own master and legally equal with others. Again the law, for the same reason, must not interfere with a man who does not interfere with his fellows. And lastly the law must protect free exchange of opinions, the making of covenants—in short every free employment which is not derogatory to others.[3]

The law, therefore, exists to protect the rational pursuits of rational men. What, then, are the ends of a rational being?

§ 12. *Perfection and happiness*

Kant holds that the ends of a rational being are, firstly, his own perfection and, secondly, his neighbour's happiness.[4]

Perfection, he explains, may be understood in an ontological or quantitative sense. In this case (which is here irrelevant) it means neither more nor less than totality. The term, however, may also be understood in a teleological or qualitative

---

[1] Introduction to the *Metaphysic of Morals*, IV (Abbott, p. 279).
[2] *Metaphysical Elements of Ethics*, Preface, II (Abbott, p. 292 n.).
[3] *Werke*, Berlin edn, vol. VI, pp. 237 *sq*.
[4] *Ibid.* p. 385.

sense and taken to indicate the adaptation of means to ends. In this sense (which is highly relevant to ethics) it behoves a man to educate and improve his brute nature, to clarify his mind and to discipline his habits and inclinations. This duty of culture, however, is always a duty of *self*-culture, for the culture must be the fruit of our own self-governance. For this reason we may not seek the culture of others. But it is otherwise with good fortune or happiness. To seek our own happiness as an end is to do obeisance to nature and to fortune (which are outside our dominion). It cannot be disinterested action, as good action must always be, and the most that can be conceded in this matter is that we are rationally entitled to preserve our own health, secure a competence and the like *as means* to our own perfection (or alternatively to avoid such grief, poverty or pain as hinder the moral life). Our concern for the happiness of others, *per contra*, is disinterested, and so there *is* a positive duty of beneficence.

It is plain from this account that a Kantian considers himself justly entitled to seek everything in the way of culture and even in the way of personal comfort that would seem reasonable on any sane theory of life. The sole condition is that such things should be sought, not for their own sakes, but in subordination to the plan and policy of a rational existence. If so, the manifest implication is that these things should be sought *on account of their worth*, not, indeed, on account of values outside personality, but on account of values regarded as possible constituents of a personality rationally governed and directed. Instead of being drawn from mere reason, they are rationally understood to be capable of being assimilated into a rational existence. In this case, Kant's so-called "excessive" rigorism disappears, and the subordinate values of sensibility may even achieve a high importance. But if this is what Kant meant all the time, much that he says must be admitted to have been stated very unfortunately.

On the other hand, Kant's account of our duties towards others seems pretty thoroughly perverse. If the question is what we *can* do to others, then, if we cannot directly make them cultured or more perfect we also cannot directly make them happy. We can put the sources of good fortune in their way, and do something to remove certain prevalent obstacles to felicity; and, in the same way, we can put the opportunities for culture and similar excellences in other people's way, or remove eyesores and many degrading things. Beneficence of this species may be quite as *disinterested* as beneficence of any other species. And if the only happiness that is good is the happiness that is earned by worthiness to be happy, we should *not* be doing good if we put any other happiness in other people's way.

I think we should conclude, therefore, that Kant's account of our duty towards others, in this part of his work, is thoroughly inadequate and confused; and that his account of our duty towards ourselves appears to demand the rational recognition of many values which are neither exclusively moral nor exclusively part of the noumenal substance of reason. The latter point may be further pursued by considering his account of personal dignity in greater detail.

§ 13. *The nature of human dignity*

Kant's account of human dignity is prefaced, in the *Elementarlehre* of the *Tugendlehre*,[1] with the explanation that when the self, as Kant always holds, is both lawgiver and subject, it is necessary to explain, in order to avoid contradiction, that the self which is lawgiver is homo noumenon, and that the self which is subject is homo phenomenon. Such an explanation takes very high ground. It remains to see whether the ground is sustained.

Suicide, Kant holds, is a degradation. It is destruction of the life whose object is the furtherance of reason. Difficulties arising out of the maxim *Volenti non fit injuria* are then discussed; and as a casuistical question, to which no answer

[1] *Werke*, vol. VI, pp. 417 *sqq*. The subsequent examples follow this discussion.

is offered, it is asked whether the Great King was or was not justified in carrying poison on his person, lest, being captured, he should be forced to give a higher ransom than his subjects could pay.

Sexual perversion is also a pollution of human dignity, but Kant very candidly admits that the utter reprobation with which vices of this type are commonly regarded is very hard to justify "upon grounds of reason".

Gluttony and intoxication are also regarded as a surrender of the dignity of a rational being. As a question in casuistry Kant asks whether the Mahommedans are right in prohibiting wine but not opium, and (with Chesterfield) whether any banquet can be dignified in which the number of the guests exceeds the number of the Muses.

Kant's treatment of lying, avarice and false humility is more noteworthy.[1] An intentional falsehood, he says, may or may not be hurtful to others, but is always a degradation to the man who utters it. For speech is in principle the expression of thought, the part of nature which comes nearest to reason itself; and the lack of candour, sincerity or fidelity is always intrinsically contemptible.

Avarice is condemned because it contracts the proper enjoyment of the goods of life; and lest this be counted as venial imprudence, it is further explained that avarice is an abject and servile enthralment to money, and that money, in the eye of reason, is but a means to a means (i.e. to commodities).

And so of false humility. As phenomenon, man is an animal of very little moment. As noumenon he is beyond all price, being an end in himself and the possessor of intrinsic worth. Accordingly, if he should remember his littleness as an animal, he should also remember his greatness as a rational being. This dignity in man is neither pride nor conceit, but a just estimate of his value as it is. Man should be humble only when he reflects on the inconsistency between his elective will and the holy principle of righteousness within him. As a corollary, Kant is contemptuous of cries of pain, prostration before idols,

[1] *Ibid.* chap. ii, pp. 428 *sqq.*

any taint of slavery, all fawning, lackeydom and the esteem of titles "in which pedantry the Germans go beyond all nations on the earth, the Indian castes alone excepted".[1] He also maintains that the disdain either of oneself or of mankind is the greatest of sins.

Although Kant insists in principle that intrinsic worth holds of all rational beings, his thought is severely restricted to mankind. Reverence towards invisible or impersonal beings, even if they are rational, he here declares to be illegitimate, or at least not a duty. For our duty concerns only those rational beings whom we know. And Kant makes short work of any supposed duty towards non-rational beings. The destruction of natural beauty is a crime *against man*, and no other sort of crime;[2] and we do not owe any duty to the lower animals, but may kill or enslave them as we will. To delight in giving them pain is indeed morally wrong, but it is wrong because it degrades *us* and not because it hurts *them*. Even gratitude to an old horse, or house-dog or other companion, is only indirectly a duty to them. Directly (actually?) it is a duty we owe to ourselves.

In all these ways it is surely plain that Kant's conception of dignity goes far beyond pure reason. For neither speech nor sexual functions are noumenal, and the abuse of them is in the main an abuse of their natural office. When a man reverences his body, he is thinking primarily of its physical perfection. And when Kant goes on to proclaim man's duty of cultivating his intellect (for that is creative), his memory, imagination and other powers of his soul, his physical activity in gymnastic exercises, it is abundantly clear that he is travelling upon a highroad broader by far than the austere and narrow pathway of pure reason and the pure ego.

---

[1] *Werke*, vol. VI, p. 437. "Das Du, Er, Ihr and Sie, oder Ew. Wohledlen, Hochedeln, Hochedelgebornen, Wohlgebornen (ohe, iam satis est!) in der Anrede."

[2] *Ibid.* p. 443.

§ 14. *Value and existence*

I shall conclude this chapter by reminding the reader of certain of the conclusions at which Kant arrived in the second part of his *Critique of Judgment*.

As we saw, Kant maintained in the first part of this work that our judgments concerning beauty, although they did not affect our scientific knowledge of nature, were evidence, nevertheless, of a certain harmony between the faculties of our minds and the panorama of natural phenomena. The other respect in which such harmony might naturally be expected is in regard to our purposes; and the most obvious case of purpose is the biological adaptation of means to ends. To many minds it seems as certain that nature does nothing in vain—at any rate in the living part of her—as that she does nothing by chance.[1]

Here Kant demurred. In his view there could be no natural science other than mechanical science. *De facto*, to be sure, mechanical principles *are* inadequate in biology. We may be quite sure that no Newton will ever arise who could show that, *without a purpose*, a single blade of grass can be made to grow by simple mechanical laws.[2] Yet the principle of purpose, or the reciprocal adaptation of means to ends, is never a piece of natural science. All that we can competently infer, in this instance also, is a general and non-specific harmony between the mind (ultimately between the mind's values) and nature. We do not know of purpose as a natural cause.

Kant's caution, in this particular, seems to be over-caution. According to him, a living being is self-formative as well as self-moving;[3] and mechanical things, because of their inertia, cannot conceivably have this property.[4] If, then, living things actually do have this important non-mechanical property it is impossible to see why science should not take cognisance of

---

[1] *Critique of Judgment*. Bernard's translation, p. 281.
[2] *Ibid.* pp. 312 *sq.*   [3] *Ibid.* p. 278.
[4] *Ibid.* pp. 304 *sq.*

the circumstance in the most scientific way. What is more (especially when we remember that Reason for Kant is a form of *Life*)[1] it is difficult to conceal the close resemblance between the "authorship" of these self-formative living things and the intrinsic worth of homo noumenon, according to which rational man has the reason for his existence within himself. Yet Kant maintained that rational man, *alone in nature*, is possessed of this self-originating and self-justifying authorship.

The reason why Kant persisted in this attitude is no doubt that he correctly refused to identify a rational ground with a natural cause. Man's dignity, we may say, gives a justifying reason for his existence, but is not the natural originator of human life. This is what most of us believe—but not upon Kantian grounds. For most of us believe that things might exist without possessing dignity at all; and we do not believe that dignity determines existence. We even believe that, granting man to have dignity *when he exists*, it is entirely possible that, at some date, men should not exist at all. And Kant himself seems to go halfway towards this conclusion, although not the whole way. Speaking of the Greenlander, the Lapp and other denizens of inclement regions who contrive to collect driftwood for fuel and blubber for food, Kant says that we do not see, speaking generally, why men should be *there* at all.[2] But do we see *à priori* why men *must* be anywhere? Granting that man's character may fit him for a place among the values, is this a sufficient or constraining reason for his existence on his planet?

In general, Kant clearly enunciated his belief that the world cannot be regarded as a place providentially fitted for man and any of his purposes. "Nature has not taken him for her special darling, and favoured him with benefit above all animals. Rather in her destructive operations—plague, hunger, perils of water, frost, assaults of other animals great and small, etc.—in these things she has spared him as little as

[1] Cf. *ante*, p. 279.
[2] *Critique of Judgment*, p. 271.

any other animal."[1] Yet he also maintained that man, *propter dignitatem suam*, is "the ultimate purpose of creation here on earth".[2] And he combined these two views by holding that we can believe only in a general agreement between the sensible (or natural) order, and the supersensible order of dignity or excellence.

The conclusion of the whole matter, therefore, is, for Kant, somewhat as follows: There is but one intelligible reason why anything should exist at all. That reason is worth or dignity. Consequently this, and this alone, is the final purpose of all creation.[3] We learn also (there is some effrontery here) that *without man* the whole creation would be a waste and have no final purpose.[4] Yet man's psychological being has no true worth. The universe has no special concern with his happiness or other private concerns. It is also relatively unconcerned with his intellect; for if man existed only to contemplate or represent the world, *this* could not be a final purpose.[5] There is no sufficient value in the contemplative repetition of what already exists. Man's final worth is his worth as an agent—the exercise of his "good" or "free" will.

The good will, which justifies in itself, needs no other support, although it may be corroborated by many subsidiary tokens. When a man, in the presence of natural beauty, is serene and at rest, he feels the need for reaching out in gratitude towards the hidden art which (as he is constrained to believe although without definite knowledge) makes this beauty possible. Similarly, in his moral capacity, he experiences gratitude, obedience and proper self-abasement towards the highest good,[6] although the highest is beyond mortal attainment. These ideals and these needs, however, although irrepressible and most firmly grounded, do not advance our scientific understanding of nature. We cannot comprehend how the moral order governs in detail, and must fain be content with the general (although essentially rational)

---

[1] *Ibid.* pp. 353 *sq.*
[2] *Ibid.* p. 348.
[3] *Ibid.* p. 372.
[4] *Ibid.* p. 370.
[5] *Ibid.*
[6] *Ibid.* p. 375.

assurance that it does govern with adequate, supreme and complete authority. In the end our small, and hardly won perquisite of *knowledge* has to make room for the larger vistas of faith, but for a faith not blind, and for a confidence which is incomprehensible only in the sense that it cannot be verified by the devices of physical science. For "faith (absolutely so called) is trust in the attainment of a design, the promotion of which is a duty, but the possibility of the fulfilment of which (and consequently also that of the only conditions of it thinkable by us) is not to be *comprehended* by us".[1]

[1] *Critique of Judgment*, p. 410.

CHAPTER IX

TOWARDS A CONCLUSION

§ 1. *Explanatory*

IN place of a formal summary of the argument of this book —always apt to be over-complicated in an *œuvre de longue haleine*—I propose to offer a free, although condensed, exposition of the substance of the book's argument and of the conclusions towards which the argument points.

Rejecting the subordinate, and proceeding to the dominant, senses of "value" we found, in the main, three principal theories of value-disvalue. These are the theories of natural election, of psychological interest and of conceptual worth or excellence. We may call them the elective, the appreciative and the timological theories.

All three theories have been defended in the past, and all are held at the present time. The elective view, however, is usually held in the restricted form of biological self-maintenance, or as a doctrine of quantity of being, life or perfection, and its initial legitimacy, to say nothing of its truth, is flatly denied by many philosophers. Of the other two theories, the appreciative is, on the whole, the most usual, with or without minor concessions to the conceptual on the one hand, and to the elective on the other hand. Believers in the timological view, however—and there are many of them —maintain that the essence of value slips through the coarse net of the elective theory and also through the finer meshes of the appreciative view.

I propose in the first instance to consider the legitimacy and the implications of the elective theory.

§ 2. *The legitimacy of the elective theory*

The elective theory rests on the simple foundation that whatever *matters* to a thing, or concerns it, is a value or disvalue to that thing; and that whatever does not matter to it, is, for it, no value but wholly indifferent. Since everything matters to itself, self-maintenance is a value to every existent.

There seems no reason for restricting this doctrine to conscious selves or even to living things. On the contrary (as we saw) there are strong grounds for believing that natural election is a very general principle in nature, far more extensive than either life or consciousness. It may lay the foundations of biology or (perhaps) of mind, but is not itself confined to life or to consciousness.

According to the appreciative view, this entire conception is necessarily far too wide. For appreciation is definitely a conscious experience. It is liking, desiring, wishing *et id genus omne*, or a special form of these. Only a conscious or spiritual being, on these assumptions, can appreciate at all; and it is metaphor or poetry, not science, to speak of value in the elections of unconscious things—as much of a metaphor as to say that the desert is athirst. To be sure, if "unconscious" wishes and the like are admitted, it seems arbitrary where we should stop once conscious boundaries have been overpassed. Even believers in the "unconscious", however, seem commonly to hold that the "unconscious" is at least hemi-demi-semi-conscious, denying the title to what is merely physiological, and, *à fortiori*, to what is frankly material.

If we keep (as is usual) to the stricter view that all appreciation is conscious (or, alternatively, spiritual) it does not immediately follow that we can appreciate only spiritual beings or conscious properties. At this point, however, another principle enters. For it is said that we appreciate only what stirs our emotions or conscious appetency, and therefore that if we appreciate living bodies or physical things we do so only in a special relationship to ourselves and not apart from this relationship. They *matter* to us only in so far as they affect our feeling and appetite, and any value ascribed on the occasion of this special relationship is accidental to *them*.

In short, the view is that only our feelings, together with things in so far as we may be said to *feel* them, are values. And it seems better (for the reasons given in Chapter I, Sect. II) to describe the matter thus than in terms of means and end. The essential distinction is between what is a value in a certain relation and what is a value without this restriction. For instance, food is a value when it is assimilated. Before it is assimilated it is a possible source (or means) of value, but *not* a value. I do not say that our feelings assimilate what they feel, but the essential distinction referred to seems the same in their case also.

To sum up. According to the appreciative view, our feelings and conscious interests are all that matter to us, and nothing can matter to a being that does not feel.

The timological theory does not necessarily imply that the character of value is found only in spirits or conscious beings, but most exponents of this doctrine maintain that they can discern either by a single intuition or by a series of intuitions (in an exhaustive survey of the values alleged to be possible), that nothing except spirits or conscious events can have the character—except instrumentally or in some such determinate relation to conscious spirits.

As it seems to me, we should be very chary of all such arguments. If, indeed, it were true that we could clearly discern the presence of value in certain spirits or in their states, and that we could clearly discern the absence of value in material and in unconscious things, there is, so far, nothing more to be said. The negative part of this thesis, however, seems more than a little dogmatic; for our powers of discerning are, after all, very limited. Again, even if both the positive and the negative parts of the contention were true, the conclusion that values pertain exclusively to spirits and to their states would not follow, because, for all we know, there may be much in the universe that is neither matter, life nor mind. Indeed, the general thesis would be exceedingly rash unless a definite connection could be discerned between spiritual nature and the character of value. Such a connection plainly exists according to the appreciative theory, but not so plainly according to the timological. It seems clear, to be sure, that *certain* values attach only to spirits or to beings very like them. But not that all values must; and we may even consider the question whether the timological theory, in these applications of it, is not surreptitiously, and quite unjustifiably, borrowing a part of the appreciative theory.

Obviously, unless either the appreciative or the timological theory can be shown to be true, the elective theory is not to be condemned on account of its inconsistency with one or other of them. And the truth of any of the theories remains to be considered. I think we may agree, however, that the elective theory is not *prima facie* absurd, and therefore are entitled to examine its implications.

§ 3. *Implications of the elective theory*

The elective view states, firstly, that everything is valuable to itself. This does not mean that it is valuable in its own eyes, for it may have no eyes, and its eyes, if it has them, may deceive it. On the contrary, the statement is intended to be purely factual and objective.

The elective view states, secondly, that whatever matters to a given thing or, in mildly metaphorical language, helps or hinders it, is a value to that thing. This statement also is intended to be purely factual and objective. There is no good reason why it should not be. If anyone says that fact and value must always be utterly distinct, he may be invited to prove his contention.

The first of the above statements appears to imply that the value of self-maintenance is intrinsic and absolute as well as objective. Such an interpretation may be superficial, however; for the qualification *to itself* is essential. The second statement is obviously relative, not absolute, and as much extrinsic as intrinsic. This, however, does not affect the objectivity of such values. For things *are* in the relation in question.

In terms of the first statement, the universe must be said to be valuable to itself. The universe, however, does not pick and choose within itself; for everything within it contributes to its characteristic being. To be sure, if any feature of the universe, say its order, could be shown to be more fundamental than any other feature, anything closely related to and sustaining this order might be said (in terms of the elective theory) to be more valuable from the universal point of view than anything else. But it is we, not the universe, that draw this distinction. Everything in the universe is equally essential to it, for if anything were different, even the least of things, the universe itself would be a different universe.

For the same reason there can be no disvalues in the universe from the universal point of view. In terms of the elective theory, a disvalue within the universe would be something opposing the universe, yet itself a part of the universe; which is absurd. A part of the universe might conceivably oppose the rest of the universe, but not itself *and* the rest.

§ 4. *The appreciative versus the elective view*

The appreciative view relies upon *interest*; and interest, as we have seen, may mean either "making a difference" or "arousing emotion, conscious appetency or excitement" (mild or tense). These two senses are not the same, even in the case of mankind. For many things (e.g. the vitamines of a former example or certain endocrine secretions) may *make* a difference to us although we have no suspicion of their existence, and may make a specific difference to us without, so far as we can tell, arousing *any* specific feelings.

Such differences as are made, whether we feel them or not, support the elective, not the appreciative, theory; and it is very surprising that writers like Mr Perry, who are (modified) behaviourists in psychology, should insist so strongly upon the conscious and psychical character of interest.

In general, we hold very strongly that what is to our advantage, and what we consciously feel to be pleasant or interesting, are closely allied; and, on any theory, our feelings are a highly important part of ourselves. Sometimes, however, we have to choose, and frankly to admit that certain things which we like are not advantageous to us, even granting that, in the main, it is good to have what we like for no other reason than because we like it. This seems to imply that the elective meaning of "interest" is more important than the psychological.

In the same way, the many attempts that have been made to establish a metaphysics of felicity point towards the same conclusion.

If so, it is surely illogical to suppose that value is in principle a human affair. Appreciation, indeed, may be entirely human, or confined to humanity together with a few of the higher animals. But interest, in the etymological sense of making a difference, has no such restriction.

It is possible, no doubt, to argue that although elective interest, in the case of humanity, is sometimes more fundamental than psychological feeling, nevertheless, value does not emerge *at all* unless and until there is sentient interest. In other words, the arousal of appreciation might be held to be a necessary, although not a self-sufficient, condition of value.

In view of what has been said, however, this opinion would seem to be entirely arbitrary, unless the appreciative view, contrary to its principles, relies upon a premiss which itself requires the timological view. This premiss would be that nothing infra-sentient can have any timological value at all.

§ 5. *The foundations of the appreciative view*

In general, exponents of the appreciative view maintain, quite simply, that value *means* appreciation (at any rate in the case of mankind) and are content to assert that this usage is confirmed by general agreement. Such an attitude can

ix] TOWARDS A CONCLUSION 307

scarcely be regarded as satisfactory. There cannot be this general agreement so long as the elective and the timological views are actually held.

Certain independent arguments, however, are sometimes adduced. Among these, one of some interest is the interjectional theory.

Words, we all know, may be very misleading, and "value" may very well be one of the worst of them. According to the interjectional view, expressions which contain the words "value", "good" or the like are not at all what they seem. They appear to be referential (i.e. to indicate a property), but are in fact emotive. That is to say, they merely express our own emotions and are like interjections long drawn out—a very big Ha! or a most prolonged Ugh![1]

This argument does not seem to me to be strong. The ambiguous use of words is, of course, very frequent, and a similar ambiguity may extend to grammatical moods. Thus, to choose Mr Braithwaite's example, when we say "Naughty" to a child we *may* mean neither more nor less than "Stop".[2] The entire distinction, however, between the emotive and the referential use of language seems very much overdrawn, and the interjectional application of it a huge exaggeration.

Take, for example, Lear's speech:[3]

> Blow, winds, and crack your cheeks! rage! blow!
> You cataracts and hurricanoes, spout
> Till you have drench'd our steeples, drown'd the cocks!
> . . . .
> Rumble thy bellyful! Spit, fire! Spout, rain!
> Nor rain, wind, thunder, fire, are my daughters:
> I tax you not, you elements, with unkindness:
> I never gave you kingdom, called you children,
> You owe me no subscription...
> ...O! O! 'tis foul!

If ever there was emotive language, this language is emotive. The imperative and the indicative moods jostle one

[1] Cf. R. B. Braithwaite, *Proceedings of the Aristotelian Society*, 1927–28, pp. 137 *sqq.*, with the references to Ogden and Richards, *The Meaning of Meaning*.
[2] Cf. the use of the word "sage" in French.   [3] Act III, Sc. 2.

another. In a sense there is as much of an interjection as if Lear spat. Yet the language is not merely interjectional, because the so-called emotive use of language is not devoid of referential meaning. Lear is characterising facts, and indicating analogies and distinctions which are congruent with his distress. His language *has* a meaning, and the foulness which he attributes to his daughters' conduct has a meaning too. He characterises both their ingratitude and the insentient hurricanoes. And he contrasts the two.

A more considerable argument is the genetic one. But this requires a separate paragraph.

§ 6. *The genetic argument*

It need not be disputed that much is to be learnt from the genesis of development of things or ideas—provided that we know what the course of this genesis is. It is, however, always an intricate matter to interpret the message of any evolution.

Regarding our present topic, it is frequently stated that value begins with individual feeling or appreciation, and that subsequently there is continuity in its development. Through the mere fact of existing, the human individual acquires a certain stability in his feelings and appreciations; and by reflection he comes to discern a species of organisation, and even some sort of standard, within them. Again, through intercourse with his fellows, he becomes socialised into a person, and so comes to participate in an over-individual organisation of appreciation. And finally, as in morals, this social, personal, and over-individual level of appreciation becomes transformed into an over-social order, so that some Athanasius is able to stand against the world.

Such, at any rate, is the picture Dr Tennant sketches,[1] and he gives us a better picture than many of the type. Let us, then, consider the several stages in this suggested development.

---

[1] *Philosophical Theology*, vol. I, chap. vii. Cf. on a larger scale the entire argument of Mr Urban's *Valuation: Its Nature and Laws*. Also H. Maier, *Psychologie des emotionalen Denkens*, Part v, chap. iv.

The starting point is dubious, because the elective theory may explain rudimentary value much better than the appreciative. And timologists need not be dismayed, because they might plausibly contend that rudimentary thinking need not occur very much later than rudimentary appreciation.

Again, the suggested development from a pre-social and sub-personal individual to a social and personal one is thoroughly unhistorical. Infants are not less social than adults, but if anything more so; and the same is true of primitive communities as compared with civilised ones.

Furthermore, advocates of the social view might perfectly well maintain, as many in fact do maintain, that *nothing* should over-ride loyalty to society, and therefore that all over-social theories are retrograde and confused.

Neither the beginning, the middle, nor the end of this alleged course of development is therefore at all certain. Suppose it correct, however. Is the logic of the theory at all to be commended?

As Dr Tennant himself admits, it would be possible for a timologist consistently to accept this picture of the development of values, and yet to maintain that feeling, the formation of individual character, and social intercourse have the function of *revealing* provinces and types of value which otherwise would remain hidden. Indeed—although Dr Tennant does not appear to admit the fact—it seems pretty plain that the so-called "over-social" values are of this order. There is no reason why social intercourse should create more than a social product, much less why it should create something better than society and rightly capable of over-riding society. And yet it is quite likely that, through intercourse with our fellows, we should come to perceive values which otherwise we might have overlooked. Mathematics is not a social product in the same sense as the British Constitution, but it is very unlikely that the science of mathematics would be what it is without organised social effort and co-operative study. Putting the question otherwise, we might say that an over-social political constitution is a mere absurdity but that over-social values are not absurd at all. The presumption, therefore, is that there *are* such values (as the timologists maintain) and that, even if we learn of these values through social transactions, the values themselves are not constituted by these transactions.

Even if Dr Tennant himself has slipped in his logic, however, it does not, of course, follow that the timological interpretation of this development, although possible, is the only possible interpretation. Our confidence is shaken, that is all. But perhaps we should consider another of Dr Tennant's damaging admissions.

His general line of argument, as with all who agree with him generally, is to trace a certain continuity—and then, *Stet pro ratione continuatio*. At the beginning of his discussion, however, he professes himself a believer in "epigenesis" or emergent evolution—"growth out of what was into what was not".[1] "What was", in this instance, is individual appreciation; and Dr Tennant maintains that such appreciation becomes something *not merely individual*, although continuing to be *appreciation*. As far as the logic of emergence or of epigenesis goes, however, it would be equally legitimate to argue that appreciation itself may develop out of something that is *not* appreciation (as on the elective theory), and that appreciation may also develop into something that is *not* or is *not merely* appreciation.

In short, the genetic argument settles very little indeed; and I have only to add, pursuant to what was said in Chapter VII, § 12, that however highly we may rate the influence of society, the logical connection between being social and being excellent is not at all close. Are the values of bees or aphides or ants or other social creatures necessarily higher than the values of the lion? And if some of our feelings become socialised while others do not, what, in the absence of a timological premiss, can we infer about the *values* of these relatively social or relatively asocial feelings?

[1] *Philosophical Theology*, p. 139.

On he passed.
"That soul hath greater cause for grief than I",
Orion thought—yet none the less was sad.

A mixture of this sort is the usual psychological phenomenon, and its value cannot be deduced from the origin of these mixed feelings.

§ 7. *The appreciative versus the timological view*

Advocates of the appreciative view (who commonly have not even considered the possibility of the elective hypothesis) are usually so thoroughly convinced of the truth of their opinion that they are frankly contemptuous of their visible enemy, timology. The character of excellence, they say, or again the character of badness, interpreted as timologists interpret it, is a mysterious, unintelligible, unverifiable, noumenal[1] predicate, out of all relation to life or actuality.

There is no great variety in these statements. Anything that is intelligible is rationally so, and in that sense noumenal. Similarly, anything that is intelligible is verified by the mere fact of being understood, and for the same reason is not mysterious. The essence of these complaints, therefore, is that the exponents of the appreciative view do not believe that there *is* a character of excellence.

The statement that value, timologically regarded, must be out of relation to life requires, perhaps, a passing mention. Fundamentally it is a simple fallacy. Because excellence is, logically speaking, an "absolute" predicate and not a "relative" one, the monstrous inference is drawn that the predicate cannot be related to, that is to say cannot hold of, anything actual or alive. This conclusion has no better warrant than the parallel argument that the predicate "blue" (which, logically speaking, is also "absolute") cannot have any relation to clear skies, delphiniums, Protestants, Cambridge, teetotallers or baby boys.

Another interpretation that is sometimes given seems to be at least equally fallacious. It is said that values, according

[1] *Ibid.* p. 141 and p. 158.

to the timological view, must constitute a realm of ideal essences wholly distinct from the world of fact, and that this mysterious ideal realm either does not exist or is nobody's concern.

The relation of ideals to facts is far too intricate to be dismissed in this cavalier fashion, but it is sufficient to note, in the present connection, that the charge thus brought is quite fantastic. All that the timological theory is logically committed to is the possibility of discriminating between good, bad and indifferent. It would be quite consistent with the theory (although I do not think it would be true) that nothing except hard fact *was* either good or bad.

A more important objection is the argument from economy of hypotheses. We ascribe excellence, it is said, only to what we appreciate, and we base our views concerning excellence, very largely at least, upon our actual appreciations. Why, then, unless we are forced into doing it, should we seriously suppose that there is anything *except* appreciation in this affair?

Before discussing this crucial argument, it is advisable to make yet another troublesome but inevitable explanation.

§ 8. *Prizing and evaluation*

The term *evaluation* naturally suggests a reflective standard of values and even an entire axiology. We evaluate anything when we think its values *out*, and determine their place on a definite scale. A presupposition of any such reflective procedure, however, is that we should possess and build upon the *idea* of value, either by passing judgment upon the character of value when we find it, or, if this is denied, by *approving* in the special sense defined by the British moralists.

It will be convenient to include these judgments or approvals under the term "evaluation" as well as the more elaborate process of determination according to a standard.

Contrasted with such evaluation is the fact of prizing, setting store by, *Werthaltung*. For, just as it is possible, and indeed quite frequent, to love without knowing that we love, so it is possible to value a thing without admitting or recognising the circumstance. Sometimes, indeed, we hold that a man's ideas of what he values are very far removed indeed from what he actually values, and that his professed principles and standards of value are remote from the principles and standards which he actually employs. If he knows the fact, or might know it readily, we call him a hypocrite—unless, indeed, his actions excel his professions. But he need not know the fact at all.

The test, we say, is his conduct and actions. What a man is set upon, what his heart craves for, that he values. He need not think about the matter at all, and, if he thinks, he may think to little purpose. Neither onlookers nor the man himself know all that is passing within him, and the man himself may often have better opportunities for judging than the onlooker. But very often an onlooker may discern a man's real values better than the man himself. These onlookers, often, are able to see what he prizes; and the man himself may be startled if he comes to see what they have seen for a long time.

The elective theory is based upon, and restricted to, the fact of prizing. In its eyes, the action of prizing is the whole circumstance in the case. Such actions, it declares, are not confined to consciousness, but widely disseminated in nature; and evaluation is only the recognition of election or prizing and the attempt to formulate it with precision.

According to the appreciative theory, there is, properly speaking, *no* prizing unless there is feeling or conscious appetency. If we infer a man's values from his actions, we are really inferring his state of mind. And, of course, we may be mistaken on the point. In general, according to the theory, "primary value" *is* his emotional reaction;[1] and evaluation is either reflection upon these primary values, or an emotion of higher order, the "secondary" emotion of calm approval.

The timological theory is concerned with the character of

[1] "Psychology bids us regard all primary value as thus constituted." Tennant, *op. cit.* p. 142.

value, but this character, when discerned, is, like other characters, discovered. Therefore it may hold when it is not discerned, just as anything else may exist before we know it to do so. Accordingly, on this theory also, it is entirely possible that our prizing should possess or be evidence of value although many who prize do not discern the character of the value.

§ 9. *Insufficiency of the appreciative view*

Returning, then, from this inevitable digression, to the point at which the main argument was temporarily abandoned, we have now to consider the contention that primary value is emotional attraction or appreciation, that all evaluations of excellence *require* this primary value, and consequently that, unless very strong reasons to the contrary can be shown, the principle of parsimony or the economy of hypothesis prohibits the addition of an otiose timology to appreciations which are, in principle, sufficient.

I propose to show that there *are* these strong contrary reasons, and that timology, so far from being otiose, is essential to the appreciative theory itself.

The main point has already appeared, but will bear reappearance. It is not true in fact that primary value, even in human beings, necessarily implies emotional attraction. Men prize what they need as much as what they desire, and they may neither know nor feel what they need. The bent of their action is evidence enough of what in fact they prize. We have no more right to presume that determinate psychological satisfaction occurs in all such instances than the Epicureans had to assert that all animal instincts are a search for pleasure. Therefore, of two things, one. Either appreciation is only a special form of elective prizing, or it is something so much more *excellent* than unfelt elective prizing that the latter is not worth calling "prizing" at all. The latter alternative is pure timology, and the timology in it is not otiose. The former alternative would forbid the belief that any election is better than any other, that the elections of a clod are either more or less worthy than the elections of a man.

The analysis of evaluation supplies further confirmation. As we saw in Chapter VI, those who were most in earnest with the appreciative view and most acute concerning it, accepted the plain truth that we esteem and approve much that we may not like, that we like much that we do not esteem, that we may esteem our enemies although they hurt us and despise traitors who may be useful—in short, that our evaluations must often be distinguished from "primary" appreciation. They maintained, however, that evaluation was a secondary or contemplative appreciation, an impartial sentiment with a general purview. Yet, as we saw, they failed to sustain this contention. In their hands the fiction of the impartial spectator scarcely attempted to disguise the timological activities of the "man within"—and certainly did not succeed in disguising these activities. When Adam Smith's theory of the sentiments is revised, as it often is at the present day, it is well to remember *all* that he said.

To be sure, if our emotions or appreciations could themselves achieve objectivity, as Brentano and Meinong declared, there would be nothing in the arguments of this paragraph to impugn such a theory. The appreciative view, we have argued, itself could not stand without somewhere presupposing objective timology. The nature of this timology, of course, is not thereby defined. But we found when we considered these attempts to make feeling potentially objective that they could not succeed, and that the objectivity of values requires the *truth*[1] of value-judgments, if it is known at all.

§ 10. *Prizing and timology*

But, it may be objected, surely there is at least a very close connection between prizing and value, and especially between appreciative human prizing and the values which humanity

[1] Cf. W. R. Sorley, *Moral Values and the Idea of God*, especially chap. IV.

can either attain or discern. Moreover, the objector may continue, is it not equally certain that this ultimate, inexpugnable intimacy between prizing and value puts a formidable barrier in the way of all objective theories of excellence? Are there not, indeed, two sides to this matter, each separately most convincing? On the one hand, if value, even supposing it to be in certain respects a singular property, is, in the end, a character which, like any other character, is discernibly present in certain entities and discernibly absent from others, how comes it that this character is something which stirs our pulses, arouses our loyalties, determines our duties? And why should other characters *not* have this momentous consequence? On the other hand, supposing the connection to exist, what confidence can we have in any of our judgments of value? To attain truth we should avoid bias, but if values are so intimately allied with our preferences, affections and loyalties, how is it possible to avoid this bias in *any* value judgment?[1] For ethical, aesthetic, religious or scientific bias is surely not less dangerous than any other bias. In short, if we cannot be disinterested (whether or not we need be selfish) in our judgments of value, how can we hope to attain truth in them?

These barriers certainly seem to be formidable. But let us examine them.

Regarding the first of them we have to say that anyone who asks why there should be this connection may be invited to consider why there should not. If our elections, preferences and loyalties really were quite irrational, then, *à priori*, we might like, or love, or admire *anything*, ludo as much as literature, slugs as much as heroes. Nothing but experience could show what, in actuality, we do appreciate; and if we do, in a measure, appreciate excellence, the fact would be neither more nor less intelligible than any other ultimate preference or loyalty.

---

[1] Mr Alexander bids us "study our prepossessions without prepossession" (Naturalism and Value, *The Personalist*, Oct. 1928). May it not, however, be a prepossession that values *are* prepossessions?

I do not suggest that this answer is adequate. On the contrary, I would suggest that, whatever we may say, we all really do believe that our sentiments and our loyalties should not, and need not, be wholly irrational. And (I think) we all believe that we ought to seek the best we can achieve just because it is the best. Thus, to employ technical language, we believe in an ultimate synthetic connection between value or excellence on the one hand, and what we ought to do or to love on the other hand; and, although it is conceivable, I do not think it is likely, that there can ever be such ultimate connections between entities that are simply and absolutely *different*.

Therefore, I think, there must be a certain affinity or natural propinquity between objective values and the human soul, and it would be heartening to us if we could divine or discern some nuance or adumbration of this affinity. Yet may we not? Is it not possible to maintain that all excellent things have a certain rapport and elective affinity with one another, and that our minds themselves have a measure of excellence? We need not hold in consequence that all our psychic activities are excellent. For the corruption of the best may be the worst, and some small part of our souls may be worth all the rest. Nevertheless there may be (I think there is) this general connection and, if there is, why should the connection be other than rational?

The second objection, I think, is also far less formidable than many people suppose. Searching for truth, we should certainly try to avoid all bias; but we should not therefore try to avoid emotion. On the contrary we may search in a spirit of tense excitement, and, as Helmholtz said, be chained by the leg to a problem. What has to be avoided is the type of excitement which disturbs or colours the clarity of our intellectual vision.

What has to be shown in support of the second objection, therefore, is that our emotions must necessarily disturb and destroy the clarity of our judgments of value *in this particular way*; and there is no convincing reason why they should. It is admitted, on any sane theory, that we can go a long way towards eliminating private bias or local and temporal perspectives in these judgments, and although we must always discern values (and everything else) from our human station, it does not follow that we cannot allow for a proper margin of human error. If human imagination is frequently neither extensive nor profound, it possesses, nevertheless, a genuine range above, beneath and around the human species; and it is false (as well as arbitrary and dogmatic) to deny the circumstance.

§ 11. *Evaluation and reason*

"I am apt to suspect", Hume said, "...that reason and sentiment concur in almost all moral determinations and conclusions"; but he added that "the final sentence, it is probable, which pronounces characters and actions amiable or odious, praiseworthy or blameable...depends on some internal sense or feeling, which nature has made universal in the whole species".[1]

Taking "moral" determinations to include all values, not merely those of righteousness, and "reason" to denote insight and understanding, not a fetish of the schools, we have concluded, in effect, that Hume's dictum ought to be reversed. Timology is our insight into values; and we have this insight, often imperfectly, to be sure, but authentically, nevertheless. It is doubtful whether Hume's "universal" sentiment exists at all, although it is not doubtful that there is an effective concurrence between our appreciations and our insight into values.

Because of this rational insight it is to be expected that a reflective or rational elaboration of timological determinations should also occur; and it does occur. To be sure, there has been a persistent tendency on the part of the greater rationalists in philosophy, both to magnify the office of reason unduly and to confound the distinctive character of reason (which should not be doubtful) with something remote and

[1] *An Enquiry Concerning the Principles of Morals*, Sect. 1, Selby-Bigge's edn. pp. 172 *sq.*

aloof. Thus, as we saw, Descartes seems to have maintained in the end that reason and mind are the same, and that minds differ from bodies by the whole diameter of being. Kant exalted the purity of reason so high that he rated the values of sensibility far too low. Geulincx and Malebranche, maintaining in their several ways that reason is *love*, were inclined, in detail, to represent this *amor rationis* as something less general and far more empirical than, on their theory, they had any right to do.

Our discussion of the views of these philosophers in Chapter VIII was designed to show that "reason" cannot, without grave peril, be over-simplified in this way, and that it takes its revenge when its purity and austerity are rarefied into pure diaphaneity. The need for caution in the interpretation of "reason", however, should never be taken to suggest that there is no such thing as reason. On the contrary, the place of insight and reflection in this matter of values is plainly so firm that nothing in the end can shake it.

For example, although there are many who have perplexed themselves out of any explicit belief in the rationality of values, there are very few who deny the reality of justice and equity, or would affirm that equity could occur in the absence of reflection or rational comparison. Yet how could there be equity without insight into value? Justice, in one of its branches, is the equitable apportionment of good and evil. There is no credit in apportioning *evils* impartially and without cause, and there is no sense in apportioning impartially we know not what. For the rest, justice is fairness in respect to what is morally relevant. It is treating those equally who are equal *in relevant respects*. And the knowledge of this relevance is insight and nothing else. In other words, justice presupposes the possibility of rational insight into the values of men and of things; and therefore it is illegitimate to believe in the reality of rational justice and yet to doubt the reality of rational values. *Quod erat demonstrandum.*

§ 12. *Natural election versus timology*

If, then, there is such a thing as rational insight into excellence, how is this rational timology related to "value" in the other senses of "value" we have discussed?

It should be evident that the issue here is ultimately between the elective and the timological theories. In essentials, the appreciative view is a special form of the elective. It asserts that what matters to anything is what matters psychologically or emotionally. No other election matters at all. But the general logic of this species of election is the same as the logic of any election.

Elective values are relative to the elective agent, and timological values are absolute. This seems a clear and inescapable distinction, but the point demands enquiry.

If a thing has a certain property in certain relations and in these relations only, it really does have the property *in these relations*, and this statement is absolute in the same sense as the statement, concerning other things, that they have a certain property in *all* relationships or that they have some property *irrespective* of their relations. We have to distinguish, in other words, between the value *of* the related, and the value *in* a relation itself.

Accordingly, the breach between absolute and relative theories of value need not always be complete, and it may be doubted whether the breach is complete even in certain apparently egregious instances. Take, for example, the spider and the fly. The spider really has a point of view and so has the fly. When the fly escapes from the spider, there is a good from the fly's point of view; i.e. because the fly *has* a point of view, we have the right to say, absolutely, that there is *a* good when this event occurs. From the spider's point of view, which is also real, the fly's escape is a calamity. Therefore, by the same reasoning, there is also *an* evil when this event occurs. This good and this evil, however, are not the same, although both have to do with the fly's escape from the spider. Consequently there is, so far, no contradiction.

There is, however, a plain contradiction between saying that anything is good *simply*, and saying that it is good *only from a certain point of view*. The elective theory is committed to the latter interpretation, whether in the general form (according to which the phrase "point of view" is interpreted without any exclusive reference to psychology) or in the special psychological form of the appreciative theory. The timological theory, on the contrary, requires the former interpretation. It has to do, in old-fashioned language, with what is excellent from God's point of view; and although, even from God's point of view, it must be held to be true that there is a tigerish good when a tiger catches a man, and a human good when a man escapes from a tiger, we could not say (as we must sometimes say) that the man's escape is a greater value than the tiger's feast unless we knew, quite simply, that the man *is* better than the tiger. It is not enough to say that the man is better from his own point of view; for he is worse from the tiger's. What has to be maintained, at least, is that the man's point of view is itself more excellent than the tiger's.

In other words, the timological theory cannot accept the kind of qualification implied in the elective theory as necessarily and always relevant, although it need not deny that there are certain values subject to this qualification. And, as we have seen, if we are in earnest with our timology, it is conceivable and not unlikely that certain genuine elections contain no excellence at all, but may be quite worthless or very bad indeed.

§ 13. *The ambiguity of "value"*

There is therefore a fundamental disparity between the timological and the elective theories. And if value has only one meaning we may accept one or other, but not both.

Our conclusion has been that the timological theory cannot be surrendered because what it states is true. Can we then abandon the elective theory?

According to what has been said, there is no need to abandon it in so far as it does not conflict with the timological theory;

but many philosophers, as we know, are prepared to abandon a great part of the elective theory—all of it, indeed, that is not conscious, emotional or appreciative election. On the other hand it would seem quite absurd to say that the elective view, at any rate in the special form of appreciative favouring, is simply an abuse of the term "value". We may appreciate much that is not *excellent*; but it is begging the question to say that value and excellence must be the same.

It might be maintained that excellence is the superlative of which value is the positive, and that election or appreciation enters into the question only because all our elections and all our appreciations have (or indicate) a certain degree of "value" timologically interpreted. This seems a possible view, correct in what it asserts if doubtful in what it denies; and I have tried to show that there are close connections between our sentiments and appreciations, on the one hand, and our insight into excellence upon the other.

It seems more likely, however, that "value" is an ambiguous term which includes both elective or appreciative prizings and timological insight. In view of the admitted ambiguity of "value" in the current speech of so many nations, it should not be at all surprising if the attempt to bring precision into the idea of value should end with a less extensive but more acute ambiguity. And I suspect that it does. I also suspect that, even if the elective view in its full range be deemed extravagant, it is arbitrary and improbable to argue that prizing should be confined to psychical appreciation.

CHAPTER X

STANDARDS AND MEASURES OF VALUE

SECTION I. THE IDEA OF MORAL ARITHMETIC

§ 1. *The earlier forms of the explicit idea*

NEITHER the general conception of balancing good against evil, nor the more special notion of a prudent reckoning of future advantages, can be supposed to be at all novel. Indeed, when Berkeley in his *Alciphron*[1] fathers upon Socrates the maxim that "rakes cannot reckon" and refers thereafter to the computations of the Epicureans, there is nothing unhistorical in his statements. It is quite another thing, however, to attempt to give precision to these common ideas, or analytically to lay bare their foundations; and in the latter respect it has to be said that the notion of a precise "moral" (or practical) arithmetic (l'arithmétique or l'espérance morale), whether from the legislator's point of view or from the private person's, is in reality the invention of the late seventeenth and eighteenth centuries.

During the period in question this moral arithmetic was elaborated in the simplified form of a thoroughgoing hedonism; that is to say, what were supposed to be calculable were "lots" of pleasures or pains. And pleasure, we know, is not the only value, or (probably) a very accurate measure of value. On the other hand, since the principles of this moral or hedonic arithmetic were examined in those days with far greater care than is now usual in accounts of our standards of value, they deserve a scrupulous examination. I propose, therefore, to consider them in the first instance, and thereafter to discuss the possibility of generalising them on assumptions more adequate than those of hedonism.

[1] Dialogue II, § 18 (Summary).

The idea of moral arithmetic, then, was characteristic of the entire epoch now under review. Among British writers, we find it in Locke ("Judging" [about probable pleasures] "is, as it were, balancing an account and determining on which side the odds lie")[1]; in Shaftesbury ("We have cast up all those particulars from whence, as by way of addition and subtraction, the main sum or general account of happiness is either augmented or diminish'd.... The subject treated may be said to have an evidence as great as that which is found in numbers, or mathematicks")[2]; and in the passage we formerly quoted from Hutcheson ("In equal degrees of happiness expected to proceed from the action...the virtue is in a compound ratio of the quantity of good and number of enjoyers....That action is best which procures the greatest happiness for the greatest numbers")[3]—in short, we find it very prevalent indeed. The same is true of continental authors, for example Helvétius and Beccaria, or, in a more general and literary way, Fontenelle in his *Traité du Bonheur* and La Rochefoucauld with his fundamental principle that glory and honour mask a conscious or unconscious calculation.

On the whole, the clearest account of the doctrine, at this stage of its development, was given by Maupertuis, the mathematician and astronomer, in his thin but pellucid *Essai de philosophie morale*, and this statement of the doctrine should suffice for our present purposes.

Maupertuis defines pleasure as "every perception which the mind would rather experience [alternatively, 'would like to rest in'] than not"[4]; and pain as the opposite of pleasure. Pleasures or pains occupy time; and good is the sum of pleasant moments, evil the sum of painful ones. In addition to duration, he holds, we must also take account of intensity, and in our reckoning must multiply (not add) intensity and duration together. Although no one can expect to make such calculations with complete precision, everyone knows that

---

[1] *Essay*, II, xxi, § 69.
[2] Conclusion of *Inquiry*.
[3] *Inquiry*, Pt. II, Concerning Moral Good and Evil, Sect. iii, § 8.
[4] *Op. cit.* chap. i.

x] STANDARDS OF VALUE 325

pleasures *are* greater or less in accordance with this product. Happiness is the favourable balance or nett advantage of pleasures, and misery the nett disadvantage. The comparison of pleasure with pleasure or of pain with pain is relatively easy, and the comparison of pain with pleasure relatively difficult. But both are possible.[1]

Maupertuis, himself notoriously morose and litigious, advocated a species of "natural" pessimism, for he maintained that, apart from the comfort and hope of Christianity, the pain of ordinary existence exceeds its pleasure; with the corollary that suicide is legitimate and may be advantageous[2] —except for a Christian. Such pessimism was alien to the doctrines of natural perfectibility and inevitable progress then beginning to captivate Europe. Otherwise he expressed, better than most, what many were thinking, although his references, in a single sentence, to the proximity of pleasures and to their probability are inadequate, even when judged by contemporary standards.

In this latter respect, an event of some importance was Daniel Bernoulli's argument "Specimen Theoriae Novae de Mensura Sortis", which appeared in the *Transactions of the Petersburg Academy*[3] and was separately published in 1738. In this argument Bernoulli maintained that, in general, it could be assumed that "moral fortune" (or happiness) was inversely proportional to "physical fortune" (or wealth), that is to say that, a minimum of subsistence being granted, happiness increases continuously with increase of wealth, but in inverse ratio in the rate of increase. To a man with 100 ducats an increase of 50 should be regarded, normally, as yielding the same increment of happiness as an increase of 500 to a man with 1000 ducats.

Bernoulli's principle played a considerable part in subsequent attempts to apply mathematical probability to conduct, but it might be treated independently of such applications. His formula, $dy = k \dfrac{dx}{x}$, it should be noted, treats happiness

[1] *Ibid.*   [2] *Op. cit.* later chapters.   [3] Vol. v (1730–31).

and wealth as *continuously* varying quantities or, in technical language,[1] deals with the "diminishing *marginal* utility" of income. Again, since this formula is equivalent to $y = k \log \frac{x}{a}$ (where k, as above, and a, the initial physical fortune, are constants), we have the result, so delightful to many subsequent theorists, that happiness increases in an arithmetical progression when the corresponding wealth increases in a geometrical progression.

§ 2. *Bentham's opinions*

M. Halévy prints as an appendix to the first volume of his *Radicalisme Philosophique* a series of extracts from MS. No. 27 in the University College collection, assigning 1782 as their approximate date. These fragments, taken together, give the fullest general account of what Bentham, in other places, calls "Value of a lot of pleasure or pain: how to be measured", and there is little reason to suppose that Bentham would have altered the manuscript appreciably if he had published it. I propose, firstly, to give the substance of these fragments, and secondly to annotate and underline their contentions by referring to what Bentham elsewhere says.

"The idea of considering happiness as resolvable into a number of individual pleasures", Bentham says, "I took from Helvétius; before whose time it can scarcely be said to have a measuring." From Beccaria he further learned that the value of each sensation contained the four ingredients of duration, intensity, certainty, and proximity.[2] A fifth ingredient was of course the extent of the pleasure, that is to say, the number of persons who had it. "It seemed to me", Bentham continues, "that such an analysis was the very thing that was wanted as the foundation for a compleat system of moral science."

---

[1] Cf. Keynes, *A Treatise on Probability*, p. 318, and Weinberger, *Die Grenznutzenschule*, pp. 7 *sqq*.

[2] Bentham also mentions Maupertuis, but found that the discussion had taken "a wrong turn" in his pages.

The ingredients of duration and intensity are "dimensions of value" in pleasures, that is to say, they constantly belong to pleasures, as breadth or thickness belong to bodies, and are the measurable aspects of pleasure. In this measurement "the limit of a pleasure in respect of intensity on the side of diminution is a state of insensibility; the degree of intensity possessed by that pleasure which is the faintest of any that can be distinguished to be pleasure, may be represented by unity"; but "there is no fixing upon any particular degree of intensity" as a maximum. Similarly, he says, a "moment" may be taken to be the minimum unit of duration; and again there is no fixed maximum. According to Bentham these two dimensions are naturally represented by whole numbers; the ingredients of certainty and proximity, however, are naturally represented by fractions. A probability is a degree or fraction of certainty, and remoteness is to be regarded as a fraction of complete proximity, i.e. actual presence. Regarding the extent of pleasures we are told that "the total value of the stock of pleasure belonging to the whole community is to be obtained by multiplying the number expressing the value of it as respecting any one person, by the number expressing the multitude of such individuals".

Bentham believed, of course, that pleasure is the only good, pain the only evil, and that the greater quantity of pleasure is all that is meant by greater good. This, however, in the language of the century is "moral fortune", and its relation to "physical fortune" must therefore be discussed. On this point the fragments are fairly full, but Bentham may not have been prepared to abide by them *au pied de la lettre*.

The legislator, aiming at the maximum advantage of the people, can only, Bentham says, "lay in a man's way some *instrument* of pleasure, and leave the application of it" to the man. These instruments are, in some sense, possessions which may be measured by money, "the current instrument of pleasure". Indeed "it is plain by incontrovertible experience that the quantity of actual pleasure follows in every instance in some proportion or other the quantity of money". "As to the law of that proportion", however, "nothing can be more indeterminate. It depends upon a great variety of circumstances".

In general, Bentham goes on, the more money a man has, the greater his happiness. But we cannot argue that if one guinea gives a man one unit of pleasure, a million guineas gives a million unit-pleasures to the same man at the same time. "Perhaps not a thousand, perhaps not a hundred: who can say? perhaps not fifty." Indeed, although there are no limits to the increase of quantity of money, there *are* such limits to the increase of pleasure in individual persons. For some men find anything more than a hundred guineas a plain distraction and misery. Regarding large fortunes, therefore, the problem is quite indeterminate, but regarding small sums, Bentham thinks, it is sensible and fair to assume that increase of wealth and increase of happiness are *directly* proportional.

If so, since money is measurable, such happiness is measurable; and with regard to happiness not produced by money, money, if not "an exact and proper" measure "is the only one such as pain and pleasure will admit of".

If of two pleasures a man, knowing what they are, would as lief enjoy the one as the other, they must be reputed equal. There is no reason for supposing them unequal. If of two pains a man had as lief escape the one as the other, such two pains must be reputed equal. If of two sensations, a pain and a pleasure, a man had as lief enjoy the pleasure and suffer the pain, as not enjoy the first and not suffer the latter, such pleasure and pain must be reputed *equal*, or, as we may say in this case, *equivalent*.

Therefore, if money and pleasure are directly proportional, the common measure of money applies with "reputed" precision.

How much money would you give to purchase such a pleasure? 5 pounds and no more. How much money would you give to purchase such another pleasure? 5 pounds and no more. The two pleasures must, as to you, be reputed equal. How much money would you give to purchase immediately such a pleasure? 5 pounds and no more. How much money would you give to exempt yourself immediately from such a pain? 5 pounds and no more. The pleasure and the pain must be reputed equivalent.

It is only from necessity, Bentham concludes, that he prompts mankind to speak this mercenary language. Politics and Morals require the measuring instrument of money, as natural philosophy requires the barometer and the thermometer. Without such instruments, adieu to both.

'Tis in this way only we can get aliquot parts to measure by. If we must not say of a pain or of a pleasure that it is worth so much money, it is in vain, in point of quantity, to say anything at all about it, there is neither proportion nor disproportion between Punishments and Crimes.

The differences between this statement respecting the relation of "physical" to "moral" fortune and a formula like Bernoulli's is too obvious to need commenting on. If Bentham's mathematics were childlike in comparison with Bernoulli's, his grasp of psychology was incomparably firmer. Yet, in the end, what he says on this question in these passages is obviously and quite candidly a piece of bluff. The legislator, we are here informed, *must* rely upon a barometer which he has very slight reason for believing accurate regarding small sums, and knows to be meaningless regarding large ones!

For the most part, Bentham did not use, and did not need to use, this piece of bluff, but he was driven to employ something rather like it. Despite occasional wavering (as when he speaks of "pleasure itself not being ponderable or measurable")[1] he maintained (on the whole consistently) that it *was* measurable, and, as we have seen, explained in some detail what the principles of the measurement were. In short, his chief contention is accurately set forth in the following passage:

Legislation, which has hitherto been founded principally upon the quicksands of instinct and prejudice, ought at length to be placed upon the immovable base of feelings and experience; a moral thermometer is required which should exhibit every degree of happiness and suffering. The feelings of men are sufficiently

[1] See quotations in O. Kraus, *Zur Theorie des Wertes: Eine Bentham-Studie*, p. 31.

regular to become the object of a science or an art; and till this is done, we can only grope our way by making irregular and ill-directed efforts.[1]

On the other hand, no one was more sensible than Bentham himself of a part of the difficulty of constructing the thermometer well. In the sixth chapter of the *Principles of Morals and Legislation* he tells us that

> pain and pleasure are produced in men's minds by the action of certain causes. But the quantity of pleasure and pain runs not uniformly in proportion to the cause....In the same mind such and such causes of pain or pleasure will produce more pain or pleasure than such or such other causes of pain or pleasure; and this proportion will in different minds be different.

What is more, he proceeds to adduce a list of thirty-two circumstances which influence (and may qualify) the effect of *any* exciting cause.[2]

In view of these complications, it is surely apparent that Bentham's psychical thermometer would be very difficult indeed to construct, and he could not pretend that it had been constructed. His "political arithmetic", under actual conditions, was therefore an arithmetic of pretence. The judge distributing penalties, and the legislator distributing instruments of happiness, had to proceed, by Bentham's own showing, on a non-mathematical basis. On the one hand, Bentham maintains that these important persons should have a list of the "circumstances affecting sensibility" by their sides, and take account of it in their decisions, and Bentham rightly denied that this was "a visionary proposal not reducible to practice".[3] On the other hand, he says, as J. S. Mill later did, "Experience, observation and experiment—these are the foundation of all well-grounded medical practice; experience, observation and experiment—such are the foundations of all well-grounded legislative practice."[4] Mill's appeal to the experience of the race,[5] and not to a psychical thermometer, is obviously in keeping with this latter statement.

---

[1] O. Kraus, *op. cit.* p. 40 n.   [2] Chap. vi.
[3] *Principles of Morals and Legislation*, chap. vi.
[4] Cf. Kraus, *op. cit.* p. 31.   [5] *Utilitarianism*, chap. ii.

§ 3. *Buffon to Fechner*

Although Buffon, in his *Essai d'arithmétique morale* (1777) attempted to give a certain numerical formula for expressing the relation between the nominal value of money and its "moral" worth, his principal contentions are usually opposed to any such reckoning. In particular, he emphasised the divergence between personal satisfaction and pecuniary fortune. To the affluent, an increase in income yields no appreciable increase of happiness. To those who have only what is necessary, increase of wealth gives a boundless prospect of joy. Since Buffon defined the "necessary" as the accustomed standard of living, the variations and the relativity of his standards are the more obvious.

Laplace was unable to accept Buffon's mathematical formulae,[1] but agreed that a man's "moral fortune" depends upon a host of circumstances. Mathematical expectation, he says, is the product of the money hoped for, multiplied by the probability of its attainment, but moral hope depends upon a thousand varying circumstances which can neither be defined nor computed.[2] In general, however, it is reasonable to adopt Bernoulli's principle, and accept the view that the relative value of a sum infinitely small is directly proportional to its "absolute" or conventional pecuniary value, and inversely proportional to the total fortune of the person interested. This "moral" value, however small, should never be null, because existence itself is a positive value to everyone.[3] As Maecenas said: vita dum superest, bene est.

Like Bernoulli, Laplace supposed himself able to draw the consequences that gambling is always unwise, that it is imprudent for an investor to have all his eggs in the same basket, and the like. The first of these conclusions depends upon the principle that when two gamblers have the same initial capital, the winner gains relatively little moral fortune

---

[1] *Essai philosophique sur les probabilités*, chap. iii.
[2] *Théorie analytique des probabilités*, 1st edn. (1812) p. 187.
[3] *Ibid.* pp. 432 sq.

on his augmented capital, while the loser has a more serious loss to happiness relatively to his diminished capital.

These speculations of Bernoulli and Laplace were destined to be applied far more widely than in the restricted field of "physical" and "moral" fortune; for Fechner, in his *Elemente der Psychophysik* (1860), not only accepted the Bernoulli formula as an accurate expression of the relation between *any* pleasure and its causes,[1] but regarded it as the key to the entire relation between body and soul. And Fechner's book had profound effects both on the philosophy and on the psychology of the later nineteenth century.

The experimental facts, formulated chiefly by Weber, on which Fechner based his sweeping conclusion were in effect that, within the normal ranges of sensation, any given physical stimulus must be increased by a determinate fraction of its strength in order to yield a mental sensation just discernibly different. This "constant" or determinate fraction differs in different sensations such as brightness, or pressure. But if these just discernible differences in any series of sensations are regarded as arithmetically equal units, we do have the result that, within normal ranges, a geometrical progression of increments in the stimuli corresponds to an arithmetical progression in the increments of the corresponding sensations.

Fechner's generalisation of these results beyond the normal range of the majority of stimuli to which men are sensitive was over-zealous, and Stumpf has given the strongest reasons for denying that these just discernible differences in sensation are, in fact, arithmetically equal units; (for two sensations not discernibly different from a third are very commonly distinguishable from one another). The effect of Stumpf's argument is, however, that sensations are to be regarded as continuously increasing quantities, just as in the Bernoulli theorem. In other words, the formula $dy = k \dfrac{dx}{x}$ remains.

Undoubtedly, therefore, Fechner's extension of the formula

---

[1] See vol. I, pp. 237 *sq.* for references to Bernoulli, Laplace and others; vol. II, pp. 549 *sq.* for explicit application to pleasure.

to so wide a field was highly significant and deserved a part at least of its author's enthusiasm. Even if the formula held for *all* sensations, however, with much greater precision than we have any sufficient reason for supposing at present, there would be serious hazards in arguing from *sensations* to the *pleasure* accompanying them. For our pleasures are incomparably more variable than even our sensations, and the great majority of Bentham's thirty-two "circumstances affecting sensibility" (which do affect pleasures) could not be estimated in psycho-physical tables. Fechner himself seems to have become aware of this circumstance, for in a later work he admits that "the pleasure-increment cannot be mathematically estimated".[1]

§ 4. *Turgot to Gossen*

These comparisons between "physical" and "moral" fortune have plainly a certain relation to "value in use", "value in exchange" and other economic notions discussed in Chapter I, § 1. For if "utility" is defined as "capacity to produce pleasure", it is the instrument of "moral fortune"; while money, or the token of the ratio of exchange, is the common denominator of "physical fortune". Bernoulli's doctrine is therefore that "value in use" does not increase in direct proportion to increase in total wealth. In other words, there is a *Sättigungskala* of pecuniary wealth, as well as a diminishing return for successive acts of enjoyment, such as the eating of gooseberries.

Again, when "natural value", as in the Pufendorf tradition,[2] is said to be a function of utility *and* scarcity, it is clear that the utility or pleasure-giving properties of anything is not identical with its value. To be sure, the possession of something that is scarce often gives the possessor a special pleasure; but this is an objection to the pleasure-theory of utility and not a confirmation of it. What is meant by the theory is that the services of anything, say the nourishment supplied

---

[1] See references to *Vorschule der Ästhetik* in O. Kraus, *op. cit.* p. 53.
[2] Cf. p. 17 of the present book.

by a loaf of bread to any particular person, is not affected by the difficulty anyone else may have in purchasing a loaf.

An interesting point in the development of the Pufendorf tradition is Turgot's insistence, in a fragment on *Valeurs et monnaies*, that individual estimates of values are based not on utility and scarcity alone but on these combined with *excellence*, and that the social or pecuniary standard is a conventional but well-grounded expression for all three of these elements.[1] Condillac's statement that it is our estimates of utility and scarcity, not their reality, that affect prices is also to be noted.[2]

For our purposes, however, the most important contribution to the subject, prior to the independent discoveries of Jevons and of the Austrian economists, is Gossen's *Entwickelung der Gesetze des menschlichen Verkehrs* (1854). The basis of this book was a theory of the measurement of pleasures.

Gossen maintained that each of us endeavours to attain the highest possible felicity, and that pleasures, as they grow, diminish in their rate of increase, eventually reaching a limit of complete satiety. Repetition of pleasures, again, diminishes the time during which these stale pleasures, in comparison with fresh ones, are felt. On the other hand, practice and facility may make certain activities more pleasurable than they were without practice.

All values, he went on to say, are entirely relative to these facts concerning human pleasures; and we are subject to these limitations. Nevertheless, below the limits of satiety, pleasures, and their increments, may very well be calculated with all the resources of the calculus. Indeed, it is correct to assume that the marginal or smallest atoms of pleasure in any person chosen at random are identical in value, and again that the smallest increment in anyone's pleasure is independent of the direction in which he seeks the pleasure. The latter assumption is, of course, simply the theory of the commensurability of all pleasures, common to all the theories we

---

[1] Cf. Weinberger, *op. cit.* pp. 38 *sqq.*
[2] *Ibid.* p. 46.

x] STANDARDS OF VALUE 335

are now considering. The former, if it could be accepted, would simplify the calculation of what Bentham called the "extent of a 'lot' of happiness".

§ 5. *Jevons*

On page 1 of this book we saw that Jevons developed Bentham's utilitarianism further than J. S. Mill had done, and on page 24 we saw that the essence of his contention was that the "ratio of utility is some continuous mathematical function of the quantity of commodity". We may now supplement these remarks by considering, in greater detail, firstly his relation to Bentham and, secondly, the precise type of measurement which he believed to be possible in the case of pleasures and pains.

Jevons accepted Bentham's ethical principle ("I have no hesitation in accepting the Utilitarian theory of morals which does uphold the effect upon the happiness of mankind as the criterion of what is right and wrong")[1], and he also accepted Bentham's psychological principle ("It is the inevitable tendency of human nature to choose that course which offers the most apparent good at the moment").[2] He agreed, again, that Utilitarianism must be quantitative. ("To me it seems that our science must be mathematical because it deals with quantities. Wherever the things treated are capable of being *more or less* in magnitude, there the laws and relations must be mathematical in nature.")[3] And he expressly commended Bentham's clear perception of the point.

Yet, having quoted Bentham's statement, "Sum up all the values of all the pleasures....The balance will give the good tendency of the act, upon the whole", Jevons remarks, "I confess that it seems to me difficult even to imagine how such estimations and summations can be made with any

[1] *Theory of Political Economy*, p. 27.
[2] *Ibid.* p. 69. Cf. Edgeworth, *Mathematical Psychics*, p. 15: "The conception of man as a pleasure-machine may justify and facilitate the employment of mechanical terms and mathematical reasoning in social science". [3] *Ibid.* p. 4.

approach to accuracy",[1] and he concludes that our pleasures must be measured indirectly by inference from human choice.

Far be it from me to say that we ever shall have the means of measuring directly the feelings of the human heart. A unit of pleasure or of pain is difficult even to conceive; but it is the amount of these feelings which is continuously prompting us to buying and selling...and it is from the quantitative effects of the feelings that we must estimate their comparative amounts.[2]

So much on the first point. On the second point (approaching the subject from the consumer's point of view) Jevons advocated "the fearless consideration of infinitely small quantities. The theory consists in applying the differential calculus to the familiar notions of wealth...and all the other notions belonging to the daily operations of industry".[3] The way in which he proposed to use the calculus is best explained in a rather lengthy quotation.

"We can seldom or never affirm," he says, "that one pleasure is a multiple of another in quantity.... The theory turns upon those critical points where pleasures are nearly, if not quite equal.... The whole amount of pleasure that a man gains by a day's labour hardly enters the question; it is when a man is doubtful whether to increase his hours of labour or not, that we discover an equality between the pain of that extension and the pleasure of the increase of possessions derived from it. The reader will find, again, that there is never, in a single instance, an attempt made to compare the amount of feeling in one mind with that in another. I see no means by which such comparison can ever be accomplished.... But...every event in the outward world is represented in the mind by a corresponding motive, and it is by the balance of these that the will is swayed.... The motives and conditions are so numerous and complicated, that the resulting actions have the appearance of caprice.... It is by examining the average consumption...in a large population that we should detect a continuous variation connected with the variation of price by a constant law. ...Accordingly questions which appear, and perhaps are quite, indeterminate as regards individuals, may be capable of exact investigation and solution in regard to great masses and wide averages."[4]

[1] *Theory of Political Economy*, p. 12.
[2] *Ibid.* pp. 13 *sq.*
[3] *Ibid.* p. 4.
[4] *Ibid.* pp. 20 *sqq.*

STANDARDS OF VALUE

On the whole, therefore, it would appear that the claims Jevons makes for his calculus are really very moderate. "Final", "marginal" and "infinitesimal" quantities have to be used because we are dealing with continuous quantities when we deal with slight oscillations of pleasure, gradually diminishing enjoyment or the growth of preference, or, again, with the exchange of individual items in a stock which, in the world's market, is very large indeed. These continuous variations, and their relations, are conveniently described in economic graphs, that is to say, in continuous curves which, because they are continuous, require the differential calculus when they are represented algebraically. This being understood Jevons asserts little rather than much in his "fearless" application of the calculus. Mr Edgeworth puts the point very fairly when he says "It is not so much a political arithmetic as a sort of economic algebra, in which the problem is not to find x and y in terms of given quantities, but rather to discover loose quantitative relations of the form: x is greater or less than y; and increases or decreases with the increase of z".[1]

§ 6. *The legitimacy of "marginalism"*

The name of "marginal", it is true, is sometimes given to theories which employ, not this loose quantitative algebra, but a species of crude arithmetic even with regard to a few items. Thus the Austrian economists, while disclaiming exact numerical measurement,[2] commonly employ arbitrary numbers such as 10, 8, 6 to illustrate their meaning, and, as we saw in Chapter I, are liable to reach conclusions which are wholly absurd.

Let us return, for a moment, to the hypothetical case of the mariner and his biscuits. Suppose a shipwrecked sailor and his dog in a boat, and suppose also that there are two biscuits in the boat, that biscuits are indivisible units, and

---

[1] *Papers relating to Political Economy*, vol. II, p. 274. Cf. the same author's *Mathematical Psychics*, pp. 2 *sqq.* and p. 87.
[2] Cf. quotations from Böhm-Bawerk and von Wieser in O. Kraus, *op. cit.* p. 91.

that one biscuit is sufficient for man or dog while more than one biscuit is superfluous for either. On these premisses it is gravely argued[1] that the value of the two biscuits is twice the value of the less useful or marginal biscuit (i.e. the dog's) on the ground that, the two biscuits being the same, no one would give more for one than for the other.

The absurdity of this conclusion can be easily shown. Suppose that the sailor and his dog had no biscuits, but that there was an avaricious sailor within hail who had plenty of biscuits, and himself needed only one. In that case the destitute sailor might be forced to surrender all that he possessed in exchange for the one biscuit he needed, but when the bargain was concluded, the avaricious sailor, if he had no other customers, might easily throw an extra biscuit to the dog, and it would not matter which of these two biscuits was eaten by the man and which by the dog. The destitute sailor would not give more for one than for the other, but he would give the same for two as for one.

In other words, the fact that either biscuit, chosen at random, would feed the man, on the one hand, or the dog, on the other, is quite irrelevant to the problem in question. The value of the two biscuits is the value of the man's biscuit *plus* the value of the dog's biscuit, and nothing else in the world. It is only when there is a large supply of biscuits in a free market that the price of *any* biscuit chosen at random can be said to be regulated by the "marginal" or cheapest biscuit.

Again, it can scarcely be doubted that many economists, from a laudable desire to show that their "curves of diminishing utility" and the like have a "real meaning",[2] have greatly exaggerated the economic effect of fine adjustments at the margin. In household economy the margin, to be sure, *is* important, as Mr Micawber's classical remarks concerning the difference between saving sixpence and spending sixpence too much on an income of twenty pounds per annum suf-

---

[1] Smart, *The Theory of Value*, p. 30.
[2] Cf. Irving Fisher in *Economic Essays Contributed in Honor of John Bates Clark*, pp. 157 sq.

ficiently showed; but Mrs Micawber's relatives were not mistaken in thinking that such major items as the rapid increase of the Micawber family were really more important than fine adjustments at the pawnbroker's. And in political economy it is reasonable to suppose that relatively fixed expenditure on debt is quite as important as fine marginal adjustments concerning the bonus in the civil service.

In short, there is a great deal of truth in Mr Hobson's contention that consumption and production, both on a large scale and on a small scale, are causally determined, in the main, by the "organic make up" of the mill, the industry, or the family income, and that, in all these cases, central things are in the centre.[1] This is legitimate criticism of the fallacy that because prices are mathematical functions of marginal prices, and because computation in terms of the marginal oscillations are mathematically convenient, therefore the marginal fluctuation should be regarded as a highly privileged causal agency in "determining" prices. Taken as a whole, however, Mr Hobson's argument is itself fallacious, because there is no inconsistency between "marginal" and "central" methods of reckoning. The question is whether differentials can be applied (without serious inaccuracy) to small finite differences, and even Mr Hobson would not deny that large finite differences are mathematical functions of small ones. In other words, causal determination is quite a different thing from mathematical equivalence.

"The great bluff which the mathematical economists have put up", Mr Hobson says, is that "they have transferred to the organised industrial system the qualities of identical nature, infinite divisibility, and absolute fluidity that belong to money",[2] and he proceeds to argue that neither physical commodities nor "subjective factors" have these qualities. Regarding commodities, it seems enough to say that boxes of matches and the like do seem to have the qualities at least as clearly as money has; and that, if the "subjective factor" be

[1] *Free Thought in the Social Sciences*, Part II, chap. iii.
[2] *Ibid.* p. 118.

pleasure, Jevons's loose algebra seems much more nearly correct than Mr Hobson's statement that the "subjective factors are finitely not infinitely divisible, and of slow and difficult mobility".[1]

At a recent by-election I heard one of the orators declare—he was speaking of an increase in the tax on tobacco by ½d. an ounce—that "every puff from the working man's pipe was a little something extra in the Chancellor's pocket". Even if the puffs are discontinuous physical quantities, the satisfaction attending them need not be supposed to be similarly discontinuous.

§ 7. *Problems in the measurement of pleasures*

After these historical explanations it ought to be possible, swiftly and rather briefly, to set down the principal perplexities that attend all attempts to reckon pleasures.

When the problem is interpreted in Bentham's rather simple-minded way we have in the first instance to consider the two "dimensions" of duration and intensity.

The measurement of duration, in the case of pleasures, should not be more difficult than in other cases. It is true that our psychological *tempo*, or experienced time, may differ from clock-time in important ways; but, in the main, it would be hypercritical to deny that the durations of some given pleasure could be measured by a stop-watch. Again, it is true that since duration is a continuous quantity, such units as a second or a minute are, in a way, arbitrary. But so are feet and inches. And no reasonable objection can be taken to the use of such units.

The "intensity" of pleasures and pains is much more dubious, and Bentham seems to have been speaking vaguely when he spoke of it. We may think, no doubt, of grief becoming more poignant, or of toothache becoming more acute within the same apparent area. Even in these cases, however, it is very unlikely that we have anything like a pure dimension of "intensity". The changes are usually qualitative or at

[1] *Free Thought in the Social Sciences*, p. 119.

least sub-qualitative, and they bear the marks of the thwarting of profounder dispositions, wider restlessness, the beginning of frenzy and the like. To distinguish the mere "intensity" of identical pleasures and pains from these embarrassing attendants is too delicate a task for most of us.

Supposing, again, that we really could discriminate "intensity" from irrelevant accompaniments, it would be very difficult indeed to have rational confidence in our measurement of it. In the case of sensations, any just discriminable difference in the sensations which arise from a given stimulus is equated with a measurable increase in the physical intensity of the relevant stimulus. This is no proof that the differences in the sensation are differences only in the sensation's *intensity*, and if it were, the pleasures accompanying sensation have, as we saw, much more complicated conditions than the sensation has. In other words, degrees in intensity of the *same pleasure* are much more arbitrary and elusive than degrees of intensity of the *same sensation*.

Something might be done, perhaps, by employing Jevons's principle and saying that we learn from "marginal" choices when a pleasure is preferable to (or really greater than) some other, although we might not otherwise have known of the fact. Any extensive application of this principle, however, would be difficult if we did not make Jevons's assumption that *all* such choices depend upon increase of pleasure; and we saw in Chapter I that this assumption is quite definitely illegitimate.

It must be conceded, therefore, that any measurement of the dimension of "intensity" in pleasures is only doubtfully feasible. Suppose, however, that the thing could be done, and even that appropriate units could be found, not less serviceable or more arbitrary than a minute or a second in the case of duration. If so, it might be as reasonable to say that if the intensity of a given pleasure is doubled we have therefore precisely twice as much pleasure as we had before (just as there is precisely twice as much pleasure in two seconds of a given enjoyment as in one second of the same). And we could go on doing these sums so long as we kept strictly to the dimension of intensity on the one hand or to the dimension of duration on the other hand. But what would happen if we tried, as Bentham tried, to multiply the two dimensions together? Can anyone pretend that he *knows*[1] that two seconds of a faint pleasure are precisely equal to one second of the same pleasure twice as intense? And if this is not the correct proportion, what *is* the correct proportion? Indeed, is there any correct proportion?

We are dealing, now, with amount of pleasure. There is more pleasure (very likely in a precise arithmetical sense) in proportion as a pleasure endures. There is more pleasure (possibly in a precise arithmetical sense) in proportion as a pleasure becomes more intense. But is there *any* numerical correlation between "intensity" and duration. If there were, we should have to lay claim to some definite intuition concerning the comparative numerical pleasure-values of "intensity" and duration, and I do not see how we could reasonably profess the least confidence in any such intuition.

Our conclusion, therefore, is that the "dimension" of duration is arithmetically measurable, and the "dimension" of "intensity" conceivably although very doubtfully so, but that the two dimensions are *not* arithmetically comparable *inter se*.

So far we have argued in terms of an increase or diminution of the same pleasure in the same individual. The next step, therefore, is to examine different pleasures in the same individual.

[1] *Pace*, I fear, Mr Edgeworth, "The unit in each dimension [of time and intensity] is the just perceivable increment. The implied equation to each other of each *minimum sensibile* is a first principle incapable of proof. It resembles the equation to each other of indistinguishable events or cases, which constitutes the first principle of the mathematical calculus of *belief*. It is doubtless a principle acquired in the course of evolution". (*Mathematical Psychics*, p. 7.) On p. 101 of the same work, however, Mr Edgeworth says (speaking again of duration and intensity taken together), "The comparison of pleasures as to quantity is here admitted to be vague"—but at least as useful as examiners' marks! On the same page Mr Edgeworth is prepared to accept as an "axiom" the statement that "Any just perceivable pleasure-increment experienced by any sentient at any time has the same value".

As we saw in Chapter v, § 7, the phrase "different pleasures" is ambiguous, for it may mean either "pleasures of different quality" or "pleasures arising from different sources". In the discussions with which we are at present concerned it is assumed that all pleasures are the same in quality, so that there is a common denominator of simple agreeableness on the one hand and of mere disagreeableness upon the other.

It is perhaps a moot point whether pleasures do differ in quality. If so, it is legitimate to argue upon the assumption that the only necessary difference in them, for present purposes, is the difference in their source.

Even so, however, certain difficulties in connection with the comparison of pleasures and pains, whether "of different quality" or "from different sources", have to be kept in mind.

It is sometimes argued, e.g. by Locke,[1] that we must be infallible judges of *present* pleasure when we have it, for the simple reason that we do have it. Pleasure *is* an experience, and the experience is the whole of it. Whatever may be thought of this argument in general, however, it must surely be admitted that the mere fact that we *experience* a pleasure does not in any way imply that we discriminate, say, its "intensity" correctly. Again, if there is any truth in Jevons's principle of unsuspected revelations at the margin, there must be a further limitation of Locke's doctrine.

In any case it is very rare for two separate pleasures to be present together in any one mind, like the clear and the yellow waters flowing together in the united Rhône. When pleasures occur simultaneously they are usually pretty thoroughly mixed (or even indissolubly fused) so far as our powers of discrimination go. For the most part, therefore, we have to compare either a present pleasure with an anticipated or remembered one, or else two remembered pleasures on the one hand or two anticipated ones on the other. Our anticipations of pleasure are notoriously untrustworthy, and our comparison between present and remembered pleasures egregi-

[1] *Essay*, Book II, chap. xxi, § 60.

ously unfair. The best test, therefore, is the comparison of two remembered pleasures, when both are recent enough to be remembered pretty well. Such a standard need not be unsatisfactory, but cannot inspire the highest confidence. For memory is never precise, and there are reasons for supposing that the memory of pleasures is less reliable than the memory of events. We have to train ourselves to remember the latter.

An additional source of perplexity must therefore be conceded here, and any attempt to equate our feelings in the one respect in which Bentham and his followers admitted a distinction of quality (i.e. to equate our pleasures with our pains) is manifestly still more dubious. Some men would rather be insensible than suffer a little pain. Others would rather have lively pleasures at the price of lively pains. A third party welcomes pain because it heightens pleasure, when the pleasure comes. And there are other individual differences in this matter.[1]

Finally, we have to consider what Bentham called extent, that is to say, the calculation of the pleasures of many different persons. What reason have we for supposing that we can measure this dimension of pleasures?

Elaborate psychological experiments on these questions concerning pleasures and pains have seldom been attempted, and present an infantile appearance. If they were attempted they would have to be either introspective or behaviouristic, that is to say, they would depend either upon certain statements concerning the feelings of particular persons, made by these persons, in certain situations, or upon an inference from human behaviour, experimentally or statistically obtained.

Even assuming, on the first method, that these introspective statements were fairly reliable, the conditions of pleasure are so intricate and complicated that it may be doubted how far general conclusions, of high probability, could be inferred from such investigations.

The alternative method is, therefore, by far the most usual

[1] E.g. Michelangelo's amazing view that "a thousand joys are not as good as a single torment".

—and is also (like Mill's appeal to "the experience of the race") very far from precise. It is difficult to see how it could be very precise, even with regard to the relatively simple case of bodily pleasures and pains. How intense was Scaevola's suffering when he held his hand stoically in the flame? Did his patriotism dull or annul the suffering, or did it not? When the Indians proved their manhood by enduring torture, was their sensibility to actual pain the same as other people's? Is the period of childbirth easier for a gipsy woman to bear than for an imaginative or opulent lady? Are the cries of young children at a dentist's evidence of really acute suffering.

It seems impossible to suppose that great exactitude can be expected in the answers (if there are any) to questions such as these. In a general way, to be sure, we have a great deal of important knowledge concerning the pleasure-yielding and the pain-yielding properties of many things to very many people. If it were not so, there would be no sense in administering anaesthetics, or in giving schoolboys a holiday. We might even construct a comparatively plausible hedonic thermometer, and apply it not unreliably in a good many cases. Yet if the thermometer were a useful working device, it could not therefore be shown to be an instrument of precision.

§ 8. *Further on the same*

As we saw, Jevons maintained that although there are no arithmetical units of the type Bentham supposed (except in respect of duration), nevertheless the calculus may be "fearlessly" employed. This is like saying that differentials should be employed although it is impossible to integrate them. What is more, Jevons surrendered his point in another way. For he assumed that we know the margins where the increments of pleasure are infinitesimal—which is to assume that we *know* when pleasures are *very nearly* equal, and that we *know* when they are very nearly equivalent to pains. Such approximate knowledge, if we had it, would be good enough for Bentham's political and moral arithmetic.

Granting, therefore, that the Bernoulli-Gossen-Jevons method is more appropriate to the continuous variations of pleasure than Bentham's rude computations, there would not seem to be any pronounced difference in point of principle.

On the whole, therefore, we should conclude (1) that we do have a good deal of knowledge about greater and less in pleasures, and about the balance of pleasure over pain; but (2) that our data are too indeterminate for precise mathematical reckoning of this knowledge.

The question then is whether pleasures themselves, although greater or less, are themselves indeterminate *quanta*, or whether all that is meant is that we do not know enough about them to determine their quantity with precision. Very often, it is not at all evident which of these two opinions is held. "Satisfaction, then", Mr Edgeworth says, quoting Poincaré, "is a magnitude but not a measurable magnitude." "Nevertheless, it is not 'par cela seul exclue de toute spéculation mathématique'." And Mr Edgeworth goes on to say, "Is it not evident that without having more exact relations than those of 'more' and 'less' we can infer that the product of a and b, ab, is greater than $a\beta$ if it is given that $a > a$, $b > \beta$? We can make this inference even without the second datum, if it is known that a is very much greater than a, while b is known not to be much greater than β".[1] Very possibly we *can* draw such inferences; but many believe that even these rough estimates of indeterminate quantity would have no meaning at all, unless there really were an exact quantitative relation in the facts themselves, supposing that, *per impossibile*, the facts themselves were fully known.

On this point it seems enough to say that the inferences *are* valid, and perfectly objective, with respect to the facts *as known*. They do not presuppose anything *except* what is known. Therefore the question whether the facts themselves are or are not more determinate in respect to quantity than our knowledge of them, is theoretically irrelevant. Everything that exists, to be sure, is determinate. But it does not

[1] *Mind*, N.S., No. 123, p. 274.

follow that all existent *quanta* are *numerically* determinate *quanta*; and perhaps some *quanta* do not have this particular species of determinateness.

Logically speaking, therefore, we have every right to believe in the validity of our beliefs concerning *greater* and *less* in pleasures, and also to believe in a certain broad arithmetic concerning them, without any necessity for making up our minds concerning the numerical precision of hedonic *quanta* in nature. Therefore, if (as should be admitted) our knowledge of the quantity of any pleasure is never numerically precise except with respect to duration, it is a luxury to speculate about a greater degree of numerical precision than we are able to attain. As a luxury-speculation, I think, we might hazard the conjecture that if intensity is a genuine "dimension" of pleasure it is probably numerically precise; but very dubiously so if intensity is really a misdescription of slight qualitative changes. We should also hold, I think, that the product obtained by multiplying duration into intensity is probably meaningless, and not unlike the empty fiction of multiplying the shape of a coloured patch into the degree of saturation. Patches of colour do have shape, and colours have a numerically measurable degree of saturation or purity. But units of shape multiplied by units of purity are vain mathematical entities and no more to be regarded than the product of Columbus's egg into Oliver Cromwell's sincerity.

§ 9. *The meaning of pleasure*

In this entire argument I have assumed that we mean by pleasure what is usually and, I think, correctly meant by it, namely, a recognisable psychological state possessing agreeable quality in a certain volume or amplitude. "Lots" of pleasure seem plainly so to be understood. "The most apparent good at the moment" (offered by any course of action) of which Jevons spoke must be understood in this way—for Jevons took the good to *be* pleasure. And similarly of "the perceptions which the mind would rather experience than not" in the definition cited from Maupertuis.

These authors accordingly held that pleasure is the *result* at which we aim, the *thing* we choose or prize or prefer; and their statements, as we have seen, are downright false, because we choose much that is not pleasure, and prefer certain excellences out of all proportion to their pleasure-yielding properties. I think, however, that a great part of the reason why the falsity of such statements was not perceived by these authors was that Bentham, Jevons and the rest frequently meant by "pleasure" something quite different from what they said. When they *said* that pleasure was the *thing* that we liked, or chose, or prized or preferred, they *meant* very often that it was our liking, prizing, choice or preference *itself*. According to the latter view, the preferring is the pleasure, the tendency to cling to anything is itself our pleasure in it.

Certainly, this interpretation makes nonsense of much that they said—which is, perhaps, why they did not say it. For example, Jevons's statement, quoted above, would become a statement to the effect that our preference is for the greatest apparent *preferring* at the moment. And this is absurd. Nevertheless, when these authors speak about "pleasure", it is apparent that preference or choice or prizing is the actual subject of their argument.

Can we then mend the situation by *saying* what they often *meant*? If we did, we should plainly have to measure a *different* quantity, viz. the duration and "intensity" of our choosing, not of what we choose—perhaps, as Mr Perry suggests,[1] a distensive magnitude in the degrees of differences in our choices. And obviously we need not expect to reach the same results.

If we interpret Jevons and others in this fashion, we should have to say that, in their opinion, measurable choice and preference is expressed in economic statistics. It is manifest, however, that economic choice or preference is only a part of

---

[1] *General Theory of Value*, p. 635. The term "distensive magnitude" is Mr W. E. Johnson's (*Logic*, Part II, chap. vii) and means degree of difference in qualities of the same sort, e.g. a greater or lesser difference between red and yellow than between green and blue.

the field of choice or preference as a whole. What is required is an examination of *all* choice and preference, "elective" as well as psychological, timological as well as "elective". Either there are other standards in this wide field, or "economics" must be interpreted far more broadly than is usual or convenient. This wider enquiry, however, is not the measurement of *pleasure*, and is appropriate to the second, or more general, section of this chapter.

SECTION II. THE GENERAL THEORY OF VALUE-MEASUREMENT

§ 1. *Axioms of value and of value-measurement*

The design of the second section of this chapter is to examine the possibility of extending the principles and conclusions of the first section to a wider field. The field *must* be wider because, as we saw, pleasures are not the only values, or pains the only disvalues. On the other hand, the principles implied in any computation of values have been much more adequately discussed in connection with pleasure-pain than in other species of value. It is therefore to be expected that something of general significance should emerge from the discussion.

Before proceeding with this task, however, it will be convenient to give some account of certain formal principles which apply to *all* values and to their computation. These formal principles may be subdivided into (*a*) Axioms of the constitution of values or disvalues, and (*b*) Axioms of the addition of independent values and disvalues.

(*a*) *Constitutive axioms*.

1. (i) The Axiom of Objectivity. If M has the value a, it has that value. And similarly of disvalue.

This axiom corresponds to the Law of Identity in formal logic. Corresponding to the Laws of Non-contradiction and of Excluded Middle we have:

(ii) If M has the value a, it cannot be without that value. And similarly of any disvalue.

(iii) M must either have the value a, or not have that value. And similarly of any disvalue.

(In (iii) M does not have the value a if either it has no value or else has a "neutral value", or some disvalue incompatible with the possession of a.)

We have also:

2. The Axiom of the Division of Values. All values are positive, negative or neutral.

The presence of neutral value must be distinguished from the absence of any value. Thus in any gradual transition from pleasure to pain there is a point or small length which belongs to the pleasure-pain series, but contains neither appreciable pleasure nor appreciable pain. This neutral value is quite different from insensibility, or the mere absence of pleasure-pain.

Again, as Kant proved in his *Essay on Negative Quantities*, the distinction between positive and negative in values is of the utmost importance. Pain is not "diminished pleasure" but opposed to pleasure as such. Vice differs from virtue, not as earth from heaven but as hell from heaven.

Once more, while the presence of a value a *is* a value, the absence of a need not be a positive disvalue. This point (which is obvious) is occasionally misrepresented in moral disquisitions. If it is right, say, to be grateful to a given person, any ingratitude, whether insensibility or positive resentment towards a benefactor, is wrong. Again, if we have the opportunity of achieving a value, and forgo the opportunity, our action is wrong because of the wickedness of useless sacrifice. What is proved in such instances, however, is that, if *only* one action is right, every *other* adjustment to the situation is wrong; and this principle is not at all inconsistent with what has been stated above.

The Axiom of Division must be carefully distinguished from what may be called the Probability of Specific Opposition in Values. Most values seem to have a single opposite disvalue, as pain and pleasure, virtue and vice, love and hatred, beauty and ugliness. It is not self-evident, however, that there must always be a one-one opposition of this order. The relation of opposition might be one-many; or again the only alternative might be between the presence of some value and its simple absence.

It is also to be noted, that if a' is a specific value and a'' its opposite specific disvalue, a'' need not be a disvalue in every respect and from every point of view. Sympathetic pain, for example, may be a disvalue *quâ* pain and a value *quâ* sympathetic.

(b) *Additive axioms for independent values.*

3. The Axiom of Addition: $a + b$ is a greater value than a. And also than b, when a and b are positive values. Similarly, if a and b are negative values $a + b$ is a greater disvalue than a. And also than b.

We have also the Commutative, Associative and Distributive Axioms.

4. The Commutative Axiom: $a \times b = b \times a$.
5. The Associative Axiom: $(a + b) + c = a + (b + c)$.
6. The Distributive Axiom: $(a + b) \times c = (a \times c) + (b \times c)$.

These axioms hold for independent comparable values and for independent comparable disvalues respectively. The great difficulty of applying them, however, is that we find it so difficult to discover whether most values are or are not independent, and that if we proceed to multiply numerically incomparable magnitudes we may reach quite fantastic (or at least egregiously arbitrary) results, as in the fictitious products examined in the last section. That is why these axioms do not really help us very much in attempts to evaluate standards of goodness. They are mentioned here because they are true, and also relevant. But they are seldom very helpful in the principal business of this section.

Two other points, however, must still be mentioned in the present connection. Firstly, we should note that the treatment of specific values as positive quantities and of their opposite disvalues as negative quantities, while legitimate in a general way, may be very arbitrary indeed when we employ the ordinary process of subtraction, or an arithmetical *plus* and *minus*. The difficulty here is to find an intelligible unit and to know when $+1$ is precisely or even approximately opposite to -1. The nature of this difficulty has been abundantly illustrated in the first section of this chapter.

A second point concerns the relation of *dependence* in value measurements. This general question will occupy us later, but it seems appropriate to consider a principle proposed by Mr Theodor Lessing[1] at the present stage of our argument. According to Mr Lessing we should accept the following additional axioms:

7. If the value of M depends upon the value of N, N has greater value than M.

8. If the disvalue of M depends upon the disvalue of N, N has greater disvalue than M.

These alleged axioms seem to me to be false. As we have seen, the value of M might depend in large measure upon the *existence* of N, although N had no value at all. Suppose, however, that this is not what is meant, and that the principle means strictly what it says, viz. that M's value depends upon N's value. If this means that M borrows its value from N, it is surely possible that M might borrow the whole of N's value. Again, it is surely possible that N does not *transfer* any part of its value to M, but that being valuable, it helps M, to be valuable also. A "good" example, as the copy-books say, may help others to be good. If so, the followers may very well be better than their masters, or for that matter, might themselves become good through their horror of some awful example set them.

[1] *Studien zur Wertaxiomatik*, chap. ii, § 3. The formulation in this work of several "axioms" seems defective.

§ 2. *The commensurability of all values*

In the language of ordinary mathematics, quantities are said to be commensurable in so far as they are comparable by means of positive whole numbers. Thus we all learned in our schooldays that 1 and $\sqrt{2}$ are incommensurable. There is sufficient authority, however, for using the term "commensurable" in a much less restricted sense; and it is convenient to do so here.

By "commensurable", then, I shall mean "comparable with precision in any metrical way", not necessarily in terms of positive integers.

In all the arguments considered in the first section of this chapter it was assumed that pleasure is the only positive value, and that "a greater good" means simply "a greater amount of pleasure". It was natural to suppose, therefore, that if pleasures are mensurable (i.e. measurable) at all, they must all be *com*mensurable. Yet we saw that although the "dimension" of duration is numerically measurable, duration may not be numerically *com*mensurable with the "dimension" of intensity.

We have therefore to distinguish, even in the case of pleasures, between numerical and non-numerical commensurability, and have to face the question whether non-numerical commensurability is, properly speaking, commensurability at all.

It seems fair to say that any two pleasure-values are commensurable if a principle corresponding to the Axiom of Archimedes holds of them, that is to say, that two pleasure-values x and y are commensurable if they are so related that some quantity of x (perhaps very large) is a greater pleasure-value than some quantity of y (perhaps very small). If, on the other hand, the pleasure-value of x is infinite in comparison with the pleasure-value of y, so that the smallest quantity of x is infinitely greater than any conceivable quantity of y, the two pleasure-values are not commensurable.

In the latter case, however, these pleasure-values may very well, in a general sense, be comparable, and indeed very easily so. For comparing x with y we should always be able to see that x has a greater pleasure-value than y.

According to this account of commensurability, commensurable values need not be *arithmetically* commensurable. The question is one of greater and less, not of greater and less in precise arithmetical units. We have therefore to distinguish between *numerical* and *mere* commensurability, as well as to distinguish between *mere* commensurability and *mere* comparability; and I propose to employ all three distinctions in the sequel. I do not think we can dispense with any of them; and, in any case, *qui bene distinguit, bene docet.*

What we have now to do, therefore, is to discard the patently false assumption that pleasures are the *only* positive values, and to consider whether *all* values are numerically commensurable, merely commensurable, merely comparable, or not even comparable. Since the term "value" is probably ambiguous it is to be understood that value, unless some other indication is expressly given, is to be interpreted in the timological sense.

It seems likely that all excellent things are, in certain ways, *quanta* of excellence. To be sure, it may seem quaint to talk of the amount of some excellence, say virtue. Yet degrees of excellence are not to be denied, and what differs in degree differs in amount. Accordingly there are no barriers in this direction.

Admitting, however, that excellences may all be quantitative, it is overwhelmingly improbable that all are numerically commensurable. For pleasures are values, and it is unlikely that the dimension of duration, in their case, is numerically commensurate with the dimension of "intensity". Even apart from this, it seems ludicrous to contend that the disvalue of "a single lie" is precisely and numerically equal to the disvalue of some specific quantity of toothache.

It might be supposed, in the latter instance, that mere commensurability is just as absurd as numerical commensurability. But is it? Neither Lecky nor Rashdall could assent to Newman's statement that

it were better for sun and moon to drop from heaven, for the earth to fail, or for all the many millions who are upon it to die of starvation in extremest agony, than that one soul—I will not say should be lost—but should commit one venial sin, should tell one wilful untruth though it harmed no one, or steal one poor farthing without excuse.[1]

They maintained, in short, that venial lies are a lesser evil than some great degree of suffering, and would probably have said the same about lies not venial. In other words, they did believe in the mere commensurability of these values.

To be sure, Newman may have been right, but he is not obviously right, and it would be difficult to choose stronger instances of so-called incommensurable values than Newman's examples.

I think, therefore, that what I have called the *mere* commensurability of all values is very hard to deny. Those who, very rightly, take beauty or love or moral worth to be immensely greater and finer values than, let us say, sensual pleasure, do not usually assert what Newman asserted—unless indeed they are simply careless in what they assert. What they mean, I think, is rather what Dr McTaggart said with some precision in a passage which I am constrained to quote. (In Dr McTaggart's view love was by far the greatest good.)

Can we say that love is incommensurably better than any other good? This seems attractive, but I cannot think it is correct. If it were so, it would follow that, starting from *any* standpoint—my own at present, for example—the smallest conceivable increase in love would be better than the greatest possible increase in knowledge, virtue, pleasure or fulness of life. And it does not seem to me that this is true.

Is there any other way in which love could hold a supreme and unique position? I think that there is. It would hold such a position if it were true that love is capable of being so good, that no possible goodness arising from knowledge, virtue, pleasure or fulness of life could equal it. And it is this view—a view which has

[1] *Anglican Difficulties*, p. 190.

been held by many people, mystics and non-mystics—which I believe to be true. It seems to me that when love reached or passed a certain point, it would be more good than any possible amount of knowledge, virtue, pleasure or fulness of life could be.[1]

As it stands, this statement appears to assert that a certain kind or degree of love *is* incommensurable with all other values although a lower kind or lesser degree of love is not incommensurable with them. If so, the statement itself could hardly be other than arbitrary; and many, no doubt, would maintain that love does not have this kind of superiority over virtue or over knowledge. If, however, the value of pleasure or of knowledge increased according to a law of diminishing value and reached or asymptotically approached an upper limiting value, while the increase in the value of love had no such restriction, Dr McTaggart's view would be what was naturally to be expected; and there is some evidence that we do believe something of the sort regarding pleasures and perhaps regarding knowledge, although few of us believe it regarding beauty or regarding virtue.

On the whole, however, it seems prudent to conclude that all values are probably commensurable, although it is improbable that the principal species of value are arithmetically commensurable *inter se*. If so, since all the entities that are commensurable are *à fortiori* comparable, it follows that all values are comparable, and (by obversion) that no values are non-comparable.

§ 3. *Further on the same*

Certain points connected with this conclusion should be noted, even if the discussion of them has perforce to be desultory. I shall treat each of them separately.

(1) Love, pleasure, beauty, truth and knowledge are very different one from another, and it may be an error to regard many of their differences as determinate varieties of certain common features. What has been argued above is only that their *values* are probably comparable because they are probably commensurable.

[1] *The Nature of Existence*, vol. II, p. 437.

(2) Nothing in this argument should be taken to imply any particular theory of the way in which the degree or amount of excellence should be computed in any of the great departments of value, such as love or beauty or felicity. Despite certain well-known objections which need not be considered here,[1] it seems reasonable, on the whole, to regard "lots" of pleasure as the sum of successive felicitous moments in this or the other man's experience. The same assumption seems also not unreasonable in the case of beauty, for the character of beauty either holds of individual precious things or belongs to individual short periods of enjoyment. On the other hand, "lots" or amounts of information seems a very poor way of evaluating knowledge, and greater excellence in this domain appears to attach to the luminosity and organising potency of principles. Regarding virtue, again, the truth may be that, in the main, degrees of purity and degrees of excellence are to be regarded as one and the same.

(3) It is not denied that relevant circumstances may alter cases.

> Where is this straw, my fellow?
> The art of our necessities is strange
> That can make vile things precious.

(4) Different values *have* to be compared if it is necessary to choose between them, and if any rational justification for the choice can be given. It is not, however, theoretically essential that a choice between values should be forced upon us in order to make comparison possible. Even if the greater values were not only the best bedfellows but inseparable companions, we might still compare their several excellences. For example, love would exclude scientific knowledge, and scientific knowledge would exclude love, if we meant by "love" some vehement and short passion directed towards a person, and by "scientific knowledge" brief, intense and enthralling concentration. Yet steady affection towards persons and habitual clarity of intellectual judgment are in

[1] E.g. T. H. Green, *Prolegomena to Ethics*, Book III, chap. iv. Even Bradley seems to have renounced these arguments. Cf. footnotes to Essay III in *Ethical Studies*, 2nd edn. (especially on p. 94).

no way opposed. Accordingly, in all such discussions, much depends upon the definition of the values compared, and too much stress may easily be laid upon the need for compromise and compensation in the enforced choices and valuations of ordinary life. Nevertheless, if a man *cannot* write or study when his children are imitating fog-horns within earshot, he *has*, at certain times, to choose between the enjoyment of family affection and the sedulous pursuit of knowledge.

(5) In any of the major domains of value, other than pleasure, the abandonment of the hedonistic myth may simplify the comparison, and in certain cases, even the numerical computation, of the special values concerned. For example, it is simpler and much more precise to compute the health-values of a scientific diet, by calories, quantity of proteins and the like, than by any bizarre arithmetic of pleasures and satisfactions. Such arithmetical reckoning is probably not feasible at all in the case of the values of knowledge or of virtue; and the standards of truth, on the one hand, or of righteousness, on the other, are more easily ascertained by intuition and by direct comparison than by dubious and enormously complicated sums concerning the quantity of pleasure reasonably to be expected from knowledge or from virtue, even in a given society during its proximate future.

(6) *Per contra*, the hedonistic myth, if it could be accepted, would probably simplify the comparison between one domain of value and another. In certain ways, however, this might not be the fact. If these domains were incommensurable, we should have to restrict our comparisons to each, and would not be entitled to begin the troublesome enterprise of comparing the values in one domain with those in another. Again, if a limited set of "higher" values were immensely (although, in theory, not incommensurably) greater than any probable amount of some "lower" kind of value, we should be entitled, for all practical purposes, to ignore the "lower" values altogether. The same result, to be sure, would follow if the pleasures resulting from these "higher" values were immensely greater than any probable amount of "lower"

pleasure. But although many would hold that the *value* of intellectual sincerity, say, was immensely (if not immeasurably) greater than the value of any prowess to be achieved in cricket, it would be merely impudent to assert that the *pleasure* of such sincerity was so very much greater than the pleasure of bowling Mr Hobbs before he had scored.

(7) Mr Perry lends countenance to an extraordinary opinion concerning intensity of interest. "All fully aroused interests", he says, "are of equal intensity."[1] Unless this statement means that *no* interest is fully aroused until it is an obsession totally possessing a man or a nation, it would imply the absurd consequence that the greatest extent of a man's interest in cabbages must have exactly the same intensity as the greatest extent of his interest in his children.

§ 4. *Lines of preference*

In the concluding paragraph of Section I of this chapter we saw that Maupertuis and certain other hedonists, when they *spoke* of pleasure, may have *meant* something quite different, namely preference. We should consider, therefore, what may legitimately be argued on these lines.

To prefer one thing to another, as Mr Perry correctly points out, is not to desire one *more* than another, but one *rather than* another.[2] In any attempt to measure preference, therefore, we do not measure intensity of "desire" or of "pleasure". Instead, we measure choice, or what we would *rather* have.

Clearly, preference is a fact, whether the preference be psychological or in the way of natural election. In considering the undoubted fact of it, however, we are faced with the entire problem with which this book has been occupied. Is the fact of preference mere brute circumstance and nothing more, or can certain preferences be justified in a rational way? Our conclusion was that our preferences are justified if we prefer what is a greater excellence in the timological sense. Otherwise they simply express the brute circumstance of private or racial constitution.

[1] *General Theory of Value*, p. 633.   [2] *Ibid.* p. 616.

The modes of our choosing, or what moralists call the "motives" of choice, may themselves be noble, or, again, may be vile. And so may the course that is chosen. It is only in certain cases, therefore, that the mode of preference *confers* value, and, in general, the logic of justifiable preference is just the logic of (timological) value. A separate discussion, therefore, is not required.

Since it has been contended, however, that certain (non-timological) lines of preference do in fact determine certain standards of value, it is politic to consider the nature of such contentions.

According to the principle of natural election, any particular thing exhibits a certain constancy and characteristic tenor in most of its elections. Such habitual patterns of action have a certain similarity to a standard of behaviour. If the pattern is common to all or to most of the member of a given species, it is not dissimilar in some respects to a racial "standard" or canon *in genere*.

When we turn from natural election to psychological interest and appreciation, we find that more elaborate principles are suggested. Among such proffered suggestions, Mr Perry's seem the most notable.

Mr Perry's fundamental principle is that preference generates a transitive, asymmetrical relation, and therefore an *order*, among its terms. This relation "is transitive", he says, "because if b is preferred to a, and c to b, then c is preferred to a; and asymmetrical because if b is preferred to a, then a is not preferred to b, but stands in a converse relation which is different from the original relation".[1]

Specious as this logic seems, it may well be doubted whether it holds *de facto* of our subjective preferences; for these may be far more whimsical and capricious than Mr Perry's principle suggests. What is more usual than for a visitor to the Kenwood Collection—the kind of visitor who "knows what he likes"—traversing this very logic regarding the Romneys, the Rembrandt and the Franz Hals within a very

[1] *General Theory of Value*, p. 636.

few minutes or even seconds? Such caprice, therefore, is not unusual concerning individual *a*'s and *b*'s and *c*'s at approximately the same time; and it is notoriously frequent at different times. Again a "standard" confined to individual *a*'s and *b*'s and *c*'s would be a feeble sort of standard. What is needed is some principle concerning the *kind* of thing *a* is rather than concerning the individual *a*. Moreover, a principle concerning the amount of *a* would be highly desirable. A man, let us say, would rather have milk than cream in his tea. This preference applies, within reason, to *any* milk and to *any* cream in *any* tea. But surely the quantity of the milk or of the cream is also relevant.

In short, any subjective order of preference worth the name requires rather more logic than Mr Perry's principle states, and very often contains rather less logic in actual fact. Nevertheless it is true that our subjective appreciations, as well as our natural elections, may exhibit a certain habitual steadiness and something like a settled order of preference. In this case we may prefer all or most things of a certain kind to all or most things of another kind, and may also, within each kind, exhibit a relatively constant order of preference. Again, as Mr Perry says, if Smith's order of preference coincides (or partially coincides) with Robinson's order of preference, there is, so far, a *common* order for the two, even if Smith is much more sensitive than Robinson. And it need not be denied that certain marked preferences are approximately universal in the human species.

In all such cases, however, there would be no *logical* standard, although there might be a customary uniformity. It is difficult, if not impossible, we may concede, for any man to welcome and to reject the same thing at the same time in the same parts and respects. Apart from this natural difficulty, however, if different people at the same time, or the same men at different times, both welcome and reject the same thing, there is nothing more to be said in terms of preference. From the point of view of preference, the question is simply what feelings people actually have. Such feelings are not the less genuine if they are whimsical, variable and capricious.

§ 5. *The commingling of values*

It is time, however, to relinquish these digressions, and to return to the principal theme of the present Section.

We have seen that all values are probably commensurable, and that there are certain laws and axioms for the comparison and addition of *independent* values. In the latter respect we found that the main difficulty was to know what values may be treated as independent, or, in other words, to apply these laws and axioms.

The central problem in this connection is what Mr Moore calls sometimes the "principle"[1] and sometimes the "paradox"[2] of *organic unities*. "The value of a whole", he says, "must not be assumed to be the same as the sum of the values of its parts."[3]

Since "part" and "whole" are logically correlative terms, this statement of the principle may not be wholly precise, and it might be more accurate to speak of the "values of the items, *taken separately*, which are comprised in the whole"— which is plainly what is meant by "the values of its parts".

In proof of his view, Mr Moore says[4] that the union of two moderate goods may be a very great good, and the union of a good with something in itself indifferent may be a good far more excellent than the item in this composite excellence which, by itself, would be good. *Ceteris paribus*, the same holds of evil. Again, it is possible that things which, separately, have no value, have great value in conjunction. This would normally be said of the cells composing a human body. And we have no right to deny the possibility that some combination of things which severally would be evil might be a very great good. Indeed, the last of these views is one of the stock solutions of the "problem of evil", and is usually illustrated

---

[1] *Principia Ethica*, p. xi.   [2] *Ibid.* p. 27.
[3] *Ibid.* p. 28.   [4] *Ibid.* pp. 27 sq.

by the dramatic interest of sinning, the glory of certain discords in great music, and the like.

In consequence of these arguments Mr Moore believes himself entitled to maintain that the value of certain wholes bears "no regular proportion"[1] to the sum of the values of the items, taken separately, which are comprised in such wholes.

According to monistic philosophers, the universe is an organic unity in this sense; and they also maintain that nothing is valuable except in its context, and that the ultimate context for any value is the organic unity of the universe as a whole. A consequence of this opinion is that particular values can never be discerned with accuracy, that all abstraction is, in the end, illegitimate and that the logical Principle of Assertion, according to which any particular truth is finally and wholly true, is false.

These consequences, being themselves false, reduce to absurdity the principle on which they are based; and it seems unnecessary to consider the principle further in this place since it has already received attention when "coherence" and "comprehensiveness" were debated. I propose therefore to assume that abstraction and separate discernment may both be entirely legitimate, and *not* to assume the very doubtful proposition that the universe *is* an organic unity in the sense required. These assumptions, of course, are also Mr Moore's.

Nevertheless, since the universe does contain many organic unities in Mr Moore's sense, and since, as we saw in the early pages of this book, the conception of intrinsic value seems less important and less generally applicable than Mr Moore contends, it is plain that the principle of organic unities may seriously perturb many particular standards of value. For how can we know for certain whether any given value is not in fact comprised in *some* organic unity?

Certainly, it may be said that the "sum of the values of the parts", when there is such a sum, is a genuine sum, and is what it is whatever the value of any organic unity may be.

[1] *Ibid.* p. 27.

This assertion is true and important. On the other hand, if we knew that the "parts" always did belong to some organic whole, and had any effective knowledge concerning the organic wholes in question, it would surely be a comparatively idle business to compute such sums. Our computations, although quite legitimate, would be known to be inadequate to the situation, and our plain duty would be to follow the more adequate and not the less adequate portions of our knowledge.

(A similar point arises in connection with the theory of probability. There is always a determinate and objective probability relative to any given piece of evidence, but it is also our business to collect *as much* relevant evidence as possible. And anyone who, except for special reasons, neglects relevant evidence in order to play with the probabilities of something *less* than he knows, is pursuing a comparatively idle, if legitimate, course.)

Accordingly, if we *know* that any item is comprised in an organic unity, it is usually sane to consider the value of the unity rather than the value of the item; and of course it may be true that things which do not appear to be comprised in *any* organic unity may really be so comprised. In ordinary affairs, however, we are able to investigate such questions with a reasonable degree of confidence. A living body has a kind of unity which a dead body does not have. A hive of bees does not have the same sort of unity as the stones in a cathedral. When the cathedral crumbles and falls, such stones as remain have a certain kind of unity, but only the unity of a heap. It is conceivable, no doubt, that the whole universe is a living animal (without an environment) and therefore that even the crumbling stones, although we do not know it, are part of this vast, unknown, but conjectured monster. Yet there is not the faintest reason for thinking so, or, on the basis of any such possibility, the shallowest ground for denying that a mass of ruins is very different indeed, in respect of unity, from a proud and mortared edifice.

The same considerations seem plainly to apply to the union

and commingling of values. It is because we know something about their commingling that we are able to make statements of the kind Mr Moore makes. A discord, taken separately, *is* ugly; incorporated in a work of musical grandeur, it *may* yield beauty. Both the separate and the commingled values must be known and discriminated before such judgments can be made. In other words, we know a great deal about the commingling of values as well as about values that are relatively isolated or combined in ways that are not "organic" at all. And there is no good reason to distrust our experience in this matter.

Indeed, it is probably an overstatement to say that "no regular proportion" is to be looked for. On the contrary we should presume the existence of a regular proportion in the items which compose the human frame or a hive of bees, or in the special discords which may enhance the beauty of some swelling and majestic harmony; and many of these regular proportions may be discovered. It is another thing, to be sure, to expect any single simple formula for all commingling of values in all "organic" unities, and it would probably be very unwise to look for one. The "emergence" from commingled values has to be ascertained empirically just like the mutations of species or the emergence of living things. Experience rather than some abstract formula seems, in the main, to determine the results of these finer combinations. Perhaps, even the "higher" values can never be deduced from the "lower" values comprised in them. Yet this is not to say that "emergent" development must be capricious or fantastic or unintelligible.

I think we should infer, therefore, that the commingling of values complicates, but does not destroy, the formulation of standards of value.

A special point should also be borne in mind. Even when values are conjoined and (in a measure) commingled, the separate discernment of them may still, on the whole, be adequate. When Shelley spoke of the "propinquity" of the good, the beautiful and the true, he referred to a notable connection; and all three of these values may further commingle with an appropriate delight. Despite all the concord between them, however, the standards of truth, beauty and moral goodness should, on the whole, be kept distinct. In the unison of these excellences, each is the nobler for a certain restrained determination within its own effective sphere.

§ 6. *The inverse estimation of commingled values*

The problem of the last paragraph was approached from the side of the items comprised in an organic unity, and the greater part of the argument, for simplicity's sake, proceeded on the assumption that what had to be considered was the intrinsic value of the items on the one hand, and the intrinsic value of the organic unity upon the other hand.

It is obvious, however, that the problem might be approached from the side of the organic unity as well as from the side of the items comprised in it; and it is likely that both methods have to be employed in practice. For the purposes of theoretical exposition, it is usual to follow the Cartesian principle, and attempt to construct wholes (intellectually) from their (relatively) simple components. The countenance of nature, however, is complex rather than simple. Analytical simplicity is not, in general, one of nature's gifts, but has to be wrung from the facts by hard intellectual toil.

If the procedure from items comprised to the comprising unity is regarded as *direct*, the converse procedure from the unity to its items must be regarded as *inverse*.

It seems frequently to be supposed that the only method open to us, whether we proceed directly or inversely, is, in the end, the method of intuitive judgment. The Winged Victory of Samothrace, we say, has very great value indeed. The particles composing it have severally no value. Careful comparison, faithful analysis and many corroborative tests may go to the making of such intuitions, but, in the end, we have to rely upon the intuitions themselves and upon them alone.

It may be so "in the end". Probably it is so. But the

"end" may be very far off; and something effective might perhaps be done by the inverse method before the "end" is reached.

Certain economists, notably von Wieser in his criticism of Menger, have attempted to indicate the rudiments of an inverse method of evaluating complementary utilities. A coal-fire, let us say, cannot be kindled without sticks and matches as well as coal. Any one of these three components, therefore, is separately valueless for this purpose. Yet each of the three components has alternative uses, and effective inferences concerning the relative values of the components are implied by the circumstance.

Proceeding symbolically, and employing rough arithmetic, they say that if $x + y = 10$, $2x + 3z = 29$ and $4y + 5z = 59$, then $x = 4$, $y = 6$ and $z = 7$.[1] In other words, they maintain that we may, in certain cases, reasonably compute the relative values of x, y and z, not from our intuitions of their separate values, but from our knowledge of a number of different wholes containing some of these ingredients in different proportions. Such inferences would hold of items which had *no* intrinsic or separate value, but possessed value in certain combinations only—an important matter if the conception of "intrinsic" value has less significance than many writers suppose.

It may be doubted whether the mathematics in these examples is very convincing. What do the variables x, y and z stand for? What significance would they have, say, in the problem of the sticks, the fire and the coal? In any case it would have to be conceded that the inferences hold only for the specific combinations in question. If any of the items were put to a fresh use, the basis of the estimate would be destroyed, as we know in industry from discoveries for utilising waste products.

Nevertheless, it seems not wholly unreasonable to maintain that the more we learned concerning the possibly valuable combinations of complementary items, the greater our legiti-

[1] This simplified example is taken from the editor's preface to von Wieser's *Natural Value* (Eng. trans.), p. 14.

mate confidence would be in our inferences according to the inverse principle. And even the mathematics of these economists is not, perhaps, more dubious or more arbitrary than many of the customary problems in inverse probability.

If so, there seems no reason why inferences of the inverse type should be restricted to economic values.

§ 7. *Perceptual evaluation*

A very large number of writers on morals are of the opinion that general moral standards carry us a certain way and a certain way only. All such general standards, they consider, are far too abstract to fit the delicate sinuosity of appropriate action, and must be supplemented by a kind of moral tact, native or acquired. Pascal's *esprit de finesse*, the trained sagacity of Aristotle's level-headed φρόνιμος, the gentleman-like poise and assurance of Hume's "man of sense", the schoolboy's sense of "good form", of what is "it" and of what is "simply not done", are necessary in addition to all general standards logically and precisely excogitated.

The implications of this opinion, if it were sound, could hardly be confined to moral affairs. Obviously the values of art and of beauty support the opinion even more strongly than moral values do. Perceptual standards, again, may yield effective methods of measurement, with a minimum of artifice, even in cases where their efficiency usually causes some surprise. The "born" cook usually disdains oven-thermometers, scales and even the clock, and is content, at the most, with "hot" or "moderate" ovens, heaped tea-spoonfuls, a "pinch" of this and a "suspicion" of that. A very little science, to be sure, would be an effective bulwark against the grosser culinary misfortunes; but a "born" cook does not have these misfortunes.

It is unnecessary, however, to give special attention to these analogous cases. For a fundamental moral principle is always to "make the best of it" where "best" is understood quite generally. An examination of the moral question, therefore, carries with it all that is essential.

In general, I think, we have to say that the opinion now under review contains a problem and does not give its solution. Let us first consider, however, what may be said in support of the opinion.

It may be argued, firstly, that habit, spontaneous or induced, may achieve the same end as reflective thought. A well-drilled squad, for example, by obeying orders with precision, reaches any assigned position in an admirably efficient manner.

Secondly, it is true that trained perception may enable us to measure with considerable precision. The example of the heaped tea-spoonfuls and the scales is not really a good one, for it compares the rough perceptual measurements in terms of instruments always accessible with the perceptual standards of a more delicate instrument not always so convenient. There are, however, plenty of other examples. We can measure pretty well by the naked eye without any clear knowledge of geometry or trigonometry, and perceptual indications may take the place of scientific schedules. There is a famous story of a Bristol pilot who led the British Fleet up the St Lawrence, judging by the colour of the water, after the French had destroyed all buoys and signals. And the pilot had never crossed the Atlantic before.

Thirdly, it may very well happen that we have to rely upon perception, either because it is the only method we have, or because it is the only method available at some given time. Aesthetic values seem to offer a plain example of the first case; for beauty, as we saw, is concerned with the shows of things, and, for the most part with their sensible or perceptual shows. We have lost it when we turn to anything except its shows. The second case occurs very frequently indeed in the ordinary conduct of life. We cannot be expected to go about with a portable moral laboratory in our hands, and often it is necessary to act promptly without any time for pondering.

Fourthly, there are instances in which perceptual methods, although not the only methods possible, seem to be by far the best. A notable example is to be found in certain types of human relationships. What is called "tact" largely consists in, as we say, "sensing the atmosphere" of our company, and, for the most part, friendly intercourse is most likely to occur if we do not think very hard, but respond, as the phrase goes, "naturally", i.e. if we are companionable in an impressionist way. Calculative good fellowship is not very likely to succeed with ingratiating canvassers, or touts, or public speakers.

These arguments, however, do not seem to prove very much. The first shows that we may be drilled or habituated into doing without reflection what *someone* could justify by reflection. The orders that the squad follows *are* planned. The second and third show that perceptual standards may be tolerably efficient, or may have to be accepted *faute de mieux* at some given time. This is no proof that the standards could not be improved, or that they could not be justified, by reflection. On the contrary, we are sure that they could be improved, and are confident that they could be justified, by taking thought, if we had the time and the opportunity for that exercise. Our admiration for the pilot does not and should not impede the advance of the science of navigation; and very few crossed the Atlantic before the compass was invented.

To be sure, all such standards require perceptual data, and the same may be granted regarding most, if not all, in our standards of value. If we did not have actual living experience of values, if we prized nothing and were drawn towards excellence by no burning and compelling aspirations, it is unlikely that we should speculate on these matters at all. Yet this also is no proof that we should not, and may not, come to understand the principles of our perceptual experience in a logical and rational way.

The fourth argument is, no doubt, the strongest; but the fourth argument, also, does not prove very much to the point. What it demonstrates, surely, is not that there are *no* principles regarding friendship and human intercourse, but only that men are likely to be better clubmates if they do not think too much about the principles of social intercourse when they are with their friends in the club. They are also more likely to trip on the steps of the club, if they think about the way they are stepping, than if they descend the steps guided only by perception. The latter circumstance does not affect the truth of the law of gravitation. The former need not affect the reality of social principle.

In short, all that appears to be proved is that, *for practical purposes*, perceptual standards may frequently be better than elaborately reflective ones, and that, probably (in a smaller number of instances) the complexities of practice may be so considerable that sensitive but unreflecting perception is almost always preferable to a reflective survey too intricate for our powers. The importance of the latter circumstance is largely diminished by the fact that tact and trained perception, in social intercourse and elsewhere, is suffused with lessons from our own experience learned at least half reflectively, and with lessons from tradition that are at least half reflective too.

In general, therefore, the fact that we may have to trust to perception does not deny the reality of principles justifying such perceptual standards. On the contrary, it should be presumed that a standard "sensed" in a perceptual way could, if we had sufficient patience and ability, be understood and justified in a reflective way. There is no essential rift between the two. And we may corroborate the presumption, I think, in a way that is very nearly conclusive, if we attend to another feature of the affair. To perceive is always to perceive something particular, but timological valuation is always general—implicitly general, if not expressly so. When we perceive anything to be excellent we are in the presence of a character which, if it be authentic at all, necessarily holds, not of the thing perceived only, but of any other thing similar in relevant respects. This is the truth even in the most individual of values, that is to say in aesthetic ones. Works of art, however intensely individual they may be, show at least a certain analogy in their appropriate excellences; and when relevant excellences are plainly similar, it is intolerably capricious not to accept them all.

Alternatively, we may say that all particular values permit of inductive generalisation. But we are never entitled to *accept* any generalisation unless the reality supports us, that is to say, unless what is generalised really *is* general. Consequently, the fact, if fact it be, that "perceptual" standards are sometimes the only practicable standards does not affect the fundamental verity that the essence of any justifiable standard is logic, reason and principle.

§ 8. *Patterns and schemata of valuation*

Briefly, our conclusion may be expressed as follows.

If all values are commensurable, there exists a single system of all values which is measurable. And it is probable that all values are commensurable, rational comparison of greater and lesser excellence being possible (in principle) throughout the entire domain of timology. In certain dimensions of certain values, numerical comparisons may be employed without undue or misleading conventions. In others it is unlikely that determinate arithmetic is feasible.

This single timological system is rational and objective, not arbitrary and relative to individual feeling, or even to corporate sentiment. When an impressionist and perceptual standard is appealed to, there is a tendency to forget the logic and the sanity allied with most of our impressions, and falsely to suppose that impressions are alogical although reflection is logical.

If these conclusions are duly admitted and duly pondered, it is permissible and important to note and explore certain affinities between rational timology and appreciative valuation, or again, between the rational standards human beings may acknowledge and certain, at least, of the natural elections of humanity.

As we saw, our perceptual impressions refer directly and immediately to particular fact, although they carry along with them certain wider implications. The same may be said of appreciations actually felt, and, probably, of choices actually made, whether consciously or unconsciously.

An important set of theories in modern psychology, moreover, lays emphasis (as many former psychologists also laid emphasis) upon the backgrounds, patterns or schemata, often unknown and not even divined, within which all particular perceptions, appreciations and choices occur.

According to the *Gestalt* psychologists, for instance, the actions and selections, say of Köhler's chimpanzees, are wholly unintelligible unless they are regarded as a response to a problem vaguely understood as a whole. This response to the problem is in the first instance a certain general pattern of adjustment, and in the second instance a finer, more discriminating adjustment within the poise and the ambit of the primary, vaguer adjustment. There is not, of course, one single pattern for *all* adjustments—a kind of general vigilance or readiness for *everything*—although even this has been suggested. On the contrary there are many patterns, themselves fluid and modifiable, although relatively definite at any given time.

Sir Henry Head calls these patterns schemata, and illustrates them very clearly by reference to sensations of posture.

"By means of perpetual alterations in position", he says, "we are always building up unwittingly a model of ourselves, which is constantly changing. Every new posture or movement is registered on this plastic schema.... The psychical act of postural recognition follows, as soon as this relation is completed on levels that are not associated with consciousness.... Unless postural impulses continuously modified these unconscious activities in consonance with every change in bodily attitude, we might will a movement that was impossible owing to the movement of the limb. This is evident in every case of ataxy."[1]

The phantom hand that is sensed after an amputation is itself an illustration of the point; but Head gives a peculiarly striking example when he tells of a little finger completely

[1] *Aphasia and Kindred Disorders of Speech*, vol. I, p. 488.

paralysed after a wound. In the end, the entire hand had to be amputated. And the phantom hand had only four phantom digits.

It is not to be supposed that this descriptive psychology of schemata and patterns itself supplies an answer to many of the problems we have raised. If these schemata determine our selections, they are also confirmed, if not established, *by* our selections. Disputes on this point resemble the classical controversy regarding the priority of the hen or the egg—or regarding Adam's navel. And fresh patterns are integrated by the dissolving and commingling of elements (or minor integrations) in the old. In general, however, the conclusion stands that all our selections, whether we know it or not, are at least partially determined by some relatively organised pattern. Since all the patterns are organised (either loosely or firmly) they resemble some variety of standard, and connote some degree of stability.

When the pattern is physiological we have the case in which natural election is the obvious principle to go by. When the pattern is emotional or sentimental, we have the type of theory considered in § 4 of this Section. And when the pattern bears the stamp of a reflective estimate concerning excellence, it has manifest affinities with what was considered in § 7.

If any such reflective estimate were our own, we may have forgotten it. If it is due to tradition, no one may be able to say how much prolonged thinking, or how much casual thinking, may have gone to the making of it. A pattern may very well be rational in its origins although we have forgotten the reasons for it. The question is whether there *is* a reason. When, like so many at the present day, we are vaguely ashamed of people who have "gone to the good" and at the same time are disquieted at the "slump in ideals", our only remedy is to renew, and in earnest, our reflection upon values. But we need not suppose that these brooms of our awakened reflection are sweeping a room that has never been swept before, or a room that has never been swept to any purpose.

Ideals themselves seem to be patterns which are also

exemplars. They are always, by profession, some organisation of values, usually exhibited in a pattern more than half pictorial. From the spark of aspiration the imagination takes fire, and the whole man may be aflame. Ideals are the poetry of values, but there is also a place for prose; and the place, I think, although certainly not unoccupied, has hitherto not been adequately filled. If the present volume clears a little rubbish away and does not add much more, it will have amply fulfilled its purpose.

INDEX

Abercrombie, L.: 152 n.
Absolute: *v.* relative, xx, 43 *sq.*, 48, 72, 89 *sq.*, 137, 181, 240 *sq.*, 311, 319 *sqq.*
Abstraction: legitimacy of, 363
Acquiescence: 81 *sq.*, 91, 107
Action: 81 *sqq.*, 144, 187, 190, 264 *sq.*
Active: *v.* passive, interest, 102; pleasure 165 *sq.*
Activity: 63, 65, 68, 90, 282
Aesthetic values: see Beauty; Taste
Affective-volitional: xiii, 102 *sqq.*
Agreeable qualities: xix, 206 *sq.*, 237
Agreement: in approval, 209 *sqq.*, 246; in knowledge, 83 *sq.*, 243, 245 *sq.*
Alexander, S.: 316 n.
Alternative: ends, 49 *sqq.*; utilities, 367
Ambiguity of value: 252 *sq.*, 307, 321 *sq.*
Amiable character of virtue: 203 *sq.*
Amor unionis: 274 *sq.*
Anger: Descartes on, 263, 266
Animals: men's attitude towards, 87, 157 *sq.*, 260, 296
Anticipated: satisfaction, 6, 13, 29 *sq.*; *v.* remembered pleasures, 343 *sq.*
Appetence: xx, 69, 71 *sq.*, 75 *sq.*, 80 *sq.*, 102, 117, 128 *sqq.*, 132, 174 *sq.*, 180, 194, 302 *sq.*, 305 *sqq.*; and beauty, 153. See also Horme
Appreciation: 176 *sqq.*, 183 *sqq.*, 301 *sqq.*, 360 *sq.*, 372 *sq.*; of poetry, 152 *sq.*, 232
Appropriate emotions: 238
Approval: xiv, xix, 172, 176, 252, 312; simplicity of, 183 *sqq.*
Aristippus: 129
Aristotle: xviii, 101, 103, 132, 168, 368

Arithmetic, moral: 25, 323 *sqq.*; *v.* sociableness, 370
Art: 45 *sq.*, 67 *sq.*, 149 *sq.*, 160, 168, 170, 249 *sq.*, 368, 371; divine, 150 *sq.*, 299
Artifice: 197, 204 *sqq.*, 214
Asceticism: 266; of reason, 267; in art, 278
Aspiration: and imagination, 375; quality of, 131; unconscious response to, 227
Assertion: principle of, 363
Association: 202, 204
Attuition: 141 *sqq.*
Austrian economists: xviii, 1, 16, 23 *sq.*, 136, 172, 334, 337
Authorship: in action, 269 *sqq.*, 291 *sq.*
Autonomy: of reason, 66, 279, 283 *sq.*; of ethics, 44 *sqq.*, 221
Avenarius, R.: 166
Axiology: xiii, 33 *sq.*, 46 *sq.*, 262, 264
Axioms of value: 140; additive, 349, 351 *sq.*; constitutive, 349 *sqq.*

Bacon, F., Baron Verulam and Viscount St Albans: 93 *sq.*, 99 *sq.*, 163
Baldwin, S.: 46
Balguy, J.: 217
Beatitude: 80 *sq.*, 91, 262 *sqq.*
Beauty: xv, xvii, xix, 134, 149 *sqq.*, 176, 183 *sq.*, 189, 193 *sq.*, 207, 276 *sqq.*; an occult quality? 222; and ugliness, 258; for Spinoza, 71 *sq.*, 74; for Shelley, 365 *sq.*; of virtue, 219; natural, 151, 207 *sq.*, 296 *sq.*, 299; physical or mental? 228 *sqq.*, 235 *sq.*; rationality of, 222 *sq.*, 225, 256
Beccaria: 324, 326
Begehren: 136
Behaviour: 38
Behaviourism: 106 *sqq.*, 305, 344 *sq.*

INDEX

Belief: and sensation, 222; in valuation, 105, 139. See also Judgment; Probability
Bell, C.: 161 *sq.*
Benevolence: 190 *sqq.*, 203 *sqq.*, 225, 268, 275, 291; as basis of approval, 187, 191 *sq.*
Bentham, J.: 148, 157 *sq.*, 326 *sqq.*, 333, 335, 340, 342, 344 *sq.*, 348
Berkeley, G.; 74, 83, 323
Bernoulli, D.: 325, 329, 331 *sqq.*, 346
Bewerten: xvi, 177
Biology: 7, 78, 93, 100 *sq.*, 104 *sq.*, 106 *sq.*, 166, 279, 297 *sq.*, 301 *sq.*
Böhm-Bawerk, E. von: 1, 25, 337 n.
Bonheur, le: 165
Bonum honestum: 88, 98, 183, 255 *sqq.*
Bonum jucundum: 88, 98, 118, 146 *sqq.*, 183 *sq.*, 272
Bonum utile: 1 *sqq.*, 88, 98 *sq.*, 272
Bosanquet, B.: 154, 156
Bouglé, C.: 52 *sq.*
Bradley, F. H.: 45, 249, 357 n.
Braithwaite, R. B.: 307
Brentano, F.: 136 *sq.*, 140, 238, 246, 315
Broad, C. D.: 97 *sq.*
Brown, W.: 25 n.
Browne, Sir T.: 150 *sq.*
Brunschvicg, L.: xvii n.
Buffon, G. L. L., Comte de: 225 n., 331
Burke, E.: 204 n., 222
Butler, J.: 79, 148, 188, 217
Butler, S.: 150
Byron, G. Gordon, Lord: 131 n.

Calm: beauty, 198; passion, 197 *sq.*, 239
Calculus: of utility, xvii, 20, 24 *sqq.*; of pleasure, 334 *sqq.*, 339, 345 *sqq.*
Cannan, E.: 11
Carey, H. C.: 17 n.
Carritt, E. F.: 151 n.
Cassel, G.: 10, 22
Catallactics: 4, 9 *sqq.*, 14
Causes: and substance, 42 *sq.*; concepts as, 279; final, 71 *sqq.* and see Purpose; in perception, 83 *sq.*, 229 *sq.*; of sensation, 332; of pleasure, 330; plurality of, 52, 232; principle of, 96 *sq.*; reasons as, 284, 286, 288
Certainty: of pleasures, 326 *sq.*
Character, moral: 195
Character, the, of value: xii *sq.*, xvii, 231, 303, 316
Cicero: 103, 195
Coherence: 84, 87, 244, 246 *sqq.*, 257, 363
Collingwood, R. G.: 156
Commensurability: 9, 25, 334, 353 *sqq.*
Commingling of values: 362 *sqq.*
Commodity: strict sense of, 19
Common property: meaning of, 159 *sq.*; in all desires? 95; in all values, 173
Communism: 11, 14, 22 *sq.*, 214
Comparability: 342, 351, 354; of motives, 336; of pleasures, 343; of preferences, 2, 336
Comparative: = subjective? 77, 89, 240 *sq.*
Comparison, nature of: 200, 253, 319, 357 *sq.*
Competing ends: 49 *sqq.*
Complementary: ends, 49 *sqq.*; goods, 27, 367
Complete: good, 36, 290; in logic, 240
Completion: 39, 109 *sqq.*, 147, 166, 255 *sqq.*
Comprehensiveness: and reason, 199 *sq.*; in knowledge, 87. See also Coherence
Condillac, E. B. de: 334
Conditions, substantial: 42 *sq.*, 47 *sqq.*, 88, 99
Confusion: 72, 74, 85, 89, 164 *sq.*
Conscience: 215 *sq.*, 223 *sq.*, 237, 271, 276, 288
Consciousness: and intrinsic value, 60, 65, 303; and natural election, xx, 5 *sq.*, 93 *sq.*, 99 *sqq.*, 104 *sq.*, 256, 289, 302 *sq.*, 313, 320, 322; and physiological action, 102; and the self, 143. See also Belief; Mind; Psychology; Spirit
Constraint: external and internal, 292

Consumer's surplus: 30
Consummations: 5 *sq.*, 12 *sq.*, 37, 42
Consumption: 5, 32 *sq.*
Contemplation: not man's final purpose, 299
Contemplative emotion: 239
Continuity: see Genetic argument: mathematical, 24, 326, 340. See also Margins
Correlative terms: 240
Correspondence theories: see Agreement
Croce, B.: 2, 63 *sqq.*, 151
Cudworth, R.: 208 *sq.* n., 217, 219
Culture, duty of: 249, 293
Cumberland, R.: 217
Cyrenaics: 29

Dare v. Strand and Savoy Properties, Ltd.: 18 n.
Demand: 26; and supply, 16 *sq.*
Dependent values: axioms concerning, 352
Desire: abstention from, 261; and beauty, 189, 279; and economics, 7, 10, 15, 20, 24, 33; and highest good, 164; and natural election, 95, 103, 314; and pleasure, 78 *sq.*, 88, 167 *sq.*; and true knowledge, 266; and value, 114 *sqq.*; common property in? 95; for Spinoza, 71, 75; rationality of, 219
Dessoir, M.: 163 n.
Dewey, J.: 153
Dictionary: argument, 224 *sq.*, meanings of value, xiii *sqq.*
Differentiation of interests: 58
Dignity: 172, 179 *sqq.*, 184, 221, 236 *sq.*, 246, 276, 279 *sqq.*, 284 *sq.*, 288 *sqq.*, 294 *sqq.*; and decorum, 212; in relation to numbers, 204
Direct passions: 194 *sq.*, 201
Discovery of excellence: 171 *sq.*, 314
Disinterestedness: of approval, 192, 207, 316; of judgments of beauty, 277; of benevolence, 293 *sqq.*
Distensive magnitude: 348
Disvalues: xvi

Dominant goods: 36
Driesch, H.: 100
Duration of pleasures: 157, 324 *sqq.*, 340 *sqq.*, 347 *sq.*, 353 *sq.*
Duty: simplex character of, 223 *sq.*; to self and others, 293 *sq.* See also Reason; Homo noumenon

Economic: activity and pleasure, 168; function, 63 *sqq.*
Economics: and ethics, xviii, 2, 7 *sqq.*, 20, 28, 33, 63 *sqq.*; and social philosophy, 59; and value, xiii, xx, 1 *sqq.*, 32 *sqq.*, 179, 281 *sq.*
Economy of hypotheses in value theory: 312, 314 *sqq.*
Edgeworth, F. Y.: 158 n., 225 n., 335 n., 337, 342 n., 346
Efficiency: xv *sqq.*, 65 *sqq.*, 169
Egence: 109 *sq.* n., 141
Egoism: see Selfish Theory; in economics, 64, 67
Ehrenfels, C. von: 1, 122 *sq.*, 136 *sqq.*, 141, 166, 168, 174 *sq.*
Elective will: 287, 295
Elizabeth, the Princess: 260 *sqq.*
Emotion: 76, 79; a single aesthetic? 154 *sq.*; nobility of, 291; patterns in, 374; and beauty, 161 *sqq.*
Emotional significance: 181, 184, 235, 246 *sq.*, 252, 302, 305 *sqq.*, 313 *sq.*, 317 *sq.*, 321 *sq.*
Emotive use of words: 307 *sq.*
Empathy: 168
End: and means, 32 *sqq.* See also Instrumental goods; Purpose; rational, 282 *sqq.*, 289
Ens realissimum: xiv
Epicureans: 129, 314, 323
Epicurus: 29, 129, 262
Epigenesis: 310
Epiphenomenalism: 76
Equality of appetences, 128 *sq.*; of pleasures, 328 *sq.*
Equity: 214, 239, 254, 268, 319
Equivalence and value, xiii, xv *sq.*, 172
Error: and desire, 139; in passion or emotion, 180, 196, 238; in sympathy, 215; margin of, 318;

INDEX

of opinion, 265 *sq.*; of valuation, 188. See also Confusion
Espérance morale: 323
Esteem: 194, 225, 231, 235 *sq.*, 315. See also Approval: values, xiv, 12 *sqq.*
Ethics: and aesthetics, xix *sq.*, 279 *sqq.*; and metaphysics, xviii, 81 n.; and social welfare, 33; and value-theory, 183 *sqq.*; in relation to truth and art, 45 *sq.*; to mechanical science, xix
Evaluation: 312 *sqq.*, 368 *sqq.*
Evil desires: 125 *sq.*; in ourselves, 81
Evil, problem of: 275, 362 *sq.*
Excellence: xx, 69, 109 *sqq.*, 127, 131 *sqq.*, 141, 169 *sqq.*, 178 *sqq.*, 184, 222 *sq.*, 236, 249, 252 *sq.*, 255 *sqq.*, 311, 314, 317, 321 *sq.*, 334, 371 *sq.* See also Perfection and Dignity: *quanta* of, 354
Exchange: 3, 18, 59, 172, 328, 333, 337 *sq.*
Exchange-value: xiii, 3 *sq.*, 10, 13 *sq.*, 21 *sq.*, 32
Existence: and value, 137, 139 *sq.*, 178, 284 *sq.*, 352; value as justifying, 288 *sq.*, 298, 312
Experience: and deduction, 365; and reason, 271, 371; human, 244, 330; personal, 55; superhuman? 196; variations in, 232
Expetition: 48 *sq.*, 124 *sq.*, 139, 148 *sqq.*, 153, 175, 267 *sq.*, 290
Expression: in art, 151 *sqq.*; of emotion, 212
"Extent": 326 *sq.*, 344

Faith: 274, 300; animal, 243, 245
Fancy value: xvii, 281 *sq.*
"Favouring": 105, 322
Fechner, G. T.: 332 *sq.*
Felicity, metaphysics of, 165 *sqq.*, 256; promotion of relative, 138
Fisher, Irving: 338 n.
Flaubert, G.: 163
Fontenelle, B. Le B. de: 324
Form: in aesthetics, 162 *sq.*
Fortune: moral and physical, 325, 329, 331 *sqq.*; gifts of, 290

Freedom: 72 *sq.*, 79, 265 *sq.*, 269 *sqq.*, 273, 275, 285 *sqq.*, 292

Generality of approval, 194 *sqq.*, 203, 237; of values, 371
Genetic argument: 101, 308 *sqq.*, 365
Gestalt-theorie: 373
Geulincx, A.: 124, 259, 268 *sqq.*, 319
Giotto, G. di B.: 161 *sq.*
Goblot, E.: 133 *sq.*, 160 *sq.*
Godwin, W.: 29, 214 n.
Goethe, J. W. von: 256
Golden section: 163, 227
Good: Geulincx's account of, 272; Green's, 141; Hobbes's, 135; Schopenhauer's, 136; Shaftesbury's, 186; Spinoza's, 70 *sqq.*, 75; Reid's, 223
Gosse, Sir E.: 278
Gossen, H. H.: xviii, 28 *sq.*, 334, 346
Gratitude: and justice, 213, 215
Green, T. H.: 141 *sqq.*, 146, 148, 357 n.
Grote, J.: 109 *sq.* n.
Guyau, M.: 40

Habituation: in desire, 121. See also Satisfaction: in perception, 369
Haering, T.: 174
Halévy, É.: 17, 326
Harmony: 131, 165, 169, 187, 189, 194, 248 *sq.*, 257, 277, 279 *sq.*, 297
Head, Sir H.: 102, 373
Hedonism: see Pleasure: deductive, 167, 169
Hegel, G. W. F.: 112, 151
Helmholtz, H. L. F. von: 317
Helvétius, C. A.: 324, 326
Herbart, J. F.: xix *sq.*
Hermann, C.: 163 n.
Heterogony of means: 52
Heyde, J. E.: 1
Higher and lower: in the soul, 265; utilities, 7 *sq.*, 20, 98 *sq.*
Hobbes, T.: 9 n., 135 *sq.*, 141, 150, 185, 208 n.
Hobson, J. A.: 339 *sq.*

INDEX

Homo noumenon: 283, 288 sqq., 298; as lawgiver v. subject, 294
Horace: 207
Horme: 88, 114 sq., 117 sq., 120, 126, 175
Hudibras: 9
Humanism in values: xix, 77, 81, 107, 111 sq., 194 sqq., 306, 318
Hume, D.: xix, 183, 193 sqq., 207 sq., 211, 214, 217, 227, 239, 318, 368
Hutcheson, F.: 17, 183, 188 sqq., 195, 198, 203 sq., 208, 211, 217 sq., 324

Ideal: sympathy, 215; the, 248 sq.; of beauty, 280 sq.
Ideals: 80, 374 sq.; and facts, 33 sq., 312
Ideas: and impressions, 202; the way of, 221, 225
Identity, law of and value: 53 sq., 349 sq.
Imagination: and beauty, 278; for Spinoza, 72 sqq.; sympathetic, 209 sqq., 215. See also Fancy value
Immediacy: of perception in morals, 218 sq.; of sensation, 191
Impartial spectator: 203 sq., 207 sqq., 216, 237, 239, 313, 315
Importance: xiv, 128 sqq. See also Natural election
Impressionism: 370 sqq.
Increments, marginal: 26, 331 sqq., 342 n.
Independent values: 351, 362
Induction: 97, 244 sq., 372
Infallible judgment of present pleasure: 164, 343
Insight: 191, 238 sq., 245 sqq., 254, 318 sq. See also Timology.
Inspiration, artistic: 150
Instinct: 38 sqq., 194, 201, 314
Instrumental goods: xvii, 5 sqq., 13, 32 sqq., 65, 101, 116, 196, 227, 293, 297 sq., 303
Intellect: and value, 220 sq., 238 sq., 273. See also Reason; Insight; Judgment
Intellectual character of desire: 139, 279

Intensity: of pleasures, etc., 25, 130 sq., 157, 324 sqq., 340 sqq., 347 sq., 353 sq.; of "interests", 359
Interesse: 103
Interest: and natural election, 102 sqq.; expansion of, 57 sq.; in Kantian sense, 279, 283; psychological, xx, 256, 301, 303, 305 sqq.; root-, 38
Intrinsic value: xvii, 34 sqq., 42 sqq., 48 sq., 61, 90, 99, 173, 200, 276, 281, 284 sq., 290, 292, 295, 304, 363, 366 sq. See also Dignity; Excellence; Perfection
Intuition: 60, 218 sq., 224 sq., 249, 303, 366 sq.; for Spinoza, 91; v. computation, 358
Inverse estimation of value: 366 sq.

Jevons, W. S.: 1, 16, 23 sq., 28 sq., 31, 34, 334 sqq., 340 sqq., 346 sqq.
John, St: 148 sq.
Johnson, W. E.: 348 n.
Joint: demand, 49; supply, 49
Jonson, B.: 113
Judgment: in Locke's sense, 324; of beauty, 276 sqq.; of value, 217, 222, 225, 247, 253 sq., 261 sq., 264 sq., 312 sq., 315 sq.
Justification: and value, 44; of existence, 284 sqq., 298 sq.

Kant, I.: xvi sqq., 36, 65, 90, 97 sq., 103, 108, 141 sqq., 149, 154, 169, 243, 245, 259, 266, 276 sqq., 319, 350
Keynes, J. M.: 23 n., 97 sq.
Kraus, O.: 329 n., 330 n., 333 n.

Labour: theories of value, 13 sq.; productive, 8, 20
Laplace, P. S., Marquis de: 331 sq.
La Rochefoucauld, F. de: 324
Lauderdale, Lord: 18 sq.
Lear: 307 sq.
Lecky, W. E. H.: 355
Leibniz, G. W.: 163 sqq., 227, 255, 259, 286
Lessing, T.: 352

INDEX

Locke, J.: 14, 17, 110, 114 *sqq.*, 118 *sqq.*, 124, 163 *sq.*, 186, 217 *sq.*, 240, 324, 343
Lotze, H.: xviii *sq.*
Love: xv, xvii, 137, 149, 170 *sq.*, 192 *sqq.*, 198, 201 *sq.*, 205, 217, 230, 234 *sq.*, 239 *sq.*, 246, 265, 267 *sq.*, 272 *sqq.*, 290 *sq.*
Lucas, E. V.: 162

Mackenzie, D. A.: 53
Maecenas, 331
Maier, H.: 308 n.
Malebranche, N.: 259, 272 *sqq.*, 319
Mandeville, B.: 188
Margins: 23 *sqq.*, 326, 337 *sqq.*, 341, 345 *sq.*
Market: a free, 15, 26 *sqq.*, 338; -value, xv, xvii, 281 *sq.*
Marshall, A.: 5, 10, 30
Marx, K.: 13, 22
Maupertuis, P. L. M. de: 324, 326 n., 347, 359
McTaggart, J. M. E.: 95 n., 170 *sq.*, 182, 355
Means and end: see Instrumental
Measurement: 2, 8, 13, 24, 64, 323 *sqq.*; of "importance", 131; of perfections, 263
Mechanical science: xix, 297 *sq.*
Meinong, A.: xvi, 1, 136, 138 n., 172 *sqq.*, 234, 237 *sq.*, 239 n., 241, 246 *sq.*, 252, 315
Memory: 107 *sq.*; of pleasures, 138, 343 *sq.*
Mendelssohn, M.: 103
Menger, C.: 1, 367
Merit: 195, 213 *sq.*, 219
Michelangelo: 344 n.
Mill, J. S.: 1, 3 *sq.*, 7 *sqq.*, 20, 33, 123, 157 *sqq.*, 330, 335, 345
Mind and Body: 42 *sq.*, 47, 60 *sq.*, 76 *sqq.*, 166 *sq.*, 264 *sq.*, 267, 269 *sq.*, 275, 281, 288 *sq.*, 319
Money: xiii, xv, 10 *sqq.*, 327 *sqq.*, 333 *sq.*
Monism: 70, 83, 363
Montaigne, M. de: 92, 95, 99 *sq.*
Moore, G. E.: 114, 362 *sq.*, 365
Mystical view: of perfection, 134; of value, 136 *sq.*

Natural: *v.* spiritual, 142 *sq.*; abilities, 195; piety, 243, 245; religion, 270
Natural election: xx, 5 *sq.*, 92 *sqq.*, 115, 122 *sq.*, 131 *sq.*, 134, 141, 143, 175, 228, 240, 252 *sq.*, 255 *sq.*, 301 *sqq.*, 309, 313 *sqq.*, 320 *sqq.*, 349, 359 *sqq.*, 374
Natural value: 16 *sqq.*
Needs: 1, 8 *sq.*, 20, 24, 314, 357; sound, 28 *sq.*, 31
Negative Quantities, Essay on: 90, 350
Neutrality: axiological, 256; ethical in physics, 285; of nature to man, 298 *sq.*
Newman, J. H.: 355
Newton, Sir I.: 240, 297
Non-economic utilities: 12
Non-indifference: see Natural election.
Non-mental values: 226 *sqq.*
Nunn, T. P.: 115

"Objective": an, 177 *sqq.*
Objective reference: 144, 176 *sqq.*, 226 *sqq.*, 242, 246, 277 *sqq.*, 315. See also Transcendence
Objectivity, axiom of: 349
Obligation: 209 n., 220, 268, 270 *sq.*, 292
Occasionalism: 269, 271 *sq.*
Opposition, principle of specific: 350 *sq.*
Order: 72, 74, 257 *sq.*, 273, 275, 305
Over-social values: 308 *sqq.*

Pascal, B.: 273 *sq.*, 368
Passion: 81 *sq.*, 84 *sqq.*, 209, 264 *sqq.*, 270 *sqq.*, 275; unjudging, 217
Past: value of, 123, 175
Paton, H. J.: 247
Patterns: 40, 80, 372 *sqq.*
Paulhan, F.: 61
Peace: 148, 290
Perceptual standards: 368 *sq.*
Perfection: xx, 69 *sq.*, 80 *sqq.*, 88, 108 *sqq.*, 132 *sqq.*, 160 *sqq.*, 222 *sq.*, 227, 247, 249, 255 *sqq.*
Perry, R. B.: 2, 103 *sqq.*, 305, 348, 359 *sqq.*

Personal character of value: 172 *sqq.*, 288 *sqq.*
Physical objects: value of, 226 *sqq.*
Pierson, N. G.: 5 n.
Plato: xv
Platonists, the Cambridge: 219
Pleasure: xv, xx, 5, 8, 64, 78 *sq.*, 88, 118, 137, 146 *sqq.*, 189 *sqq.*, 202 *sqq.*, 219 *sq.*, 231 *sq.*, 239, 256, 276 *sqq.*, 290 *sqq.*, 306, 323 *sqq.*, 353, 356 *sqq.*; identical with good? 34, 119 *sq.*; witness of perfection, 164 *sqq.*, 263, 275
Plotinus: 257
Poincaré, H.: 346
Polytelism: 52 *sq.*
Pope, A.: 184
"Position" in values: 172 *sq.*
Praeter passionem: 272
Pragmatism: 96, 106
Prall, D. W.: 105 *sqq.*
Preference: 138, 337, 348 *sq.*, comparability in, 2, 359 *sqq.*
Price, R.: 183, 217 *sqq.*, 225
Prices: xv; differential, 26; market, 26; natural, 21
Pride: 193 *sqq.*, 201
"Primary" value: 313 *sqq.*
Prizing: 54, 177, 182, 253, 312 *sqq.*, 322, 370
Probability: 97 *sq.*, 261, 263, 325, 327, 331, 342 n., 364; inverse, 368
Production, cost of: 13 *sqq.*
Progressions, geometrical and arithmetical: 326, 332
Propinquity of values: 317, 365
Proportion: see Harmony; Perfection
Propriety, 209 *sq.*
Protopathic and epicritic: 78
Psychologism: 176
Psychology: 93 *sqq.*, 104 *sqq.*, 220 *sq.*, 299, 321 *sq.*, 359 *sq.*
Psychophobia: 106
Psycho-physical parallelism: 74, 76, 78, 84 *sqq.*
Pufendorf, S.: 17, 333 *sq.*
Pulchritudo vaga and *adhaerens*: 277 *sq.*
Punishment: 213 *sqq.*

Purpose: xvi *sq.*, 7, 38 *sqq.*, 63 *sqq.*, 70 *sqq.*, 99 *sqq.*; and beauty, 279; and mechanism, 64, 297 *sq.*; and reason, 282, 285; final of creation, 299

Quality: of desires, 126 *sqq.*, 133 *sq.*; of pleasures, 157 *sqq.*, 343 *sq.*; in perfection theories, 292 *sq.*
Quantity: nature of, 346 *sq.*; of being, 75 *sqq.*, 134, 227, 257; of pleasure, 157 *sqq.*, 343 *sqq.*

Rashdall, H.: 282 n., 355
Reason: xviii, xx, 66, 73, 79, 81 *sqq.*, 165, 184 *sqq.*, 194 *sqq.*, 206, 208 *sq.* n., 214 *sqq.*, 226 *sq.*, 244 *sq.*, 252 *sqq.*, 318 *sqq.*, 359 *sq.*, 372; and inclination, 287
Recessive judgments: 234 *sqq.*
Reflection: 38 *sq.*, 144, 184, 197 *sq.*, 370, 374
Reflexion (Locke's sense of): 181 *sq.*
Reid, T.: 183, 217 *sq.*, 221 *sqq.*, 227, 256
Relativity of good and evil: xiv, xx, 72, 77, 89 *sq.*, 135 *sq.*, 173, 179 *sqq.*, 200, 240 *sq.*, 311, 320 *sq.*; in natural election, 93 *sqq.*, 304
Respect (Kant's sense of): 279 *sq.*, 283
Ricardo, D.: 2 *sq.*, 13, 15
Richards, I. A.: 128 *sq.*, 134, 154
Rights: of man, 288 *sq.*; natural, 14
Ritschl, A.: xviii *sq.*
Ross, W. D.: 125 *sq.*
Rousseau, J. J.: 259, 288 *sq.*
Rules, general: 197, 209
Ruskin, J.: 32 *sqq.*
Russell, Hon. B. A. W.: 114

Satiety, 28 *sq.*, 156, 334
Satisfaction: 5 *sqq.*, 13, 24 *sq.*, 28 *sqq.*, 64 *sq.*, 88, 118 *sqq.*, 146 *sqq.*, 175, 256, 261, 314, 331, 340, 346
Sättigungskala: 24 *sqq.*, 64, 333
Scarcity: 17 *sq.*, 22 *sq.*, 333 *sq.*
Scheler, M.: 140

INDEX

Schemata: 40, 372 sqq.
Schiller, F. C. S.: 96 n.
Schopenhauer, A.: 136
Science, and philosophy: 285 sq., 299 sq.
Selby-Bigge, Sir L. A.: 193, 204 sq.
Self: as lawgiver, 294; in pride, 201 sq.; unifying, 143; -assertion, 75, 79 sq.; -justifying goods, 36, 44 sqq., 298; -realisation, 143, 257; -revealing knowledge, 84; -sufficient goods, 36, 44 sqq.
Selfish theory, the: 145,191 sq., 203
Selflessness of beauty: 156
Sense: 73 sq., 228 sqq., 281, 286; good, 260, 262; internal, 190; pleasures of, 164 sqq., 176, 333, 341; stimulus and, 341
Sense, the moral: 186 sq., 189 sqq., 194, 197 sq., 201, 205 sqq., 218 sq., 223, 225
Sentiment: 184, 195 sqq., 203 sqq., 225, 239, 273, 276, 289, 315, 318, 322, 374
Shaftesbury, A. A. Cooper, Earl of: 183 sqq., 204, 222, 237, 324
Shand, A. F.: 114 sqq., 246
Shelley, P. B.: 146, 170, 365
Sidgwick, H.: 114, 167, 213
Significant: ideas, 242 sq.; form, 162
Sirven, J.: 273 n.
Smart, W.: 338 n., 357
Smith, Adam: 3, 7 sqq., 13, 17, 183, 207 sqq., 239, 315
Sociality and value: 61 sq., 185, 190 sqq., 202 sq., 209 sqq., 233 sq., 248 sqq., 264, 276, 308 sq.
Socrates: 127, 323
Sorley, W. R.: 315 n.
Specific variety: 113
Spencer, H.: 166
Spinoza, B. de: xx, 40, 69 sqq., 101, 166, 232 sq., 255, 257, 259
Spirit: and value, 173, 303 sq.
Spontaneity: 282 sq., 298
Stephen, Sir L.: 3
Stoics: 82, 92, 124, 211, 272
Stumpf, C.: 332
Subject: in valuation, 105 sq., 108, 172 sqq., 235, 282 sqq.

Subjectivity in value: 71 sqq., 137, 161, 163, 226 sqq., 277 sqq., 360 sq.
Sublime, the: 222, 237, 278, 280
Substitute goods: 27, 49 sq., 282
Suicide: 270 sq., 294 sq., 325
Summum bonum: xviii, 259, 264, 266
Superfluity: 18 sqq., 27
Superlative: 241, 258, 322
Supersensible, the: 284 sqq., 299
Supplementary goods: 49 sq.
Sympathy: 202 sqq., 208 sqq., 239, 291
Synthetic connection in value theory: 285, 317

Taste: 153, 183 sqq., 201, 221 sq., 227, 231
Taylor, A. E.: xiv sq.
Tennant, F. R.: 308 sqq., 313 n.
Termination and climax: 41 sq., 48
Tetens, J. N.: 103
Theognis: xv
Thermometer, hedonic: 329 sq., 345
Time: 86, 89, 145, 200, 257; in economic value, 15 sq., 30; in means and end, 41; in pleasant experience, 166; in satisfaction, 29 sq.
Timology: xiii, 179 sqq., 301, 303 sq., 306 sq., 309 sq., 311 sqq., 321 sq., 349, 359 sq., 371 sq.
Torquemada, T.: 232 sq.
Tragedy: 170, 237
Transcendence of ideas: 242 sqq.
Transvaluations: 53 sqq.
Tripartite division in psychology: 103
Trollope, A.: 158
Truth: xv, 45 sq., 54, 74 sq., 142, 161, 181 sqq., 191, 210, 219 sq., 224, 238, 242 sqq., 265, 315 sqq., 356, 358, 363 sqq.
Tucker, A.: 114, 118 sqq., 214
Turgot, A. R. J., Baron de Laune: 333 sq.

Ultra-recessive judgments: 236 sqq.
Unconditional good: 36, 43 sq., 48; value, 81 sq., 286, 290

INDEX

Unconscious, the: 100, 302
Unconscious desires: 122; values, 5 *sq.*, 54 *sq.*, 305
Uneasiness: 116 *sqq.*, 120 *sq.*, 124
Understanding, the: 218, 220 *sq.*, 261 *sq.*, 273. See also Reason
Units: of pleasure, 328, 336, 341, 345, 352, 354
Universal: good, 36; law, 283 *sq.*; sentiment, 318
Universality: 244; 249; aesthetic, 277; and objectivity, 248 *sq.*; of approval, 207, 216
Universe, the: and natural election, 305; and values, 112 *sq.*, 256, 363; man's attitude to, 264
Urban, W. M.: 308 n.
Utilitarian: 9, 34, 134, 249; formula, 204
Utilitarians: 1, 5, 8, 67
Utility: xiv, xix *sq.*, 2 *sqq.*, 72 *sq.*, 88, 98 *sq.*, 133 *sq.*, 172, 183, 186, 197, 202 *sq.*, 206 *sqq.*, 265, 333 *sqq.* See also Instrumental; *Bonum utile*

V*aleo:* xv
Valeur: xv, xvii, 262 n.
Validity: 180 *sqq.*, 226, 243 *sqq.*
Valore: xv
Value-experience: 176, 180
Valuta: xv
Variations of standards: 74 *sq.*, 231 *sqq.*, 277

Vaughan, H.: 55 n.
Vigilance: 373
Virtue: xviii, 82 *sq.*, 186 *sq.*, 190, 193 *sqq.*, 201, 203, 207, 219, 263, 266, 268, 273, 350, 355 *sqq.*

W*allas, G.:* 39
Walras, L.: xviii, 16
Wants: 143 *sqq.*, 282. See also Needs
Ward, J.: 114 *sqq.*, 121, 168
Weber, E. H.: 332
Wert: xvi, 172
Werten: xvi, 177
Werterlebnis: xvi
Wertgefühl: 177
Werthaltung: xvi, 177, 312 *sq.*
Westermarck, E.: 233
Whately, R.: 4
Whitehead, A. N.: 69 *sq.*, 93 *sq.*
Wicksteed, P. H.: 2, 24, 29
Wieser, F. von: 1, 18 *sqq.*, 27 *sqq.*, 32, 337 n., 367
Will: 31, 71, 76, 103, 116, 145 *sqq.*, 164, 195, 220, 247 *sqq.*, 259, 264, 266, 269 *sqq.*
Witasek, S.: 177
Wohlgemuth, A.: 138 n.
Wundt, W.: 52

Y*oung, Allyn:* 26

Z*eno:* 262

BD
232
L188   Laird, J.
              Idea of value.

31289

SOUTH COLLEGE
709 Mall Blvd.
Savannah, GA 31406